*Maximum MIDI*

## DATE DUE

| | | |
|---|---|---|
| JY 13 00 | | |
| AG 3 00 | | |
| AG 9 00 | | |
| ~~DE~~ | | |
| OC 2 03 | | |
| JY 23 | | |
| | | |
| | | |
| | | |
| | | |
| | | |
| | | |
| | | |
| | | |
| | | |

# *Maximum MIDI*

## *Music Applications in C++*

PAUL MESSICK

/▮▮ **MANNING**

GREENWICH
(74° W. LONG.)

his book, see http://www.browsebooks.com

ok when ordered in quantity. For

Special Sales Department
Manning Publications Co.
3 Lewis Street
Greenwich, CT 06830

Fax: (203) 661-9018
e-mail: orders@manning.com

**Library of Congress Cataloging-in-Publication Data**
Messick, Paul.
    Maximum MIDI: music applications in C++ / Paul Messick.
       p.   cm.
    Includes index.
    ISBN 1-884777-44-9
    1.  MIDI (Standard)   2.  Computer sound processing.  I. Title.
    MT723.M48   1997
    784.19'0285'5711--dc21                              97-23268
                                                              CIP
                                                                MN

Manning Publications Co.
    3 Lewis Street
    Greenwich, CT 06830

    Copyeditor: Margaret Marynowski
    Typesetter: Tony Roberts
    Cover design: Leslie Haimes

Printed in the United States of America
    2  3  4  5  6  7  8  9  10 - CR - 00  99  98

*For my mother, Patricia,*

*whose inner fire warms my heart,*

*and for my father, Vernon,*

*whose quiet dignity inspires me every day.*

# contents

# *preface*

The seed for this book was planted in 1993. I found myself frustrated by the obstinate, poorly documented, and woefully inadequate MIDI functions available to me as a Windows programmer. So, I set out to write a set of routines that would allow me to write music applications without sweating the MIDI details.

This seemed like a straightforward goal at the time. Giddy with hubris and a false sense of security, I embarked on my mission. I expected to knock out this bit of code in a few days.

After hundreds of development hours (the long-suffering spousal unit estimates thousands), watered with the purest rainwater, bathed in golden-hour sunlight, and fertilized using the highest quality bovine output, a simple "toolkit" of MIDI functions took root. Since that first version, copious quantities of hair-pulling, testing, writing, and rewriting have helped improve it and along the way produced the book you hold in your hands and the software that is supplied on the accompanying CDROM.

Many programmers long to write applications that combine two powerful life forces: music and computers. Because of the scarcity of information about MIDI programming this has been a difficult task to do well. As a result, only the most fanatical have succeeded. But now, armed with this book and the MaxMidi ToolKit, musically-inclined programmers of all abilities can make their MIDI dreams reality. You can use the ToolKit, royalty-free, to write your own C and C++ MIDI applications to provide accompaniment for games and multimedia; aid you in writing music; control musical instruments, stage lighting, video- and audio-tape machines; and provide a basis for musical experimentation. May this ToolKit and book be as entertaining for you to use as they have been for me to create. Enjoy!

# *acknowledgments*

Like a film *auteur*, I receive sole credit on the book cover as the author of this tome. But, as in filmmaking, publishing a book involves the hard work of many individuals. I'd like to thank these people, all of whom deserve great credit for making this book as good as it is and none of the blame for any of its shortcomings.

Thanks to Len Dorfman, for his encouragement at the start; David Rowe for redrawing all of the illustrations from smudged and faded hand drawings, and for insightful comments above and beyond the call of duty; and Phil Sours for supplying comments instead of sleeping or eating. Thanks also to the other readers for their helpful comments: Bret Costin, Casey Palowitch and Jeff Fried.

Many programmers have used the ToolKit over the years, and their comments and suggestions have helped to improve it. But I'm especially grateful to Jeff Cazel, Jon Coopersmith, and Gary Muller for pointing out bugs that appeared in early versions of the ToolKit code.

Thanks are also bestowed on Mary Piergies for shepherding this book through production, and Tony Roberts and Margaret Marynowski for their efforts in producing the final product. And I especially wish to thank Mary Courtney, for her razor-sharp editing eye, her on-the-money comments, and her boundless love. Without her, this book would never have been finished.

# author online

Purchase of the Maximum MIDI book includes free access to a private Internet forum where you can make comments about the book, ask technical questions, and receive help from the author and from other ToolKit users. To access the Maximum MIDI forum, point your Web browser to http://www.manning.com/Messick/forum/. There you will be able to subscribe to the forum. This site also provides information on how to access the forum once you are registered, what kind of help is available, and the rules of conduct on the forum.

# about the reader

This book makes a few assumptions about you, the reader. It assumes you know:

- How to connect and use MIDI instruments and sound cards. While simple MIDI connections are covered—briefly—for completeness, the book assumes that you know enough about MIDI to be able to connect instruments together.
- Enough C and C++ to be dangerous. Even really dangerous. Line-by-line explanations of the C and C++ code are not found here.

The C++ examples are written using the Microsoft Foundation Classes (MFC) application framework, and all of the examples are supplied with makefiles for the Microsoft Visual C++ 4.x and 5.x compilers. And, if you have and know how to use the Microsoft compiler and MFC you'll find ToolKit more useful and the book easier to understand.

Maximum MIDI also assumes that you want to:

- Write music programs in C or C++.
- Learn how MIDI is implemented in Windows 95.
- Understand the algorithms used for synchronization, tracks, and Standard MIDI Files.
- Use the ToolKit functions as they are, modify them, or write your own MIDI routines from scratch.

Maximum MIDI offers something for programmers of every experience level and is all that most MIDI programmers will need. The examples and code are for Windows 95, but with all of the source code supplied, the C functions and C++ classes can be adapted to other operating systems or modified to do special tasks. While it's not necessary to look at the ToolKit source code to write MIDI programs, it is comforting to know that it can be modified and ported to perform all sorts of new tricks. And programmers at all levels can benefit from the supplied source code. After all, the best way to learn new tricks is to steal them from someone else!

# guide to the book

*Maximum MIDI* is intended as a thorough sourcebook that programmers can use when writing MIDI applications. It uses a set of routines, written in C and C++, as a working, concrete example of how to handle MIDI in a wide range of applications. While these routines, called the *Maximum MIDI Programmer's ToolKit*, are designed to work in Windows 95, they can be easily adapted to other systems. The book includes all of the algorithms used in the ToolKit, along with the ToolKit source. So, programmers are free to use the ToolKit routines as they are, modify the source to add new features, or strike out into uncharted territory by writing new routines from scratch.

The book is organized in three parts. The first section (chapters 1 through 8) covers how MIDI is used in Windows 95, including the MIDI protocol, algorithms to carry out all the basic tasks, the DLLs that implement those algorithms, and examples to use those routines in C. The second section (chapters 9 through 15) covers the MaxMidi C++ classes, including Microsoft MFC-based example programs using these classes. The third section encompasses four appendices that document the ToolKit C-language API and C++ classes, along with the complete source code for the classes, source code for the two MaxMidi DLLs, and three of the larger example programs.

It's not necessary to read every chapter, or even to read them in order. For example, if you are most interested in how Standard MIDI Files work, jump ahead to chapter 13 where they are discussed. A glossary is included to help with terms that might be defined in as-yet-unread chapters. But, of course, the most complete understanding comes to those who read everything and experiment thoroughly. To best understand everything about MIDI in Windows 95, study the book and pore over the code.

Chapter 1 covers some basic MIDI information, explaining simple interconnections and how the Windows 95 MIDI implementation is organized. Start with this chapter for a MIDI refresher, and a quick subterranean peak at how MIDI works in Windows 95.

The MIDI protocol is dissected in detail in chapter 2. While this chapter is not intended to replace the MIDI specification, it does provide enough detail for programmers to intelligently use the MIDI protocol. Topics such as Channel Voice messages, System Exclusive messages, MIDI Time Code, and General MIDI are thoroughly explored.

Chapter 3 delves into the internal workings of Windows 95, DLLs, Timers, and the MMSYSTEM API. This technically advanced chapter sets the stage for the low-level MIDI routines used in the ToolKit. Look here when trying to understand why MIDI is implemented the way it is in Windows 95.

The first half of chapter 4 introduces the ToolKit's C-language API for sending MIDI events, while the second half provides a map of these functions as implemented in the MaxMidi DLL internals.

Chapter 5 covers MIDI input much as chapter 4 covers MIDI output. The first half of the chapter covers the C-language API and a guide to the DLL's internal workings consumes the second half.

System Exclusive Messages are the topic of chapter 6. It is built on the foundation laid by the previous two chapters, and covers how these messages are handled using the ToolKit. Like the earlier chapters, it includes a guide to the inner workings of the ToolKit sysex-handling code, and explains how the DLL code has been extended to support sysexes.

The fundamental algorithms for musical timing are covered in chapter 7. Timestamps, ticks, SMPTE/MTC sync, and MIDI sync are all covered. Be sure to at least skim this chapter before moving on to chapter 8, where ToolKit-based synchronization is introduced.

The sync functions that are implemented in the MaxMidi DLLs (using the algorithms introduced in chapter 7) are shown in chapter 8. Recording and playing MIDI events is covered, along with an explanation of the internals of the ToolKit sync engine.

C++ finally rears its head in chapter 9. The three essential ToolKit classes, CMaxMidiIn, CMaxMidiOut, and CMaxMidiSync are introduced and examined. These classes enable C++ applications to easily support MIDI input and output, with and without synchronization.

Chapter 10 documents how MIDI support is added to an MFC-based application and uses two simple example programs to illustrate the process.

Chapter 11 explores sysex message handling using the ToolKit. A simple System Exclusive librarian program is the end result of these explorations.

Tracks make their first appearance in chapter 12. The CMaxMidiTrack class explored in this chapter makes writing sequencers a breeze. A quick and easy one-track sequencer example program illustrates the point.

Standard MIDI Files are the topic of chapter 13 where this popular file format is examined from soup to nuts. The file organization, C routines for reading and writing SMFs, and a C++ class to handle these files are all explained.

Chapter 14 expands our simple one-track sequencer by adding multiple tracks and support for reading and writing Standard MIDI Files. Along the way, a track merging algorithm is introduced that allows ToolKit-based applications to play back any number of tracks without hassle.

Chapter 15 encourages readers to strike out on their own by using the ToolKit—possibly adding features and modifying it along the way—in their own MIDI creations.

A glossary provides answers to those all important "huh?" questions that sometimes arise. This section is especially useful when reading chapters out of order, since normally each chapter builds on the last. When in doubt, look it up here.

Finally, four appendixes completely document the ToolKit source, the C-language API, and the C++ classes. Appendix A provides detailed documentation for the ToolKit's C-language API and C++ classes. This documentation is also included in two help files that are on the accompanying CDROM. Appendix B is the complete source code for the two MaxMidi DLLs, while appendix C provides a source code listing of all of the ToolKit C++ classes. And, appendix D includes the source code for three of the example programs: *MidiSpy*, *SxLib*, and *MaxSeq*. Of course, all of the source code is also supplied on the CDROM.

**CHAPTER 1**

# MIDI and Windows 95

In less than 10 years, MIDI—the Musical Instrument Digital Interface—has taken the music world by storm. MIDI interfaces—the hardware that makes MIDI available to an instrument or computer—appear on keyboards, sound cards, computer motherboards, guitars, tape recorders, saxophones, violins, and all manner of boxes that go beep in the night.

MIDI's first name is *musical*, and music is its primary focus. There are limitless possibilities for musical expression with a MIDI-equipped computer, one or more MIDI instruments, and some software. Using a sequencer program, you can record and edit musical performances and save them in disk files. While each sequencer generally uses its own proprietary file format, most sequencers also support a common format, the *Standard MIDI File* format. This standard file format allows compositions to be shared with other listeners, regardless of what kind of sequencer or playback program they use.

Such standard-format files are commonly available on the Internet from web pages, Usenet newsgroups, and ftp sites. Recording, posting, and sharing MIDI compositions has become a popular hobby for many musicians. Using a web-browser plug-in made for the task, some web pages even play MIDI songs in real time.

There are other MIDI programs which allow users to edit instrument settings to create new sounds. Instrument settings, called *patches*, *programs*, or *sounds*, are retrieved from the instrument (via MIDI) and modified using a *patch editor* program. The edited patches are then sent back to the instrument and stored in its memory, providing a new ready-to-play sound. Another program, called a *patch* or *sysex librarian*, can store individual patches or banks of patches in disk files and transfer these patches to and from MIDI instruments.

Games and multimedia titles often use MIDI to provide background music and sound effects. While digital (waveform) audio is often used in these programs as well, MIDI provides a compact way to make sound. For example, a 10-minute segment of background music might occupy 100 Kb of disk space, while 10 minutes of CD-quality digital audio would occupy more than 100 MB. In addition, playing MIDI data requires far less CPU processing power than is needed to play digital audio.

MIDI programs have found a home in music education. Used properly, computers enhance music training, making learning easier and more enjoyable. For example, MIDI provides an interactive connection between a music student and a computer. The computer can interpret the student's performance and provide appropriate feedback to speed the learning process. Of course, a computer can never replace a good human teacher, but computer-based music education helps bring music into more people's lives.

The uses for MIDI have moved beyond the strictly musical realm. For example, stage lighting for theater and musical events is often controlled via MIDI. In some setups, MIDI cables are connected to each light, carrying messages that control the lamp's intensity.

A sequencer or MIDI playback program then controls the lighting by sending the proper MIDI messages with the same timing as originally recorded. Controlling lighting using MIDI is so popular that the process is codified in the MIDI Show Control section of the MIDI specification.

Many audio and video tape machines, digital audio and video workstations, and other mechanical synchronized devices can also be controlled via MIDI. For example, a controller or sequencer can command a tape machine to shuttle, stop, play, and record by sending the appropriate MIDI messages. All of the machine control commands are detailed in the MIDI Machine Control section of the MIDI specification.

# What is MIDI, Anyway?

With the growth of uses for MIDI has come confusion of what MIDI is and what it can do. Here are some lists to help clarify what MIDI is and is not.

MIDI is

- A way to interconnect musical instruments, computers, and other devices
- A way to play synthesized sounds on a sound card
- A standardized communications protocol
- A way to control nonmusical devices, such as theater lighting, tape recorders, etc.

MIDI is

- Concerned with performance but not with audio
- A compact representation of a musical performance
- Changeable: a sequenced performance can be easily edited to change the notes, timing, and even the sounds made by an instrument

MIDI is not

- Audio: only a receiving MIDI instrument can make sound
- Waveform audio: sound cards record and play waveform audio
- A panacea: some tasks are best done using waveform audio, while some tasks can use MIDI

MIDI is not

- Only for sound cards on computers
- Too slow for good timing: MIDI events are sent very quickly, quick enough for most sequences to play with the proper human feel
- Infinitely fast: too many notes, Herr Mozart, can clog the works and cause delays

One source of confusion about MIDI's possibilities is the merging of waveform audio playback, synthesis, and MIDI technology. Many sound cards and synthesizers create realistic sounds using *wavetable synthesis*. In a sound device, a wavetable is a permanent block of digital audio data, often stored in a ROM. This audio is broken up into small portions, each covering a pitch or range of pitches. When the device receives MIDI notes, it plays digital audio *samples* corresponding to those particular pitches. Sampling keyboards are similar, but they usually retrieve their sounds from disk storage instead of from ROM. Since many computer sound cards have waveform audio record and play capabilities in addition to a wavetable synthesizer, it's no wonder users are confused about where waveform audio ends and MIDI begins. MIDI can trigger a wavetable or sampling sound device, but it is not audio.

There are endless combinations of ways to interconnect MIDI devices, limited only by the user's budget for MIDI instruments. The most basic way to use MIDI is to connect two instruments using two MIDI cables. Most instruments have a MIDI output port, a MIDI input port, and a MIDI thru port. MIDI data is sent by a device's output and thru ports, and is received by its input port. The thru port, which does not appear on all instruments, simply outputs exactly what is received by the device's input port.

MIDI cables always connect a MIDI output port to a MIDI input port. Avoid connecting input to input or output to output. Connecting a MIDI input to another MIDI input won't hurt anything, but the system won't work correctly. However, connecting two outputs together can cause ground loops resulting in an annoying hum in both devices' audio outputs. In the worst case, the difference between ground potentials between the two devices can even cause hardware damage. Therefore, ensure MIDI happiness by only connecting outputs to inputs.

## *Simple Connections*

The drawing below shows two keyboards connected together. Instrument A's output is connected to instrument B's input. Thus, assuming the two keyboards are properly adjusted, notes played on A will trigger sounds in B.

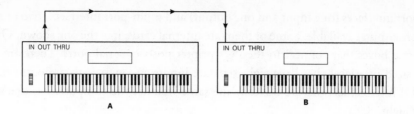

**Figure 1-1 Two-keyboard interconnection**

After years of practicing, writing songs, and gigging in bars and nightclubs for virtually no money, our long-awaited record deal finally gets inked. Advance check in hand, we head for the nearest music emporium and load-up on new toys. A couple of much cooler keyboards and a sound module replace our old, outdated instruments. Here's one way we might interconnect our new MIDI setup:

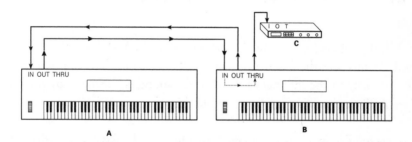

**Figure 1-2   A more advanced setup**

Keyboard A can send MIDI to keyboard B. It also sends the same MIDI data to sound module C via B's MIDI thru port. Keyboard B can play sounds on A, but not on C. Remember, the thru port's data is simply a copy of the input port's data. Nothing from the B keyboard's output will appear in its thru port.

Connecting keyboards and sound modules is fun, but it is more interesting to connect MIDI devices to a computer and use the computer to process MIDI events. Figure 1-3 shows the simplest way to connect a keyboard to a PC.

Here, the computer has a MIDI interface that is on a card plugged into one of the computer's expansion slots. This interface might be part of a sound card or might be a hardware card unto itself. This example shows two connections—an input and an output—but other options are possible. For example, there are many different kinds of single-port interfaces (one input and one output) and multi-port interfaces (two or more inputs or outputs) available. Some of them are internal cards, like the one shown. Others are external boxes that connect to the PC's printer ports or serial ports. There are even mondo-sized interfaces that have eight separate inputs and eight separate outputs. But the MIDI interconnections are basically the same whether the computer has one set of ports or eight.

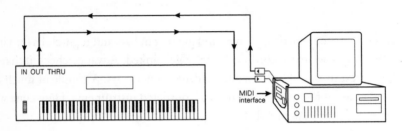

**Figure 1-3  Keyboard and computer**

Many MIDI programs are intended to be used with the MIDI functions available on sound cards. In this case, there is no external MIDI connection. The computer routes the MIDI data directly to the internal card where the sound is generated by the on-board synthesizer. A given computer can have any combination of internal and external MIDI devices.

The connections shown here only scratch the surface. There is a wide variety of MIDI devices available, each device presenting unique opportunities and tradeoffs. The topic of how to *use* MIDI is beyond the scope of this book. Many other books are available on how to interconnect MIDI instruments and how to use particular instruments and programs. Connecting and using MIDI devices is best tackled with owner's manuals and one of these how-to books in one hand, and a strong cup of coffee in the other. Writing MIDI programs to control those instruments is the topic of the rest of this book.

# Why Not Use the MCI Sequencer or Streams?

Windows 95 has two different, but related, ways to handle MIDI. One is a high-level programming interface, called the Media Control Interface (MCI), that includes a MIDI playback capability called the MCI Sequencer. The MCI Sequencer provides simple sequence playback, but it is unable to record or synchronize to other processes or sync sources. However, it is simple to use, and for some applications it may be all that is needed to do the job. Luckily, this Windows component is fully documented in the manuals that accompany most Windows-specific development tools and compilers.

The other method for handling MIDI data is included in a set of low-level functions that comprise the core of Windows' multimedia subsystem. Any imaginable MIDI program can be written using these general-purpose functions. In fact, the MCI sequencer is implemented using these exact function calls. But, as many diligent programmers have found, using such low-level functions in an application can be difficult and frustrating. Luckily, all of the Nasty Bits have been taken care of by the MaxMidi ToolKit. Applications need only make a few simple calls to the ToolKit to implement MIDI features.

Windows 95 includes one other tempting MIDI programming feature. *Streams* provide another method to play sequenced MIDI events. To use streams, applications place MIDI events in a buffer, including timing information for each event. A simple set of functions will accept the data and play the sequence. These functions are similar to the low-level functions provided by the ToolKit. However, like the MCI Sequencer, streams can only *play* sequences, limiting their usefulness for full-featured MIDI applications. The ToolKit functions provide easy-to-use record and play features supporting multiple tracks of MIDI, Standard MIDI Files, MIDI Clock synchronization, and more.

# *The Windows MIDI Connection*

MIDI support, as implemented in Windows 95, is organized in layers. Each layer is built on top of the layers below, increasing in abstraction and functionality as the layers rise. The following diagram shows how each of these layers is interconnected.

At the very bottom of the hierarchy is the MIDI interface. The interface physically connects external MIDI devices to the computer, or in the case of a sound card's built-in synthesizer, it directly makes sound based on MIDI data that the card receives. Often, this piece of hardware is a plug-in card that connects directly to the computer's bus (where data and control signals are transferred between the CPU on the motherboard and various input/output cards, such as disk drive interfaces and video cards). Typical MIDI interface cards connect to external MIDI devices via short MIDI cables (sometimes called pigtails). The diagram shows two cables, one for input and one for output, but there may be more connections available on a particular card. Many sound cards include both an on-board synthesizer and an external MIDI interface (usually requiring an optional special adapter cable).

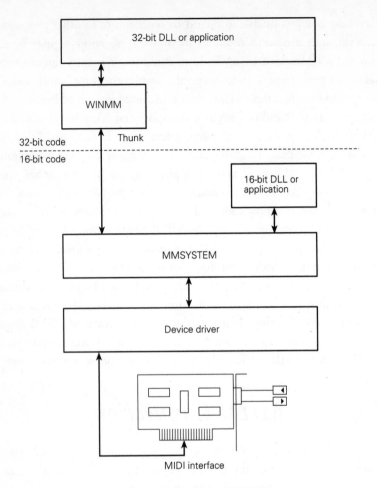

**Figure 1-4 Windows 95 MIDI**

But other possibilities for MIDI interfaces are available. Instead of an internal card, some MIDI interfaces connect to the computer via serial COM ports or parallel printer ports. In these cases, all of the hardware is in an external unit and the interface is connected without opening the computer's case—a popular feature with many users. And some interfaces do more than just send and receive MIDI data. In addition to the sound cards whose synthesizers respond to MIDI events, some interfaces can read and write various forms of tape synchronization—where musical timing is driven by signals recorded onto audio or video tape. Other interfaces can perform complex routing and filtering operations, even without a computer attached. Other, more advanced interfaces process video signals directly, reading timing information directly from the video and providing a visual indication of timing called a *burn-in window*. Maniacally power-hungry users can even connect several MIDI interfaces to a single computer.

But, no matter what kind of MIDI interfaces are installed on a system, as far as MIDI applications are concerned they are all accessed the same way. That is, each type, brand, or model of interface may use radically different technology to do its job, but Windows will access each interface using identical function calls. This feat of magic—mapping dissimilar hardware devices to a common software interface—is done using a piece of software called a *device driver*. The manufacturers of Windows-compatible MIDI interfaces supply these device drivers with their hardware. Users install these drivers using the Add New Hardware applet, located in the Control Panel.

Using such a device driver layer for MIDI hardware means that Windows does not need to "know" anything about the actual hardware MIDI device available on the system. The driver hides the details of the hardware from Windows, presenting a well-defined method for accessing any MIDI hardware device, regardless of how the hardware works.

Once installed, a device driver communicates with the hardware MIDI device to send and receive MIDI data. The driver presents a specific set of functions implementing the basic MIDI input, output, and control functions that Windows needs to access the device. But applications never call device driver functions directly. Another software layer, called MMSYSTEM, implements higher level multimedia (including MIDI) functions. MMSYSTEM communicates with MIDI device drivers as needed to send and receive MIDI events.

The MMSYSTEM layer is implemented in a Dynamic Link Library (DLL) that is part of Windows. This multimedia subsystem provides more than just MIDI device driver access. It also implements high precision timer services, waveform audio playback and record features, specialized file access features that access RIFF format disk files, and other multimedia-related functions.

MMSYSTEM is implemented as a 16-bit code module. All MIDI device drivers are also 16-bit code, although some drivers include a 32-bit portion, called a *VxD*. Windows 95 32-bit applications call 16-bit functions, including MMSYSTEM, using a process called *thunking*. Thunks allow 32-bit processes to call 16-bit code (and vice versa). Thunks and thunking are covered in detail in chapter 3.

Since 32-bit DLLs and applications cannot call MMSYSTEM directly, Windows 95 provides a special thunking DLL, called WINMM. WINMM makes all of the features of MMSYSTEM available to the 32-bit universe. Unfortunately, WINMM is almost useless for MIDI applications. The reasons for this are discussed in detail in chapter 3. In a nutshell, any applications that are timing sensitive—such as sequencers—will find the timing facilities available via WINMM unsuitable. Luckily, 16-bit applications and DLLs use MMSYSTEM's high-precision timers without the drawbacks inherent in accessing them using WINMM. Since timing done in 16-bit code is rock solid, the MaxMidi ToolKit implements all of its timing-sensitive features in a 16-bit DLL, called MxMidi16.

The MxMidi16 DLL is paired with a 32-bit DLL, MxMidi32. Like WINMM, this MxMidi32 uses thunks to provide 32-bit applications with access to 16-bit code. But since MxMidi32 calls MxMidi16, where all the ToolKit's timing and MIDI functions are implemented, native 32-bit Windows 95 applications get the best of both worlds—the ToolKit's fast, tight timing coupled with the speed and features available to native 32-bit code.

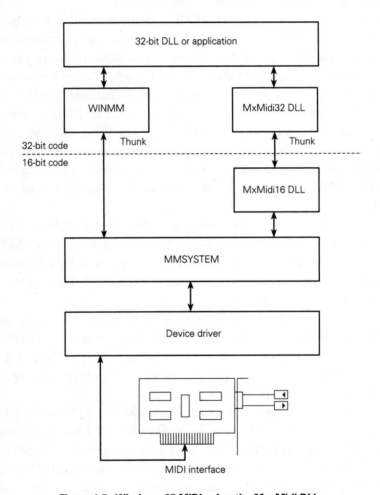

**Figure 1-5  Windows 95 MIDI using the MaxMidi DLLs**

# The MaxMidi ToolKit

The MaxMidi ToolKit accompanying this book consists of two Dynamic Link Libraries and seven C++ classes that give Windows 95 applications easy access to MIDI functions. The functions and classes are both easy to use and powerful. Unmodified, the ToolKit provides enough features to implement nearly any MIDI program. But since the ToolKit includes full source code for the DLLs and classes, programmers can add new features and modify existing ones without having to start from scratch.

The ToolKit also contains over a dozen example programs that illustrate how to use the available features and provide jumping-off points for developing new applications. Three of the examples are full-featured programs in their own right. These examples concentrate on the ToolKit's MIDI features and implement basic user interfaces. Start with the MidiSpy, SxLib, and MaxSeq programs, and then add friendlier user interfaces, to produce advanced, full-featured MIDI programs.

# Rolling Your Own

This book includes tons of source code, example programs, help files, documentation, and algorithms for writing MIDI programs. Use these tools to write your own programs. Take the code apart and look at it. Modify it, step through it in a debugger, understand it. But above all, use it.

Most programmers will be able to use the ToolKit as-is to write the perfect program. But sometimes extreme measures are required. This is when the supplied source code becomes crucial. Programmers are an iconoclastic lot. It's axiomatic that programmers can't resist changing other people's code. There's always a better way. You are strongly encouraged to take the ToolKit code and make it your own.

Given such a head-start, any imaginable MIDI program is just around the corner. What could you possibly be waiting for?

**C H A P T E R   2**

# The Musical Instrument Digital Interface

# Overview

The Musical Instrument Digital Interface standard—MIDI to you and me—came about in 1983. Originally conceived by a consortium of synthesizer manufacturers (Roland, Yamaha, Oberheim, and Sequential Circuits) as a way to connect instruments together to layer sounds, it has evolved into the protocol of choice to control everything from sound generators to stage lighting.

In the most basic sense, MIDI is nothing more than a communications protocol. It is used to transmit information about a musical *performance*, but it knows nothing about the actual *sound* of the notes. MIDI tells us what notes are played, and when and how. A noisemaker, such as a synthesizer, receives the MIDI data and produces a sound in response. If the synthesizer is set to sound like a trumpet, the MIDI events cause it to make trumpet-like sounds. In this sense, MIDI is like sheet music—it's not the sound, it's the notes. Unlike sheet music, however, MIDI messages can flow along a wire and cause a synthesizer to make sound.

# Get the Spec

While this chapter provides enough information for you to be able to intelligently write many MIDI programs, it is not a replacement for the actual MIDI specification. Most of the fundamentals are here, but there are many advanced features of MIDI that this chapter sidesteps, simplifies, or even omits entirely. *The Complete MIDI 1.0 Detailed Specification* includes seven sections: a tutorial, the basic specification, MIDI Time Code, Standard MIDI Files, General MIDI, MIDI Show Control, and MIDI Machine Control. It is published by the MIDI Manufacturers Association as the ultimate source of technical information about how MIDI works.

There are at least two ways to get a copy of the MIDI specification. The MIDI Manufacturers Association (MMA) distributes copies of the specification (currently about $50). They can be reached at:

MIDI Manufacturers Association
PO Box 3173
La Habra, California 90632-3173
http://home.earthlink.net/~mma/

However, since the MMA is primarily concerned with providing services to their members, they prefer that purchasers buy the specification from MIX Bookshelf. MIX Bookshelf can be reached at:

MIX Bookshelf
6400 Hollis Street #10
Emeryville, California 94608
Order Line: 800-233-9604 or 510-653-3307
Fax: 510-653-5142
http://www.mixbookshelf.com/

# The MIDI Protocol

MIDI is a serial protocol. That is, each bit of information flows along a wire and one bit follows the next in sequence. Each byte is sent at 31,250 baud and occupies 10 bits; a start bit, eight data bits, and a stop bit. So, 3,125 bytes can be sent each second, or each byte takes 320 microseconds to transmit.

A MIDI message is a packet of data that fully specifies an event. Most messages are one, two, or three bytes in length, although some may be longer. A three-byte message— a Note On, for example—takes 960 microseconds, nearly a millisecond, to transmit. Slightly more than 1,000 such notes could be sent in one second.

Each MIDI message, regardless of its length, contains a single status byte (specifying what kind of event it is) and zero or more data bytes. The numerical value of a status byte is always between 128 and 255 (0x80 to 0xFF). All data bytes fall between 0 and 127 (0x00 to 0x7F). This provides easy identification of status and data, but limits the range of a single data value to seven bits.

There are two basic types of MIDI messages: Channel messages and System messages. Channel messages are directed at a particular destination and are subdivided into Channel Voice messages (ones that specify or modify a note) and Channel Mode messages (ones that configure the receiver). System messages come in three flavors: System Common messages (specifying data of interest to all devices in the system), System Real-Time messages (timing-related events), and System Exclusive messages (a catch-all for anything the MIDI inventors did not think of first).

# Channel Voice Messages

By far, the most common type of data sent using MIDI is the Channel Voice message, or simply, the Channel message. These messages can be directed to a particular device (by specifying a channel). All of the Channel messages specify performance information: what note is played or how the sound of the note is affected. For example, a Note On message tells what note is played and how, and a Pitch Bend message affects the pitch of the currently sounding note.

Four bits of a Channel message status byte specify the channel. The other four bits indicate what kind of Channel message it is. To minimize the number of bits needed (and to maximize confusion) channels 1 through 16 are encoded as 0 to 15 (0x00 to 0x0F) in the lower four bits of the status byte. There are seven different Channel messages, having either one or two associated data bytes. These messages are shown in table 2-1.

**Table 2-1   Channel Voice Messages**

| Status Byte (Hex)* | Data Bytes | Message |
|---|---|---|
| 0x8n | NOTE, VEL | Note Off |
| 0x9n | NOTE, VEL | Note On |
| 0xAn | NOTE, PRESSURE | Key Aftertouch |
| 0xBn | CTRL, VALUE | Control Change |
| 0xCn | PROG# | Program Change |
| 0xDn | PRESSURE | Channel Aftertouch |
| 0xEn | LSB, MSB | Pitch Bend |

\* n=channel, 0 for channel 1, F for channel 16

## *Note On/Note Off*

These two messages are the noise-makers of MIDI. Each specifies the pitch of the note and its velocity. On most keyboards, middle C corresponds to a MIDI note number of 60. Notice that pitches outside of the range of hearing can be played using MIDI, possibly causing unexpected canine or seismic activity. Velocity is generally interpreted as corresponding to loudness: where 0 is silent, 64 is mezzo piano (*mp*) and 127 is fortississimo (*fff*).

A Note On will start sounding a note at the given pitch. Once started, a note must be silenced, otherwise it becomes a stuck note. MIDI provides two ways to stop a note from sounding: the Note Off message and the Note On message with a velocity of 0. A Note Off message is similar to a Note On message. It specifies the particular note and a velocity. However, this velocity specifies how the note is to be released. Alternatively, a Note On with a 0 velocity will work just as well. If velocity corresponds to loudness, it makes sense that 0 velocity produces silence. Ending a note by using a Note On message with 0 velocity is common. A Note On and its corresponding Note Off would both have the

**Table 2-2   Control Change Messages**

| Controller (decimal) | Function | Controller (decimal) | Function |
|---|---|---|---|
| 0 | Bank select | 69 | Hold 2 |
| 1 | Modulation wheel | 70 | Sound controller 1 (sound variation) |
| 2 | Breath controller | 71 | Sound controller 2 (timbre/har-monic intensity) |
| 3 | Undefined | | |
| 4 | Foot controller | 72 | Sound controller 3 (release time) |
| 5 | Portamento time | 73 | Sound controller 4 (attack time) |
| 6 | Data entry MSB | 74 | Sound controller 4 (brightness) |
| 7 | Channel volume | 75–79 | Sound controllers 5–10 |
| 8 | Balance | 80–83 | General purpose controllers |
| 9 | Undefined | 84 | Portamento control |
| 10 | Pan | 85–90 | Undefined |
| 11 | Expression controller | 91 | Effects 1 depth |
| 12 | Effect control 1 | 92 | Effects 2 depth |
| 13 | Effect control 2 | 93 | Effects 3 depth |
| 14–15 | Undefined | 94 | Effects 4 depth |
| 16–19 | General purpose controllers | 95 | Effects 5 depth |
| 20–31 | Undefined | 96 | Data increment |
| 32–63 | LSB for controllers 0-31 | 97 | Data decrement |
| 64 | Damper pedal (sustain) | 98 | Non-registered parameter LSB |
| 65 | Portamento on/off | 99 | Non-registered parameter MSB |
| 66 | Sostenuto | 100 | Registered parameter LSB |
| 67 | Soft pedal | 101 | Registered parameter MSB |
| 68 | Legato footswitch | 102–119 | Undefined |
| | | 120–127 | Reserved for channel mode mes-sages |

same status value. This allows the use of *running status* (described later) to compress the number of bytes needed to start and end each note. The duration of a note is the elapsed time between a Note On and the matching Note Off (or Note On with 0 velocity).

## *Aftertouch*

Aftertouch messages are sent by some keyboards after a key bottoms out. Varying the horizontal or vertical pressure on the key while the note is sounding will result in a flood of Aftertouch messages. A given instrument may assign these messages to any parameter it desires. Key Aftertouch, sometimes referred to as Polyphonic Key Pressure, affects only the specified note, while Channel Aftertouch (*aka* Channel Pressure) affects all notes playing on a given channel.

## Control Change

Control Change messages are used to change the volume, pan, portamento time, modulation, and many other qualities of the sound of a sound-making MIDI device. There are 120 possible controllers, as shown in table 2-2. Many of them are undefined. Controller numbers 0 to 31 specify the Most Signifigant Byte (MSB) of a given controller, providing seven bits of resolution. If finer control is needed, controllers 32 to 63 give an extra seven bits of resolution for controllers 0 to 31. Controller numbers 120 to 127 are reserved for Channel Mode messages and are discussed later in this chapter.

Controller numbers greater than 63 are used as "switches," where values less than 64 correspond to "off," and values greater than or equal to 64 are "on." But, the MIDI specification also allows these controllers to be used as continuous controllers.

## Program Change

This channel message selects the desired program or patch on the receiving instrument. By changing the program, a flute can become a saxophone, a pipe-organ, or any other sound that the instrument has available. The program number does not include any information concerning the actual sound of the patch, it merely specifies a particular number. A program number of 0 selects the first program in the receiving instrument.

## Pitch Bend

All of the notes playing on a given channel can be bent in pitch using the Pitch Bend message. The pitch is specified as a 14-bit number, using two 7-bit bytes, least significant byte first. It is centered at 0x00, 0x40, and the most negative bend (down in pitch) is 0x00, 0x00, while the

## Running Status

There is considerable redundancy in a typical stream of MIDI messages. Note Ons on a given channel are sent, followed some time later by corresponding Note Offs. Twisting on a pitch bend wheel generates dozens or even hundreds of Pitch Bend messages. Since each byte is sent serially, and since, as both lawyers and musicians say, time is of the essence, it would be useful to squeeze out some of the redundant data. Luckily, the MIDI protocol provides a simple and effective way to do just that: *running status*.

Take the example of three Note On messages, followed by three more Note Ons with velocity 0 (serving as Note Offs). For simplicity, all of these bytes are shown in hex, and are on channel 1. Remember, a Note On's status on channel 1 is 0x90. This simple sequence requires 18 bytes.

```
90 3C 40 90 3B 62 90
39 27 ... 90 3C 00 90
3B 00 90 39 00
```

Since the status value for each of the events is the same (all of them are Note Ons on channel 1), there are redundant status bytes in the example. Running status is a form of data compression, so we can omit the redundant status bytes.

A new status byte must be sent whenever the status changes, either because of a new message type or the same message type on a new channel. In practice, it's a good idea to refresh the status byte periodically, even when it is not strictly necessary. If a receiving device were to come on line in the middle of a sequence, or lose track of the status byte, it would refuse to make any sound until the status was refreshed. Updating once every 16 or 32 events is adequate.

By applying running status to our sequence, we can shorten it to 13 bytes.

```
90 3C 40 3B 62 39 27
... 3C 00 3B 00 39 00
```

Running status can only be used with Channel Messages, and is terminated whenever the status byte changes. Note that System Real-Time messages are "invisible" to running status. They never require the status to be refreshed. But more on that later.

most positive bend is 0x7F, 0x7F. The bend is relative to the bend range that is selected in the receiving device. For example, if the receiver's bend range is set to three MIDI notes (or semitones) then 0x7F, 0x7F will bend the pitch up three semitones. Likewise, 0x00, 0x00 will bend the pitch down three semitones. The same MIDI messages sent to a receiver with a bend range of five will bend its notes up and down five semitones. The bend range of most instruments can be adjusted from the front panel.

# Channel Mode Messages

Channel Mode messages change the behavior of a receiving device. Some of these messages serve to set the receiving device to a particular state, while others affect how the device interprets subsequent Channel Voice messages. Channel Mode messages are actually Control Change messages for controllers 120 to 127. These messages are outlined in table 2-3.

**Table 2-3   Channel Mode Messages**

| Mode Message (decimal) | Status/Data Bytes* | Usage |
|---|---|---|
| All Sound Off (120) | 0xBn 0x78 0x00 | |
| Reset All Controllers (121) | 0xBn 0x79 0x00 | |
| Local Control (122) | 0xBn 0x7A VAL | VAL = 0 for off, VAL = 127 for on |
| All Notes Off (123) | 0xBn 0x7B 0x00 | |
| Omni Off (124) | 0xBn 0x7C 0x00 | |
| Omni On (125) | 0xBn 0x7D 0x00 | |
| Mono On (Poly Off) (126) | 0xBn 0x7E VAL | VAL = number of channels, or 0 to set the number of channels to the number of voices available |
| Poly On (Mono Off) (127) | 0xBn 0x7F 0x00 | |

*n = Basic Channel, 0 for channel 1, F for channel 16

Channel Mode messages are sent to the Basic Channel of the receiving instrument. The Basic Channel is a particular channel (sometimes called the Global Channel) of the device and is either permanently hardwired in the device or can be set from its front panel. Channel Mode messages sent to any other channel will be ignored.

A receiving device can be in one of four modes, which are set using four mode messages: Omni On, Omni Off, Mono On, and Poly On. These modes are outlined in table 2-4.

**Table 2-4   Receiving Modes**

|          | *Poly*   | *Mono*   |
|----------|----------|----------|
| *Omni On*  | **Mode 1**<br>Omni On<br>Poly  | **Mode 2**<br>Omni On<br>Mono  |
| *Omni Off* | **Mode 3**<br>Omni Off<br>Poly | **Mode 4**<br>Omni Off<br>Mono |

For example, to set a receiver to Mode 1, send the Omni On message, followed by the Poly On message.

Turning Omni On allows the receiver to respond to messages sent on any channel. If Omni is off the receiver will respond to messages on the Basic Channel, but will ignore messages sent on any other channel.

*Poly* is short for *polyphonic*. A polyphonic instrument is capable of sounding more than one note at a time. Selecting Mono mode forces the receiver to play only a single note at a time. The use of Poly or Mono mode is often determined by the type of sound being played. Piano is clearly a polyphonic instrument, while playing chords on a tuba is physically difficult at best.

There are four other Channel Mode messages in addition to the four Mode messages described above. Reset All Controllers will force all of the controllers, such as Pitch Bend and Modulation Wheel, to their default positions. The All Notes Off message will silence any sounding or stuck notes. However, these two messages are ignored by any receiver that has Omni turned on. Because of this, All Notes Off is rarely useful as a panic button message. Like the All Notes Off message, the All Sound Off message silences all notes that are currently playing. All Sound Off is a recent addition to MIDI, so many older devices may not respond to this message. In an emergency situation, the surest way to fix any stuck notes is to send a Note Off (or Note On, velocity zero) command for all 128 notes on all 16 channels. Notice that sending these 2,048 notes can take several seconds, even using running status.

Local Control refers not to the behavior of a micromanaging government agency or overzealous police force, but to the internal connection between a musical keyboard and its internal sound module. Normally, Local Control is on, and playing keys on the instrument will make the internal sound module sound the notes. Turning Local Control off separates the two functions. That way, a keyboard can be used as a controller, while the sound module in the instrument can be played using MIDI from a sequencer.

# System Messages

System Common messages, as shown in table 2-5, are used to coordinate the activities of all of the devices connected to a given system. Of the seven System Common messages, two are undefined. The EOX, or End Of Exclusive message, and the MTC Quarter Frame message are covered later.

The Song Position Pointer message (SPP) tells a sequencer or drum machine the position where sequence playback is about to begin. This position, as a 14-bit value, is a count of time since the beginning of the sequence. Each of these units of time equals six MIDI Clocks. Since there are 24 MIDI Clocks per quarter note, one SPP unit of time is a sixteenth note. Therefore, the SPP message specifies the sequence position on a sixteenth-note boundary. This message is sent before a System Real-Time message such as Start or Continue is sent. This message has no meaning if the MIDI system is not synchronizing to MIDI sync, as discussed in the next section.

The Song Select message specifies which sequence or drum pattern is played, if the receiver is set to synchronize to MIDI sync. The song number is an index that starts at 0. The message is ignored if the receiver does not handle multiple sequences or drum patterns.

Tune Request is a now-defunct message that dates from the days of analog synthesizers. These instruments were notorious for drifting out of tune (some more than others), and the Tune Request message forced them to retune their oscillators. This message is rarely used now that most synthesizers and sound modules are little more than computers with audio outputs.

**Table 2-5   System Common Messages**

| Status Byte (Hex) | Data Byte(s) | Message |
|---|---|---|
| 0xF1 | VAL | MIDI Time Code Quarter Frame |
| 0xF2 | LSB, MSB | Song Position Pointer |
| 0xF3 | SONG# | Song Select |
| 0xF4 | | Undefined |
| 0xF5 | | Undefined |
| 0xF6 | | Tune Request |
| 0xF7 | | EOX, End of Exclusive |

# System Real-Time Messages

System Real-Time messages indicate that something is happening *right now*. They are all single-byte messages, and they have the unique ability to appear anywhere, even between the status byte and the data bytes of a MIDI message.

MIDI Timing Clock messages (0xF8), often called MIDI Clock messages, are sent when a system is synchronizing timing to another MIDI device. Typically, this type of MIDI sync is used with drum machines and with some types of tape synchronization. Twenty-four MIDI Clocks are sent for every quarter note. The rate at which they are sent is determined by the tempo: faster tempos reduce the time between clocks. MIDI sync is noted for its ease of use and lack of precision. With only 24 clocks per beat there is plenty of room for error.

Start (0xFA), Continue (0xFB), and Stop (0xFC) are real-time messages that control synchronization when using MIDI sync. The Start message indicates that timing is about to begin at the beginning of the current sequence. However, timing does not actually start until the next MIDI Clock message.

The Stop message halts playback or record immediately, even if MIDI Clocks continue to be received. A receiver must hold its current position and ignore MIDI Clocks until either a Start message or Continue message is received.

A Continue message causes timing to resume from its current position on the next MIDI Clock. This message allows a sequence to be paused (using Stop) and then unpaused. Sending a Start message after a Stop message will cause the sequence to begin again at the very beginning.

Active Sensing (0xFE) messages are vestigial annoyances that date back to the original Yamaha DX-7. Active Sensing is supposed to work like this: if an instrument is equipped with Active Sensing, it sends 0xFEs at least every 300 milliseconds, unless it is sending other MIDI messages more often. If this instrument is connected to another Active Sensing-equipped device, the receiver will recognize these bytes and will send its own Active Sensing bytes back to the other instrument. If either one stops sending Active Sensing, for whatever reason, both devices assume that the MIDI cable has been unplugged and they will turn off all sounding notes.

The System Reset (0xFF) message is another rarely used MIDI message. If received and recognized by a device, a System Reset message should force the device into its power-on reset condition, clear running status, turn off any sounding notes, set Local Control on, and otherwise clean up the state of things.

# System Exclusive Messages

System Exclusive messages (sysex messages) are the black sheep of the MIDI protocol. They are of arbitrarily large size and can be used for nearly any purpose imaginable. Originally, they were designed as a method to transfer all of the stored settings of one instrument to another instrument, in so-called *bulk dumps*. Our founding fathers did not intend sysex messages to be used in real time—for example, while Channel Voice messages are being sent—but they are increasingly being put to this use.

All sysex messages conform to a simple structure. They begin with the System Exclusive status byte, 0xF0. A one- or three-byte Manufacturer ID number serves to identify the instrument for which the message is intended. If the first byte is a 0, the following two bytes form a 16-bit ID. Any number of data bytes may follow (all 7-bit, with the eighth bit set to 0). Normally, one or more of the early data bytes specify the instrument model and the type of sysex message. The entire message is terminated by an End of Exclusive status byte, an EOX (0xF7).

Manufacturers obtain ID numbers from the MIDI Manufacturer's Association (MMA). The ID-holders must publish the format of any sysex messages that are used on any released product. This information should be found in the user's manual for a given instrument.

Because of their potentially large size, merging sysex messages into a stream of Channel messages during playback can be risky. It will take more than a second for a 4,096-byte message to be transmitted. During that time, no other messages can be sent, possibly disrupting the smooth playback of the musical events. *Caveat emptor.*

A sysex message is terminated by either the trailing EOX status byte, or when any other status byte—other than a Real-Time message—is encountered. Real-Time messages will not affect a sysex message; they are effectively filtered out. In fact, when using

MIDI sync, MIDI Clocks can appear in the middle of sysex messages to maintain synchronization.

# MIDI Time Code and SMPTE

MIDI Time Code (MTC) and SMPTE are not the same thing, although the terms often are used interchangeably. SMPTE is an acronym for the Society of Motion Picture and Television Engineers, a group that generates technical standards for the audio, broadcast, and film industries. Some of the standards that SMPTE originates become so useful that they are adopted by the American National Standards Institute (ANSI). The particular standard that is useful for music is published as ANSI/SMPTE 12M-1986, and titled, *Time and Control Code*. This specification describes how time code is to be recorded on audio and video tape, as well as the proper format of the data that are recorded.

The audio or video tape that is used to synchronize sequencers is commonly striped with SMPTE time code. This audio signal marks on the tape the start of each "frame," and gives each frame a unique serial number. Frames occur at a specific, fixed rate. The four most common frame rates are 30 frames per second (fps), 29.97 fps (also known as 30-frame drop), 25 fps, and 24 fps. These frames correspond to frame rates used in television and film:

- 30 fps. B/W television and audio that will not be synced to video
- 29.97 fps. Color television and any audio synced to video
- 25 fps. European color television
- 24 fps. Film and any audio synced to film

Each frame has a serial number, given in hours, minutes, seconds, and frames. The frame number of each consecutive frame is incremented until it reaches the value of the frame rate. At that point the seconds number is incremented and, if necessary, the time rolls over into the minutes and hours fields as well. For example, while reading 30 fps time code, the frame number increments from 0 to 29. Instead of counting 30, it rolls over to 0 and the seconds field is incremented (because one second has elapsed). When 60 seconds go by, the minutes field is incremented, and so on.

The same thing happens for the other frame rates, with one exception. If the frame rate is 29.97 fps (actually, 29.97002617 fps), then slightly less than thirty frames will elapse each second. Another way of looking at it is that thirty frames will elapse in slightly more than one second. If no corrections are made to the counting of frames, then over time the frame number, viewed as hours, minutes, seconds, and frames will differ from time as measured with a stopwatch or wall clock. In fact, at the end of an hour, the frame numbers will differ from the stopwatch time by 108 frames, or about 3.6 seconds.

To make the frame numbers agree with a stopwatch, over time, a scheme of skipping (or dropping) frame numbers was devised by the all-knowing folks at SMPTE. The first two frames of every minute are skipped (i.e., 1:27:00:00 and 1:27:00:01). However, this subtracts 120 frames from the count every hour. This is too many; we only need to skip 108 frames. Therefore, no frames are dropped on minutes 0, 10, 20, 30, 40, and 50. This results in exactly 108 frames being dropped each hour, compensating for the difference between the time code frame numbers and the wall clock time.

This can be very confusing. It is important to remember that the dropped frames are not actually dropped. Nothing is removed and thrown away and no data are lost. It is simply that in counting the frames some of the frame numbers are skipped to make the numbers agree.

But what does all this have to do with MIDI Time Code? MIDI Time Code is the MIDI representation of SMPTE time code. Remember, SMPTE time code is the analog signal that marks each frame of time on a piece of audio or video tape. MIDI Time Code events occur at times corresponding to the frames that are striped on the tape. To convert SMPTE time code into MIDI Time Code you must use a SMPTE time code reader. Luckily, these are commonly available, either as standalone units or as MIDI interface built-ins. Even better, most of these readers can also write SMPTE time code so that tapes can be striped for later SMPTE/MTC synchronization.

MIDI Time Code takes two forms. The first, *Full messages*, are special 10-byte System Exclusive messages that fully specify the frame number for a given frame. Full messages can be used to update a MIDI receiver with the current frame number using a single message, or when receiving stalled SMPTE. Stalled SMPTE occurs when a reader sees the exact same frame number over and over again, as when syncing to video while the tape is paused. But not all devices respond to Full messages, so use them with caution.

*Quarter Frame messages*, on the other hand, are useful while tape is rolling. As the name implies, four Quarter Frame messages are sent for each frame of SMPTE that is read. Each message specifies which of eight messages in a series is being sent (the message type) and part of the frame number for this frame (the frame data). It takes eight Quarter Frame messages to fully specify a given frame, but since they come at the rate of four messages per frame, two frames' worth of messages are needed to get the complete frame number. Once an application that is reading MTC gets a complete frame, it can increment the frame number on every fourth Quarter Frame message, to get the frame number for the intermediate frames.

All Quarter Frame messages begin with the status byte 0xF1. They have one data byte that contains the message type and the frame data. The data byte is formatted like this:

0*nnndddd*

where *nnn* is binary 0–7 and *dddd* are 4 bits of frame data. Bits 4–6 have the following meaning:

*nnn*

0    Frame count low nibble

1    Frame count high nibble

2    Seconds count low nibble

3    Seconds count high nibble

4    Minutes count low nibble

5    Minutes count high nibble

6    Hours count low nibble

7    Hours count high nibble/frame rate

The nibbles from message types 0 and 1 are combined to find the frame count. Only the low 5 bits are significant; all others will be 0. Likewise, nibbles from types 2 and 3 are combined to find the seconds value, and nibbles from types 4 and 5 specify the minutes. The two nibbles from types 6 and 7 messages are also combined to find the hours value. However, bits 5 and 6 of the hours value are treated specially, since they indicate the frame rate:

0*ffhhhhh*

where *ff* is 00 for 24 fps, 01 for 25 fps, 10 for 30 fps drop (i.e., 29.97 fps), and 11 for 30 fps non-drop. The frame count ranges from 0 to one less than the frame rate. The highest frame number that can be specified is 23:59:59:29 for 30 fps MTC: the next frame in the sequence is 00:00:00:00.

A Full message is a 10-byte sysex message that specifies the frame time and format in a single packet. The sysex is formatted like this:

```
F0 7F 7F 01 01 hr mn sc fr F7
```

where *hr* (hours), *mn* (minutes), *sc* (seconds), and *fr* (frames) are the same format as outlined above.

MIDI Time Code (MTC) is a much more accurate timebase for tape synchronization than MIDI Clock messages. Assuming a tempo of 120 bpm, a MIDI Clock message would occur every 20.833 milliseconds. On the other hand, 30 fps non-drop MTC messages occur every 8.333 milliseconds. Additionally, MTC messages are more accurate because they are generated from a sequence of 80 bits per frame (as recorded on the tape) versus the 24 MIDI Clocks-per-quarter-note timebase for MIDI Clock synchronization. These advantages—combined with the high quality and low cost of some SMPTE/MTC readers—have made SMPTE/MTC the preferred tape synchronization method in modern music production.

# General MIDI

Imagine for a moment—if you will—the perfect symphony, recorded for all posterity as a MIDI sequence. When recording the sequence, we select certain sounds from the best-sounding MIDI device at our disposal: program 32 for violin sounds, program 55 for timpani, program 1 for grand piano. We choose these program numbers because these are the locations of the sounds we wish to use. The result is a performance worthy of a standing ovation.

Proudly, we take our new sequence to our friend's studio to hear it play on his far superior sound module. However, the results are not everything we hoped for. The piano sounds like a trumpet and the violins have morphed into pipe organs. And what must have once been timpani now sounds remarkably like a tortured cat. Not a happy sound.

The problem is that even though the two sound modules might have similar sounds available, they are organized in different ways. Program 1 on our instrument is a grand piano, but the same program number is assigned to a trumpet sound in our friend's sound module. Likewise, program 32 on the newer, better instrument produces pipe organ sounds instead of violins. And, program 55 is now the, well, tortured cat patch. How are we to ever hope that a sequence created for one set of sound modules will ever play properly on another?

The answer is called General MIDI. General MIDI specifies a minimum set of capabilities that a sound module should provide. Sound modules don't have to support General MIDI, but if they do they get to sport a nifty GM logo, and users get to record and play sequences without worrying about how they will sound on someone else's system.

## The General MIDI Mode

To be declared General MIDI-compliant, a sound module must possess a number of minimum features. It must have a GM sound set containing 128 different sounds, or presets, arranged in a particular order. It also must have a separate set of drum sounds, with each different sound mapped to particular key numbers. All of these sounds, both presets and drum, must be playable via a certain number of voices, and affected by a minimum set of controllers and other MIDI messages. Assured of these basic capabilities, music authors can create MIDI files that will sound right when played on a wide variety of systems.

General MIDI is also a mode. GM-compliant instruments can have multiple sound sets and operating modes. General MIDI does not limit what a given instrument can do. Because of this, there are two System Exclusive messages that switch an instrument in and out of the General MIDI mode. These messages are:

**General MIDI On:**    F0 7E *<device ID>* 09 01 F7

This message turns General MIDI mode on. The instrument will provide at least the minimum set of General MIDI functionality, and use the GM Sound Set and Percussion Map as the list of available sounds.

**General MIDI Off:**    F0 7E *<device ID>* 09 02 F7

This message turns General MIDI mode off. The receiving instrument will revert to its normal mode of operation.

In both cases, the *<device ID>* byte is either the device ID for the target instrument (available from the device's owner's manual), or 7F to broadcast the message to all devices. The 7F (broadcast) ID is recommended for most uses since it guarantees that all GM-capable devices on the system are in the proper mode.

## General MIDI Requirements

A GM sound device must have at least 24 voices that can be dynamically allocated across all 16 MIDI channels. Each channel can be assigned to a different preset sound. Channel 10 is always used for key-based percussion sounds. The 24 voices can either be dynamically allocated across all 16 channels (including the percussion sounds), or 8 of them can be allocated to the percussion sounds while the remaining 16 voices are dynamically allocated to the other channels.

**Table 2-6    General MIDI Controllers**

| Controller | Description |
|------------|-------------|
| 1 | Modulation |
| 7 | Volume |
| 10 | Pan |
| 11 | Expression |
| 64 | Sustain Pedal |
| 121 | Reset All Controllers |
| 123 | All Notes Off |

In addition, all of the channels respond to Pitch Bend (over a default range of ±2 semitones), Aftertouch, and a minimum set of controllers (shown in table 2-6). Of course, a given device may respond to a wider range of MIDI messages while in GM mode, but all GM sound devices will respond to these commands.

## The GM Sound Set

The General MIDI sound set is organized into 16 logical groups, and each group occupies 8 presets (table 2-7). The sound names serve as guidelines, so the sounds in one particular instrument may not be exactly like the sounds in another. Sound module manufacturers are free to use different architectures and sound synthesis methods in their products, so the sound quality may differ between devices. But a trumpet preset will be identifiable as a trumpet and a violin will sound like a violin, even if a little imagination might be needed in some cases. However, in all devices the presets are organized as shown in table 2-8.

## The Percussion Map

Except for the chromatic percussion presets in programs 9 through 16, all of the percussion sounds are played on channel 10. These sounds are mapped to particular keys, so that note number 36 sounds a bass drum while note number 70 plays maracas. There are 47 different percussion sounds that provide a basic "kit" that is suitable for most musical styles, (table 2-9).

**Table 2-7  General MIDI Instrument Groups**

| Preset | Instrument group | Preset | Instrument group |
|--------|------------------|--------|------------------|
| 1–8 | Piano | 65–72 | Reed |
| 9–16 | Chromatic Percussion | 73–80 | Pipe |
| 17–24 | Organ | 81-88 | Synth Lead |
| 25-32 | Guitar | 89–96 | Synth Pad |
| 33–40 | Bass | 97–104 | Synth Effects |
| 41–48 | Strings | 105-112 | Ethnic |
| 49–56 | Ensemble | 113–120 | Percussive |
| 57–64 | Brass | 121–128 | Sound Effects |

Copyright © 1991, 1994 MIDI Manufacturers Association—Used with Permission

**Table 2-8   General MIDI Sound Set**

| Preset | Sound | Preset | Sound | Preset | Sound | Preset | Sound |
|---|---|---|---|---|---|---|---|
| 1 | Acoustic Grand Piano | 33 | Acoustic Bass | 65 | Soprano Sax | 97 | Fx 1 (train) |
| 2 | Bright Acoustic Piano | 34 | Electric Bass (finger) | 66 | Alto Sax | 98 | Fx 2 (soundtrack) |
| 3 | Electric Grand Piano | 35 | Electric Bass (pick) | 67 | Tenor Sax | 99 | Fx 3 (crystal) |
| 4 | Honky-tonk Piano | 36 | Fretless Bass | 68 | Baritone Sax | 100 | Fx 4 (atmosphere) |
| 5 | Electric Piano 1 | 37 | Slap Bass 1 | 69 | Oboe | 101 | Fx 5 (brightness) |
| 6 | Electric Piano 2 | 38 | Slap Bass 2 | 70 | English Horn | 102 | Fx 6 (goblins) |
| 7 | Harpsichord | 39 | Synth Bass 1 | 71 | Bassoon | 103 | Fx 7 (echoes) |
| 8 | Clavi | 40 | Synth Bass 2 | 72 | Clarinet | 104 | Fx 8 (sci-fi) |
| 9 | Celesta | 41 | Violin | 73 | Piccolo | 105 | Sitar |
| 10 | Glockenspiel | 42 | Viola | 74 | Flute | 106 | Banjo |
| 11 | Music Box | 43 | Cello | 75 | Recorder | 107 | Shamisen |
| 12 | Vibraphone | 44 | Contrabass | 76 | Pan Flute | 108 | Koto |
| 13 | Marimba | 45 | Tremolo Strings | 77 | Blown Bottle | 109 | Kalimba |
| 14 | Xylophone | 46 | Pizzicato Strings | 78 | Shakuhachi | 110 | Bag Pipe |
| 15 | Tubular Bells | 47 | Orchestral Harp | 79 | Whistle | 111 | Fiddle |
| 16 | Dulcimer | 48 | Timpani | 80 | Ocarina | 112 | Shanai |
| 17 | Drawbar Organ | 49 | String Ensemble 1 | 81 | Lead 1 (square) | 113 | Tinkle Bell |
| 18 | Percussive Organ | 50 | String Ensemble 2 | 82 | Lead 2 (sawtooth) | 114 | Agogo |
| 19 | Rock Organ | 51 | Synthstrings 1 | 83 | Lead 3 (calliope) | 115 | Steel Drums |
| 20 | Church Organ | 52 | Synthstrings 2 | 84 | Lead 4 (chiff) | 116 | Woodblock |
| 21 | Reed Organ | 53 | Choir Aahs | 85 | Lead 5 (charang) | 117 | Taiko Drum |
| 22 | Accordion | 54 | Voice Oohs | 86 | Lead 6 (voice) | 118 | Melodic Tom |
| 23 | Harmonica | 55 | Synth Voice | 87 | Lead 7 (fifths) | 119 | Synth Drum |
| 24 | Tango Accordion | 56 | Orchestra Hit | 88 | Lead 8 (bass + lead) | 120 | Reverse Cymbal |
| 25 | Acoustic Guitar (nylon) | 57 | Trumpet | 89 | Pad 1 (new age) | 121 | Guitar Fret Noise |
| 26 | Acoustic Guitar (steel) | 58 | Trombone | 90 | Pad 2 (warm) | 122 | Breath Noise |
| 27 | Electric Guitar (jazz) | 59 | Tuba | 91 | Pad 3 (polysynth) | 123 | Seashore |
| 28 | Electric Guitar (clean) | 60 | Muted Trumpet | 92 | Pad 4 (choir) | 124 | Bird Tweet |
| 29 | Electric Guitar (muted) | 61 | French Horn | 93 | Pad 5 (bowed) | 125 | Telephone Ring |
| 30 | Overdriven Guitar | 62 | Brass Section | 94 | Pad 6 (metallic) | 126 | Helicopter |
| 31 | Distortion Guitar | 63 | SynthBrass 1 | 95 | Pad 7 (halo) | 127 | Applause |
| 32 | Guitar Harmonics | 64 | SynthBrass 2 | 96 | Pad 8 (sweep) | 128 | Gunshot |

**Table 2-9  Percussion Key Map**

| Key | Drum Sound | Key | Drum Sound | Key | Drum Sound |
|-----|------------|-----|------------|-----|------------|
| 35 | Acoustic Bass Drum | 51 | Ride Cymbal 1 | 67 | High Agogo |
| 36 | Bass Drum 1 | 52 | Chinese Cymbal | 68 | Low Agogo |
| 37 | Side Stick | 53 | Ride Bell | 69 | Cabasa |
| 38 | Acoustic Snare | 54 | Tambourine | 70 | Maracas |
| 39 | Hand Clap | 55 | Splash Cymbal | 71 | Short Whistle |
| 40 | Electric Snare | 56 | Cowbell | 72 | Long Whistle |
| 41 | Low Floor Tom | 57 | Crash Cymbal 2 | 73 | Short Guiro |
| 42 | Closed Hi Hat | 58 | Vibraslap | 74 | Long Guiro |
| 43 | High Floor Tom | 59 | Ride Cymbal 2 | 75 | Claves |
| 44 | Pedal Hi Hat | 60 | Hi Bongo | 76 | Hi Wood Block |
| 45 | Low Tom | 61 | Low Bongo | 77 | Low Wood Block |
| 46 | Open Hi Hat | 62 | Mute Hi Conga | 78 | Mute Cuica |
| 47 | Low-Mid Tom | 63 | Open Hi Conga | 79 | Open Cuica |
| 48 | Hi-Mid Tom | 64 | Low Conga | 80 | Mute Triangle |
| 49 | Crash Cymbal 1 | 65 | High Timbale | 81 | Open Triangle |
| 50 | High Tom | 66 | Low Timbale | | |

# MIDI Evolution

From the first simple implementations to the latest spec additions, MIDI has continuously evolved. In its current state it encourages a wide range of musical and control uses: many of them were never imagined by MIDI's creators. And it accomplishes these tasks with minimum cost, adequate performance, and maximum compatibility.

New features and popularity continue to drive MIDI's path of evolution as it becomes more mainstream. MIDI interfaces and MIDI file players appear on many new computers. Low-cost keyboards are available in high-volume discount stores, electronic emporiums, and perhaps even a few grocery stores. But there is still work to be done on the software side. Let's begin.

# CHAPTER 3

# Using MIDI in Windows

# Organization of the ToolKit

The software described in this book and supplied on the accompanying CDROM is a set of routines that allows you to write robust, high-performance MIDI applications for composition, musical experimentation, education, and games. The source code falls into three logical categories:

- Two Dynamic Link Libraries (DLLs) that handle MIDI input, MIDI output, and synchronization, and that provide support for Standard MIDI Files (SMFs).

- C++ classes that use the functions provided by the DLLs. These classes implement MIDI input, MIDI output, synchronization, SMF, track, and device menu objects for use in Microsoft Foundation Class (MFC) -based applications.

- C++ example programs that are written using these classes. Included are a MIDI spy program, a System Exclusive librarian, and a multitrack sequencer.

The low-level functions that locate and open input and output devices, and record and play back with synchronization are located in a 16-bit DLL, called MxMidi16. This is where functions inside of Windows are called to make MIDI happen. A second, 32-bit DLL, called MxMidi32, is used as an interface between 32-bit Windows 95 applications and the 16-bit DLL. This DLL also contains the functions that read and write Standard MIDI Files. Since these two DLLs are inseparable, they are collectively referred to as the MaxMidi DLLs (or DLL) throughout the rest of this book.

You don't need to understand what is going on inside of these two DLLs to use them in your programs. But there are some interesting things going on in there. Complete source code for the DLLs is included in appendix B (as well as on the disk), and a roadmap-style overview of what is going on in each set of functions appears at the end of chapters 4, 5, 6 and 8.

These DLLs can be called from any C or C++ program just as they are. But C++ *aficionados* get to write their programs using MFC-ready classes that provide an even easier and more extensive MIDI implementation. These classes include ones for MIDI input, output, and synchronization—all of which call the MaxMidi DLLs directly in their implementation. In addition, an SMF class adds support for reading and writing Standard MIDI Files, a track class manages MIDI data, and a couple of menu classes add easy support for pop-up menus for selecting input and output devices.

There are numerous example programs—all written in MFC—for use with Microsoft Visual C++ 4.x and 5.x. You can use these programs as starting points to develop your own killer MIDI applications. Each example builds on earlier ones, adding features and illustrating ToolKit features along the way. These examples culminate in three full-fledged, almost-ready-for-prime-time applications; a MIDI trace program, a System Exclusive librarian, and a simple multitrack sequencer.

The MIDI trace program, called *MidiSpy*, displays incoming MIDI data as either hexadecimal bytes or as an interpreted trace that indicates the type of message and data values. It can also echo received data to a selected output. This example shows the use of the ToolKit with simple non-synchronized input and output, and is a good place to start when trying to understand how to use the ToolKit functions.

A slightly more advanced program is a System Exclusive librarian called *SxLib*. This example will receive and send system exclusive bulk dumps and store them in standard format disk files. SxLib is a good place to start when developing that patch editor for your favorite synthesizer.

Finally, a simple multitrack sequencer, called *MaxSeq*, ties all of the concepts and features of the ToolKit together. This sequencer will record and play any number of tracks of MIDI at any tempo and save the data in Standard MIDI Files. Starting from this example, a world-class sequencer is only a user interface away. All of the MIDI functions are taken care of by the ToolKit. The MaxMidi C++ classes even have basic track editing functions built in.

# Windows and DLLs

But what are DLLs, and why are there two of them for the ToolKit functions? And why do we need DLLs at all?

In its most common use, a Dynamic Link Library—DLL, for those in the know—is an executable module that contains functions that can be called by any program. All a caller needs to know is the name of the DLL and what functions it makes available—*exports,* in DLL parlance. Lurking inside this simple definition are some remarkable capabilities. More than one application can call functions in a given DLL and, in Windows 95 at least, there is normally only one copy of the code that is shared by all callers. A program does not need to know anything about functions in the DLL, other than their names and the parameters they expect (and, of course, what they do), to call them. While the program is running, the DLL may not even be loaded from disk until it is needed. This saves memory and helps programs start faster. By not needing to know such plebeian details as the address in memory where a given function resides, applications can easily perform all sorts of programming marvels. For example, assume you wrote the wildly popular intergalactic word processor, StarWord. Marketing comes to you and says

## What's a Thunk?

A thunk is a small piece of code that allows a 32-bit process (i.e., a 32-bit DLL which is called from a 32-bit application) to execute code in a 16-bit process (i.e., a 16-bit DLL), or vice versa. Windows 95 uses a *flat* thunk that allows calls to occur in either direction. Windows 95 also supports *generic* thunks, which are also used in Windows NT. But generic thunks only allow 16-bit code to call 32-bit code.

A flat thunk is created using a *thunk compiler*. A thunk script—essentially a list of prototypes for the functions to be thunked—is processed by the thunk compiler, resulting in a short assembly language file. This file must then be assembled twice—once to generate the 16-bit side of the thunk layer and once to produce the 32-bit version. The 16-bit object file is linked into the 16-bit DLL, while the 32-bit file is linked into the 32-bit DLL. The two DLLs must each call a special *thunk connect* function so that the system can initialize the two thunk layers. One final embellishment makes the process complete. The 16-bit DLL must be tagged in a special way so that the Windows 95 module loader will handle the DLL properly. This tagging is done using a special version of the resource compiler.

Each object file contains several short code fragments. Two short pieces of code appear for each function that can be called in the other DLL—one for when the function is called, and one for when it returns. And a single thunk connect function is provided to initialize the thunk layer.

Thunking occurs in three phases. First, when the 32- and 16-bit DLLs load, their DLL entry points are called. The 32-bit

they have made a huge sale to the Klingon Federation. If you were clever and put all of your text display routines in a DLL, you could simply replace the English version DLL with a new Klingon version that uses the same function calls. Marketing is happy, you are happy, and best of all, the Klingons won't vaporize you for selling vaporware.

In the case of the ToolKit, some of the functions *must* be put in a DLL, no matter what the cost. There are two reasons for this. One is straightforward. To understand the other will require a discussion of the 32-bit universe, the infamous Win16Mutex, and thunking.

First the easy part. While a MIDI device is open, Windows sends messages that indicate that interesting things are happening. For example, every time a MIDI message is received by a hardware MIDI interface, the message is sent to a device driver. The device driver then sends the MIDI data to any application that has opened the device.

The catch is that the MIDI message could be received at any time, even while Windows is in the middle of something critical, like accessing a disk drive or allocating memory. The device driver will call the application (that is, whoever opened the device) at interrupt time. This code is called right then, no questions asked. If that part of the application's code is paged out to disk, the system would not be able to reload the code from disk and it would most likely crash.

As a result, the code to be called by the device driver must reside in a fixed, pagelocked segment. Any global data that the code expects to have access to must be fixed and locked as well. The easiest and best way to fix code like that is to place it in a DLL and set the FIXED attribute in the DLL's .def file. That way, the DLL will be loaded by the system and locked down so that it is never moved or paged out. Any time the device driver needs to call code in the DLL, it knows that the code will be present.

# Windows 95 and the Win16Mutex

During the design phase of Windows 95, the folks in Redmond had a problem and it wasn't just "Cappuccino or nonfat Latte?" They wanted to add the Win32 API for 32-bit applications while still supporting older Win16 applications. Windows 95 is preemptively multitasking, and each running program or task has at least one thread. Thus, a given piece of code can be in the middle of processing a call from one thread when it gets called from another thread. This works great if the code was designed to be reentrant. It is a disaster if the code is not reentrant.

Earlier versions of Windows were not preemptively multitasking. (That is, your program had to call `GetMessage`, `PeekMessage`, or `Yield`; otherwise Windows ground to a halt.) Therefore, any Win16 application running under Windows 95 has to be treated with kid gloves. This is done using a special flag, variously called the Win16Mutex, Win16Lock, or that [expletive deleted] Mutex. Any thread can claim the Win16Mutex, and while it has possession, no other thread can claim it without being blocked, since there can only be one owner of a mutex. When the mutex is released, the blocked thread will run.

In the context of 32-bit Windows 95, when 16-bit code runs, it claims the Win16Mutex, does its business, and then releases the mutex just before returning. But which 16-bit code are we talking about, exactly? Well, back in Redmond, the clever, hard-working programmers were given many (often conflicting) requirements for Windows 95. It needed to run 16-bit applications at least as well as Windows 3.1, operate "acceptably well" in only 4 MB of RAM, and ship on August 24th. Given those restrictions, they (wisely) chose to keep major portions of the system as 16-bit code and only wrote 32-bit code where it made

DLL's entry point is normally called `DLLMain()`. This function calls the thunk connect function which, in turn, calls a Windows system function to connect the thunk. Connecting, in this case, means replacing some of the thunk code with direct calls to Windows functions that actually perform the hard work. When the 16-bit DLL loads, its entry point is also called. But in this case, when the loader finds that the DLL has been specially tagged, an entry point called `DllEntryPoint()` is called. This entry point then calls the 16-bit version of the thunk connect function to initialize the 16-bit side of the thunk.

The second phase occurs when either the 16- or 32-bit DLL wishes to call a function in the other DLL. The caller's thunk code fragment converts each of the parameters into the proper form for the other DLL. Signed and unsigned integer (`int`) variables must be converted since integers are 16-bit in a 16-bit process and 32-bit in a 32-bit process. Likewise, pointers must be converted between 32-bit `near` pointers and 16-bit `far` (16:16) representations. Once the conversions are complete, and the parameters copied to a new stack, the processor is switched to the proper data-size mode, and the corresponding function is called in the destination DLL.

This "other side" function processes the call and eventually returns back to the caller, which in this case is the thunk layer code. This last phase converts any return values back into the proper representations, copies them to the proper stack, switches back to the original processor mode, and returns to the original caller. *Fait Accompli.*

## Creating and Using Thunks

Several unique tools are needed to build DLLs that use flat thunks. Two of them, the thunk compiler and a special version of the resource compiler, are distributed as part of the Win32 Software Development Kit (SDK). The Win32 SDK is included with the Microsoft Development Network (MSDN) Professional subscription. The SDK is supplied with some compilers, so you may already have these files. If not, you will need to purchase a MSDN subscription to get them. The MSDN comes on a stack of CDROMs, and includes versions of every operating system that Microsoft sells, along with gigabytes and gigabytes of example programs, documentation, SDKs, DDKs, tools, and more.

The thunk compiler accepts a thunk script file for input. This script specifies the function name and parameters for each function that will be thunked, which direction each pointer parameter can be passed through the thunk layer (input, output, or both), and other thunk compiler settings. The output of the thunk compiler is an assembly language file. This file must be assembled using the Microsoft assembler, MASM (version 6.11 or later), to create the two object files that implement the thunk layer. It may be possible to use other assemblers by careful editing of the assembly file.

But it is not necessary to have or use any of these tools to use the MaxMidi ToolKit. The two DLLs that contain the low-level MIDI functions are ready to go. Pre-thunked, you might say. However, you will need the thunk compiler, resource

the biggest improvement.

One of the parts of the system that remains 16-bit is the multimedia subsystem.* Most of the waveform audio, MIDI, and high-precision timing support resides in a 16-bit DLL called MMSYSTEM. Win32 provides a 32-bit module, called WINMM, that calls into MMSYSTEM using 32- to 16-bit thunks so that 32-bit applications can call multimedia API functions. However, this is of little value, as we shall see.

MMSYSTEM makes calls into device drivers to communicate with hardware devices, such as MIDI interfaces. A device driver is a 16-bit DLL that exports certain functions that MMSYSTEM knows to call. Such drivers can also have a special 32-bit portion, in the form of a VxD, that can provide improved performance and robustness, but MMSYSTEM never calls directly into such a VxD.

Every time that a 32-bit application calls one of the functions exported by WINMM, the corresponding function in MMSYSTEM is called via a *thunk*. A thunk is a small piece of code that takes any parameters passed and converts them into 16-bit versions (i.e., 32-bit integers and HANDLE become 16-bit versions), copies them to a 16-bit stack, switches stacks, changes the processor mode from 32-bit to 16-bit, claims the Win16Mutex, and calls the 16-bit function. When that function returns, the thunk reverses the process, converting parameters, switching stacks, releasing the mutex, etc. This thunking business takes a bit of time, but speed is not the major issue.

---

* The next version of Windows (aka Memphis, Windows 97, Windows 98, etc.) may change this. The Windows Driver Model (WDM), a device-driver architecture similar to that used in Windows NT, might eventually replace the 16-bit multimedia drivers used in previous versions of Windows. If this happens, two things are likely to be true: a new 32-bit multimedia subsystem will mean multimedia applications will have to be modified in order to support the new capabilities; and the old 16-bit drivers will continue to be supported so that existing programs will still work. But whether the WDM appears in any future version of Windows will remain a mystery until it is actually released in a retail version of our Favorite Operating System.

# Timers and Windows 95

Hardware timers are used by multimedia programs to achieve high-accuracy timing. The ToolKit uses a timer, started by a call to `timeSetEvent()`, when playing or recording MIDI with synchronization. This timer can have an accuracy as fine as 1 millisecond per interrupt; in such a case the timer callback function would be called every millisecond. This works great in a cooperatively multitasking operating system such as Windows 3.1.

But what about Windows 95? A fancy preemptive multitasking architecture demands a fancy timer architecture. In Windows 3.1 a timer callback is called when the PC's timing hardware interrupts the processor. In other words, the callback occurs at interrupt time. In Windows 95, however, the hardware interrupt causes a separate timer thread to execute. The callback function is then called when that thread receives a time slice from the operating system. This has two effects. First, it releases the restrictions on which functions can be called inside such a callback function. Second, it makes the timer completely useless if musical timing is needed.

For example, assume that your 32-bit program starts a multimedia timer so that it calls a callback function every 10 milliseconds. Normally, Windows 95 switches from thread to thread every 20 milliseconds. Assume for the moment there are three threads running in the system, including the blocked timer thread, which is last in the list of threads. When 10 milliseconds have passed, the timer thread becomes unblocked. The first thread executes, consuming its allotted 20 milliseconds. Then the second thread executes—another 20 milliseconds. Finally, the third thread, the one for the timer, gets to execute, but 40 milliseconds have passed. The system has already missed three other timer interrupts before it has even started to process the first one. But wait, there's more. There is no guarantee that each thread will use all of its allotted timeslice. It

compiler, and assembler if you wish to modify the MaxMidi DLLs and create new versions.

Given these three tools, you can create thunks in your own DLLs, or modify and build the MaxMidi DLLs by following these steps:

- Create or modify the thunk script as needed. The script that accompanies the ToolKit files (called MxMidi.thk and located in the ToolKit's Thunk folder) is a good example of a thunk script.
- Compile the thunk script using the thunk.exe compiler. This will generate an assembly file.
- Assemble the output of the thunk compiler. This must be done twice, once for the 16-bit side of the thunk (specifying /DIS_16 on the command line), and once for the 32-bit side (specifying /DIS_32).
- Add the resulting object files to the corresponding projects for the 16- and 32-bit DLLs.
- Add a new entry-point function, called `DllEntryPoint()`, to the 16-bit DLL. Call the thunk connect function from inside `DLLEntryPoint()`. See the MidiIn.c source module (located in the ToolKit's MxMidi16 folder) for an example of how this is done.
- Likewise, call the proper thunk connect function in the `DllMain()` entry point of the 32-bit DLL. The MxMidi32.c file (located in the MxMidi32 folder) provides an example.
- Add the following imports and exports to the 16-bit DLL's .def file:

```
EXPORTS
DLLENTRYPOINT @1
      RESIDENTNAME
MXMIDI_THUNKDATA16  @2
      RESIDENTNAME

IMPORTS
C16THKSL01=KERNEL.631
THUNKCONNECT16=KERNEL.651
```

- Add the Thunk32.lib library to the 32-bit DLL's project and add the following export to its .def file:

```
EXPORTS
MidiSy32_ThunkData32
```

- Compile and link the two DLLs.
- Tag the 16-bit DLL as subsystem 4 compatible using the version of the resource compiler (RC.EXE) that is found in the Win32sdk\MSTools\Binw16 folder of the Microsoft Win32 SDK CDROM. No other version will work for this task. The file is tagged like this:

```
rc -40 MxMidi16.res
          MxMidi16.dll
```

A batch file called rctag.bat is provided (in the ToolKit's MxMidi16 folder) as an example.

For more information on the use of the thunk compiler and thunking in general, see the Microsoft Knowledge Base articles Q125710, Q125715, and Q142564. Also, search for the keyword *thunk* in the Developer Network Library CDROM (part of the MSDN subscription) or on the Microsoft WWW site (`http://www.microsoft.com`).

might use all of it, none of it, or some amount in between. Since the duration of each thread is changing all the time, our poor timer thread gets timeslices at wildly varying intervals. If another thread starts—bringing the total to four threads—things get even worse!

The only good way out of this morass is to put all of the timing code in a 16-bit DLL. That way, the timer will behave like the old Windows 3.1 timer—thanks to the Win16Mutex. Because the MIDI input and output functions are so closely tied to timing, all of those functions belong in the DLL, too. Then, we can write 32-bit applications and get rock-solid timing as well, all thanks to our new-found friend, the Win16Mutex.

# *Low-Level MMSYSTEM MIDI Functions*

Any MIDI application is ultimately built on top of the low-level functions provided by Window's multimedia subsystem, MMSYSTEM. For example, the ToolKit DLLs call MMSYSTEM functions to open and close MIDI devices, send and receive MIDI events, and manage the MIDI interface hardware. The ToolKit source code is a good real-world example of how to use these Windows functions.

These functions use several data structures and handles during their operation. They are:

- `MIDIHDR`, which manages System Exclusive data blocks:

```
typedef struct midihdr_tag {
  LPSTR    lpData;                     // pointer to data
  DWORD    dwBufferLength;             // length of data
  DWORD    dwBytesRecorded;            // used for input
  DWORD    dwUser;                     // user data
  DWORD    dwFlags;
  struct midihdr_tag FAR *lpNext;      // reserved
  DWORD    reserved;                   // reserved
  DWORD    dwOffset;                   // callback offset
  DWORD    dwReserved[8];              // reserved
} MIDIHDR, *PMIDIHDR, FAR *LPMIDIHDR;
```

- `MIDIINCAPS`, which describes the capabilities of a MIDI input device:

```
typedef struct midiincaps_tag {
  WORD     wMid;                       // manufacturer ID
  WORD     wPid;                       // product ID
  VERSION  vDriverVersion;             // driver version
  char     szPname[MAXPNAMELEN];       // product name
  DWORD    dwSupport;                  // driver support flags
} MIDIINCAPS, *PMIDIINCAPS, FAR *LPMIDIINCAPS;
```

- `MIDIOUTCAPS`, which describes the capabilities of a MIDI output device:

```
typedef struct midioutcaps_tag {
  WORD     wMid;                       // manufacturer ID
  WORD     wPid;                       // product ID
  VERSION  vDriverVersion;             // driver version
  char     szPname[MAXPNAMELEN];       // product name
  WORD     wTechnology;                // device type
  WORD     wVoices;                    // # of voices
  WORD     wNotes;                     // max # of notes
  WORD     wChannelMask;               // channels used
  DWORD    dwSupport;                  // driver support flags
} MIDIOUTCAPS, *PMIDIOUTCAPS, FAR *LPMIDIOUTCAPS;
```

- `HMIDIIN`, a handle to a MIDI input device
- `HMIDIOUT`, a handle to a MIDI output device

The MMSYSTEM MIDI input and output functions are fully documented in compiler help files and other documentation available from Microsoft. But to make life easier when writing MIDI programs or reviewing the ToolKit source code, here is a quick reference guide to the most frequently used functions.

Notice that in these function lists the `wDeviceID` parameter always specifies the desired device. This value ranges from 0 up to the number of devices available on the system. Additionally, the `wSize` parameter specifies the size (in bytes) of the structure used by a particular function.

All of the functions return a `UINT` value. The `midiInGetNumDevs()` and `midiOutGetNumDevs()` functions return the specified number of devices. All of the other functions return code that indicates the outcome of the function call. The most common return codes are:

- `MMSYSERR_NOERROR (0)`

  The function completed normally.

- `MMSYSERR_BADDEVICEID (2)`

  An out-of-range device ID was specified.

- `MMSYSERR_ALLOCATED (4)`

  Device is already allocated and is not available.

- `MMSYSERR_INVALHANDLE (5)`

  An illegal device handle was specified.

- `MMSYSERR_NODRIVER (6)`

  No device driver is present for this device.

- `MMSYSERR_NOMEM (7)`

  Driver memory allocation error.

- `MIDIERR_UNPREPARED (64)`

  Header is not prepared.

- `MIDIERR_STILLPLAYING (65)`

  Attempt to close device while still playing.

- `MIDIERR_NOTREADY (67)`

  Hardware is busy.

## MIDI Input Functions

- `UINT` ***midiInGetNumDevs***`();`

  Returns the number of input devices available on the system.

- `UINT` ***midiInGetDevCaps***`(UINT wDeviceID, LPMIDIINCAPS lpCaps, UINT wSize);`

Fills the MIDIINCAPS structure, pointed to by lpCaps, with the capabilities for the specified device.

- UINT *midiInOpen*(LPHMIDIIN lphMidiIn, UINT wDeviceID, DWORD
                    dwCallback, DWORD dwCallbackInstance, DWORD dwFlags);

Opens the specified device for input. A handle to the device is returned in lphMidiIn. dwFlags specifies the type of callback that is used to alert the application to events. Common callback types are CALLBACK_WINDOW and CALLBACK_FUNCTION. dwCallback specifies the callback function address or window handle, while dwCallbackInstance specifies user data that are passed to callback functions (but not to window callbacks).

- UINT *midiInClose*(HMIDIIN hMidiIn);

Closes the specified input device.

- UINT *midiInPrepareHeader*(HMIDIIN hMidiIn, LPMIDIHDR lpMidiInHdr,
                             UINT wSize);

Prepares a header, normally used for sysex messages, for processing by the device. The header structure and data buffer (lpData field of MIDIHDR structure) must be allocated using GlobalAlloc() using the GMEM_MOVEABLE and GMEM_SHARE flags.

- UINT *midiInUnprepareHeader*(HMIDIIN hMidiIn, LPMIDIHDR lpMidiInHdr,
                               UINT wSize);

Cleans up the preparation done by a previous call to midiInPrepareHeader().

- UINT *midiInAddBuffer*(HMIDIIN hMidiIn, LPMIDIHDR lpMidiInHdr, UINT
                         wSize);

Sends the buffer managed by the specified MIDIHDR structure to the device. Received sysex data are stored in the buffer which is returned to the application when filled.

- UINT *midiInStart*(HMIDIIN hMidiIn);

Enables MIDI input from the already-opened device.

- UINT *midiInStop*(HMIDIIN hMidiIn);

Stops MIDI input from the device.

- UINT *midiInReset*(HMIDIIN hMidiIn);

Flushes any pending input buffers and stops input.

# MIDI Output Functions

- UINT ***midiOutGetNumDevs***();

Returns the number of output devices available on the system.

- UINT ***midiOutGetDevCaps***(UINT wDeviceID, LPMIDIOUTCAPS lpCaps, UINT wSize);

Fills the MIDIOUTCAPS structure, pointed to by lpCaps, with the capabilities for the specified device.

- UINT ***midiOutOpen***(LPHMIDIOUT lphMidiOut, UINT wDeviceID, DWORD dwCallback, DWORD dwCallbackInstance, DWORD dwFlags);

Opens the specified device for output. A handle to the device is returned in lphMidiOut. dwFlags specifies the type of callback that is used to alert the application. Common callback types are CALLBACK_WINDOW and CALLBACK_FUNCTION. dwCallback specifies the callback function address or window handle, while dwCallbackInstance specifies user data that are passed to callback functions (but not to window callbacks).

- UINT ***midiOutClose***(HMIDIOUT hMidiOut);

Closes the specified output device.

- UINT ***midiOutShortMsg***(HMIDIOUT hMidiOut, DWORD dwMsg);

Sends a short (non-sysex) message to the specified device. The message is packed into a DWORD, with the first byte of the message in the least significant byte.

- UINT ***midiOutLongMsg***(HMIDIOUT hMidiOut, LPMIDIHDR lpMidiOutHdr, UINT wSize);

Sends a buffer of data, generally part or all of a sysex, to the specified device. The MIDIHDR structure must be properly initialized and prepared before calling this function.

- UINT ***midiOutPrepareHeader***(HMIDIOUT hMidiOut, LPMIDIHDR lpMidiOutHdr, UINT wSize);

Prepares a header, normally used for sysex messages, for processing by the device. The header structure and data buffer (lpData field of MIDIHDR structure) must be allocated using GlobalAlloc() using the GMEM_MOVEABLE and GMEM_SHARE flags.

- UINT ***midiOutUnprepareHeader***(HMIDIOUT hMidiOut, LPMIDIHDR lpMidiOutHdr, UINT wSize);

Cleans up the preparation done by a previous call to midiOutPrepareHeader().

- UINT *midiOutReset*(HMIDIOUT hMidiOut);

    Flushes any pending output buffers and, with some drivers, also sends Note Off messages for all notes on all channels.

# Putting MIDI to Use

We've seen some of the ins and outs of MIDI under Windows 95. Armed with this background we can begin to write useful programs to perform death-defying MIDI feats. Future chapters will attempt to perform such feats, first using the low-level MMSYSTEM functions and then with the much easier-to-use ToolKit functions.

**CHAPTER 4**

# Sending MIDI

# It's An Event

MIDI is a stream of bytes that make up events. For most (though not all) MIDI messages, a single byte does not contain enough information to be complete. Complete events can take one, or two, and often three bytes to give you enough to do the job.

In the ToolKit, a single event—containing a complete MIDI message—is contained in a `MidiEvent` structure. The structure contains a 32-bit timestamp that is used to specify the record or playback time, and four bytes that specify the message.

The structure is defined like this:

```
typedef struct {
    DWORD   time;   // time in ticks since last event
    BYTE    status; // status byte of this midi message
    BYTE    data1;  // first data byte of message
    BYTE    data2;  // second data byte of message
    BYTE    data3;  // third data byte, used for tempo changes
} MidiEvent;


typedef MidiEvent* LPMIDIEVENT;
```

For the moment, we will ignore the `time` value. It will become useful later when we need to play or record MIDI with sync. The `status` value must always be set to the status value for the message, even if we wish to use running status. The other three values, `data1`, `data2`, and `data3` are used depending on the number of data bytes for the message type specified in `status`. For messages that don't have any data bytes, such as Active Sensing or Start, all three bytes are ignored. Other messages, like MIDI Time Code, use a single data byte, always in `data1`. Most messages use two data bytes. These include Note On and Note Off messages. Set `data1` to the first byte (i.e., the note number) and set `data2` to the second byte (i.e., the velocity). The `data3` value is used by the ToolKit to contain tempo change events. These events are discussed later in the book.

But what about System Exclusive messages? They take more than three or four bytes. How do they fit in here? Well, they are contained in the `MidiEvent` structure, one byte per structure. For example, the sysex message F0 7E 00 06 01 F7 would be sent using six `MidiEvent` structures, one for the SYSEX (F0), one for each of the four data bytes, and one for the EOX (F7).

Does something seem fishy here? The four data bytes cannot go into the `status` member of the `MidiEvent`. They each have to go into the `data1` member. In the ToolKit, the `status` value must always be the message status: F0 must appear in all six `MidiEvent` structures that make up the sysex. So, `data1` will be F0 for the first event, and will be F7 for the last, while `status` will be F0 for all of them. It's a small price to pay for being able to merge sysex messages in with other MIDI messages. And, the F0 in the `status` member lets the ToolKit know that all of the data are part of a single System Exclusive message. System Exclusive messages are such an interesting subject that they get dissected in great detail later in this book.

# Devices and Drivers

Part of the appeal of using Windows for music is the wide range of different types of MIDI devices that can be connected to a Windows-based computer. Sound cards, internal MIDI interfaces, interfaces connected to printer ports and serial ports, virtual pianos, and even guitars can be connected to PCs. And with the right magic (in the form of a device driver) they will appear as MIDI input or output devices for your program to use.

Such multimedia device drivers are small programs, usually written in C and Assembler, that are automatically loaded by Windows and thus become part of the operating system. They send and receive data to and from the hardware interface, and convert data into a form suitable for use by a Windows application. Every type of interface wants to be "talked" to in a certain way for it to function correctly. In the Bad Old DOS days, each MIDI program had to be written specifically to support whatever hardware was desired. If a program didn't support your new XYZ brand of interface it was tough luck—at least until the overworked and underpaid programmers had time to add support for your interface.

Those days ended with Windows 3.1, when Microsoft added Multimedia Extensions to every system by including a system for device drivers. Now, if your program uses the proper Multimedia API functions, it works with all MIDI interfaces, including ones that are just a gleam in the eyes of a friendly engineer.

# Identifying Devices

So, what MIDI interfaces are available and how do we get at them? First, we need to find out if there are *any* interfaces available in a system, and if so, how many. This is easily done by calling the MMSYSTEM function `midiOutGetNumDevs()`. It returns the number of devices present on the system. Unfortunately, it tells us nothing about the actual availability of a device. The device could be in use by another program, and won't allow itself to be shared, or it might not even be connected to the computer or turned on. We will have to content ourselves with simply knowing we *might* be able to use it and wait until later (when opening the device) to find out if we actually *can*. A given piece of hardware may have more than one input or output—normally called ports. Each port is considered to be a separate device, even though it may be physically part of an interface with other, similar ports.

Getting the names of the devices is the next order of business. This is very useful information, especially when available in a drop-down menu or as a list of devices in a dialog. Helpfully, MMSYSTEM supplies another function that will return the name of a particular device, along with several other, less useful, bits of information. Getting a list of device names is a simple matter of iterating through all of the present devices and saving the name strings or inserting them into a menu.

Each device is specified as a number, called a device ID, ranging from 0 to one less than the number of devices present (i.e., the number returned by `midiOutGetNumDevs()`). The device ID for a particular device can change from session to session, but will be constant during the running life of a program. It may change when new devices and device drivers are added or removed from the system.

This means that identifying a device by its ID is a necessary but tenuous enterprise. Normally, a program will want to save the user's device selections. It's best to save the device's string name instead of the device ID. Then, when reopening the device later, the program can search through the list of device names to find the proper device ID and select the correct device. This ensures that the addition of a new device will not cause the program to break.

Getting the name of a device is so common and useful that MaxMidi supplies a function to make it easy:

```
BOOL GetMidiOutDescription(WORD wDeviceID, LPSTR lpszDesc);
```

This function gets the name of the specified device and copies it to the string that is pointed to by `lpszDesc`. Make sure that `lpszDesc` points to enough memory to hold the entire name, which will be no longer then `MAXPNAMELEN` (32) bytes. `GetMidiOutDescription()` returns TRUE if the device exists and FALSE if it does not. But avoid attempting to retrieve the name of a device that is outside the range of devices returned by `midiOutGetNumDevs()`, or the system may become unstable.

Getting the device ID when we have the device name is almost as easy. This function will appear later in the `CMaxMidiOut` class. Here is a C function that does the trick:

```
WORD GetIDFromName(LPSTR lpszDesc)
{
    WORD id;
```

```
char thisDesc[MAXPNAMELEN];
WORD MaxDevs = midiOutGetNumDevs();

for(id = 0; id < MaxDevs; id++)
{
        GetMidiOutDescription(id, thisDesc);
        if(strcmp(thisDesc, lpszDesc) == 0)
                return id;

        id++;
}

return ERR_NOMATCH;
}
```

The function returns an ID of ERR_NOMATCH if it cannot find a match. This usually means that the device has been removed from the system. A kind word to the user is advisable in that case.

# Initializing the MaxMidi System

The MaxMidi system needs to be initialized by applications that use its functions. To initialize MaxMidi, call the GetMaxMidiVersion() function. GetMaxMidiVersion() performs two tasks: it resizes the window message queue and it returns the version number of the MaxMidi DLLs. This C-language function should be called even if your application uses only ToolKit C++ classes (described in later chapters), since these classes call functions in the MaxMidi DLLs.

For MaxMidi to work best, the message queue should be enlarged from the default 8 message size to a more spacious 64 messages. MaxMidi posts messages to alert the client application of events and for internal housekeeping, and having a larger message queue improves performance. This is the major benefit of the GetMaxMidiVersion() function. The function is prototyped like this:

```
WORD GetMaxMidiVersion(void);
```

This function must be called—once only—before any application windows are created. If it is called after one or more windows exist, the system will likely crash, since the message queue—which is already in use—will be deleted and recreated in a larger form.

The return value contains the DLL version number, encoded in two bytes of a word value. The high-order byte holds the major version number, while the low byte specifies the minor (hundredths) version number.

# Opening the MIDI Output Device

It's time to open the device and get down to business. To open the device, call the `OpenMidiOut()` function. It is prototyped like this:

```
HMOUT OpenMidiOut(HWND hWnd, WORD wDeviceID, HSYNC hSync, DWORD dwFlags);
```

The `wDeviceID` parameter is the device ID that we found above. For simple MIDI output we don't need to use any synchronization. In this case, set the `hSync` parameter to 0 to indicate that sync will not be used. Synchronization is discussed in chapters 7 and 8.

The MIDI output device will need to send messages to the client application. The `hWnd` parameter specifies a window handle to the window that will receive these messages. Two messages are sent by the device: `MOM_CLOSE` indicates that the device has been closed, while `OUTBUFFER_READY` indicates that the output buffer is ready to accept more data. `OUTBUFFER_READY` is used to "pump" data to the device and is sent when the device is ready for more data. This message is most useful when using synchronization.

`OpenMidiOut()` performs several tasks. First, it does a bit of sanity checking to see if the requested device ID is valid. *Valid* in this case means that the ID is less than the number of devices installed in the system or is the special value of `MIDI_MAPPER` (−1). By specifying `MIDI_MAPPER` you can use Windows' built-in MIDI mapper to map channels to different instruments. If the mapper is not present, then specifying `MIDI_MAPPER` will cause the open request to fail.

Next, `OpenMidiOut()` allocates a block of memory to contain a `MidiOutStruct` structure. This structure has oodles of members that keep track of a given MIDI output device. After initializing the structure, the device driver is opened by calling the MMSYSTEM function `midiOutOpen()`. If the open succeeds, it allocates one or more queues that will hold MIDI events during output.

The open function always creates a queue that will receive non-sysex events. The size of the queue is specified in the `dwFlags` parameter; bits 12–15 encode the size, which ranges from 64 events to 32,768 events. The default size is 512 events. Other queues (really just buffers) are created if the `ENABLE_SYSEX` flag is set in `dwFlags`. If that flag is not set, then the buffers are not created (thus saving memory) and any sysex messages are ignored. Chapter 6 has more information on handling System Exclusive messages. Symbolic names for the event and sysex queue sizes are shown in table 4-1.

**Table 4-1 Queue Size Flags**

| | | |
|---|---|---|
| QUEUE_64 | SXBUF_64 | 64 messages |
| QUEUE_128 | SXBUF_128 | 128 messages |
| QUEUE_256 | SXBUF_256 | 256 messages |
| QUEUE_512 | SXBUF_512 | 512 messages |
| QUEUE_1K | SXBUF_1K | 1,024 messages |
| QUEUE_2K | SXBUF_2K | 2,048 messages |
| QUEUE_4K | SXBUF_4K | 4,096 messages |
| QUEUE_8K | SXBUF_8K | 8,192 messages |
| QUEUE_16K | SXBUF_16K | 16,384 messages |
| QUEUE_32K | SXBUF_32K | 32,768 messages |

After all of the necessary queues are allocated, the open function has one final task. It creates a hidden window that is used internally to deal with the device driver when sending sysex messages and when performing other internal housekeeping chores.

If the open request is successful, the function returns a handle to the MIDI output device, an HMOUT. This handle is opaque. That is, it is just a numerical value and has no meaning in your application except to identify the particular output device. You pass this "magic cookie" to any of the MIDI output functions when you want to do something to a particular device.

## Sending An Event

Once the device is open, sending MIDI is simple. Just fill a MidiEvent structure with the proper values and call PutMidiOut(), like this:

```
HMOUT hMidiOut;
MidiEvent Evt;

hMidiOut = OpenMidiOut(hMyWnd, 0, 0, QUEUE_512);
if(hMidiOut != 0)
{
    Evt.status = 0x90;
    Evt.data1 = 0x3C;
    Evt.data2 = 0x40;
    PutMidiOut(hMidiOut, &Evt);
}
```

A Note On message for middle C on channel 1, with a velocity of 64 just went out the MIDI port. That's all there is to it! Notice that the open function specifies a handle to your application's window (hMyWnd above), the first output MIDI device (with a device ID of 0), no synchronization, and a MIDI queue of 512 events. The call to PutMidiOut() passes the handle to the opened device and a pointer to the MidiEvent structure.

PutMidiOut() then puts the event in the queue (into one of the 512 possible locations) and returns. Actually, that's a bit of a simplification. PutMidiOut() handles the event in one of several ways, depending on the type of event and whether synchronization is being used. In our simple example—sending a Note On event without synchronization—the event is placed in the queue, but is removed from the queue right away and sent directly to the MIDI driver. If synchronization is being used, the event is queued until it is time to play the event. System Exclusive messages are queued in a different way (but your program never knows the difference).

The more observant reader has, no doubt, noticed something slightly askew in the example above. A MidiEvent structure is eight bytes long, but the example only initializes three of these bytes. In fact, the first four bytes are a timestamp and the last byte is an extended data byte that is used to handle tempo changes. These structure members only have meaning during synchronization and are ignored if no sync device is specified when the output device is opened. So, in this case it is safe to only set the three bytes that make up the MIDI message. In general, the output device will ignore any members of a MidiEvent structure that don't apply in a given instance. For example, not all MIDI messages use three bytes; many of them are only one or two bytes long. PutMidiOut() will ignore the extra data bytes in the structure if the message does not need them.

However, there is one hard, fast rule that applies. All events must have a status byte. No exceptions. PutMidiOut() does not know about running status; it needs the status of every message to know how to handle the event. In fact, the only place in Windows where running status can be honestly applied is in the device driver. If the device driver or the hardware device can handle running status, it will. Status bytes must be supplied everywhere else.

One other detail is omitted from the example: PutMidiOut() has an important return value. It returns 0 if the event was accepted (queued or sent to the driver) or –1 if the queue is full and no more events can be accepted until some of the events are output by the driver. A well-written program (that is, not a simplified example in a book) should check the return value and act accordingly.

# Closing the MIDI Output

To paraphrase a popular protest song from the 1960s: Everybody must get closed. When the output device is no longer needed, it must be closed. Otherwise, other applications may not be able to access the MIDI device and a potentially large amount of memory will leak onto the floor and stain the carpeting. Keep in mind that MIDI is a 16-bit subsystem—even in Windows 95. Windows can clean up after errant 32-bit processes, since resources used in these processes are tagged with corresponding process IDs. A 16-bit process doesn't have this luxury, so its resources (including open MIDI devices) will not be automatically freed when the application terminates.

To close the device, simply call `CloseMidiOut()` and pass the handle that you received when you opened the device. Make sure to never call `CloseMidiOut()` on an already closed handle, since the function will attempt to free memory that does not exist, with disastrous results. All ToolKit functions ignore NULL handles, so setting a closed handle to 0 is a good safety practice. To continue our simple example:

```
CloseMidiOut(hMidiOut);
hMidiOut = 0;                    // for safety!
```

When `CloseMidiOut()` executes, it sends Note Off messages for any notes that are still sounding, closes the device driver, and frees all of the memory that it was using to manage the MIDI output device.

Because most MIDI drivers close very quickly and normally purge themselves of any pending events in the process, closing the device soon after sending data will generally cause MIDI messages to be lost. Instead, open a device when your program finds it needs to use a MIDI output, use that device, and then close the device when your program terminates or when you are sure that enough time has passed for all of the MIDI events to have been sent. Remember, MIDI is glacially slow compared to a 100-MHz Pentium computer.

# Other Useful MIDI Output Functions

The MaxMidi DLLs export two other MIDI output-related functions; `FlushMidiOut()` and `ResetMidiOut()`. These functions provide extra control of the MIDI output stream.

`ResetMidiOut()` does everything that `CloseMidiOut()` does, except actually close the device. In fact, `CloseMidiOut()` calls `ResetMidiOut()` when it wants to stop MIDI from playing and needs to send Note Off messages for any currently sounding notes. Some device drivers—including one for an extremely popular sound card—will send a Note Off message for every note on every channel in response to being reset. These 2,048 MIDI messages can take several seconds to be output by the driver, causing the call to `ResetMidiOut()` or `CloseMidiOut()` to not return for quite a long time. The only known cure for this malady is to contact the manufacturer of the offending device and request a driver that does not send these Note Off messages.

The `FlushMidiOut()` function merely empties the outgoing MIDI queue of all events. This can be used to stop output without closing the device. For example, when implementing a panic button, use `FlushMidiOut()` to purge any pending events before preparing to output a block of Note Off messages.

# Inside MIDI Output

Buried deep down in the MaxMidi DLLs are secrets and treasures, waiting for the programming adventurer to discover. This section provides a pirate's map to help you navigate through deeper waters. It is not necessary to understand what goes on inside the DLLs to use the functions they export. But if you want to modify them to do something special, or if you just want to know more, read on.

## Callbacks and Fixed Code Segments

At some point when sending or receiving MIDI, Windows inevitably needs to notify your program of interesting things. A received MIDI message, notification of a sent sysex buffer (more on that later), or an indication that a device was successfully opened or closed are some of the messages that Windows might want to send to your program. There are two ways to receive these messages.

The easy method is to pass a window handle to the open function and process these messages in your window procedure. While easy to implement, this method has several major problems. The messages must pass through the Windows message queue and be read out of the queue by `GetMessage()` or `PeekMessage()` in your application's message loop. This means that these messages may take a long time to be received and processed by your window proc, with disastrous results. Using this method means that your program does not know when a message arrived, so recording or playing back with synchronization is out of the question. It also means that the message might be delayed or lost whenever your application is not spinning in its message loop. Imagine dragging a window on the screen and having MIDI playback stop.

A better way of handling these messages is to allow Windows to call a callback function whenever it wants to let you know something is happening. The callback is called immediately and your code can respond to the message quickly. In fact, the callback is called so quickly that there are serious restrictions on which functions you can call inside of such a callback function. This is part of what makes MIDI in Windows such a joy!

These callback functions are called at interrupt time, and this is the source of most of the restrictions. Interrupts happen *right now,* and as the name so cleverly hints, they interrupt whatever might be going on. The system might be allocating memory, accessing a disk drive, drawing on the screen, or making tea. Since the system might be interrupted while executing a function that your callback might want to call, the list of Windows API functions that can be called at interrupt time is depressingly short.

The functions that can be called were written to be reentrant. This means that if they are executing and are interrupted and called again by the interrupting code, they will behave themselves. Most of the internals of Windows were written *not* to be reentrant. Rewriting Windows to be reentrant would be a grand pain in the neck and would make it even slower and more memory hungry than it already is. So the designers of Windows wisely choose to limit the number of reentrant-capable functions. In fact, reentrancy issue is the origin of the much-maligned Win16Mutex flag.

From this short list, two classes of functions stand out as most useful. First, a callback can call `PostMessage()`. Second, a callback can call several MMSYSTEM functions, including ones for sending MIDI to a driver. Almost everything else you might want to do is off-limits, including memory allocation, GUI drawing or painting functions, and file access.

The code for such a callback must always be present in memory and can never be moved by the system. This rule means that the code and data segments must be fixed and pagelocked. The easiest and best way to do that is to place the code in a DLL and set the FIXED attribute in the DLL's .def file. Conveniently, the 16-bit MaxMidi DLL, MxMidi16, where these callbacks reside already has the proper attributes set in its .def file.

## MIDI Output Data Flow

The data flow diagram below shows the logical flow of information through the system when sending non-sysex MIDI messages. (Chapter 6 expands this diagram for handling sysex data.) On one side is the Client App, your program. The Client App is the sender of MIDI messages and receiver of window messages. On the other side is the hardware MIDI interface; it receives MIDI from the system and sends it to the outside world.

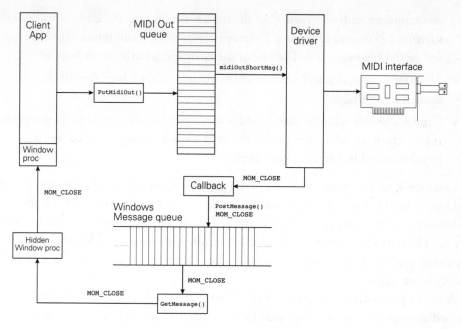

**Figure 4-1    MIDI output data flow (non-sysex)**

To use the MIDI output capabilities of the ToolKit, a device must be chosen and opened by the Client App. The `OpenMidiOut()` function performs the following steps:

- Checks the requested device ID to see if it is valid. If the requested device does not exist, the open request fails. The MIDI Mapper is handled as a special case.

- Allocates memory for a structure that holds all of the variables needed to control this device. The returned HMOUT handle is actually a DWORD that was the same numerical value as a pointer to this structure. But don't try to de-reference this handle to get to the structure; it is only valid as a pointer on the 16-bit side of the Windows universe.

- Calls `midiOutOpen()` to open the device driver for the requested interface, like this:

```
wLastError = midiOutOpen(&lpMO->hMidiOut, wDeviceID,
           (DWORD)MidiOutCallback, (DWORD)lpMO, CALLBACK_FUNCTION);
```

Calling `midiOutOpen()` will fill the `hMidiOut` member of our `MidiOut` structure with a handle to the device, based on the requested device ID. Anytime it needs to communicate with the "owner" of the device, in this case the DLL, it will call the `MidiOutCallback()` function. If the open request succeeds, the `wLastError` value will be 0. Otherwise, it will be one of the error codes outlined on page 40.

- Allocates a queue that will receive `MidiEvents` from the Client App (if the device is opened successfully).

- Creates a hidden window that is used internally to handle certain messages; primarily to clean up when the device driver is closed—using the `CloseMidiOut()` function—and in handling sysex buffers.

Once the device is open, sending a MIDI message is simple. The Client App fills the eight-byte `MidiEvent` structure with the event to be sent. The first four-bytes of a `MidiEvent` are a timestamp, which is ignored if the device is not attached to a sync device. The status byte must always be filled in; the system needs to know the status of each message to know how best to process it. The other bytes are filled in as needed by the particular message.

A call to `PutMidiOut()` gets the ball rolling. `PutMidiOut()`, located in MxMidi32, immediately thunks down to PutMidiOut16, located in MxMidi32. After a few validity checks, the function checks the timestamp of the event. If it is –1 (0xFFFFFFFF) the event is output immediately and the function returns. This serves as an escape valve to allow a Client App to send events without queueing. This is mostly useful when playing back with synchronization, since it bypasses the playback queue and outputs the event right away.

Otherwise, the event is added to the queue, if there is room. Since we opened the device without synchronization, the event is read right back out of the queue and sent to the MIDI driver by calling `midiOutShortMsg()`. What (you might well ask) is the point of putting the event into a queue and then taking it right back out? None, I say, when you are not using synchronization. Everything, however, when you are. Synchronization is covered later, in chapters 7 and 8.

`PutMidiOut()` performs one last trick before it returns. It calls an internal function, `TrackMidiOut()`, which sets or clears a bit in a table (kept in the `MidiOutStruct` for the device) that indicates whether the corresponding note is sounding. There is one bit per possible MIDI note on each channel, 2,048 bits (256 bytes) in all. This table will come in handy when closing or resetting the output device.

The call to `midiOutShortMsg()` that happened above looks like this:

```
midiOutShortMsg(lpMidiOut->hMidiOut, dwMsg);
```

lpMidiOut is the pointer to the MidiOutStruct for this device. It was obtained by casting the HMOUT that was passed from the Client App to an LPMIDIOUT. Remember, the HMOUT handle is numerically the same as a pointer to the structure, but is only valid as a pointer inside a 16-bit process. Since PutMidiOut16() *is* in a 16-bit process we can use this sleight-of-hand cast to get the pointer.

The MIDI message itself is passed in a DWORD called dwMsg. The message is encoded in the right-most three bytes of the DWORD, with the status byte on the right. This can make viewing the event in a debugger something of a brain-twister, since the message 90 3C 40 would be 0x00403C90 when sent to midiOutShortMsg().

The ResetMidiOut() function is simple; it flushes any pending events in the output queue and then calls the internal function TurnOffNotes(). This function iterates through the table maintained by TrackMidiOut() and sends a Note Off message for any note in the table whose bit is set. This will turn off any notes that might be playing, preventing stuck notes and relieving the Client App from having to keep track of which notes are still sounding.

FlushMidiOut() is even simpler. It forces the input and output pointers for the MIDI queue (and the span count of the number of events in the queue) to be 0. What more could we ask for?

Closing the MIDI output device is the reverse of opening it. CloseMidiOut(), after thunking down to CloseMidiOut16(), resets the output by calling ResetMidiOut() and then closes the device driver by calling midiOutClose(). This will cause the device driver to send a MOM_CLOSE message to our callback function, MidiOutCallback(). Since this happens at interrupt time, there is not much that can be done that is interesting. So, PostMessage() sends a corresponding MOM_CLOSE message to the hidden window.

Eventually, the Client App, which is dutifully fishing messages out of the window message queue by periodically calling GetMessage(), passes the MOM_CLOSE message to the hidden window's window proc. There, a MOM_CLOSE message is posted to the Client App's window (the one registered when OpenMidiOut() was called), and all the memory used by the MIDI output device is freed. Finally, the hidden window destroys itself, bringing to a close this MIDI output device (pun intended).

# CHAPTER 5

# Receiving MIDI

MIDI input—as implemented in the MaxMidi ToolKit—is very similar to MIDI output. The functions that identify, open, and close these two kinds of devices are almost identical. Likewise, both input and output devices use the same `MidiEvent` structure for handling MIDI data.

But there are important differences between MIDI input and output. From a program's point of view, the input process is passive—the program waits patiently for a MIDI event to arrive. On the other hand, output is active—events are sent as a result of direct action by the program. These differences are handled using two mechanisms: the application controls MIDI input by turning on or off the input device, and window messages notify the application when MIDI events are received. The program's ability to apply brakes to MIDI input ensures that events arrive only when it is ready to receive them. When events are received, they are retrieved from MaxMidi in response to window messages. Thus, the application becomes an active partner in handling MIDI input.

# Opening and Using MIDI Input

The steps needed to open an input device are almost the same we used to open an output device. Let's write a short example to illustrate the process. This program will receive MIDI events and echo them out to a MIDI output device. For the sake of simplicity, the program will open the first available input and output devices (using device IDs of 0). Here we go!

```
//
//    Maximum MIDI — Chapter 5: Receiving MIDI
//                              Echo Example Program
//

#include <windows.h>
#include "MaxMidi.h"

#define INPUT_DEVICE 0
#define OUTPUT_DEVICE 0

HMIN hMidiIn = 0;
HMOUT hMidiOut = 0;

LRESULT CALLBACK EchoWndProc(HWND hWnd, UINT iMsg, WPARAM wParam, LPARAM
lParam)
{
    LPMIDIEVENT lpMsg;

    switch (iMsg)
```

```
        {
            case WM_CREATE:
                // try to open the first input device
                if((hMidiIn = OpenMidiIn(hWnd, INPUT_DEVICE, 0,
                        MIDIIN_DEFAULT)) == 0)
                    return -1;

                // midi in must be started before messages will be
                // processed
                StartMidiIn(hMidiIn);

                if((hMidiOut = OpenMidiOut(hWnd, OUTPUT_DEVICE, 0,
                        MIDIOUT_DEFAULT)) == 0)
                {
                    // error opening MIDI out—close MIDI in
                    CloseMidiIn(hMidiIn);
                    return -1;
                }

                return 0;

            case MIDI_DATA:
                while((lpMsg = GetMidiIn(hMidiIn)) != NULL)
                    PutMidiOut(hMidiOut, lpMsg);
                return 0;

            case WM_CLOSE:
                CloseMidiIn(hMidiIn);
                CloseMidiOut(hMidiOut);
                DestroyWindow(hWnd);
                return 0;

            case WM_DESTROY:
                PostQuitMessage(0);
                return 0;
        }

    // All messages that are not completely processed above
    // must be processed here.
    return DefWindowProc(hWnd, iMsg, wParam, lParam);
}

int PASCAL WinMain(HINSTANCE hInstance, HINSTANCE hPrevInstance,
            LPSTR lpszCmdLine, int nCmdShow)
{
    WNDCLASS wndclass;
    MSG msg;
    HWND hWnd;

    // register the window class
    wndclass.style             = 0;
    wndclass.lpfnWndProc       = EchoWndProc;
    wndclass.cbClsExtra        = 0;
```

```
wndclass.cbWndExtra            = 0;
wndclass.hInstance             = hInstance;
wndclass.hIcon                 = NULL;
wndclass.hCursor               = LoadCursor(NULL, IDC_ARROW);
wndclass.hbrBackground         = (HBRUSH)(COLOR_WINDOW+1);
wndclass.lpszMenuName          = NULL;
wndclass.lpszClassName         = "Ch5EchoExample";

RegisterClass(&wndclass);

// Create and display the main window
hWnd = CreateWindow("Ch5EchoExample",
                    "Maximum MIDI Echo Example",
                    WS_OVERLAPPEDWINDOW | WS_VISIBLE,

                    CW_USEDEFAULT, CW_USEDEFAULT,
                    CW_USEDEFAULT, CW_USEDEFAULT,
                    NULL, NULL, hInstance, NULL);


// our friend, the message loop
while(GetMessage(&msg, NULL, 0, 0))
{
        TranslateMessage(&msg);
        DispatchMessage(&msg);
}

return msg.wParam;
}
```

Inspection of our deceptively simple program reveals several characteristics. WinMain, and its attendant message loop, create and maintain the main window. The window proc, EchoWndProc, processes four different messages. The WM_CREATE message handler attempts to open the MIDI input and output devices. If either one cannot be opened (if, for example, one does not exist), the handler will return −1, forcing the application to terminate, since the main window will not be created.

Once the main window is displayed, the program waits for something interesting to happen. Whenever a MIDI event is received by the input device, MaxMidi posts a MIDI_DATA message to our window. The GetMessage() function (in WinMain) retrieves it from Window's message queue and dispatches it to the window procedure. There, the MIDI_DATA case calls the MaxMidi function, GetMidiIn(), to retrieve the MIDI data. Each time GetMidiIn() is called, it returns a pointer to the next MIDI event (contained in a MidiEvent structure). The function returns a NULL pointer if there are no events to retrieve.

Each event that is retrieved using GetMidiIn() is echoed to the output device by calling PutMidiOut(). This method of echoing MIDI events allows an application to easily filter, modify, or route events as it sees fit. But it is not without drawbacks. Since the events are retrieved in response to window messages, there will be some delay. But this delay is generally small, and for the purposes of our example program it is not a problem. A more timing-sensitive program might echo events from inside of the input device's interrupt-time callback function. The MaxMidi DLLs don't implement such an echo function, but an intrepid programmer can easily add this application-specific feature to the DLLs.

The other two message cases handled in the window procedure come into play during program shutdown. A WM_CLOSE message is sent to the window proc when the program begins to close. In this example, the WM_CLOSE handler's response is to close the two MIDI devices. It then calls DestroyWindow(), which removes the window from the screen and sends a WM_DESTROY message. This final message is handled in the usual manner: a quit message is sent which causes the message loop in WinMain to exit, causing the application to terminate.

## Opening in Greater Detail

As the example shows, the OpenMidiIn() function accepts the same parameters as OpenMidiOut(). A window handle identifies the window that handles the MIDI_DATA and MIM_CLOSE messages. We've seen MIDI_DATA in action already. MIM_CLOSE, like the MOM_CLOSE message, is sent when the device is closed. Most applications ignore this message, but it can be useful. For example, during shutdown it can be used to pace the orderly release of resources that are related to a particular input device. The OpenMidiIn() function is prototyped like this:

```
HMIN OpenMidiIn(HWND hWnd, WORD wDeviceID, HSYNC hSync, DWORD dwFlags);
```

The device ID serves the same function as the output device's ID (as used in OpenMidiOut()): it uniquely identifies a particular device. The device ID ranges from 0 (for the first device) to one less than the number of devices present in the system. The number of available devices is returned by the MMSYSTEM API function midiInGetNumDevs(). As in the output device case, the device ID for a particular input device is always unique, but can change from session to session. The ID will never change during the lifetime of an application; the value can change—as a result of device drivers being added or removed—only when Windows starts.

As a consequence of this behavior, applications should not save the device ID as an identification for reopening the device later. The ID may have changed, causing the program to open the wrong device. Instead, save the description of the device, as returned by `GetMidiInDescription()`.

```
BOOL GetMidiInDescription(WORD wDeviceID, LPSTR lpszDesc);
```

This function gets the name of the specified device and copies it to the string that is pointed to by `lpszDesc`. Make sure that `lpszDesc` points to enough memory to hold the entire name, which will be no longer than MAXPNAMELEN (32) bytes. `GetMidiInDescription()` returns TRUE if the device exists and FALSE if it does not. But avoid attempting to retrieve the name of a device that is outside the range of devices returned by `midiInGetNumDevs()`, or the system may become unstable.

Getting the device ID when we have the device name is almost as easy. This function will appear later in the `CMaxMidiIn` class. Here is a C function that does the trick:

```
WORD GetIDFromName(LPSTR lpszDesc)
{
        WORD id;
        char thisDesc[MAXPNAMELEN];
        WORD MaxDevs = midiInGetNumDevs();

        for(id = 0; id < MaxDevs; id++)
        {
                GetMidiInDescription(id, thisDesc);
                if(strcmp(thisDesc, lpszDesc) == 0)
                        return id;

                id++;
        }

        return ERR_NOMATCH;
}
```

The function returns an ID of ERR_NOMATCH if it cannot find a match. This usually means that the device has been removed from the system. A gentle word to the user, and a chance to choose another device, will help correct the problem.

The next parameter to `OpenMidiIn()` is a handle to a sync device. If the handle passed is nonzero, the sync device will timestamp each received event with the time in ticks since the last received event. Synchronization, timestamps, and ticks are discussed in elaborate detail in chapter 7. If no synchronization is desired, pass 0 in place of the sync device handle. In this case, each received event is still timestamped, but with the number of milliseconds since MIDI input was started.

Last, but not least, are a set of flags (contained in bits 12–15 of the `dwFlags` parameter) that allow an application to customize the behavior of the input device. The MIDI input device stores received events in one or more queues. The default size of the non-sysex event queue is 512 events. Other queue sizes can be selected using one of the QUEUE_ flags. These flags are the same as the ones used when opening MIDI output, and are shown in table 4.1. However, the default queue works well for most applications. Likewise, if ENABLE_SYSEX is specified, the size and number of System Exclusive buffers can be set using the SXBUF_ group of flags. If ENABLE_SYSEX is not set, then these extra buffers are not created (thus saving memory) and any received sysex messages are ignored. These flags, and sysex handling in general, are discussed in chapter 6.

If the open request is successful, the function returns a handle to the MIDI input devce, an HMIN. This handle is opaque. That is, it is just a numerical value and has no meaning in your application except to uniquely identify a particular output device. The *Inside MIDI Input* section below reveals how this handle is used inside the MaxMidi DLLs.

## Controlling MIDI Input

Simply opening a MIDI input device is not enough; input must also be enabled for the application to receive events. Events are ignored by the device—as if they were never received—until the application calls StartMidiIn(). If no sync device is attached, each received event is timestamped with the number of milliseconds since StartMidiIn() was last called. If synchronization is being used, the value of the timestamp is controlled by the sync device (attached by specifying a valid sync handle when opening the input device), as discussed in chapter 7.

Whenever the application needs to temporarily halt MIDI input, it calls StopMidiIn(). In response, the MaxMidi DLLs will ignore further MIDI events. The application can continue to retrieve any queued events from MaxMidi by calling GetMidiIn(). For example, a sequencer needs to stop input when not recording so that it doesn't continue to process MIDI_DATA messages. If it simply ignores the MIDI_DATA messages while stopped—and leaves MIDI input running—when it starts to record again, it may erroneously insert a queue-full of garbage events at the beginning of the new sequence.

Alternatively, MIDI input could remain enabled while the sequencer is stopped if any queued events are flushed before recording. This is useful when the sequencer is set to echo received events to a selected output. By continuing to process received MIDI events, the user is able to play "thru" the sequencer. Flushing events that are queued while the sequencer is not recording ensures that subsequent recording begins cleanly.

# The Input Queue

A queue allows one process—receiving data, in this case—to be decoupled from another process—such as doing something with the data. The two tasks are then asynchronous; they don't need to happen at the same time. In the case of the MaxMidi DLLs, data is received from the hardware MIDI interface—through the interface's device driver—at interrupt time. But, it would be almost impossible to do anything useful with the data if processing could only happen at interrupt time. An interrupt-time callback function, running in a 16-bit process (as it must for handling time-critical events such as MIDI), cannot call any disk I/O, memory allocation, or screen drawing functions. Unfortunately, those are *exactly* the kind of functions we want to call in response to received MIDI events. Luckily, circular queues come to the rescue.

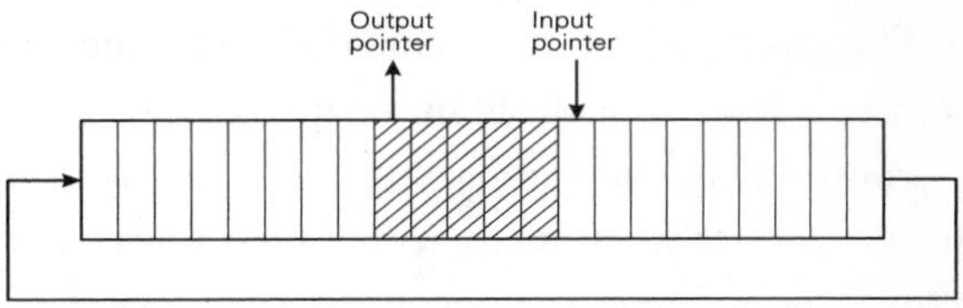

When the input device receives an event, it is put into a `MidiEvent`

**Figure 5-1    A queue**

structure and stored in a circular queue. The size of the queue is set, using the flags shown in table 4.1, when the device is opened. The default size is 512 events.

A circular queue is a memory buffer that wraps around, giving the appearance of an infinitely long buffer. Such a queue has an input pointer (that locates the next available storage location) and an output pointer (that locates the next location to read from the queue). When data is written to the queue, the input pointer indicates where in the queue the data will be stored. The pointer is then incremented to the next location. If the pointer reaches the end of the queue, it is repositioned to the beginning of the queue. Likewise, when reading data from the queue, the output pointer indicates the location to read the next piece of data. After the data is read from the queue, the output pointer is incremented, and wrapped around to the beginning of the queue, if necessary. Around and around the pointers go, with data being added to the queue by one part of a program and removed by another.

It is said that a greyhound—the racing dog, not the bus—must never catch the rabbit that it chases around the track. If the dog ever does catch the rabbit, it will be so disappointed to find the rabbit is nothing but a stuffed animal that it will lose the will to run. Handled with a good, strong leash, these racing retirees make excellent house pets: clean, quiet, but with a certain wistful melancholy.

Like the greyhound, if the input pointer ever catches up with the output pointer the queue's career is over. This happens when data is being removed from the queue slower (over time) than it is being added to the queue; the queue is then said to be *overrun*. A queue can handle this condition in one of two ways. It can refuse or ignore new data until there is room in the queue, or it can rely on the rest of the system to prevent an overrun condition.

On the other hand, the queue is empty whenever the input and output pointers are equal. The pointers are equal when the output pointer (where data are being read) reaches the input pointer (where data will be written). Thus, all of the data in the queue has been read when the output pointer reaches the input pointer. Remember that the input pointer must never reach the output pointer, since this results in an overrun queue.

The input pointer is incremented each time an event is inserted into the queue. The pointer is reset to the head of the queue when it reaches the end of the queue, wrapping it around to the beginning. On the other hand, if the input pointer would equal the output pointer when incremented (and possibly wrapped around), the event should be refused, or else an overrun would occur, since the queue is already full.

Events are removed from the queue in a similar manner. There are no events to retrieve if the input and output pointers are the same. But if they are different, the output pointer is used to retrieve the event data from the queue. Then, the pointer is incremented and wrapped around to the head of the queue, if necessary, in the same way the input pointer is handled.

Events are put into the receive queue, in the form of `MidiEvent` structures, when they are received from the MIDI interface's device driver. For non-sysex messages, the device driver calls a callback function in the MaxMidi DLLs—at interrupt time—and passes the entire MIDI message. Events coming from a device driver will always have a valid status byte, accompanied by all of the data bytes that were received for that message. The callback function in MaxMidi puts the received event into the queue—incrementing and wrapping the input pointer, if necessary—and posts a `MIDI_DATA` message to let the client application know there is an event to process.

Using the MaxMidi DLL functions, events are retrieved from the input queue by calling `GetMidiIn()`. Normally, this function is called in response to a `MIDI_DATA` message. Since the `MIDI_DATA` window message passes through the Windows event queue—and thus through the application's message queue—it may take some time for the message to be processed. There are no ill effects caused by this delay, since the MIDI data is waiting patiently to be retrieved from the MIDI input queue. But, it is possible that more than one MIDI event can be received and queued before the first `MIDI_DATA` message is processed. To optimize the performance of MIDI input and prevent data loss, call `GetMidiIn()`

inside of a loop. This will quickly retrieve all events that are waiting in the MIDI input queue and ensure that events are removed from the queue as quickly as they are inserted.

For each retrieved event, `GetMidiIn()` will return a pointer to a `MidiEvent` structure. Use this pointer to read the members of the structure, but don't hold on to or write data using this pointer. Since it is a pointer into the MIDI input queue inside of MaxMidi, the data at this address will eventually be overwritten by a newly received MIDI event. Process the event immediately, or if necessary, copy the data for later processing. If there are no events in the queue, `GetMidiIn()` returns a NULL pointer.

# Closing the MIDI Input

Just as with MIDI output devices, input devices that are left open when an application terminates will cause annoying memory leaks. And just as in the case of MIDI output, orphaned input devices will prevent other applications from accessing the MIDI input hardware. The only remedy for an orphaned MIDI device, other than a sharp slap on the wrist, is to reboot the computer. Since users generally classify that sort of behavior in the same category as tax audits and traffic tickets, always be sure to close the input device.

Closing the MIDI input device is done by calling `CloseMidiIn()`. This function will close the MIDI input driver and release the memory that MaxMidi allocated for the device. It is always a good idea to set the device handle to 0 after closing the device, since MaxMidi will ignore any calls made with a NULL device handle. Never attempt to close a device that has already been closed. Otherwise, the close function will attempt to free memory that has already been freed. Since ToolKit functions ignore NULL handles, setting the handle to 0 after closing the device is a good safety practice. For example:

```
CloseMidiIn(hMidiIn);
hMidiIn = 0;            // for safety!
```

That is all that's involved with receiving MIDI input using the MaxMidi ToolKit. Now, MIDI input and output are just a few function calls away. But read on to understand what goes on underneath the hood of the MaxMidi input routines. Although you don't need to know more to use these functions, a firm understanding of how MaxMidi handles the Windows multimedia API for MIDI input will help make using and modifying the ToolKit even easier.

# Inside MIDI Input

Like the MIDI output routines in the ToolKit, the input functions must reside in fixed code segments. The device driver that handles the MIDI hardware sends data to the ToolKit at interrupt time via a callback. Since the callback can be called at any time, the code segment for the callback function must always be present in memory and must never move. The only way to guarantee this is to put the code into a fixed segment. And the easiest way to do this is to put the code into a DLL and set the FIXED attribute for its code and data segments.

Luckily, the MaxMidi DLL—specifically MxMidi16.dll—already has these attributes, since the same restrictions apply for the MIDI output functions. For more detail on these requirements and restrictions, see the *Callbacks and Fixed Code Segments* topic in chapter 4.

## MIDI Input Data Flow

The data flow diagram shown in figure 5-2 illustrates how data—both MIDI events and window messages—flows through the MIDI input routines. In the interest of clarity, this diagram omits handling of System Exclusive messages; these are discussed in chapter 6.

On the left side is the Client App, your program. Data flows from right to left. Thus, the Client App receives both MIDI messages and window messages from the input routines. On the right side is the MIDI interface hardware. The MIDI interface is managed by its device driver, which is part of the Windows 95 system software.

To use the MIDI input capabilities of the ToolKit, a device must be chosen and opened by the Client App. The OpenMidiIn() function performs the following steps:

- Checks the requested device ID to see if it is valid. If the requested device does not exist, the open request fails.

- Allocates memory for the structure that holds all of the variables needed to control this device. The returned HMIN handle is actually a DWORD that has the same numerical value as a pointer to this structure. But don't try to de-reference this handle to get to the structure; it is only valid as a pointer on the 16-bit side of the Windows universe.

- Calls midiInOpen() to open the device driver for the requested interface, like this:

```
wLastError = midiInOpen(&(lpMI->hMidiIn), wDeviceId,
                (DWORD)MidiInCallback, CALLBACK_FUNCTION);
```

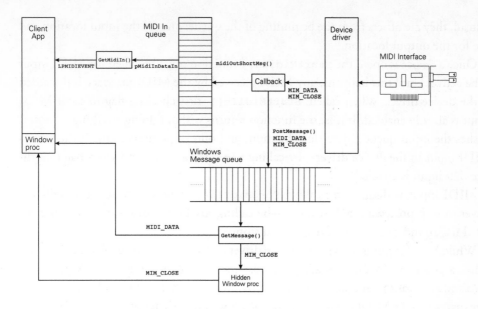

**Figure 5-2  Midi input data flow (non-sysex)**

Calling `midiInOpen()` will fill the `hMidiIn` member of our `MidiIn` structure with a handle to the device, based on the requested device ID. Any time it needs to communicate with the "owner" of the device, in this case the DLL, it will call the `MidiInCallback()` function. If the open request succeeds, the `wLastError` value will be 0. Otherwise, it will be one of the MMSYSTEM error messages outlined in chapter 3.

- Allocates the MIDI input queue. This queue will receive MIDI events as they arrive from the device driver. The `GetMidiIn()` function retrieves events from the queue and returns pointers to these events to the Client App.

- Creates a hidden window that is used internally to handle the `MIM_CLOSE` message. This message is sent by the device driver when it closes—in response to `CloseMidiIn()` being called by the client. In turn, the hidden window cleans up by releasing memory allocated by the input routines and sends an `MIM_CLOSE` message to the Client App to let it know the device is closed.

The input queue consists of a block of memory containing a number of `MidiEvent` structures; 512 of them in the default case. Two pointers serve to access the input and output locations in the queue. These two values are not actual memory pointers, though.

Instead, they are offsets from the beginning of the queue: one for the input location and one for the output location.

Once a device is open, the StartMidiIn() function must be called for MIDI input to be active. Until this happens, any MIDI received by the MIDI interface is discarded in the device driver. When called, StartMidiIn() first checks a flag to see if MIDI input is already enabled. If it is, the function returns without doing anything. If not, it flushes the input queue (by setting the input and output pointers to 0). It then starts MIDI input in the device driver—by calling midiInStart()—and sets a flag to indicate that input is enabled.

MIDI input is disabled by calling StopMidiIn(). This simple function tells the driver to stop processing MIDI input—by calling midiInStop()—and clears the enabled flag to indicate that MIDI is indeed stopped.

While MIDI input is active, the device driver collects the received MIDI bytes until it has a complete MIDI message. It sends that one- to three-byte message to the MidiInCallback() function as an MIM_DATA message. MIM_DATA is a Windows message that passes the MIDI event, encoded in the lowest three bytes of a DWORD. In response to this message, MidiInCallback() finds the next available location in the input queue for the new event and inserts it into the queue. Then it increments the pointer, wrapping it—if it reaches the end of the queue—by setting it to 0 (the first offset in the queue). Finally, the callback function posts a MIDI_DATA message to the window that the Client App specified when opening the input device. This will trigger the Client App to read any events waiting in the queue by calling GetMidiIn().

Each event that is placed in the queue is given a timestamp by calling GetEventTimeInTicks(). Since the MIDI input was not opened with synchronization (which is discussed in chapters 7 and 8), this function simply returns the timestamp that was provided by the device driver. This timestamp is the time in milliseconds (not in ticks, as the function name would suggest) since midiInStart() was last called. This happened, of course, when the Client App called StartMidiIn().

Notice that no queue overrun error checking is done. If the Client App does not read data out of the queue quickly enough, MIDI events will be lost. But this is not a problem for even the most turtle-like computer, as long as GetMidiIn() is called inside of a while loop by the Client App—as shown in the example earlier in this chapter.

The GetMidiIn() function is quite straightforward when handling non-sysex MIDI events. It checks to see if any events are in the queue. If the input and output pointers are equal, the function returns NULL to indicate that the queue is empty. Otherwise, the pointer to the next event to retrieve is calculated by adding the output offset value to the address of the start of the queue. This pointer is saved, and the output offset is incremented to the next `MidiEvent` in the queue. The output pointer is wrapped around, if necessary, by resetting it to 0 if it reaches the end of the queue. Finally, `GetMidiIn()` returns the saved pointer. The Client App uses that pointer to access the data in the `MidiEvent`.

The Client App calls `CloseMidiIn()` when it no longer needs the input device. First, `CloseMidiIn()` makes sure the input device is stopped. Then it resets the device driver—to flush any pending events—and closes the driver. In response, when the device driver is finished closing down, it sends an `MIM_CLOSE` message to the `MidiInCallback()` function. This happens at interrupt time, so all that `MidiInCallback()` can do is post a message to the hidden window that was created by `OpenMidiIn()`. The hidden window's window procedure, `MidiInProc()`, receives that `MIM_CLOSE` message and frees the memory used by the input device. It then destroys itself, and sends an `MIM_CLOSE` message to the Client App, notifying it that the input device is completely closed.

**CHAPTER 6**

# *System Exclusive Messages*

Support for MIDI in the Windows operating system—made up of device drivers, an API, and MIDI hardware—was originally adapted from the drivers and API designed for waveform (digital) audio. In fact, many MIDI interface device drivers are simply modified versions of a wave audio card driver. Wave audio record and playback involves handling many large blocks of data, each usually several kilobytes in size. While this data model does not fit normal MIDI messages very well (since they are short, one- to three-byte events), it is tantalizingly close to the System Exclusive message case. As a result, the designers of Windows Multimedia Extensions choose to separate the "long" System Exclusive messages from the other "short" one- to three-byte messages.

Short messages are handled using special, MIDI-only functions and messages. We've beat those functions into submission elsewhere in this book. Now it is time to flog long messages, and to understand how they are handled in Windows.

But before the flogging commences, let's look at how the MaxMidi ToolKit handles System Exclusive data.

# One Stream—Handling Short and Long Messages

One of the design goals of the MaxMidi ToolKit is to present a unified MIDI data interface for application programs. The method of handling long messages differently than short ones is a convenience for the Windows system, but it's not very convenient for an application programmer. MIDI data flows in a stream—one byte following the next—and having two streams to deal with is, well, inconvenient. The MaxMidi DLLs recombine the two streams—below the surface, so to speak—so that the MIDI applications need only deal with MIDI events through one mechanism.

There is one minor difference between the handling of sysex data and other MIDI messages. An entire MIDI event—a short one—fits nicely into a single MidiEvent structure. But a sysex message can be very long indeed, too long to fit into one MidiEvent. To accommodate the profligate nature of System Exclusive messages, the ToolKit requires that each byte of a sysex occupy a single MidiEvent. The data byte goes into the data1 field of the structure and the status byte must be 0xF0, so that the MaxMidi DLLs can tell that the data is part of a sysex. (Remember, *all* MidiEvents must have a valid status byte.) This is sensible enough. Both the initial sysex status byte (0xF0) and the terminating EOX (0xF7) must be sent in the data1 field of the first and last MidiEvent, respectively. Sysex data is received from the ToolKit using this same format. Perhaps an example will make this clearer.

# Sending and Receiving Sysexes

Here is a short example program that sends a single, fixed sysex message each time it is run. In true don't-ask-don't-tell spirit, this sysex does absolutely nothing useful. But it's sent out of the selected MIDI output, so it illustrates the process. The program also displays a received sysex in the application's main window. If the selected MIDI input port is connected to the specified MIDI output port, the program will display the 7-byte sysex.

```
//
// Maximum MIDI — Chapter 6: System Exclusive Messages
//              Sysex Example Program
//

#include <windows.h>
#include "MaxMidi.h"

#define OUTPUT_DEVICE 0
#define INPUT_DEVICE 0

HMOUT hMidiOut = 0;
HMIN hMidiIn = 0;

// Manufacturer ID 0x7D is for non-commercial use (e.g. research)
BYTE sx[] = { 0xF0, 0x7D, 0x50, 0x61, 0x75, 0x6C, 0xF7 };

LRESULT CALLBACK SysexWndProc(HWND hWnd, UINT iMsg, WPARAM wParam, LPARAM
lParam)
{
    int i;
    MidiEvent Evt;
    HDC hDC;
    LPMIDIEVENT lpMsg;
    char text[4];
    SIZE TextSize;
    static int x = 0;

    switch (iMsg)
    {
      case WM_CREATE:
        // open the input device
        if((hMidiIn = OpenMidiIn(hWnd, INPUT_DEVICE, 0, MIDIIN_DEFAULT))
           == 0)
           return -1;

        // midi in must be started before messages will be processed
        StartMidiIn(hMidiIn);
```

```
        // open the output device
        if((hMidiOut = OpenMidiOut(hWnd, OUTPUT_DEVICE, 0,
            MIDIOUT_DEFAULT)) == 0)
            return -1;

        // send the sysex
        // initialize the MidiEvent's status field
        Evt.status = 0xF0;

        // output bytes until the EOX is sent
        i = 0;
        do {
            Evt.data1 = sx[i++];
            PutMidiOut(hMidiOut, &Evt);
        } while(Evt.data1 != 0xF7);

        return 0;

    case MIDI_DATA:
        while((lpMsg = GetMidiIn(hMidiIn)) != NULL)
        {
            // If this is part of a sysex, display the hex bytes
            if(lpMsg->status == 0xF0)
            {
                hDC = GetDC(hWnd);
                wsprintf(text, "%2.2X ", lpMsg->data1);
                TextOut(hDC, x, 0, text, strlen(text));
                GetTextExtentPoint(hDC, text, strlen(text), &TextSize);
                x += TextSize.cx;
                ReleaseDC(hWnd, hDC);
            }
        }
        return 0;

    case WM_CLOSE:
        CloseMidiOut(hMidiOut);
        DestroyWindow(hWnd);
        return 0;

    case WM_DESTROY:
        PostQuitMessage(0);
        return 0;
    }

    // All messages that are not completely processed above
    // must be processed here.
    return DefWindowProc(hWnd, iMsg, wParam, lParam);
}
```

```
int PASCAL WinMain(HINSTANCE hInstance, HINSTANCE hPrevInstance,
        LPSTR lpszCmdLine, int nCmdShow)
{
    WNDCLASS wndclass;
    MSG msg;
    HWND hWnd;

    // register the window class
    wndclass.style              = 0;
    wndclass.lpfnWndProc        = SysexWndProc;
    wndclass.cbClsExtra         = 0;
    wndclass.cbWndExtra         = 0;
    wndclass.hInstance          = hInstance;
    wndclass.hIcon              = NULL;
    wndclass.hCursor            = LoadCursor(NULL, IDC_ARROW);
    wndclass.hbrBackground      = (HBRUSH)(COLOR_WINDOW+1);
    wndclass.lpszMenuName       = NULL;
    wndclass.lpszClassName      = "Ch6SysexExample";

    RegisterClass(&wndclass);

    // Create and display the main window
    hWnd = CreateWindow("Ch6SysexExample",
            "Maximum MIDI Sysex Example",
            WS_OVERLAPPEDWINDOW | WS_VISIBLE,
            CW_USEDEFAULT, CW_USEDEFAULT,
            CW_USEDEFAULT, CW_USEDEFAULT,
            NULL, NULL, hInstance, NULL);


    // our friend, the message loop
    while(GetMessage(&msg, NULL, 0, 0))
    {
        TranslateMessage(&msg);
        DispatchMessage(&msg);
    }

    return msg.wParam;
}
```

The Windows-specific code in this example is the same as the *Echo* example in chapter 5, so we won't dwell on those details here.

What is new and interesting are the few lines of code that output the sysex and that process the received data. The sysex in question uses a manufacturer's ID of 0x7D, which is reserved in the MIDI specification for noncommercial uses. These uses include research, education, and books about writing MIDI applications. This ID is guaranteed to be ignored by any device that can be handled by mere mortals, so the sysex is safe to send, since it will be completely ignored.

It will, however, be sent by the specified MIDI output port, and be received by the MIDI input port if the two ports are connected together. The received bytes are retrieved by the GetMidiIn() call in the MIDI_DATA switch case. If the bytes are from a System Exclusive message—and they will be—then each byte will be displayed in hex in the main window.

Notice that the input and output devices are opened using the MIDIIN_DEFAULT and MIDIOUT_DEFAULT flags, respectively. These flags specify default values for the size of the MIDI queues (512 events), the number of sysex buffers (32), the size of these buffers (512 bytes each), and very importantly for our example, specify that handling System Exclusive messages is enabled. This last option is specified by setting the ENABLE_SYSEX flag. If this flag is not set, all sysex messages are filtered, just as if they were never encountered. Disabling sysex support can save memory for applications that are not expected to support System Exclusive messages.

By design, this example has nearly as many limitations as it has features. It will send its single, fixed sysex message, and will display a single, one-line sysex in the main window. To expand upon Yeats, things fall apart, the center cannot hold, when a longer sysex is received, since the text output routine will handle only a single line of data. In spite of its shortcomings, the program serves as a good starting place for understanding how to handle System Exclusive messages using the MaxMidi ToolKit.

# Long Messages and Buffers

As outlined earlier, inside Windows, long messages follow a different path than short messages. The two diagrams below—one for MIDI input and one for MIDI output—show the behind-the-scenes handling of long messages. Both cases are similar. Sysex data is stored in buffers—depicted here as "bit buckets." There are a number of buffers, kept in a list of buffers, that are ready to accept data. When a particular buffer is filled—or the EOX byte of the sysex is encountered—the buffer is sent on its way and another one steps up to take its place.

In the case of sending sysex data, the Client App calls PutMidiOut() once for each byte in the sysex. The MIDI output device has a list of buffers available, ready to go. As bytes are received from the application, they are stored in the next available buffer. When the buffer is full—or the EOX byte is received, indicating the end of the sysex—the buffer is detached from the list of buffers and is sent to the device driver by calling midiOutLongMsg(). The driver sends the buffer's data to the MIDI interface, and returns the buffer to the MIDI output device—through the MidiOutCallback() function—where it is added back to the end of the list of available buffers.

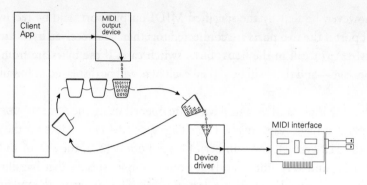

**Figure 6-1 Sending sysex data**

Receiving sysex data is a similar process. The device driver has a number of buffers—given to it by the MIDI input device when the driver is opened—that are filled with data as it arrives from the MIDI interface. When a given buffer is full, or the EOX of the message is received, the buffer is sent to the MIDI input device. More accurately, the driver calls the `MidiInCallback()` callback function, passing a pointer to a structure that includes a pointer to the buffer. In turn, the callback function posts a `MIDI_DATA` message to the Client App, which then reads the sysex data, one byte at a time, by calling `GetMidiIn()`. Finally, when the Client App is finished retrieving the data from the buffer, it is sent back to the device driver, ready to accept more.

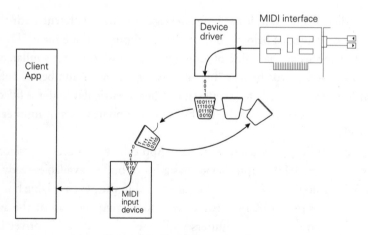

**Figure 6-2 Receiving sysex data**

# MIDI Headers and Buffers

Each of these buffers is managed by a structure, called a MIDIHDR. This "header" contains a pointer to the buffer data, the number of bytes—both used and available—in the buffer, flags, and other values needed for the system to properly handle the data. Study the header structure shown here. It is central to understanding how System Exclusive data is handled inside of Windows. Notice that this structure is slightly different from the one shown in chapter 3. The structure documented in chapter 3 is for 32-bit applications, while the version shown here is used in 16-bit processes, such as the 16-bit MaxMidi DLL.

```
typedef struct midihdr_tag {
    LPSTR   lpData;                         // far pointer to data buffer
    DWORD   dwBufferLength;                 // size of data buffer
    DWORD   dwBytesRecorded;                // input buffer byte count
    DWORD   dwUser;                         // user data—anything goes!
    DWORD   dwFlags;                        // Buffer-related flags
    struct midihdr_tag far * lpNext;        // pointer to next buffer
                                            // in list maintained by
                                            // device driver.
    DWORD   reserved;                       // reserved for device driver
} MIDIHDR;
```

Let's look at each of the elements of this structure to see what we can learn. The first element, lpData, is a far pointer to the data buffer. This buffer must be allocated as a block of global memory—with the GMEM_MOVEABLE and GMEM_SHARE flags set—and the memory must be locked. For example:

```
lpMidiHdr = (LPMIDIHDR)GlobalLock(GlobalAlloc(GMEM_MOVEABLE | GMEM_SHARE,
            sizeof(MIDIHDR)));
lpData = (LPSTR)GlobalLock(GlobalAlloc(GMEM_MOVEABLE | GMEM_SHARE,
            BUFFER_SIZE));
lpMidiHdr->lpData = lpData;
```

The buffer can be any size. The dwBufferLength structure member lets the device driver know the buffer's exact size. Small buffers are useful when handling short sysexes, since it is likely each one fits into a buffer, without wasting memory. Larger buffers are better at handling longer System Exclusive messages, such as bulk dumps of instrument settings. It is not necessary for an entire sysex to fit in a single buffer; any number of buffers (and their headers) can be handled by a device driver.

The dwBytesRecorded structure member is used when receiving sysex messages. When a buffer is filled, or the end of the sysex occurs, the buffer is sent to the MidiInCallback() function. Before the driver returns the header and buffer, it sets dwBytesRecorded to reflect the number of significant bytes in the buffer. If the entire buffer is filled with sysex data, the number of recorded bytes will equal the buffer's size. If the number of recorded bytes is less than the size of the buffer, the unused bytes at the end of the buffer will be filled with garbage.

The dwUser value can hold any 32-bit value that a program might desire. It is ignored by Windows (and the device driver). This field is not used by MaxMidi.

Out of the 32 possible flags in dwFlags, two flag bits are used to indicate the status of the header. Other flags are used by the device driver, while the rest of the flag bits are reserved. The MHDR_DONE flag is set when the buffer is returned to the callback function. It indicates that the driver is finished with the header. This flag must be cleared before the buffer can be used again by the device driver. This is normally done by calling midiOutPrepareHeader() or midiInPrepareHeader(), as described later.

The last two fields of the MIDIHDR structure are used internally by the device driver. The driver keeps the headers in a linked list, using the lpNext pointer as the link to the next buffer in the list. The reserved DWORD may hold a pointer to an internal structure, or it may be unused, depending on the particular device driver. In any case, never change these two fields. Unless, of course, you *like* to see Windows crash.

Once a header and its data buffer has been allocated, it must be *prepared* by MMSYSTEM before it can be used. This is done by calling midiInPrepareHeader() or midiOutPrepareHeader(). These two functions are prototyped like this:

```
UINT midiOutPrepareHeader(HMIDIOUT hMO, LPMIDIHDR lpMidiOutHdr, UINT wSize);
UINT midiInPrepareHeader(HMIDIIN hMI, LPMIDIHDR lpMidiInHdr, UINT wSize);
```

The HMIDIIN and HMIDIOUT parameters are the device handles returned by the midiInOpen() and midiOutOpen() functions, not the HMIN and HMOUT handles used by the MaxMidi DLL functions. In both prototypes, the LPMIDIHDR parameter specifies a pointer to the unprepared header, while the UINT value indicates the size of the header. These functions prepare the header by setting appropriate flags, and pagelocking the header and buffer. Both functions return 0 if the prepare operation was successful. MMSYSERR_INVALHANDLE is returned if the device handle is invalid, and MMSYSERR_NOMEM is returned if the memory cannot be pagelocked.

For sysex input, one or more prepared headers have to be passed to the device driver so that it can fill (and return) them as data are received. This is done by calling `midiInAddBuffer()`, which is prototyped as shown.

```
UINT midiInAddBuffer(HMIDIIN hMI, LPMIDIHDR lpMidiInHdr, UINT wSize);
```

Again, `HMIDIIN` specifies the input device handle, `LPMIDIHDR` points to the prepared header, and the `UINT` indicates the size of the header. The function returns 0 if the header is successfully added to the device driver's list of input headers, while a return value of `MMSYSERR_INVALHANDLE` indicates that the device handle is invalid, and `MIDIERR_UNPREPARED` means that the header was not properly prepared.

In the case of sysex output, the sending application fills one or more buffers with data, including the leading SYSEX (0xF0) and trailing EOX (0xF7) status bytes, and calls `midiOutLongMsg()` for each buffer.

```
UINT midiOutLongMsg(HMIDIOUT hMO, LPMIDIHDR lpMidiOutHdr, UINT wSize);
```

The parameters are the same as for the other buffer-related functions. The return value is 0 if successful. If there is an error, the return value is `MMSYSERR_INVALHANDLE`, `MIDIERR_UNPREPARED`, or `MIDIERR_NOTREADY`. The latter error code indicates that the device driver is busy and cannot accept this buffer at this time.

There are two features of `midiOutLongMsg()` that are not immediately obvious. First, the function may not return until the buffer has been sent by the MIDI hardware. Some device drivers will return immediately and continue to output the buffer in the background (they handle the data asynchronously), but many drivers will not return until the buffer is sent. This mildly complicates sysex output, since the buffer might be sent during an interrupt callback—for example, during synchronization, as described in chapter 8. It would be extremely disruptive for Windows to be stuck waiting for a sysex buffer to be output during an interrupt. The MaxMidi DLLs handle this by posting a message to an internal, hidden window that will cause the buffer to be sent when not inside of an interrupt handler.

The second hidden feature of long messages is that such buffers are not limited to sending System Exclusive data. Any valid MIDI data can be placed in a buffer and output using `midiOutLongMsg()`. All of the events in the buffer will be output at once, and only one call is needed to do the job.

# MIDI Input Data Flow Changes

The MaxMidi DLLs provide a complete example of how long message handling is implemented. The parallel nature of long and short message handling complicates the internals of the DLLs. But the end result—unified MIDI message handling—is worth the extra trouble.

In the case of MIDI input, the data flow diagram (figure 6-3) is modified by adding a list of sysex buffers (headers, actually) between the MidiInCallback() function and GetMidiIn(). Each of these buffers is passed to the device driver to be filled with data. Two pointers are maintained by the MIDI input device; one to indicate which buffer currently has data to be read by the Client App, and one to indicate which buffer has just been returned, filled with data, by the device driver. Notice that these two pointers indicate position in the list of headers, not the location of data in a buffer. Each time GetMidiIn() is called, a byte from the buffer pointed to by the output pointer is returned. When that buffer is emptied, it is reprepared and added back to the device driver, and the pointer moves to the next buffer in the list. Each time the device driver returns a filled buffer to the callback function, the address of the header is put in the list at the location specified by the list input pointer. Then, the pointer is incremented to the next position in the list, wrapping around to the beginning when the pointer reaches the end. There are no more sysex events available for the Client App when the input and output pointers are equal.

The DLL source code changes needed to support long messages propagate through nearly all of the MIDI input functions. In the OpenMidiIn() function, memory is allocated for the list of headers. The number of sysex buffers and their sizes is retrieved from the dwFlags parameter passed to the open function by the Client App. The size of each buffer is determined by bits 8 through 11. These bits specify one of ten different buffer sizes, ranging from 64 bytes up to 32K, by serving as an index into an array. Bits 0 through 7 of the dwFlags value specify the number of buffers to allocate. Each of these headers—and the attached data buffers—is allocated, prepared, and added to the device driver by calling AllocateMidiInSysexBuffer(), once for each header.

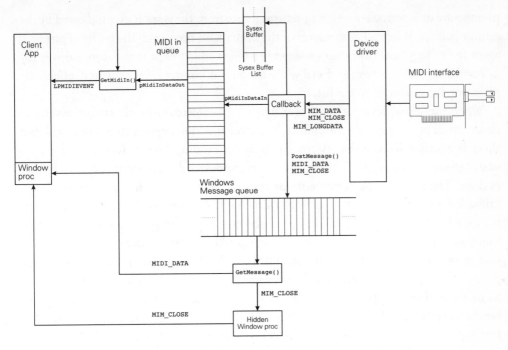

**Figure 6-3    MIDI input data flow (with sysex)**

As sysex bytes are received by the device driver, they are placed into one of the buffers that were allocated and added when the device was opened. When a buffer becomes full, or the end of the sysex is reached, a pointer to the header is sent to the MidiInCallback() as part of an MIM_LONGDATA message. The callback function places the buffer into the header list and increments the header input pointer, wrapping if necessary. If there is any data in the buffer, it posts a MIDI_DATA message to the Client App, who will retrieve the data by calling GetMidiIn().

Buffers are returned to the MIDI input device for two other conditions. If there is an error in receiving the sysex data (i.e., the sysex is malformed or corrupted, or a non-Real Time event is received in the middle of the sysex data), the driver will return the buffer using an MIM_LONGERROR message. The callback function handles the error message just like the MIM_LONGDATA message, in support of the theory that it is better for the application to see and handle the error condition than to never know. Buffers are also returned, possibly empty, when midiInReset() is called.

If the buffer list input and output pointers are equal, GetMidiIn() returns the next non-sysex event that is waiting in the MIDI queue, as described in chapter 5. If the two pointers are different, `GetMidiIn()` returns a byte from the sysex buffer indicated by the output pointer. When all of the bytes in the buffer have been read, the buffer is prepared again (by calling `midiInPrepareHeader()`) and is added back to the device driver (by calling `midiInAddBuffer()`). Finally, the list output pointer is incremented, effectively removing the header from the list.

When the input device is no longer needed, `CloseMidiIn()` closes the driver and cleans up all of the memory allocations. The close function appears straightforward, but there is a subtle feature that is crucial to understanding how it works. The call to `midiInReset()` stops MIDI input, and forces the device driver to mark all of its buffers as done. The driver, in turn, immediately returns the buffers to the MIDI input device callback function using an `MIM_LONGDATA` message. Any unused buffers will be empty, but one buffer might contain data if the driver was receiving a sysex when the reset function was called. In either event, the buffer is added to the header list. The subtlety is that all of the buffers will be returned, and thus added to the list of headers, before the `midiInReset()` function returns. This is significant, because the close function expects all of the buffers to appear in the header list so that they can be freed. Thankfully, the synchronous nature of the `midiInReset()` function guarantees that this is the case. This function accepts a single parameter, the opened device handle, and returns 0 if the reset is successful, or `MMSYSERR_INVALHANDLE` if the handle is improper.

```
UINT midiInReset(HMIDIIN hMI);
```

Once all of the headers have been returned, `CloseMidiIn()` unprepares each one by calling `midiInUnprepareHeader()`, like this:

```
UINT midiInUnprepareHeader(HMIDIIN hMI, LPMIDIHDR lpMidiInHdr, UINT wSize);
```

The three parameters are the same ones used with the other MMSYSTEM MIDI input functions. The return value is 0 (if successful), or either `MMSYSERR_INVALHANDLE` or `MIDIERR_STILLPLAYING`. The latter error return code means that the header cannot be unprepared because it is still being used by the driver. This should never occur if the `midiInReset()` function was successful.

After each header is unprepared, its buffer's memory is freed. Then the header itself is freed. Once all of the memory allocations have been unwound, the device driver is closed. The remaining memory used by the MIDI input device will be freed inside of the callback function, in response to the `MIM_CLOSE` message sent by the driver.

# MIDI Output Data Flow Changes

The changes to the MIDI Output data flow diagram are similar to the ones required to support sysex messages during MIDI input. A list of long message headers is maintained, just as in the MIDI input case. But in this case, events are put into the various buffers inside of the `PutMidiOut()` function. As the buffers become full, they are sent to the device driver to be output to the MIDI hardware.

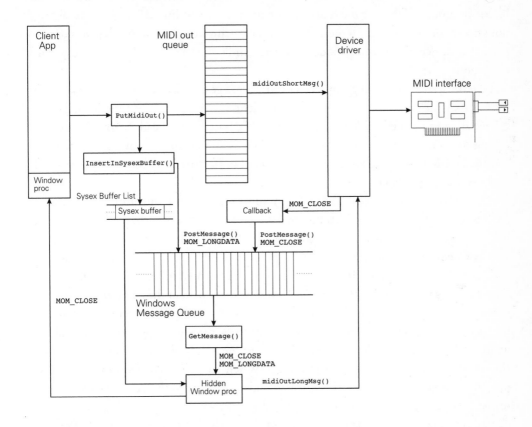

**Figure 6-4    MIDI output data flow (with sysex)**

Each header and buffer must be allocated and prepared, just as in the MIDI input case. However, the buffers are not "added" to the driver. Instead, pointers to the headers are stored in the header list. Once a given buffer is filled, it is not immediately sent to the driver to be output. Instead, a message (MOM_LONGDATA) is posted to a hidden window where the buffer will be sent to the driver, by calling midiOutLongMsg(). This circuitous route is traveled because the midiOutLongMsg() call may not return until all of the data in the buffer is output by the MIDI hardware. If the function is called inside of an interrupt process—for example, during synchronization—Windows performance might become erratic, or even unstable, since the call might take a second or more to complete. This much time spent inside of an interrupt handler is a recipe for disaster. To prevent such problems, the function is called inside of a window procedure, which is not an interrupt process. Whether the midiOutLongMsg() returns immediately (an asynchronous operation) or waits until the data is sent (a synchronous operation) depends on the particular device driver. Most modern drivers handle the midiOutLongMsg() call synchronously.

Like the MIDI input long message case, the changes needed in the 16-bit MaxMidi DLL (MxMidi16) for sysex support are evident in all of the key functions. In the OpenMidiOut() function, for example, the sysex buffers and headers are allocated by calling AllocateMidiOutSysexBuffer(). This is similar to the way that buffers are allocated for MIDI input. The size and number of buffers are determined by flags passed in the dwFlags parameter.

The AllocateMidiOutSysexBuffer() function allocates and initializes a header and buffer and then prepares the buffer by calling midiOutPrepareHeader(). A pointer to the header is stored in a list of headers as each buffer is allocated.

The Client App outputs events by calling PutMidiOut(). This function examines the status field for each event. If the event is a sysex, it is stored in a sysex buffer by calling InsertInSysexBuffer(). In that function, the data1 field of the MidiEvent is stored in the next available location in one of the buffers. If that buffer then becomes full, or the byte stored was an EOX (0xF7), an MOM_LONGDATA message is posted to the hidden window. A pointer to the header and a pointer to the MIDI output device are sent with the message in the lParam parameter. When the hidden window's window procedure receives the message, it dutifully sends the buffer to the device driver by calling midiOutLongMsg().

PutMidiOut() will refuse the sysex event if it finds that too many sysex buffers are waiting to be output by the device driver. The maximum number of pending buffers is calculated as one-half the size of Windows message queue. For example, if the message queue is 64 events in size, the maximum number of pending buffers is 32. This restriction is necessary to prevent the message queue from overflowing and possibly losing one or more of the posted MOM_LONGDATA messages. For instance, in the example above, if 65 messages were posted—due to 65 buffers becoming full—one of the MOM_LONGDATA messages would be lost by the window message queue. This buffer of data would become unrecoverable, orphaned forever, since the hidden window would never know that the buffer needed to be sent. Restrict the number of pending buffers to one-half the size of the queue and the queue will never become overrun.

Once the driver is finished sending a buffer to the MIDI hardware, it returns the buffer to the MidiOutCallback() callback function using an MOM_DONE message. The callback function prepares the buffer again by calling midiOutPrepareHeader(). The pointer to this header remains in the list of available headers, ready to be used again. If a sysex message is being sent without synchronization, the callback posts an OUTBUFFER_READY message to the client window, letting the application know that the output device can accept more sysex data.

The final act for MIDI output comes when CloseMidiOut() is called. The close function first resets the device driver. This forces it to return any buffers that are currently being output to MidiOutCallback(). It then iterates through all of the allocated buffers, unpreparing them and freeing the allocated memory. Then, it frees the other memory used by the MIDI device and closes the device driver. The headers are unprepared by calling the (predictably named) function midiOutUnprepareHeader(). This function is prototyped like this:

```
UINT midiOutUnprepareHeader(HMIDIOUT hMO, LPMIDIHDR lpMidiOutHdr, UINT wSize);
```

The three parameters are the same ones used with the other MMSYSTEM MIDI output functions. The return value is 0 if successful, or either MMSYSERR_INVALHANDLE or MIDIERR_STILLPLAYING. The latter error return code means that the header cannot be unprepared because it is still being output by the driver. This should never happen if the device driver was reset successfully.

CHAPTER 7

# Keeping Time

While playing music, foot tapping provides a timebase for the musician—a reference beat against which all other beats are measured. An orchestra conductor serves the same purpose. The musicians play faster when the conductor waves his baton more rapidly because they are synchronizing their tempo to the conductor's timebase. The metaphor of the orchestra conductor supplying the timebase for music is so powerful that many sequencer programs call their tempo track the *conductor* track.

Since timing in music is so important, this chapter will delve deeply into the method—and madness, perhaps—of timing. The subject is not difficult, but some of the algorithms for achieving solid, high-resolution timing are, well, less than obvious. But the journey is worth it, so fasten your seat belts for a wild ride!

# Timestamps

Each event in a MIDI sequence has a timestamp—a value that indicates *when* the event is to be played. Timestamps can take many forms, and each type of timestamp has its own advantages and disadvantages. For example, a timestamp could be the time in milliseconds since the beginning of the sequence. Using such a timestamp, it would be easy to determine the location in a sequence for any given event. But, with time measured in absolute, wall-clock time, changing the tempo of the sequence would involve recalculating every timestamp. Large sequences may contain thousands of events, and recalculating all these timestamps would take a long time. It's even worse if a tempo change occurs during playback or record; all of the timestamps would need to be recalculated precisely when time is at a premium.

An alternative is to devise a timebase that is not tied to absolute, wall-clock time. Since musical timing is defined as fractions of a musical beat, it makes sense to create a timebase that also measures time as fractions of a beat. A quarter note is always one fourth of a whole note—regardless of the tempo. Likewise, a sixteenth note is always the same fraction of a beat. The rate at which the notes occur can change as the tempo changes, but the relative durations are always the same. An ideal timebase divides a musical beat into many small bits that occur at a rate determined by the current tempo. Each of these tiny fractions of a beat is called a *tick*, and the number of ticks per beat is independent of the tempo.

This timebase can be further refined by making the value of each timestamp relative to the previous timestamp. Such timestamps are measured in *delta ticks*. For example, two events in a sequence that have a timestamp of 0 will be played at the same time. If the next event in the sequence has a timestamp of 100, it will play 100 ticks later. Then, if an event is inserted between the second and third events, only the timestamp of the third event must be changed. In this example, to put a note half way between the two events with timestamps of 0 and 100, set the timestamp for the new event to 50 and change the timestamp of the last event from 100 to 50. Notice that the total time, in ticks, from the first two events to the last one is still 100 ticks.

Alternatively, event timestamps could be measured in units of absolute ticks. In this case, the beginning of a sequence corresponds to time zero, and the timestamp values increase as events progress through the sequence. This method has the advantage of easy event insertion, since no timestamp recalculation is necessary. But Standard MIDI Files, as discussed in chapter 13, use delta timestamps, so conversions are necessary with either type of timebase.

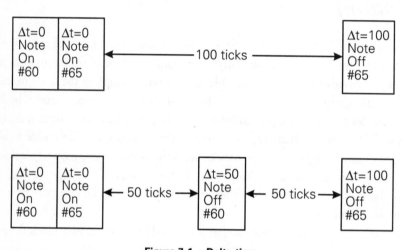

**Figure 7-1    Delta time**

The MaxMidi DLLs use a delta tick-based timebase to provide accurate and flexible timing and easy support for Standard MIDI Files. The number of ticks per beat—the *granularity* or *resolution*—can be adjusted over a wide range, and tempo can be changed, quickly and without any calculations, whenever desired.

# Of Ticks and Tempo

Tempo is the gas pedal of musical timing; it determines how fast ticks occur. When the tempo increases, the number of ticks in a unit of time increases. Then, when a sequencer plays back the events, the events are output faster. The timestamp for each event remains the same, but the rate at which ticks are produced increases.

Ticks are measured in ticks per beat (tpb). Normally, a beat can be any convenient unit of time, but in the rest of this book and in the MaxMidi ToolKit, a beat is chosen to be a quarter note. The lowest *resolution* that is meaningful is 24 ticks per beat. There is no theoretical upper limit to the number of ticks that can divide a beat, but there are practical limits. The lower limit is a result of the way MIDI Timing Clock messages work. These messages occur at a rate of 24 clocks per MIDI beat when MIDI Timing Clock synchronization is used. Since a sequencer might need to generate—or synchronize to— MIDI Clock messages, timing resolutions below 24 are not useful. For this same reason, resolution should always be a multiple of 24. Common resolutions are 96 tpb, 192 tpb, 240 tpb, and 480 tpb.

The sync algorithm used in the MaxMidi ToolKit supports resolutions as high as 960 ticks per beat. While this sounds great in a marketing sort of way, such high resolutions may be misleading. Because the calculations done in the timing routines use a limited number of bits, 32 in this case, very high resolutions at very low tempos can cause these calculations to underflow or overflow. The algorithm used in the MaxMidi ToolKit is optimized to allow tempos between 10 beats per minute (bpm) and 250 bpm at 960 ticks per beat. An even wider range of tempos is possible when using a lower timing resolution. The default resolution used by the ToolKit is 480 ticks per beat.

For a musician, tempo is normally specified in beats per minute, although sometimes Italian words are used instead. While the romance of Italy is irresistible, let's stick to numbers, since they are easier for silicon-based computers to process. It is desirable to be able to specify tempo as a fractional value (e.g., 110.3 bpm). To support fractional tempos and avoid the use of floating-point math, the MaxMidi routines specify tempo in microseconds per beat. Thus, by inverting and scaling the tempo, fractional tempos are supported without resorting to floating-point math.

To convert tempo in beats per minute into tempo in microseconds (µS) per beat, simply divide the tempo into 60,000,000. This scale factor is chosen because there are 60 seconds in a minute, and 1,000,000 microseconds in a second. Therefore,

$$tempo(\mu S / beat) = \frac{\dfrac{60\,seconds}{minute} \times \dfrac{1,000,000\mu S}{second}}{tempo(bpm)} = 60,000,000 / tempo(bpm)$$

Notice that the tempo in bpm *is* a floating-point number, but it is converted into a long integer value after dividing. The same process can be used to convert tempo in microseconds per beat into tempo in beats per minute.

# Resolution and Accuracy

It is easy to confuse the terms *resolution* and *accuracy*. Both concepts involve the "fineness" of something—in this case, of timing—but they are not the same thing. *Resolution* refers to the number of time slices into which a beat has been divided. Obviously, more divisions of a beat—higher resolution—allow a recorded performance to be a better representation of the actual performance. This is analogous to the number of bits used to sample digital audio. Sixteen-bit audio sounds better than 8-bit audio; 16-bit audio is higher resolution.

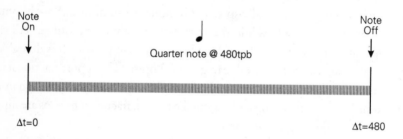

**Figure 7-2   Resolution**

*Accuracy*—as it applies to timing—refers to how close in time an event occurs in relation to when it should have occurred. Qualitatively, if a MIDI note should have played exactly on the third beat of the 11th measure, but it actually played an eighth note later, then the accuracy of the playback engine is shockingly poor. It is possible to have high accuracy with low resolution: the events fall very closely to where they *should*, but there are not many positions in time where the events *could* occur.

In addition, there are two kinds of accuracy. Short-term accuracy affects events as they are played, and is often called *jitter*. Poor short-term accuracy causes events to jitter back and forth in time from when they should occur—sometimes falling too early, sometimes too late. This can be easily heard by playing a track in sync with a known standard, such as a click track. Small variations in the timing will sound like flanging, while large variations will become more distinct to the ear, with a flam-like sound.

Long-term accuracy—also called *drift*—is a measure of how well a sync engine keeps time over a long period, such as an entire musical composition. Poor long-term accuracy will cause a sequencer to gradually drift out of sync. This type of error is usually the result of accumulated calculation errors. Even a tiny error, repeated over hundreds of beats, can add up to a sizable amount of drift. Mathematical round-off errors are the most common cause of drift. These errors are reduced by improving the synchronization algorithm to account for any rounding off that might occur. The drift of a well-designed sync engine is less than a single tick, measured over the duration of any reasonably-sized sequence.

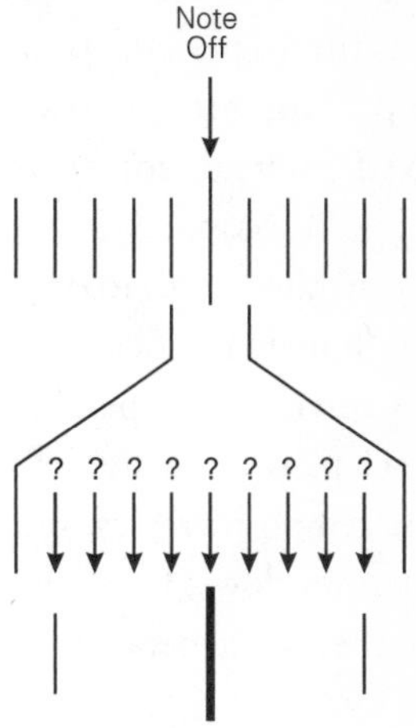

In the real world, a musical system must balance the needs of high accuracy, high resolution, and limited system resources (such as CPU speed and memory). Knowing the difference between resolution and accuracy will ensure that the proper trade-offs are made, and provide bountiful fodder for cocktail party conversation.

**Figure 7-3   Accuracy**

# Generating Ticks

Ticks may be numbers, but they are easily perceived as concrete objects. Ticks are "generated" by an algorithm called a *tick generator*. A tick generator creates ticks—by adding new ticks to an accumulated count of ticks—at a rate determined by the current tempo. For the time being, let's look at a tick generator as a black box having three inputs—resolution, tempo, and time—and a single output (ticks).

The resolution is in ticks per beat and fixes the granularity for the generation of ticks. The tempo is in microseconds per beat and determines the rate at which ticks are generated. We've discussed these already. Time, however, is a new quantity. It provides a fixed timebase for the tick timebase. That is, for the tick generator to generate ticks at a given rate it must have something against which to measure that rate.

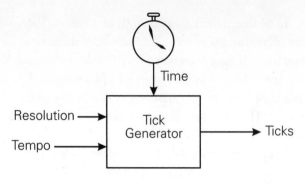

**Figure 7-4    Tick generator**

In the case of the MaxMidi tick generator, the time input comes from a periodic timer interrupt. This interrupt occurs at a fixed interval, for example, every millisecond. All that the tick generator needs to do is calculate how many ticks have elapsed, at the current tempo and resolution, since the last timer interrupt. Depending on the tempo and resolution, only a fraction of a tick may have elapsed, or many ticks may need to be generated in response to the timer interrupt. If the tempo increases, more ticks are generated on each timer interrupt. Conversely, if the tempo slows, fewer ticks are counted. But something must be done with these ticks once they are generated.

## Processing Timestamps

During playback, the current tick count is compared to the timestamp for the next event to be played. The event is output when the number of ticks reaches or exceeds the timestamp. The count of ticks is then set to 0 (or more accurately, to the difference between the current time and the event's timestamp)—these are delta ticks, remember— and the process begins again.

Timestamping during record is nearly the same process. The timestamp is set to the current tick value every time an event is received, and the tick count is cleared. The tick generator continues to increment the tick count and this count is applied to incoming events as delta timestamps.

## Inside the Tick Generator

In its simplest form, a tick generator works as follows. Given the resolution in ticks/beat, tempo in microseconds/beat, and timer period in milliseconds, the number of ticks per interrupt, *genTicks*, is calculated from:

$$gen\,Ticks = resolution \times \frac{1}{tempo} \times 1000 \times period$$

This can be derived by simply writing the units of each variable so that they cancel, leaving the number of ticks in units of ticks/interrupt:

$$\frac{ticks}{interrupt} = \frac{ticks}{beat} \times \frac{beats}{\mu S} \times \frac{1000\mu S}{mS} \times \frac{mS}{interrupt}$$

or,

$$gen\,Ticks = resolution \times \frac{1}{tempo} \times 1000 \times period$$

This looks straightforward enough. A simple divide, followed by a couple of multiplies. The problem here is that these multiplies and divides need to be integer operations. The number of ticks consists of an integer portion (that is used as the newly generated count of ticks) and a fractional part (that is the part of a tick that will be added on the next interrupt). If the fractional part is not properly accounted for, an error of up to one tick *per interrupt* will render the tick generator useless.

It is tempting to use floating-point math routines to calculate the number of ticks. After all, floating point would seem to handle the integer and fractional part of the calculation properly. But because of rounding errors, floating-point math is not accurate enough. And, floating-point math routines are notoriously slow, much too slow for our purposes here, since these routines would be called at a time-critical point—during a timer interrupt. To do this job correctly we need a fast and accurate way to calculate the number of ticks.

The goal in our case is to divide a fixed timebase into the number of ticks that correspond to the current tempo for each interrupt of the timebase. The MaxMidi sync engine does the job by splitting the problem into two parts. On each iteration, it calculates the integer count of ticks separately from the fractional portion. The fraction of a tick from the last iteration—scaled so that it is accurately represented in a 32-bit integer—is added to the "whole" number of ticks during the next interrupt.

All of the calculations are simple integer operations. The accuracy of the math is only limited by the number of bits used—no floating-point operations are needed.

Here's a simple example to illustrate how the process works. For the sake of clarity, we choose a tempo and resolution such that the number of interrupts per tick is exactly 4. (Admittedly, fancy math is not necessary in this case, but the algorithm works the same for any combination of input values.) The two equations for the number of whole ticks and the number of fractional ticks are:

$$nticks = (fticks + period \times resolution) / tempo$$
$$fticks \mathrel{+}= (period \times resolution) - (nticks \times tempo)$$

where the period is in microseconds, resolution is in ticks/beat, and tempo is in microseconds/beat. Notice that the fractional tick value (*fticks*) is an accumulator. When the algorithm starts, *fticks* is set to 0. On each iteration the newly calculated fraction is added to the current *fticks* value. For the sake of example, we choose a tempo of 4, a period of 1, and resolution of 1. We should see one tick generated for every four iterations since at a resolution of 1 tick per beat and a tempo of 4 microseconds per beat, using a timer period of 1 microsecond, one tick occurs every 4 timer periods.

$$tempo = 4$$
$$period = 1$$
$$resolution = 1$$
$$fticks = 0$$

therefore,

$$nticks = (fticks + 1) / 4$$
$$fticks \mathrel{+}= 1 - (nticks * 4)$$

| Iteration | *nticks* | *fticks* | Comment |
|-----------|----------|----------|----------------|
| 0 | x | 0 | Initialize |
| 1 | 0 | 1 | |
| 2 | 0 | 2 | |
| 3 | 0 | 3 | |
| 4 | 1 | 0 | Tick generated |

Looking closer at the two equations, there are several features worth noting. Since the (*period* × *resolution*) does not change while the algorithm is running, it can be calculated in advance. Therefore:

$$trtime = (period \times resolution)$$

and the equations become:

$$nticks = ( fticks + trtime ) / tempo$$
$$fticks\ += \ trtime - nticks \times tempo$$

For reasonable values of tempo, resolution, and period, all of the calculations above involve 24-bit operations. This leaves 8 bits unused. But they are not wasted. By shifting all of the values over by 8 bits, the algorithm can support fractional values for the timebase period. This is useful when synchronizing to SMPTE/MTC, where the timebase is driven by the reception of MTC Quarter Frame messages. The period of MIDI Time Code messages, at 30 frames per second, is 8.33333 milliseconds. That extra 1/3 of a millisecond is significant. By adding an extra eight bits to the period and scaling all of the other values accordingly, any error in the calculations—due to rounding off—is reduced to 1.3 nanoseconds per MTC quarter frame, or more than 26 minutes of elapsed time per tick.

Applying this new scaling to the algorithm, we get:

| | |
|---|---|
| $fticks = 0$ | *Initialize fractional part* |
| $trtime = resolution \times period \times 256$ | *Calculated in advance* |
| $tempo = tempo \times 256$ | *Scale tempo to match* |

$$nticks = (fticks + trtime)/tempo$$
$$fticks\ += \ trtime - nticks \times tempo$$

# MIDI Time Code Synchronization

This tick generator algorithm can also be used to synchronize MIDI recording and playback to MIDI Time Code. The timer interrupt timebase is replaced by the periodic reception of MTC Quarter Frame messages. Setting the period to the proper value—corresponding to the incoming MTC frame rate—causes the tick generator to run in sync with the received timecode.

Replacing the timer interrupt is easy. Open a MIDI input device and monitor the received MIDI data in the callback function. Every time a Quarter Frame message is received, call the same tick generator routine that the timer interrupt used to call. The period must be set to the proper value, based on the expected frame rate. The periods for the four most common frame rates are shown in the following table.

**Table 7-1  MIDI Time Code Periods**

| Frame rate | Period | Tick generator period |
|---|---|---|
| 30 Non-drop | 8.333333 mS | 2,133,333 |
| 30 Drop (29.97002617) | 8.341667 mS | 2,135,467 |
| 25 Frame | 10.000000 mS | 2,560,000 |
| 24 Frame | 10.416667 mS | 2,666,667 |

The rightmost column is the scaled value that is used as the timer period in the tick generator algorithm. It is calculated using the formula

$$tickPeriod = \frac{(1,000,000 \times 256)}{(4 \times framerate)}$$

A more refined MTC sync algorithm could achieve better short-term accuracy by interpolating between MTC events. An example of this kind of interpolating algorithm is found in the section on *MIDI Timing Clock Synchronization* that appears later in this chapter.

# Starting SMPTE/MTC Synchronization

For SMPTE/MTC sync to be useful, a mechanism must exist for synchronization to begin precisely when a particular frame—the *start frame* or *origin frame*—is received. Frames must be assembled as the MTC messages are received, since it takes 8 separate Quarter Frame messages to fully specify a frame number.

Each Quarter Frame message includes a message type, which identifies where in the sequence of 8 messages this one belongs, and a nibble of data. The frame number and type are known when all 8 messages in the sequence are received. The very first Quarter Frame message (type 0) occurs at the beginning of a frame. It is not until two frame times later that the frame number corresponding to the frame where the first quarter frame message was sent is completely known. This means that at least two complete frames of data must be processed before the incoming timecode makes sense.

Once a frame has been read, the MTC reading routine does not need to continue to assemble frames, except as a sanity check or to detect stalled or broken timecode. Instead, it simply increments the frame number every four Quarter Frame messages. A frame fits nicely into a DWORD value, so that the lowest 8 bits are used for the frame number, the next

8 bits contain the seconds, followed by 8 bits of minutes and 8 bits of hours. All four values can be accessed using a union, like this:

```
union {
      DWORD dwFrame;
      struct fr_tag {
            BYTE hr;
            BYTE mn;
            BYTE sc;
            BYTE fr; };
      } Frame;
```

Incrementing frames is easy. Simply add 1 to the count of frames. If the value is equal to the nominal number of frames per second for the received SMPTE format (e.g., 30 for 30ND or 30D, 25 for 25 frame, and 24 for 24 frame), then set the frame byte to 0 and increment the seconds value. When the seconds value hits 60, set that value to 0 and increment the minutes. Continue this process up through the hours field. Assuming a format of 30 non-drop, the highest frame number possible, in hr:mn:sc:fr, is 23:59:59:29. The next frame would be 00:00:00:00.

# Chasing SMPTE/MTC

Performing the proper calculations and starting on the correct frame is all that is necessary if sync always starts at the beginning of the sequence. Things get more complicated when playback or record must begin in the middle of the sequence. The process for calculating the proper start frame, when starting somewhere other than the beginning, is called *chasing*.

Chasing to incoming MIDI Time Code involves several steps. Although the MaxMidi DLLs do not support synchronizing or chasing SMPTE/MTC, the steps needed are outlined here, providing the algorithms needed to implement the chasing process. The basic steps for chasing a sequencer to MTC are:

- Stop synchronization while performing the chasing calculations. Flush any MIDI events that may still be in the output queues by calling `FlushMidiOut()` for each of the open output devices.

- Construct a new starting frame number by reading the incoming MIDI Time Code Quarter Frame messages.

- Subtract the original start frame (the sequence start time) from the new start frame to get the start position in the sequence as a count of frames.

- Add a fixed amount of time to allow the program to search event buffers and perform calculations. One-half second should be enough in most circumstances. This value becomes the new start frame.

- Loop through the sequence tracks and calculate elapsed time and ticks, accounting for tempo changes, until the elapsed sequence time reaches or exceeds the new start frame time.

- If this frame does not fall on a MIDI Clock boundary (i.e., the number of elapsed ticks is not divisible by 24), continue looping until such a frame is found. This frame becomes the new start frame. The next MIDI event in the sequence will be the first event to be output when sync begins.

- Set the delta time for the starting event in each track to be equal to the corresponding number of ticks since the MIDI Clock boundary.

- Send MIDI events to the output devices, starting at the event found above.

- Set the start frame to the new start frame found above. Start synchronization.

Synchronization will begin when the incoming MIDI Time Code reaches the new frame number. Notice that when recording, the timestamp of the first received event is corrected by adding the elapsed time in ticks up to the start frame.

# MIDI Timing Clock Synchronization

MIDI Time Code provides one method of synchronizing to an external timebase. MIDI Timing Clocks (or, more commonly, MIDI Clocks) provide another method. MIDI Clocks can be generated by drum machines, other sequencers, or tape readers. They are single-byte System Real-Time messages that occur at a rate determined by the tempo. Twenty-four MIDI Clocks are sent every quarter note or beat. If the tempo changes, the time between each MIDI Clock byte changes. But there are always 24 clocks per beat.

MIDI sync works like this: One device—for example, a drum machine—acts as a master. It sends a MIDI Start message to begin synchronization, MIDI Clocks to indicate tempo, and a MIDI Stop message to end synchronization. Another device—say, a computer running a MIDI application—is the slave. It receives the messages from the master and uses them as a timebase.

But this timebase varies as the master's tempo changes. This means that the algorithm used to synchronize to MTC will not work with MIDI sync. Another algorithm must be used—one that derives its tempo from the rate of incoming MIDI Clocks.

Conceptually, this algorithm is simple. First, the sync engine begins generating ticks, at a nominal starting tempo, using a periodic timer interrupt as a timebase. Then, it measures the time between each of the MIDI Clocks and calculates the incoming tempo. Finally, it compares the calculated tempo to the tempo used to generate ticks. If the two tempos are not equal, the algorithm corrects the tick generator's tempo to match the incoming tempo.

It is imperative that the number of ticks generated for each incoming MIDI Clock always be correct. The master and slave devices would gradually drift out of sync if the slave generated a different number of ticks per clock than the master. Remember, there are always 24 MIDI Clocks per beat, and the sequencer's resolution is set to a fixed number of ticks per beat. The sequencer generates *resolution/24* ticks per received MIDI Clock. For this reason, the resolution must be a multiple of 24; otherwise a fraction of a tick would be lost for every clock received.

The best way to generate the right number of ticks is to never generate too many or not enough. That seems obvious, of course, but it is central to making MIDI sync work. Let's explore an example to see how this should work.

Imagine a master, connected to a slave. The master sends MIDI Clocks at a tempo of 120 beats per minute; 2,880 clocks per minute, or 48 clocks per second. Suppose the slave's current tempo is slower than 120 bpm, say 100 bpm, and its resolution is 240 ticks per beat. The slave receives 24 clocks from the master and during that time generates 200 ticks, 40 fewer than expected. In order to stay in sync with the master, the slave must generate 40 ticks right away. It then recalculates its tempo, to match the 120 bpm incoming tempo, so that the error in ticks will be smaller when the next MIDI Clock is received.

Similarly, if the slave's tempo were too high, it would attempt to generate more ticks than necessary before the MIDI Clock is received from the master. In this case, the slave would need to hold off generating any more ticks until the clock message is received.

When MIDI sync is running properly, it will alternate between holding (if the tempo is slightly too high) or generating a catch-up tick (if the tempo is slightly too low) each

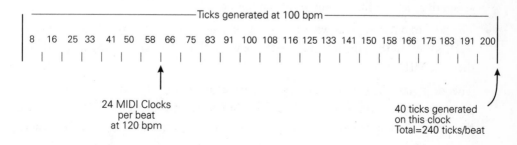

Figure 7-5   MIDI sync

time a MIDI Clock is received. Because of this, MIDI sync—even at its theoretical best—suffers from timing jitter. As a result, MIDI sync has fallen into disfavor, and for most uses has been replaced by SMPTE/MTC synchronization. It is still used extensively by drum machines, however, so most sequencers still support MIDI sync.

The equations used in the MIDI Clock tick generator are the same ones used in the tick generator described earlier in this chapter. Ticks are generated using a timer interrupt, exactly like the internal sync algorithm. Several flags and counter values keep track of the tick generator so that the proper number of ticks is generated for every MIDI Clock received.

This algorithm, as implemented in the MaxMidi DLLs, works this way:

- Before synchronization begins, several variables and flags are initialized. In addition to the variables that are used in the tick generator (fTicks, trtime, and tempo), two other variables are used by the algorithm:
  - nTicksPerClock holds the expected number of ticks per MIDI Clock at the current resolution. It is calculated by dividing the resolution by 24.
  - TempoTicks is used to recalculate the tempo each time a MIDI Clock is received. It counts the number of ticks generated since the last MIDI Clock.

  In addition, two flags control the state of the tick generator.
  - If MC_HOLD is TRUE, the tick generator stops processing ticks that are generated, but continues to accumulate the count of ticks in the TempoTicks variable. This happens when the tick generator's tempo is faster than the incoming MIDI Clock tempo.
  - The MC_RESYNC flag is set when a MIDI Clock message is received by a MIDI input device. The tick generator will then recalculate the tempo and update the tick count as needed to resynchronize to the incoming MIDI Clock tempo.
- Initially, synchronization is halted. The tick generator waits until a MIDI Start message is received. When the first MIDI Clock arrives, the tick generator begins generating ticks at the default 120 bpm tempo.
- The MC_HOLD flag is set as whenever the tick count—since the last MIDI Clock—reaches one less than the nTicksPerClock value. This last tick will be generated on the next MIDI Clock.
- The MC_HOLD flag is tested during each timer interrupt. If it is TRUE, the tick generator will continue to calculate ticks, but will not process them. This means that when the flag is set, the tick generator will not output any more MIDI data

(during playback), nor will it increment the timestamp that is applied to incoming MIDI events (during record) until a MIDI Clock is received.

- The `MC_RESYNC` flag is set each time a MIDI Clock is received by the input device. An updated tempo is calculated based on the number of ticks that have elapsed since the last MIDI Clock. The tempo will increase if the tick generator did not generate enough ticks during this interval, or decrease if the tick generator tried to generate too many ticks. Notice that any "extra" ticks are counted only for the purpose of calculating a new tempo. Then, they are discarded by the tick generator, since it is held in stasis by the `MC_HOLD` flag.

- The `MC_RESYNC` flag is tested during each timer interrupt. If it is TRUE, the tick generator resynchronizes the number of generated ticks to match the number that should have been generated since the last MIDI Clock. If the tick generator was too slow, the number of ticks needed to catch up is immediately generated. If the tick generator was too fast, exactly one tick is generated (since the count was held at `nTicksPerClock-1`). The hold flag is cleared and synchronization continues normally.

- When the MIDI input device receives a MIDI Stop message it stops synchronization.

This algorithm is fully implemented in the MaxMidi DLLs. For even more detail on this implementation, see the fully commented source code in appendix B.

# Chasing MIDI Sync

Whenever the sequencer receives a MIDI Start message—followed by a MIDI Clock message—while synchronizing to MIDI Clock messages, it must begin playback or record at the beginning of the sequence. Of course, a sequencer—while synchronized to MIDI Clocks—may need to start somewhere in the middle of the sequence. Two MIDI messages make this possible: Continue and Song Position Pointer.

The MIDI Continue message indicates that the receiving sequencer should begin synchronization—on the next MIDI Clock message—wherever it is currently located in the sequence. It can be used to unpause a sequencer, or to continue playback after a new sync location has been specified using the Song Position Pointer (SPP) message.

An SPP message consists of a status byte (0xF2) followed by two data bytes that specify the new sync location for the sequence. Record or playback will begin at this location when a MIDI Continue message is received. The location is specified as a 14-bit count of

16th notes since the beginning of the sequence.

To chase a sequencer to a new SPP location, perform the following steps:

- Stop any currently active synchronization and flush any data out of all MIDI output devices.

- When the new location is received via the Song Position Pointer message, calculate the number of ticks since the beginning of the sequence using these equations:

```
SppLoc = (RxEvent.data2 << 7) + RxEvent.data1;
SeqTicks = SppLoc * 6 * (resolution / 24);
```

- For playback, search through the sequence event list, adding up the delta tick counts of all of the events, until the accumulated tick count is greater than or equal to the SeqTicks value. The event where this occurs will be the first event played.

- Correct the timestamp of this event by setting it to the difference between the accumulated tick count and SeqTicks. This will cause the event to be output the proper number of ticks after the 16th note boundary specified by SeqTicks.

- Begin sending MIDI events, if any, to the MIDI output devices and enable synchronization. Playback or recording will begin when a MIDI Continue, followed by a MIDI Clock message is received. If recording, offset the timestamp of the first recorded event by the SeqTicks value.

While SPP chasing is not built into the MaxMidi DLLs, these steps—along with the DLL's MIDI sync support—are all a program needs to handle this type of synchronization.

**CHAPTER 8**

# *MaxMidi Synchronization*

The MaxMidi DLLs provide a rich set of functions that implement a sync engine, supporting both internal sync and MIDI sync. Resolution can range from 24 ticks per beat to 960 ticks per beat or more. Tempo can be set at any time during playback or record—as often as once per tick, if desired. In addition, whenever the tempo is changed while recording, a special tempo change event is automatically inserted into the recorded data stream. During playback, the sync device encounters such tempo events in the outgoing event list and updates the tempo.

Additionally, the sync device provides functions to start, stop, and restart synchronization. By connecting the sync device to an input device (that has been opened as a sync input), it can be slaved to incoming MIDI sync. In this case, the sync device will automatically respond to the MIDI Start, Stop, and Continue messages. Other functions allow an application to set or get the current tempo, and set or get the timing resolution.

The sync device must be opened before it is ready to be used. This should be done before opening any MIDI input and output devices that will utilize sync, since a handle to the sync device must be specified when opening sync-enabled input and output devices. While it is possible to open more than one sync device, most applications should use only a single sync device. Each sync device uses a periodic timer—a limited system resource. Because each sync device uses its own timer, it is difficult to synchronize these devices to each other. But, since a single sync device can handle multiple output devices, there is little need for multiple sync devices.

Use the OpenSync() function to open a device. Four parameters are needed: a handle to an already opened sync device (pass 0 when initially opening the device), a window handle, the sync mode, and the timer period. If successful, OpenSync() returns a non-zero handle to the sync device. This handle is used by other sync, input, and output functions to specify the particular sync device. If the open fails, the returned handle will be 0. The prototype for the open function looks like this:

```
HSYNC OpenSync(HSYNC hSync, HWND hWnd, WORD mode, WORD timerPeriod);
```

Two sync modes are supported by the ToolKit—internal sync (selected by specifying S_INT) and MIDI sync (selected by specifying S_MIDI). The timer period is specified in milliseconds. It can be as small as 1 millisecond, but such a rapid timer gains short-term accuracy at the expense of system performance. On slower systems, a 1-millisecond timer can slow screen updates, interfere with disk access, and even cause the mouse to become erratic. In that case, a more reasonable timer period of 10 milliseconds would give the computer time to handle all of its tasks smoothly. Many programs make the timer period user-selectable, so that the program can be optimized for both fast and slow machines.

However, for most systems, a 1 millisecond timer is preferred in order to provide the best possible timing accuracy.

The window handle specifies a window that will receive messages from the sync device. Two messages are possible—MIDI_BEAT and SYNC_DONE. The MIDI_BEAT message is posted on every beat (quarter note) while sync is running. The message's wParam value is always 0, and lParam contains the handle to the sync device. This message can be used to update a beat counter or to drive a simple metronome.

The SYNC_DONE message is posted when the sync device finds that there are no events remaining to be played. Like the MIDI_BEAT message, the wParam value is always 0, and lParam contains the handle to the sync device. It is often used to stop synchronization at the end of a sequence during playback. The sync device will post this message as soon as it starts if there are no messages to be played when sync begins. As a result, the SYNC_DONE message should be ignored when recording, to prevent sync from stopping inappropriately.

Just like the other messages sent to an application by the MaxMidi DLLs, these two messages are posted—instead of sent—to the window proc of the window that is specified when the sync device is originally opened. These messages must be posted since they originate inside the timer interrupt that drives the sync engine. There are few Windows API functions that can be called during an interrupt; SendMessage() is not one of them. Thus, these messages pass through Windows message queue, and are dispatched to the proper window proc in the application's GetMessage() loop. This means that the timing of these messages is not precise, and the application should avoid any assumptions about when the messages will arrive.

The final parameter, a handle to a sync device, serves an important purpose. It is normally set to 0 when OpenSync() is called. However, when an application wishes to change the settings of a sync device without closing the device first, it passes the handle that was returned when the device was initially opened—along with the window handle that was specified for the original open—and specifies the new values for the sync parameters. Using this method, the sync mode or timer period can be changed without invalidating the sync device handle. A special value, USE_CURRENT, can be specified for either the sync mode or timer period. This flag tells OpenSync() to keep the current value for that parameter, so that the application need not keep track of these settings. Changing sync settings by reopening the sync device is useful when one or more input or output devices have been opened with synchronization, since these devices have copies of the sync device handle. If the handle were to change, all of the input and output devices would need to be closed and reopened—a slow and disruptive process.

Once a sync device is open, synchronization is started by calling StartSync( ). If the sync mode is internal (S_INT), the sync engine immediately begins generating ticks. If, instead, the sync device is set to MIDI sync (S_MIDI), calling StartSync( ) will arm the sync device. In this case, synchronization will not start until a MIDI Start message, followed by a MIDI Clock, is received.

When a sync device is opened, the default values for resolution and tempo are set to 480 ticks per beat and 120 beats per minute, respectively. To change the resolution, call SetResolution( ) and specify the new resolution in ticks per beat. The resolution should only be changed when synchronization is stopped. The current resolution can be retrieved from the sync device by calling GetResolution( ).

The tempo can be changed, and the current value retrieved, any time before or during synchronization. SetTempo( ) changes the tempo, specified in microseconds per beat (where a beat is a quarter note), while GetTempo( ) returns the current tempo (also in microseconds per beat).

When SetTempo( ) changes the tempo, it checks to see if there is an input device attached to the sync device. If there is, SetTempo( ) inserts a tempo change event (with the proper timestamp) into the MIDI stream that is being sent by the input device to the application. This event is contained in a MidiEvent structure. The status byte is set to 0 to indicate that it is a tempo change event. Tempo is specified as a 24-bit value. The three bytes of the new tempo are put into the three data bytes of the tempo change event, where data1 contains the most significant byte.

During playback, when the sync device encounters a tempo change event in the outgoing MIDI data, the tempo is automatically changed to the new value. Thus, a sequence containing tempo changes will play exactly as intended, tempo changes and all. Enter these tempo events by calling SetTempo( ) during recording or by inserting them directly into the event list.

Tempo changes (caused either by SetTempo( ) or by tempo change events in the outgoing MIDI data) have no effect when synchronizing to MIDI sync. The sync device is slaved to the incoming MIDI Clock tempo, so the tempo used for synchronization *is* the MIDI Clock tempo. The current tempo during MIDI sync can be retrieved by calling GetTempo( ).

Synchronization can be stopped by calling StopSync( ), or can be paused by calling PauseSync( ). The StopSync( ) function halts synchronization and resets any attached MIDI output devices. Resetting a MIDI output causes it to flush any pending MIDI events and send Note Off messages for any notes that were sounding when the reset occurred. PauseSync( ) also stops synchronization. But it does not reset any output devices. PauseSync( ) also accepts a flag that, if TRUE, causes the function to send Note

Offs for any sounding notes. If the flag is FALSE, notes that are sounding continue to sound. This case is useful for momentarily halting sync—to send a short sysex, for example—without stopping any sounding notes. If the sequence is to be paused for a longer period, the hanging notes should be stopped by specifying TRUE for the reset flag.

Restart a paused sync device by calling `ReStartSync()`. The sequence will continue playing from its paused location as if it had never been halted.

When a sync device is no longer needed, release it by calling `CloseSync()`. This will stop the device (if running), destroy the periodic timer, and free the memory that is associated with the sync device. Any output devices that are attached to the sync device are automatically detached when the sync device is closed.

## Using the Sync Functions

To play back MIDI events using synchronization, start by opening a sync device. Pass the handle to the sync device to each output device that is to be synchronized as it is opened. Sync will then be automatic for those devices. For example:

```
HSYNC hSync;

hSync = OpenSync(0, hWnd, S_INT, DEFAULT_TIMERPERIOD);
hMidiOut = OpenMidiOut(hWnd, wDevID, hSync, MIDIOUT_DEFAULT);
hMidiIn = OpenMidiIn(hWnd, wDevID, hSync, MIDIIN_DEFAULT);
```

In this case, the sync device is being opened for internal sync. The handle will be 0 if the open is unsuccessful.

Once the sync device is opened, the tempo and resolution may be changed from their default values. If the resolution is to be changed, it must be set before beginning to play or record. Resolution can be set between 1 and 960 ticks per beat, and should normally be a multiple of 24. For example:

```
SetResolution(hSync, 240);
```

The tempo may be changed at any time, before or after synchronization is started. Tempo is set in microseconds (µS) per beat. This allows very accurate fractional tempos to be set and is compatible with the Standard MIDI File format for tempos. The tempo in beats per minute can be converted to tempo in µS/beat by dividing 60,000,000 by the tempo. For example:

```
DWORD tempo;
double dTempo;

dTempo = 121.53;
tempo = (DWORD)(60000000.0/dTempo);
SetTempo(hSync, tempo);
```

The current tempo and resolution may be retrieved by calling `GetTempo()` and `GetResolution()`, respectively.

The MaxMidi DLLs automatically generate MIDI Start, Stop, Continue, and Clock messages during synchronization for internal sync. In order for an output to automatically send these messages, it must be opened with the `SYNC_OUTPUT` flag set in the `dwFlags` parameter of `OpenMidiOut()`. Any number of output devices may serve as sync outputs.

# Playing Back in Time

To start synchronization for playback, first send events to the output devices that have data to send. Send data until either all data have been sent or `PutMidiOut()` indicates that the queue is full by returning −1. For example:

```
LPMIDIEVENT lpMidiBuffer;
DWORD eventCount;
DWORD nBufferEvents;

// Events are in a buffer, pointed to by lpMidiBuffer
// Number of events in the buffer is nBufferEvents

eventCount = 0L;
while((eventCount < nBufferEvents) && (PutMidiOut(hMidiOut,
    (lpMidiBuffer + eventCount)) == 0))
        eventCount++;
```

Next, start synchronization by calling `StartSync()`.

```
StartSync(hSync);
```

Playback will begin, starting with the event having the smallest timestamp value. When a MIDI output queue that is being synchronized falls below 25% of its capacity, MaxMidi will send an `OUTBUFFER_READY` message to the application window procedure. Process this message by sending more events, if available, to the output device. The `lParam` of the message is the pointer to the originating output device. For example:

```
case OUTBUFFER_READY:
   while((eventCount < nBufferEvents) &&
      (PutMidiOut(hMidiOut,(lpMidiBuffer + eventCount))== 0))
         eventCount++;

   return 0;
```

Synchronization should be stopped when playback is complete. The SYNC_DONE message is sent by the sync device when playback is finished:

```
case SYNC_DONE:
   StopSync(hSync);
   return 0;
```

# Recording

To record MIDI events with tick-based timestamps, first open a sync device. Open a MIDI input device and pass the handle to the sync device. Then, start sync by calling StartSync( ). Finally, start MIDI input by calling StartMidiIn( ). For example:

```
HSYNC hSync;

hSync = OpenSync(0, hWnd, S_INT, DEFAULT_TIMERPERIOD);
hMidiIn = OpenMidiIn(hWnd, wDevID, hSync, MIDIIN_DEFAULT);
StartSync(hSync);
StartMidiIn(hMidiIn);
```

If desired, one or more output devices can be opened, as shown in the previous section. Previously recorded MIDI events can then be played at the same time that new events are recorded.

Tempo changes made while recording will cause timestamped tempo events to be placed in the incoming stream of MIDI data that is sent to the application. Note that a starting tempo event is not inserted into the event stream unless the tempo is set after sync has been started.

A MIDI_DATA message is sent to the application window procedure as each complete MIDI event is received. The application should retrieve each event using the same method described in chapter 5. The timestamp associated with each event is in units of ticks since the last event, or delta ticks. For example:

```
case MIDI_DATA:
   while((lpMsg = GetMidiIn(hMidiIn)) != NULL)
   {
      // process the message pointed to by lpMsg
   }

   return 0;
```

When recording is complete, both synchronization and MIDI input for all input devices associated with the sync device should be stopped.

```
StopSync(hSync);
StopMidiIn(hMidiIn);
```

## Sync Data Flow

The data flow diagram in figure 8-1 shows how the sync device is organized. The client application is on the left. It sets the tempo and resolution of the tick generator and receives SYNC_DONE and MIDI_BEAT messages. The tick generator code runs when the periodic timer interrupt calls the syncTimer() callback function. In response to the interrupt, the tick generator (located in the sync() function) calculates a new value of elapsed ticks, based on the resolution and current tempo.

The timer interrupt works the same way during MIDI sync. In addition, the MIDI sync handler receives MIDI Clock messages from a MIDI input device. This handler calculates a new tempo and updates the state of the tick generator via the MC_HOLD and MC_RESYNC flags. Later, during the next interrupt cycle, the tick generator calculates the new ticks, just as in the internal sync case, but using the newly calculated tempo.

Three variables accumulate ticks: the TempoTicks variable is used to recalculate tempo during MIDI sync, the Tick Accumulator (dwTicks) maintains a count of elapsed ticks, and the TicksSinceBeat counter is used to output MIDI Clocks at the proper rate during internal sync. The accumulated count of elapsed ticks—dwTicks—is compared to the timestamp of the next event queued in each of the MIDI output devices in the MIDI Output Device list. Any event whose timestamp is equal to or less than the tick count is sent to the device driver to be output by the MIDI hardware. But let's not get ahead of ourselves; the details of synchronized MIDI output are discussed later in this chapter.

A sync device is opened by calling OpenSync(). OpenSync() performs the following steps:

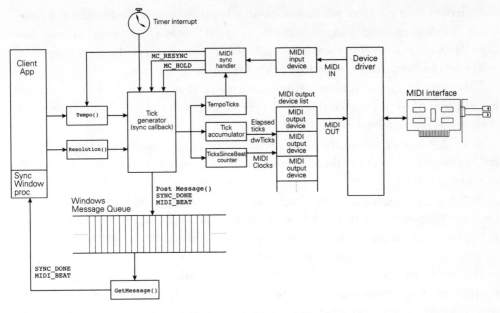

**Figure 8-1    Sync device data flow**

- Checks the `hsync` parameter to see if the device is already open. The sync device is being reopened with new parameters if the handle is valid. In that case, the timer is stopped and the new values are used to reopen the device.

- Allocates memory for the `SyncStruct` structure that is used to maintain the sync device, if the `hsync` parameter is 0 or is an invalid handle. If the `hsync` handle is valid, `OpenSync()` uses the structure corresponding to this handle, instead of allocating a new structure.

- Initializes the `SyncStruct` and sets the default resolution and tempo.

- Creates a list of MIDI output devices that will be filled with pointers to devices that are attached to this sync device.

- Creates and starts the timer that will drive the tick generator.

The timer created by `OpenSync()` periodically calls `syncTimer()`. The `syncTimer()` function, in turn, calls the sync engine which is contained in the `sync()` function. The sync engine generates ticks, outputs MIDI Clocks as necessary, and searches the buffers in each of the output devices in the device list. For each of the output devices in the list, it compares the timestamps of the events in the buffer with the elapsed count of ticks since the last event was output (`dwTicks - dwLastEventTicks`). It sends to the hardware device driver any event whose timestamp is less than or equal to the delta tick time; either as a short message (using midiOutShortMsg()), or as a long (sysex) message (using midiOutLongMsg()). It then sets dwLastEventTicks equal to the elapsed count of ticks (dwTicks), so that the new delta tick value will be 0.

Whenever the sync() function encounters a tempo change event (a MIDI event with a status byte of 0), it uses the three data bytes to assemble the new 24-bit tempo and directly update the tempo value.

StartSync() initializes members of the SyncStruct structure, along with the dwLastEventTicks value in the MIDI output device's MidiOutStruct structure. It then calls ReStartSync().

ReStartSync() adjusts various flags to allow the timer interrupts to be processed by the sync() function. It then sends a MIDI Start message—if the sync mode is not S_MIDI—to any output devices that were opened with the SYNC_OUTPUT flag set.

StopSync() stops the sync() function from processing any further timer interrupts by clearing the appropriate flags, thus stopping synchronization. Even when sync is stopped, the timer continues running, but since the SYNC_RUNNING flag is 0, the sync() function returns without doing anything. Next, StopSync() sends a MIDI Stop message to any output devices that were opened with the SYNC_OUTPUT flag set. Finally, it resets each output device to flush any pending MIDI data and turn off any sounding notes.

PauseSync(), on the other hand, saves the state of the sync flags and then stops sync by clearing the appropriate flags. If the reset flag parameter is TRUE when PauseSync() is called, the function then sends a MIDI Stop message to any output devices that were opened with the SYNC_OUTPUT flag set and turns off any sounding notes.

The SetTempo() function scales the new tempo to minimize round-off errors in the calculations used by the tick generator. If synchronization is running (i.e., if StartSync() has been called) and a MIDI input device is attached to the sync device, a tempo change event is inserted into the receive buffer of the input device. Then, a MIDI_DATA message is sent to the client application, just as if the event were received as a MIDI message.

SetResolution() calculates resolution-dependent values in the SyncStruct structure. GetTempo() and GetResolution() simply return the appropriate values from the same structure.

When the musical party is over and the sync device is no longer needed, CloseSync() shuts it down by stopping and destroying the timer. Finally, after searching through the MIDI output device list and detaching each device from the sync device, it frees the memory associated with the sync device. As they say in the movies: The End.

# MIDI Input Data Flow Changes

Well, it's not quite the end after all. The MIDI input and MIDI output data flow diagrams require a few changes to show how synchronization affects these two devices. The updated MIDI input data flow diagram shown below illustrates the simple changes needed for the input device to support synchronization. This diagram illustrates non-sysex data flow using synchronization. For sysex reception, the first buffer of a message is timestamped. Any other buffers occupied by the message receive a timestamp of 0. In all cases the timestamp is applied in the same manner, so only the non-sysex data flow is shown.

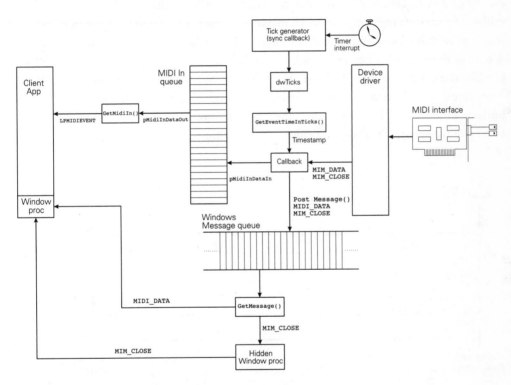

**Figure 8-2    MIDI input data flow with sync (non-sysex)**

The tick generator in the `sync()` callback function generates ticks that are accumulated in the `dwTicks` variable. Whenever an event is received, the device driver calls the `MidiInCallback()` callback function. The callback then calls `GetEventTimeInTicks()` to get the timestamp for the event. This function calculates (and returns) the number of ticks that have elapsed since the last received event. It does this by subtracting the number of ticks that had elapsed when the last event was received (stored in the dwLastEventTicks member of the input device's MidiInStruct structure) from dwTicks (a member of the sync device's SyncStruct structure). It then sets dwLastEventTicks to the value in dwTicks, so that the timestamp for the next event will be relative to this event.

The returned timestamp is stored in the time member of the MidiEvent structure for this event. The other members of the structure—status and data bytes—are set as in the non-sync case.

The timestamp is calculated slightly differently for the case of System Exclusive buffers. Sysex data is collected by the device driver in buffers, which are then sent to the callback function using MIM_LONGDATA messages—one per buffer. A given sysex message might be contained in a single buffer, or might be spread across multiple buffers. A buffer is sent to the callback when either it becomes full (i.e., all available bytes in the buffer contain sysex data), or the EOX byte is received. Since the timestamp used for MIDI events applies to the first byte of an event, and the sysex buffer does not arrive until the buffer is full, the calculated timestamp must be corrected to account for the time it took to receive the event. The diagram below shows how this works.

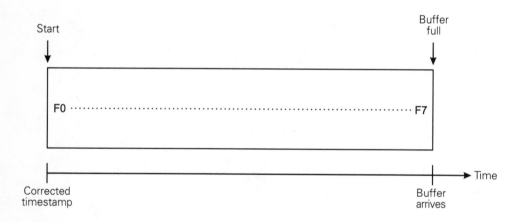

Figure 8-3  Sysex buffer timestamping

The timestamp corresponding to the beginning of the buffer is calculated like this:

```
duration = (320 * dwBytesRecorded * resolution) / tempo
timestamp = dwTicks - dwLastEventTicks - duration
```

The duration of the sysex is calculated by converting the number of bytes in the buffer into a time in microseconds (since each MIDI byte takes 320 microseconds to transmit). This value is converted into time in ticks using the same tick generator math discussed in chapter 7. The accumulated number of ticks (`dwTicks`) corresponds to the time at the end of the sysex buffer. It is corrected by subtracting the duration of the buffer, calculated in ticks.

Unfortunately, this is an imperfect scheme. It assumes that each byte received in the sysex buffer takes exactly 320 microseconds. But a MIDI instrument might insert gaps between sysex bytes, either to pace the transmission of data or because of its own internal processing delays. In other words, there is no way of knowing how long it took to receive the buffer; the best we can do is make a guess. The guess that the MaxMidi routines make is that the sysex data was received at full MIDI bandwidth, with no gaps between bytes.

This works well enough for short sysex messages. Although the sync engine will do the best it can with long sysex messages, it's best to avoid them while recording or playing back with synchronization—not just because the timestamps become questionable, but also because long sysexes will interfere with playing back musical events.

## MIDI Output Data Flow Changes

The changes needed for synchronized MIDI output are more extensive. Whether sync is used or not, MIDI events are sent to the output device by calling `PutMidiOut()`. Without synchronization, the MIDI event is either sent directly to the device driver or, in the case of a System Exclusive message, put in a sysex buffer which is sent to the driver when the buffer becomes full.

With synchronization, the `PutMidiOut()` function simply puts the event, whether a short MIDI message or a byte of a sysex message, into a circular queue. If the queue is full, the function returns −1 to let the client application know that the event was refused. Everything else associated with MIDI output occurs inside the sync callback function. The updated data flow diagram for MIDI output shows that the sync callback is between the MIDI output queue (where `PutMidiOut()` stores the outgoing events) and the device driver.

A single sync device can manage multiple MIDI output devices. A pointer to the `MidiOutStruct` structure for each output device is stored in a list of output devices (the MIDI Output List). The sync callback function services each of the output devices in the list, one at a time. Each output device attached to the sync device is handled the same way by accessing it through its pointer in the MIDI Output List. For clarity, the data flow diagram shows the logical flow of data for a single output device.

On each timer interrupt, the tick generator calculates elapsed ticks, just as it has always done. Then, it checks the MIDI output queues of each of the devices in the MIDI Output List. For each output device, it compares the timestamps of the events in the queue to the elapsed time since the last event that was sent from this particular output device. Any events whose timestamps are less than or equal to this delta time are sent to the device driver.

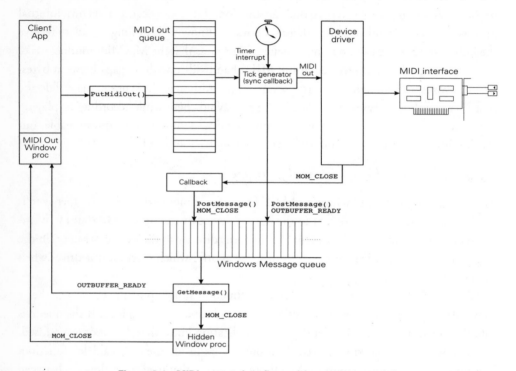

**Figure 8-4   MIDI output data flow with sync (non-sysex)**

Whenever the output queue for a particular device falls below 25% full, the sync callback posts an OUTBUFFER_READY message to the client window for that output device. This message will be retrieved by the application's message loop and routed to the proper window. Normally, the window proc that receives this message will output more data, if it has more for the particular output device, by calling PutMidiOut().

System Exclusive messages are handled much like short messages during synchronized output. The bytes of the sysex message appear in the MIDI output queue as a series of

`MidiEvents`, one event per byte. Each byte has a timestamp, just like any other `MidiEvent`. Normally, the first byte of the sysex will have a nonzero timestamp, while all of the other events—up to a sysex buffer-full—have zero timestamps. This indicates that all of the sysex bytes, up to the next one having a nonzero timestamp, are to be sent at the same time. The sync callback reads each of these zero-timestamp events from the output queue and puts them into a sysex buffer. When the buffer is full—or an EOX is encountered—the entire buffer is sent to the device driver as a long message by calling `midiOutLongMsg()`.

# CHAPTER 9

# I Want My C++

So far, all of the code in this book has been written in plain, old-fashioned C. This is good; the low-level MIDI functions—input, output, and sync—need to be lean and mean. And, being low-level functions, there is little to be gained by trying to force these functions into the object-class paradigm. But now it is time to write applications to perform MIDI.

All programmers—the good ones at least—ask themselves several questions before starting to design, much less code, a new program. The first question is "What should it do?" This might be answered by a client, a boss, an interest in solving a problem, or a desire to learn about something. Programs that completely answer this question are often useful and can be rewarding to write.

The next question, "How should it do it?" starts the design of the program. A good program is truly designed, not just written. When writing the program, the design serves as a blueprint and guides the program's development. The blueprint could be as simple as a block diagram that shows how information will flow (a data flow diagram), to a full set of detailed flowcharts, or even pages of pseudo code.

The design of the program determines the answer to the question, "Which tools should I use?" Should the program be written in C, C++, or some other language? On which operating systems should this program be capable of running? What choices must be made to provide the desired features and performance versus the amount of programming effort to implement these features? Almost anything is possible considering the wide variety of available tools, but some problems are best solved by carefully selecting the proper tools. After all, in surgery a scalpel is a better cutting tool than an ax—but a scalpel won't get very far on a tree!

So, just as C nicely matched the requirements for the low-level DLL functions, C++ solves the needs of a Windows MIDI program with perfect harmony. Logically, there are MIDI inputs, MIDI outputs, Standard MIDI Files, synchronization devices, and tracks. These all fit well into the object-oriented paradigm of C++. From a design standpoint, there are one or more of each of these *objects*, and they interconnect in various ways to create useful programs.

For example, a simple sequencer can be created using a MIDI input object, a track object, a MIDI output object, and a sync object. Encapsulating the MaxMidi DLL functions in C++ objects makes designing and writing such programs very easy.

The rest of this chapter describes the implementation of the MIDI input, MIDI output, and sync C++ classes. Other classes, such as the Standard MIDI File and track objects, are described in later chapters.

# Microsoft Visual C++ and the Microsoft Foundation Classes

The classes described in this book specifically support Microsoft Visual C++ versions 4.x and 5.x, and are implemented using the Microsoft Foundation Classes (MFC). They have been used successfully in other environments, with suitable modifications—such as in earlier 16-bit versions of MFC, Borland C++ 5.0, Windows NT, and even on the Macintosh. The principles of operation are the same in all of these cases, and most of the source code can be used unchanged. In fact, most of the changes necessary (especially for use in 16-bit Windows environments or for the Macintosh) involve the low-level code that is called by these classes. These classes can be ported to other systems and tools by simply providing functions that are equivalent to the MaxMidi DLL functions. It is usually possible to port the low-level functions and make them work with only minor changes. Because these classes are so broadly useful, this book will present an implementation in MFC for MSVC++ 4.x and 5.x. You are free to adapt these classes to other systems.

A brief note on the naming of classes in the ToolKit: most of the classes begin with CMaxMidi—designating that these are ToolKit classes—followed by the type of the class. For example, the MIDI input class is called CMaxMidiIn, while the track class is called CMaxMidiTrack. The exceptions to this naming rule are the two menu classes, CMidiInDeviceMenu and CMidiOutDeviceMenu.

In MFC, classes that expect to receive window messages need four characteristics in order to work properly. They must

- Be derived from the CWnd class

- Have an afx_msg message map defined in the class definition

- Have a matching message map in the implementation file for the class

- Have a message function for each window message that the class will process

Remember, the windows that are used by the ToolKit function are invisible; they serve as conduits for window messages from the MaxMidi DLLs, and are never displayed.

In the ToolKit, three classes need to receive window messages: CMaxMidiIn, CMaxMidiOut, and CMaxMidiSync. These classes are declared with CWnd as their base class and receive messages such as WM_CREATE or MIDI_DATA. The messages are mapped to the appropriate message functions by the message map that is declared in each class definition.

The other classes, such as CMaxMidiTrack and CMaxMidiSMF, are not derived from CWnd. In fact, they do not use any MFC-specific features at all. These classes are pure C++ and are not tied to MFC, although they do use Win32 function calls to do their jobs.

Some of the classes are dependent on other classes in the ToolKit. For example, CMaxMidiIn and CMaxMidiOut "know about" the CMaxMidiSync class since they are often attached to a sync object when recording or playing MIDI. But there are times when you need to use a MIDI input or output object without sync. Fortunately, in this case it is not necessary to include the CMaxMidiSync object.

In order to let the ToolKit classes know which classes are used in a given application, each of the classes has a corresponding conditional that must be defined if the class is included. Some classes imply other classes (for example, SMF objects *require* Track objects in order to contain data from the SMF) and defining the conditional for one will define the conditional for the other and require that it be included. These conditionals are defined in the table below:

**Table 9-1  CMaxMidi Class Conditionals**

| Conditional | Class |
| --- | --- |
| _MIDIIN | CMaxMidiIn |
| _MIDIOUT | CMaxMidiOut |
| _SYNC | CMaxMidiSync |
| _TRACK | CMaxMidiTrack |
| _SMF | CMaxMidiSMF (requires CMaxMidiTrack) |

Some of the classes work best as base classes. These classes contain virtual functions that can be redefined in corresponding derived classes. The table below shows these classes and the virtual functions that can be redefined when deriving other classes from them.

**Table 9-2  CMaxMidi Virtual Functions**

| Classes | Virtual functions |
| --- | --- |
| CMaxMidiIn | ProcessMidiData() |
| CMaxMidiOut | ProcessOutBufferReady() |
| CMaxMidiSync | ProcessMidiBeat(), ProcessSyncDone() |

However, it is not necessary to derive classes at all if your application does not need to replace these virtual functions.

## Encapsulating the DLL in C++ Classes

I originally started to write the ToolKit C++ classes as simple wrapper classes around the existing C DLL function calls. "Gee," I thought, "this will only take a couple of days and then I can get back to my regularly scheduled program(ming)." In hindsight, I couldn't have been more wrong. But what came out of all of the gnashing and grinding are a set of classes that are dramatic testimony to the power of C++. These objects do much more than simply encapsulate the C functions.

# The CMaxMidiIn Class

This class implements a MIDI input object. If desired, a sync object can be attached to provide timestamping features for recording MIDI. Likewise, a single track object (described in chapter 12) can be attached to contain any MIDI events that are received by the input.

Follow these simple steps to use this class in a program:

- Globally define the conditional _MIDIIN.
- Add the class and its implementation (contained in CMaxMidiIn.cpp) to the project.
- Optionally create another class—derived from CMaxMidiIn—that implements the virtual function ProcessMidiData().

This last step—deriving a class from CMaxMidiIn—is only necessary if the application needs to override the default behavior of the ProcessMidiData() virtual function or to add additional functionality. Here's an example of a simple MIDI input class:

```
//=====================================================================
//   MyMidiIn Class Definition
//=====================================================================
class MyMidiIn : public CMaxMidiIn
{
public:
    MyMidiIn();
    MyMidiIn(HWND hParentWnd, WORD wDeviceID = 0);

    //{{AFX_VIRTUAL(MyMidiIn)
    virtual BOOL ProcessMidiData(LPMIDIEVENT lpEvent);
    //}}AFX_VIRTUAL

protected:
    //{{AFX_MSG(MyMidiIn)
    //}}AFX_MSG
    DECLARE_MESSAGE_MAP()
};
```

```
//=====================================================================
//    MyMidiIn Class Implementation
//=====================================================================
BEGIN_MESSAGE_MAP(MyMidiIn, CMaxMidiIn)
    //{{AFX_MSG_MAP(MyMidiIn)
    //}}AFX_MSG_MAP
END_MESSAGE_MAP()

//--------------------------------------
//    Constructors
//--------------------------------------
MyMidiIn::MyMidiIn()
{
}

MyMidiIn::MyMidiIn(HWND hParentWnd, WORD wDeviceID) :
    CMaxMidiIn(hParentWnd, wDeviceID)
{
}

//--------------------------------------
//    ProcessMidiData
//--------------------------------------
BOOL MyMidiIn::ProcessMidiData(LPMIDIEVENT lpEvent)
{
    return TRUE;
}
```

ProcessMidiData() is called whenever a MIDI event is received from the input device. The function is passed a pointer to the MIDI event. It has first right of refusal; if it returns TRUE, the event is placed in the track object or queue. The event is discarded—as if it were never received—if ProcessMidiData() returns FALSE. Since the function gets a crack at the event before it is queued, any changes made by your implementation of ProcessMidiData() appear in the received data.

In the example above, there are two ways to create an instance of the MyMidiIn class. An object can be created using the default constructor. This creates an instance that has not been opened; the result of MyMidiIn::IsOpen() is FALSE in this case. Such a deaf-dumb-and-blind object is not terribly useful, however. The object must be attached to a parent window (since the CWnd class requires a parent) and the particular MIDI device must be specified. The parent window is specified by calling MyMidiIn::Attach() and specifying the HWND to attach. The MIDI device is selected (and opened) by calling MyMidiIn::Open() and specifying the device ID, along with an optional set of flags. These flags are the same as those passed to the OpenMidiIn() function in the MaxMidi DLL.

`MyMidiIn::GetNumDevices()` returns the number of MIDI input devices that are available on the system. You must specify a device ID that is less than the count of devices when calling `MyMidiIn::Open()`. For example, if `GetNumDevices()` reports that there are three devices available, then valid device IDs are 0, 1, and 2. Once the device is open, `MyMidiIn::GetDescription()` returns a pointer to a string that describes the device.

The other constructor can be used to do all of these steps at once:

```
MyMidiIn::MyMidiIn(HWND hParentWnd, WORD nDeviceID);
```

In either case, `MyMidiIn::IsOpen()` will return TRUE if the MIDI device is opened successfully.

Even though the object has been created and the MIDI device is open, no MIDI events will be received until `MyMidiIn::Start()` is called. Any events received can be retrieved by calling `MyMidiIn::Get()`. Finally, when recording is no longer desired, `MyMidiIn::Stop()` halts reception without closing the device.

# The CMaxMidiOut Class

This class implements a MIDI output object. In many respects it is very similar to `CMaxMidiIn`. Like the input class, a sync object can be attached to provide timestamping features for playing MIDI. Likewise, one or more track objects (described in chapter 12) can be attached that will be merged and sent to the MIDI output.

The steps to use this class in a program are almost the same as those for `CMaxMidiIn`:

- Globally define the conditional `_MIDIOUT`.
- Add the class and its implementation (contained in CMaxMidiOut.cpp) to the project.
- Optionally create another class, derived from `CMaxMidiOut`, that implements the virtual function `ProcessOutBufferReady()`.

This last step—deriving a class from `CMaxMidiOut`—is only necessary if the application needs to override the default behavior of the `ProcessOutBufferReady()` virtual function or to add additional functionality. For example, here's a simple MIDI output class:

```
//=================================================================
//    MyMidiOut Class Definition
//=================================================================
class MyMidiOut : public CMaxMidiOut
{
public:
    MyMidiOut();
    MyMidiOut(HWND hParentWnd, WORD wDeviceID = 0);

    //{{AFX_VIRTUAL(MyMidiOut)
    virtual void ProcessOutBufferReady(void);
    //}}AFX_VIRTUAL

protected:
    //{{AFX_MSG(MyMidiOut)
    //}}AFX_MSG
    DECLARE_MESSAGE_MAP()
};


//=================================================================
//    MyMidiOut Class Implementation
//=================================================================
BEGIN_MESSAGE_MAP(MyMidiOut, CMaxMidiOut)
    //{{AFX_MSG_MAP(MyMidiOut)
    //}}AFX_MSG_MAP
END_MESSAGE_MAP()

//------------------------------
//    Constructors
//------------------------------
MyMidiOut::MyMidiOut() : CMaxMidiOut()
{
}

MyMidiOut::MyMidiOut(HWND hParentWnd, WORD wDeviceID) :
    CMaxMidiOut(hParentWnd, wDeviceID)
{
}

//------------------------------
//    ProcessOutBufferReady
//------------------------------
void MyMidiOut::ProcessOutBufferReady(void)
{
}
```

ProcessOutBufferReady() corresponds to the OUTBUFFER_READY message that is received from the MaxMidi DLL during MIDI output. When synchronization is being used (i.e., when a CMaxMidiSync object is attached to MyMidiOut), the OUTBUFFER_READY message is sent—causing the ProcessOutBufferReady() function to be called—when the MIDI output queue in the MaxMidi DLL falls below 25% full. If synchronization is not being used, the virtual function is called—only while a sysex message is being sent—when the output device is ready to accept more sysex data. Sending non-sysex MIDI events without synchronization is always synchronous, so no OUTBUFFER_READY messages will be generated.

The `ProcessOutBufferReady()` function is normally used as a data pump to keep the output device supplied with MIDI events. Applications that use the `CMaxMidiTrack` and `CMaxMidiSync` classes do not need to override this function, since these classes internally handle the orderly output of MIDI events.

There are two ways to create an instance of `MyMidiOut`. The default constructor creates an instance that has not been opened and the result of `MyMidiOut::IsOpen()` is FALSE in this case.

The object must be attached to a parent window (since the `CWnd` class requires a parent) and the particular MIDI device must be specified to do anything useful. The parent window is specified by calling `MyMidiOut::Attach()` and specifying the `HWND` to attach. The MIDI device is specified by calling `MyMidiOut::Open()` and specifying the device ID, along with an optional set of flags. These flags are the same as those passed to the `OpenMidiOut()` function in the MaxMidi DLL.

`MyMidiOut::GetNumDevices()` returns the number of MIDI output devices available on the system. Just as in the `MyMidiIn` class, valid device IDs for `MyMidiOut::Open()` range from 0 to one less than the number of devices. `MyMidiOut::GetDescription()` returns a pointer to a string that describes the device.

The other constructor can be used to do all of these steps at once:

```
MyMidiOut::MyMidiOut(HWND hParentWnd, WORD nDeviceID);
```

In either case, `MyMidiOut::IsOpen()` returns TRUE if the MIDI device is opened successfully.

Once the output device is open, events are output by calling `MyMidiOut::Put()`. If a sync object is attached, the event is output at the time specified by the timestamp. (Timestamps are discussed in chapter 7.) Otherwise, the event is output immediately.

Well, perhaps *immediately* is not the right word. If a sync object is attached, the event is placed in a queue and the function *does* return immediately. On the other hand, in the absence of sync the event is sent directly to the MIDI output driver. But, most drivers are synchronous. That is, the call to `modShortMsg()` (down in the MaxMidi DLL) that sends the event to the driver may not return until the event has been sent by the MIDI hardware.

It is possible that the hardware will accept the event, buffer it internally, and allow `modShortMsg()` to return right away. But if events come fast enough long enough, no matter how large the buffer in the hardware, it eventually becomes full. The hardware then tells the driver to hold on, only accepting a byte when there is room in its buffer. At this point, calls to `modShortMsg()`—and thus calls to `CMaxMidiOut::Put()`—are paced by the speed at which the hardware can output MIDI bytes. Remember, MIDI is output no faster than 3,125 bytes per second.

What does all this mean? If the hardware and driver did not behave this way, MIDI events would be lost and there would be chaos in the streets. But since the hardware is able to pace data from the application, all is well in the Heavens and in Redmond. Life is good, since this is all taken care of.

# The CMaxMidiSync Class

Rounding out the triumvirate of `CWnd`-derived classes is the `CMaxMidiSync` class. It encapsulates the synchronization engine from the MaxMidi DLLs and provides services to start, stop and pause sync. Internally, the ToolKit handles tempo in units of microseconds per beat (where beats are quarter notes). Humans—musicians, anyway—think of tempo in beats per minute. So, `CMaxMidiSync` includes functions to set and get the current tempo and to convert between beats per minute and microseconds per beat.

The steps to use this class are eerily similar to the ones for the other two classes:

- Globally define the conditional _SYNC.
- Add the class and its implementation (contained in CMaxMidiSync.cpp) to the project.
- Optionally create another class, derived from `CMaxMidiSync`, that implements the virtual functions `ProcessSyncDone()` and `ProcessMidiBeat()`.

As in the case for the other two `CWnd`-derived classes, this last step—deriving a class from `CMaxMidiSync`—is only necessary if the application needs to override the default behavior of the two virtual functions or to add additional functionality. Here is an example of a derived sync class:

```
//=================================================================
//   MySync Class
//=================================================================
class MySync : public CMaxMidiSync
{
public:
     MySync();

     //{{AFX_VIRTUAL(MySync)
     virtual void ProcessMidiBeat(void);
     virtual void ProcessSyncDone(void);
     //}}AFX_VIRTUAL

protected:
     //{{AFX_MSG(MySync)
     //}}AFX_MSG
     DECLARE_MESSAGE_MAP()
};


//=================================================================
//   MySync Class Implementation
//=================================================================
BEGIN_MESSAGE_MAP(MySync, CMaxMidiSync)
     //{{AFX_MSG_MAP(MySync)
     //}}AFX_MSG_MAP
END_MESSAGE_MAP()

//-----------------------------------
//   Constructor
//-----------------------------------
MySync::MySync() : CMaxMidiSync()
{
}

//-----------------------------------
//   ProcessMidiBeat
//-----------------------------------
void MySync::ProcessMidiBeat(void)
{
}

//-----------------------------------
//   ProcessSyncDone
//-----------------------------------
void MySync::ProcessSyncDone(void)
{
     Stop();
}
```

ProcessSyncDone() is called when the sync device finds that there are no more MIDI
events to be output. The example above stops the sync device. This is useful for playing

back a sequence, but not for recording, where usually sync must continue until record is stopped by the user. A more complete MySync class would keep track of the state of record or playback and handle ProcessSyncDone() accordingly.

ProcessMidiBeat() is called on every beat. A beat occurs every quarter note, at the current tempo, while sync is running. This event can be used to keep track of progress during playback or record.

# Attaching the Sync Device

To be useful, the sync device must be attached to either a CMaxMidiIn (or derived) input object or a CMaxMidiOut (or derived) output object. Once it is attached (by calling the Attach() function and specifying a pointer to the sync object), all synchronization for that device will be automatically handled by the sync object. Here's an example that timestamps MIDI events that are received by an instance of MyMidiIn:

```
MyMidiIn MidiIn;
MySync SyncDev;

// open the first available input device
MidiIn.Open(hParent, 0);

// initialize the sync device to internal sync and a 10ms period
SyncDev.Open(S_INT, DEFAULT_TIMERPERIOD);

// attach the sync device
MidiIn.Attach(&SyncDev);

// start recording!
MidiIn.Start();
SyncDev.Start();
```

That's all there is to it. By attaching the sync device, any MIDI events received by the input device are timestamped by the sync device and are passed to MyMidiIn::ProcessMidiData().

However, there is an error in the example above. Can you find it?

No? As soon as the sync device is started, it calls ProcessSyncDone(), since there are no MIDI events to be played. MySync implements ProcessSyncDone() by stopping the sync device. While there may be Guitar Deities fast enough to record an entire record between the call to start sync and the call to ProcessSyncDone(), prematurely stopping sync is not what is intended here.

For this example, we only want to stop recording when the user is finished. In a real program we would keep track of the mode of the program (either playback or record) and handle `ProcessSyncDone()` appropriately. But for now, we can just remove the `Stop()` call (or replace the `MySync` class with `CMaxMidiSync`), and continue with the example.

Recording is stopped when the user is finished recording, like this:

```
SyncDev.Stop();
MyInput.Stop();
```

This stops the sync device and causes the input device to ignore further MIDI messages.

Playback is similar. Simply open an output device, attach a sync device, call `CMaxMidiOut::Put()` for each `MidiEvent` (with the proper timestamp) to be played and start the sync device running. The process is even easier when the MIDI events are stored in `CMaxMidiTrack` objects, as we'll see in chapter 12.

A sync device can generate timing based on the timer hardware built into the PC, known as *internal sync*, by specifying `S_INT` when calling the `Open()` member function. On the other hand, a sync device can generate timing that is slaved to an external device—such as a drum machine—by specifying `S_MIDI`. To do this, create a MIDI input object, open it with `SYNC_INPUT` specified in the `dwFlags` parameter, and attach the sync device. The input device then routes received MIDI Start, Stop, and Clock messages to the sync device. The sync device uses these messages as the timebase for synchronization.

## *Tempo and Resolution*

The `CMaxMidiSync` class has several member functions that handle tempo and resolution. When the object is created, it is set to a resolution of 480 ticks per beat at a tempo of 120 bpm. The timing resolution, as discussed in chapter 8, can be changed to any desired value before recording or playing a sequence. It is usually best to choose a resolution that is a multiple of 24, since MIDI Clocks occur at a rate of 24 clocks per beat.

An output device automatically outputs MIDI Start, Stop, and Clock messages if the `SYNC_OUTPUT` flag is specified when opening the device. If the sync device's timing resolution is not a multiple of 24, MIDI Clock messages are output at the wrong rate and external devices, such as drum machines or other sequencers, will not stay in sync.

Likewise, an input device can be used to synchronize the sync device to MIDI Clocks by specifying the `SYNC_INPUT` when the device is opened and specifying the `S_MIDI` mode when opening the sync device. For example:

```
// Open the first available input device
MidiIn.Open(hParent, 0, MIDIIN_DEFAULT | SYNC_INPUT);

// Initialize the sync device to internal sync and a 10ms period
SyncDev.Open(S_MIDI, DEFAULT_TIMERPERIOD);

// Attach the sync device
MidiIn.Attach(&SyncDev);

// Start recording using MIDI Clock sync
MidiIn.Start();
SyncDev.Start();
```

If the resolution is not a multiple of 24, the sync device is not able to properly synchronize recording to the incoming MIDI Clock rate.

The timing resolution is set by calling the `Resolution()` member function, which returns the previous resolution. The current resolution is returned by calling `Resolution()` without any parameter. The resolution cannot be changed while sync is running, though the current resolution can be read at any time.

```
oldRes = SyncDev.Resolution(192);
currentRes = SyncDev.Resolution();
```

Tempo, on the other hand, can be changed at any time—before, during, or after sync is running. If the tempo is changed while recording, a tempo change event is inserted—with the proper timestamp—into the received stream of events that is sent to the input object. A tempo event is a `MidiEvent` where the status value is 0 and `data1`, `data2`, and `data3` contain the 24-bit tempo in microseconds per beat. If such a tempo event is encountered by the sync device during playback, the tempo is automatically set to the specified value.

To set the tempo, call the `Tempo()` member function and specify the desired tempo in microseconds per beat. When called without any parameters, `Tempo()` will return the current tempo value, also in microseconds per beat. To convert between microseconds per beat and beats per minute, use the `Convert()` member function. `Convert()` will return the tempo in beats per minute (as a floating-point `double`) by specifying microseconds per beat (as a `DWORD`). Conversely, it will convert from beats per minute (as a `double`) to microseconds per beat (as a `DWORD`). For example, the following code snippet gets the current tempo and then sets the tempo to 160.5 bpm.

```
double oldTempo;
oldTempo = SyncDev.Convert(SyncDev.Tempo());
SyncDev.Tempo(SyncDev.Convert(160.5));
```

# Summary

These three classes form the core of the C++ version of the MaxMidi ToolKit. Later chapters will introduce other classes, such as the track class and the Standard MIDI File class, that will make writing MIDI programs even easier. But now that we have a few useful MIDI classes, let's put them to use. The next chapter introduces a simple MFC application that is used as the basis for all of the C++ example programs in the book and uses the `CMaxMidiIn` and `CMaxMidiOut` classes to perform easy MIDI input and output operations.

**CHAPTER 10**

# Using the ToolKit with Microsoft Visual C++

It's time to start using the MaxMidi C++ classes to build real MIDI applications. This chapter covers the basic steps needed to create an MFC-based MIDI program using the Maximum MIDI ToolKit. Here we'll get the lay of the land, explore the MIDI input and MIDI output classes, introduce two menu classes, and use these classes in three example programs. In later chapters, we'll expand on these simple programs to make a Sysex Librarian and a MIDI sequencer.

All of these example projects are created using the AppWizard feature of the Microsoft Visual C++ compiler. Here's the basic recipe we need to make a MIDI program:

- Create a project, either manually or using the AppWizard.
- Derive classes, as needed, from the ToolKit classes. The MIDI input, MIDI output, and sync device classes include virtual functions, so derived classes are needed if these functions are redefined.
- Add all the necessary files to the project, including the MxMidi32.lib import library file and any ToolKit class implementations of classes that are used.
- Define conditionals for each of the ToolKit classes that the program uses.
- Use the ToolKit classes to implement MIDI support in the program.

It is amazingly easy to create the application skeleton using AppWizard. It creates all of the basic files and classes that are needed to build a working MFC application. Granted, the resulting program is shockingly dull, since it doesn't do anything useful, but it gets the ball rolling. Let's create one of these dull-as-rock programs and take a look at the organization of the code that the AppWizard generates. Once we understand the "free" boilerplate code, we can start adding MIDI support to make the program do something useful.

# The Application Framework

All of the C++ examples in this book will begin life in the same way. In each case, we'll use the AppWizard to create the simplest possible program framework. For our first example, let's walk through all of the steps to create a proto-app. This is the only time we will do this; in every other example only the changes will be shown. All of the files for this project and all of the other examples in the book are included on the accompanying disk.

To build this first program, create a new project workspace by selecting New... from the Developer Studio's File menu. Highlight Project Workspace in the dialog box and click OK. In the next dialog, choose MFC AppWizard (exe) as the project type and give it a name. For this example, call it *Ch10Ex1*. Click OK to create the project and start the AppWizard.

Choose the simplest possible options for the program in each of the six steps of the AppWizard. No Toolbars, no printing, no Status Bar. Databases, MAPI, OLE, ActiveX controls and sockets need not apply, either. Of course, you are free to use any or all of these features in your own programs, but for the purposes of these examples, simplicity is best. Following the *Prime Directive*, select Single Document for the application type and choose the appropriate resource language in AppWizard's Step 1 dialog. (English is the default setting.) Click Next to move to Step 2. There, select None for the database support and click Next. In Step 3, select None for OLE container support, clear the ActiveX controls checkbox, and click Next again. Step 4 lists features and support options. Deselect everything except 3D Controls, which will provide that nifty chiseled look. Click Next to move to the next step.

In Step 5, select "No, thank you" to eliminate the source file comments, and choose Shared DLL for the MFC library. AppWizard will add useful *TODO* comments to the source code if source file comments are selected. These comments can serve to remind you of things to add to the framework. However, for readability, these comments do not appear in the example projects supplied on the accompanying diskette.

The example programs link to the MFC library in its DLL form—instead of as a static library—to reduce the size of the executable. This requires that the proper version of the MFC DLL be installed on the system. Since there is a different version of this DLL for each version of the Microsoft compiler, you may wish to reduce the chance of confusion by linking to the MFC library statically. However, this will greatly increase the size of the executable. After making appropriate selections, click Next to move to the final step.

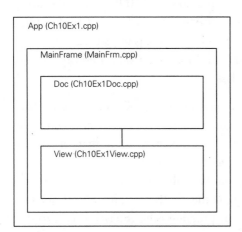

**Figure 10-1   MFC file relationship**

Step 6 shows the names of the classes and files that AppWizard will create and allows the base class name to be changed. Normally, the default names are readable enough. Click Finish, then click OK to make AppWizard create the files and open the new project.

Build the project to be sure everything came out correctly. For real excitement, run the resulting executable. Wow.

The AppWizard creates more than 15 files, but the most interesting ones are the four C++ source files. These files (Ch10Ex1.cpp, MainFrm.cpp, Ch10Ex1Doc.cpp, and

Ch10Ex1View.cpp) correspond to the four logical parts (and classes) of the program. The diagram shows how these four files interrelate.

The application itself is represented by the `CCh10Ex1App` class, which is contained in the Ch10Ex1.cpp file. All of the code needed to get the program started and keep it running is in this class, including creating other class instances, parsing the command line, and maintaining the message loop. The `Ch10Ex1App` class creates instances of three other classes:

- The `CMainFrame` class (contained in MainFrm.cpp and MainFrm.h). This class encapsulates the main window and menu, toolbars, status bars, etc.

- The document class, `CCh10Ex1Doc` (contained in Ch10Ex1Doc.cpp and Ch10Ex1Doc.h). This class manages the data associated with the program—the document in MFC parlance—which often are stored in a disk file. In this simple example, while a document class exists, it doesn't do anything, since the program does not save any data or read and write disk files.

- The view class, `CCh10Ex1View` (contained in Ch10Ex1View.doc and Ch10Ex1View.h). The view class provides a way to view the data stored in the document. In this example, the view class encapsulates the MIDI input and output "views" of the MIDI world. The view class is used to receive, process, and output MIDI events. Here, the document class is empty (i.e., data is not stored in a document), but in more sophisticated programs the MIDI data would be kept in the document class and accessed by the view class.

Keep in mind that this organization of files applies to our simple example program. Other MFC applications might have more than one view (e.g., a sequencer might have an event list view and a notation view of a given track), or even more than one main window (i.e., a Multiple Document Interface (MDI) app). But let's start with this simple Single Document Interface (SDI) example program. We will modify it to output a single MIDI event—a program change—to illustrate how the ToolKit handles MIDI output. Later, we'll add MIDI input support and make the program echo received events to the output device.

## Adding MIDI to MFC Applications

The ToolKit's MIDI output class—`CMaxMidiOut`—is a virtual class, since it has a virtual function, `ProcessOutBufferReady()`. This function is called when the MaxMidi DLL sends an `OUTBUFFER_READY` message to the window associated with the MIDI output device. This window is encapsulated by the MFC class CWnd, and CMaxMidiOut is derived from that class, so the message is sent to the message handler in CMaxMidiOut. CMaxMidiOut's version of this function does nothing. To do something useful in response to this message, derive a class from CMaxMidiOut and redefine ProcessOutBufferReady(). However, no special handling of OUTBUFFER_READY is needed in this example program. We will use the CMaxMidiOut class as is.

Three things need to be done to add MIDI support to the example program. First, the compiler must be configured properly. Next, the ToolKit class implementation and library files must be added to the project. Finally, MIDI must be implemented in the application by creating instances of the ToolKit classes and making calls to their member functions.

# Compiler Configuration

Setting the include directory (giving the compiler access to the ToolKit classes and the MaxMidi.h header) and defining the proper preprocessor definitions (so that the appropriate ToolKit classes are included) make the compiler ToolKit-ready.

To do this with Microsoft Visual C++, open the Project Settings dialog by selecting the Settings... menu item from the Developer Studio's Build menu. Click on the C/C++ tab and choose Preprocessor from the Category drop down list. This will reveal several preprocessor options, including a list of preprocessor definitions and additional include directories. Add the definition for the MIDI output class, _MIDIOUT, to the existing list of Preprocessor definitions, separating it from the others with a comma. Then, add the path to the ToolKit include directory in the Additional include directories edit control, separating the new path from any existing paths using a semicolon. If the ToolKit files are installed in their default locations, the new include path is C:\Maximum MIDI\Include.

# Add the ToolKit Files

Any MaxMidi classes that the program uses must be added to the application's project, along with the corresponding implementation files. In addition, the MaxMidi import library (MxMidi32.lib) is needed for the program (through the C++ classes) to access the MaxMidi DLLs.

Adding the import library is easy: select Add to Project|Files... from the Project menu (or, select Files into Project... from the Insert menu, for MSVC++ 4.x). Set the file type to

Library file (*.lib) and change folders to locate the MxMidi32.lib file. In the default ToolKit installation, the file is located in the `C:\Maximum MIDI\Lib` folder. Select this file and click OK (or Add) to add it to the project.

Next, add each of the MaxMidi classes that the program uses. Insert the implementation file for each class into the project. The class name, header filename, and implementation filename for each MaxMidi class are shown in table 10-1.

**Table 10-1   MaxMidi Classes**

| Class | Header | Implementation |
|---|---|---|
| CMaxMidiIn | CMaxMidiIn.h | CMaxMidiIn.cpp |
| CMaxMidiOut | CMaxMidiOut.h | CMaxMidiOut.cpp |
| CMaxMidiSync | CMaxMidiSync.h | CMaxMidiSync.cpp |
| CMaxMidiTrack | CMaxMidiTrack.h | CMaxMidiTrack.cpp |
| CMaxMidiSMF | CMaxMidiSMF.h | CMaxMidiSMF.cpp |
| CMidiInDeviceMenu | CMidiInDeviceMenu.h | CMidiInDeviceMenu.cpp |
| CMidiOutDeviceMenu | CMidiOutDeviceMenu.h | CMidiOutDeviceMenu.cpp |

For our MIDI output example program, we need to add the `CMaxMidiOut` class. We'll use the other classes in later examples.

# Use the ToolKit Classes

Now that we've dispensed with all of the preliminaries, it's time to write some code. Some aspects of the ToolKit—and of MIDI in general—desire, nay, demand to be implemented in certain sections of a MFC application. Although it is possible to organize the MIDI implementation in different ways, the diagram below shows the most logical organization, given the four MFC-generated classes that make up our example program.

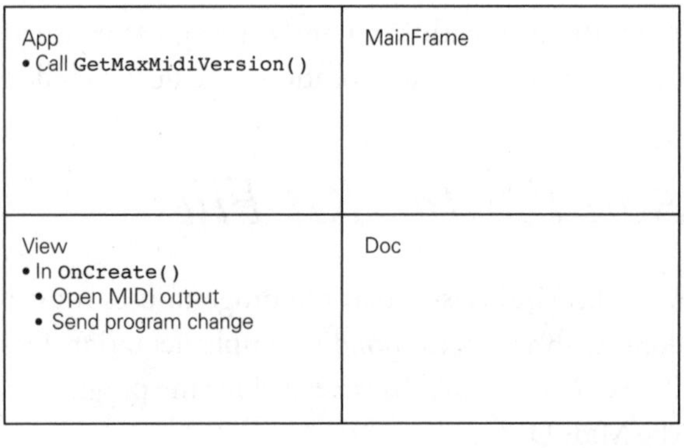

Figure 10-2   Example 1 MIDI organization

The only MaxMidi-related change needed in the application class (`CCh10Ex1App`) is to modify the classes' `InitInstance()` function to call `GetMaxMidiVersion()`, like this:

```cpp
// from Ch10Ex1.h — Ch10Ex1App class header file
class CCh10Ex1App : public CWinApp
{
public:
    WORD MaxMidiVersion;
    CCh10Ex1App();
```
*class declaration continues...*
```cpp
}

// from Ch10Ex1.cpp — Ch10Ex1App implementation file
BOOL CCh10Ex1App::InitInstance()
{
    // get the version before doing anything else, since this
    // resizes the message queue
    MaxMidiVersion = GetMaxMidiVersion();

    // Standard initialization

#ifdef _AFXDLL
    Enable3dControls();         // Call this when using MFC in a shared DLL
#else
    Enable3dControlsStatic();   // Call this when linking to MFC statically
#endif

    LoadStdProfileSettings();   // Load standard INI file options
                                // (including MRU)

    // Register document templates

    CSingleDocTemplate* pDocTemplate;
    pDocTemplate = new CSingleDocTemplate(
        IDR_MAINFRAME,
        RUNTIME_CLASS(CCh10Ex1Doc),
        RUNTIME_CLASS(CMainFrame),      // main SDI frame window
        RUNTIME_CLASS(CCh10Ex1View));
    AddDocTemplate(pDocTemplate);

    // Parse command line for standard shell commands, DDE, file open
    CCommandLineInfo cmdInfo;
    ParseCommandLine(cmdInfo);

    // Dispatch commands specified on the command line
    if (!ProcessShellCommand(cmdInfo))
        return FALSE;
    return TRUE;
}
```

The class declaration is modified by adding the version number variable, MaxMidiVersion. The version number returned by GetMaxMidiVersion() is interesting, and it is saved into this class member variable (which will be used in other example programs as part of an about box). But the important action here is that this function resizes the application message queue, making it much larger than the default. Although MaxMidi will work fine with the standard eight-message-deep queue, it works more efficiently with a relatively spacious 64-message size.

For this example, there are no changes needed in the MainFrame and document classes. Although the simple task of creating a CMaxMidiOut object and sending a program change event could be done in either of these two classes, here these tasks are implemented in the view class.

The view's OnCreate() message handler is implemented as shown. The first available MIDI output device (device ID 0) is opened, and a program change event is sent. This event sets any receiving sound device that is listening to channel 1 to its first program. The MIDI device will be closed when the CMaxMidiOut object is destroyed, when the program terminates.

```cpp
// from CCh10Ex1View.h — view class declaration header
#include "MaxMidi.h"

class CCh10Ex1View : public CView
{
public:
    CMaxMidiOut MidiOut;

protected: // create from serialization only
    CCh10Ex1View();

    class declaration continues...
}

// from CCh10Ex1View.cpp — view class implementation file
int CCh10Ex1View::OnCreate(LPCREATESTRUCT lpCreateStruct)
{
    MidiEvent evt;

    if (CView::OnCreate(lpCreateStruct) == -1)
            return -1;

    // open the first MIDI output
    MidiOut.Attach(GetSafeHwnd());
    MidiOut.Open(0);

    // output a program change on channel 1
    evt.status = 0xC0;
```

```
        evt.data1 = 0;                // program #1
        MidiOut.Put(&evt);

        return 0;
}
```

The `CCh10Ex1View` class is derived from the `CView` class, which is derived from `CWnd`, which in turn encapsulates the behavior of a window. The `OnCreate()` function is called when a `WM_CREATE` message is sent to the window during its creation phase. At this point, the window exists, so its window handle is valid. The `MidiOut` object, declared in the view's class definition, exists but has not been fully initialized or opened. It must be attached to a parent window, in this case, the view's window, before it can be opened.

Once the device is opened, it is a simple matter to initialize a `MidiEvent` structure to contain a program change event, where the status (0xC0) indicates the event is destined for channel 1, and the single data byte (0x00) specifies the first program number. The `Put()` member function sends the event.

# Receiving and Sending MIDI

Unlike walking and chewing gum at the same time, sending and receiving MIDI at the same time is easy, especially using the ToolKit's C++ functions. Let's modify our example program so it accepts MIDI from an input device and echoes it back to the output device. This will illustrate how to receive MIDI using the `CMaxMidiIn` class, and how to create a derived class and override a virtual function. A complete version of this example is on the accompanying disk.

Since this is the second example program in this chapter, the project and the application are named *Ch10Ex2*. As a result, all of the MFC boilerplate classes have slightly different names from the versions in the first example. But other than the difference in names, the boilerplate code is the same between the two programs. Only the code that is different (other than in class name) is shown here.

```
// from Ch10Ex2View.h — CCh10Ex2View class declaration header
#include "MaxMidi.h"
#include "MyMidiIn.h"

class CCh10Ex2View : public CView
{
public:
    CMaxMidiOut MidiOut;
    MyMidiIn MidiIn;
```

```
protected: // create from serialization only
     CCh10Ex2View();

     class declaration continues...

}

// from CCh10Ex2View.cpp — view class implementation file
int CCh10Ex2View::OnCreate(LPCREATESTRUCT lpCreateStruct)
{
     if (CView::OnCreate(lpCreateStruct) == -1)
             return -1;

     // open the first MIDI output
     MidiOut.Attach(GetSafeHwnd());
     MidiOut.Open(0);

     // open and start the first MIDI input
     MidiIn.Attach(GetSafeHwnd());
     MidiIn.Open(0);
     MidiIn.Start();

     // let the input object know about the output object
     // so it can echo received events
     MidiIn.SetEchoOutput(&MidiOut);

     return 0;
}
```

In addition to these changes, there is a new file to add to the project. Since the
ProcessMidiData() virtual function needs to be overridden (this is where the received
MIDI data will be echoed to the output), another class must be derived from the original
CMaxMidiIn class. This class, MyMidiIn, is shown here:

```
// from MyMidiIn.h — class declaration header file
#ifndef __MYMIDIIN__
#define __MYMIDIIN__
//====================================================================
//    MyMidiIn Class
//====================================================================
class MyMidiIn : public CMaxMidiIn
{
public:
     CMaxMidiOut* EchoOut;
     MyMidiIn();
     void SetEchoOutput(CMaxMidiOut* moDevice) { EchoOut = moDevice; };

// Overrides
     // ClassWizard generated virtual function overrides
     //{{AFX_VIRTUAL(MyMidiIn)
     virtual BOOL ProcessMidiData(LPMIDIEVENT lpEvent);
```

```
        //}}AFX_VIRTUAL

protected:
        //{{AFX_MSG(MyMidiIn)
        //}}AFX_MSG
        DECLARE_MESSAGE_MAP()
};
#endif //!__MYMIDIIN__

// from MyMidiIn.cpp — class implementation file
//======================================================================
//    MyMidiIn Class
//======================================================================
#include "stdafx.h"
#include "MaxMidi.h"
#include "MyMidiIn.h"

BEGIN_MESSAGE_MAP(MyMidiIn, CMaxMidiIn)
        //{{AFX_MSG_MAP(MyMidiIn)
        //}}AFX_MSG_MAP
END_MESSAGE_MAP()

//─────────────────────────────
//    Constructor
//─────────────────────────────
MyMidiIn::MyMidiIn()
{
        EchoOut = NULL;
}


////////////////////////////////////////////////////////////////////////
// MyMidiIn virtual functions

//─────────────────────────────
//    ProcessMidiData
//─────────────────────────────
BOOL MyMidiIn::ProcessMidiData(LPMIDIEVENT lpEvent)
{
        if(EchoOut)
                EchoOut->Put(lpEvent);

        return TRUE;
}
```

This derived class implements two major features. First, it provides a function, SetEchoOutput(), that accepts a pointer to the CMaxMidiOut object that will serve as the output device for echoed data. Second, it implements a new version of ProcessMidiData(), overriding the default (empty) one in the CMaxMidiIn base class. This new implementation is called for each received MIDI event. If the echo output device exists (i.e., if SetEchoOutput() has been called), the event is sent to that device.

# Adding Device Menus

By now, our simple MIDI application has reached the almost-useful state. Let's take it one step further and allow the user to select the desired MIDI input and MIDI output devices from two drop-down menus. These menu lists are built dynamically—when the program starts up—and list all of the devices that are available on the system. All of the menu construction and selection handling are done by two classes: CMidiInDeviceMenu and CMidiOutDeviceMenu. The drop-down lists are automatically created by these classes, and devices are opened and closed as needed in response to menu selections.

The third example program, *Ch10Ex3*, adds instances of these two classes, along with the necessary changes to hook them into the proper menu messages. There are changes to the CMainFrame class as well as changes to the view class. The two menu class implementation files are added to the project. Here is the modified source code for the new program. Although the class names have changed (again!), most of the code is the same as example 2.

```
// from MainFrm.cpp — MainFrame class implementation file
int CMainFrame::OnCreate(LPCREATESTRUCT lpCreateStruct)
{
    if (CFrameWnd::OnCreate(lpCreateStruct) == -1)
        return -1;

    // since we don't have separate ON_UPDATE_COMMAND_UI handlers
    // or ON_COMMAND handlers for the device menu items we must
    // clear this flag so that the Input Device and Output Device
    // menu items are all enabled
    m_bAutoMenuEnable = FALSE;
    return 0;
}

// from Ch10Ex3View.h — CCh10Ex3View class declaration header
#include "MaxMidi.h"
#include "MyMidiIn.h"

class CCh10Ex3View : public CView
{
public:
    CMaxMidiOut     MidiOut;
    MyMidiIn        MidiIn;

    // Input and Output Device Menus
    CMidiInDeviceMenu InMenu;
    CMidiOutDeviceMenu OutMenu;

protected: // create from serialization only
    CCh10Ex3View();

}
```

```
// from CCh10Ex3View.cpp — view class implementation file
int CCh10Ex3View::OnCreate(LPCREATESTRUCT lpCreateStruct)
{
    if (CView::OnCreate(lpCreateStruct) == -1)
            return -1;

    // attach the input and output devices to this window
    MidiOut.Attach(GetSafeHwnd());
    MidiIn.Attach(GetSafeHwnd());

    // get the parent menu
    CMenu* ParentMenu = GetParent()->GetMenu();

    // create the device menus and select the first devices
    InMenu.Create(ParentMenu->GetSafeHmenu(),
                    ParentMenu->GetMenuItemCount() - 1,
                    "&Input Device", IDM_INPUT);
    InMenu.Attach(&MidiIn);
    InMenu.SelectDevice(0);

    OutMenu.Create(ParentMenu->GetSafeHmenu(),
                    ParentMenu->GetMenuItemCount() - 1,
                    "&Output Device", IDM_OUTPUT);
    OutMenu.Attach(&MidiOut);
    OutMenu.SelectDevice(0);

    // let the input object know about the output object
    // so it can echo received events
    MidiIn.SetEchoOutput(&MidiOut);

    return 0;
}

BOOL CCh10Ex3View::OnCmdMsg(UINT nID, int nCode, void* pExtra,
AFX_CMDHANDLERINFO* pHandlerInfo)
{
    // check to see if one of the device menus has been selected
    if(nCode == 0)
    {
            InMenu.SelectDevice(nID);

            // if it's an output device, change the echo device too
            if(OutMenu.SelectDevice(nID))
                    MidiIn.SetEchoOutput(&MidiOut);
    }

    return CView::OnCmdMsg(nID, nCode, pExtra, pHandlerInfo);
}
```

The first notable change is in the `CMainFrame` class. Since the device menu classes cannot know how many MIDI devices are available until runtime (on some systems there may be nearly a dozen inputs and outputs), these classes do not implement separate `ON_UPDATE_COMMAND_UI` or `ON_COMMAND` handlers for each menu item. Instead, the classes check every `WM_COMMAND` message, and respond to the range of messages that correspond to the devices in the menu.

Normally, MFC disables menu items by default. They are enabled when the menu is shown by MFC-generated calls to `ON_UPDATE_COMMAND_UI` handlers, one for each item in the menu. To change the MFC's default behavior, the `CMainFrame` class provides the `m_bAutoMenuEnable` member variable. Setting this Boolean value to FALSE will prevent MFC from disabling the menu items.

The modified view class adds an instance of each of the two menu classes, `CMidiInDeviceMenu` and `CMidiOutDeviceMenu`. These classes are created and attached to the main menu during the `OnCreate()` function. Each class' `Create()` function accepts four parameters: a menu handle, the relative position in the menu for the new menu item, the item's display name, and a base message number. The new menu item will be inserted at the specified location, where 0 specifies the leftmost item. In this example, each menu, with the specified name, is inserted just to the left of the Help menu item by specifying `GetMenuItemCount() - 1` as the relative location. The base message number is used to number each of the devices in the menu. The first device's menu item will have a message ID equal to the base message number and each subsequent device will have a higher value.

In the example, the base input ID is `IDM_INPUT` (101), and the base output ID is `IDM_OUTPUT` (201). These two symbols are specified using the Resource Symbols dialog box. To do this, select Resource Symbols... from the compiler's View menu. Click on the New... button and type in the symbol name and value for each of the two symbols.

The final modification is to add the `OnCmdMsg()` function in the view class—using the ClassWizard—and to insert the two device menu class `SelectDevice()` calls. The `nCode` parameter is 0 if the corresponding `WM_COMMAND` message originates from a menu. If it does, both of the `SelectDevice()` functions are called; one for input devices and one for output devices. These functions ignore any message IDs outside of their valid range (i.e., from the base message number up to the base value plus the number of devices) and return FALSE. If the ID is inside the range handled by the device menu class, the corresponding input or output device will be selected and the function returns TRUE.

With these changes, the example program will echo incoming MIDI messages from any user-selected input device to any selected output device. This program illustrates how to handle MIDI input and output, without synchronization, using the ToolKit's C++ classes. In the next chapter, we'll take this program and expand it into a System Exclusive librarian that will receive sysex bulk dumps, store the data in a widely supported file format, and send those saved sysex messages back out.

# CHAPTER 11

# Handling Sysex Messages in C++

System Exclusive message handling programs are a popular category of MIDI applications. Patch editors, sysex librarians, and sample editors are all examples of programs that need to send and receive sysex messages.

MaxMidi-based applications deal with sysex messages the same way as with other MIDI messages. However, there is one difference in the way these messages are handled using the MaxMidi ToolKit. System Exclusive messages are often long—arbitrarily long—so the scheme of fitting an entire MIDI message into a MidiEvent structure must be modified to cope with these behemoths. Instead of trying to cram a single sysex into an 8-byte MidiEvent structure, the ToolKit puts each sysex byte into its own MidiEvent.

Each MidiEvent must have a valid status value (i.e., the MidiEvent.status field must be properly filled in). Since a sysex begins with a status value of 0xF0, the status field of each byte in the message is set to this value. Each of the bytes in the message—the data bytes, the leading sysex status (0xF0), and the trailing End Of Exclusive status (0xF7)—is put in the data1 field of a MidiEvent. All this is covered in more detail in chapter 6.

But in the case of a program that only handles System Exclusive messages (or treats them separately from other MIDI messages), it doesn't make sense to keep each of the bytes in its own MidiEvent. After all, a MidiEvent is 8 bytes in size. Every opportunity to minimize resources without giving up performance and features is an opportunity worth seizing. The solution in this case is to store the sysex data as a series of bytes in an array. Then, when communicating with the ToolKit routines, the program moves the bytes into and out of properly formatted MidiEvents.

To see how this process works, we'll write a simple sysex librarian program. When finished, the program will receive a sysex message, store the message on disk in a format readable by other popular MIDI programs, read such files from disk, and send the sysex messages back out to the original device. First, we'll make an example that receives a sysex message and puts it into an array. Later examples will add other features until the program is complete.

# Receiving Sysex Messages

The first sysex application example, *Ch11Ex1*, is based on chapter 10's *Ch10Ex3* example program. Like the other MFC-based examples, this program is organized around four files (containing the four fundamental classes). The application class, main frame class, document class, and view class are similar to the ones already described in other examples in this book. In fact, the only files that are changed (besides the different application and class names) are the document, view, and derived MIDI input device class (MyMidiIn) files. All of the files that make up the project are included on the accompanying CDROM.

This is the first example that puts the document class to use. In this case, the document object holds the sysex data as an array of bytes. The object allocates the memory for the array. In later examples, the document class will also load and save disk files in response to user requests. Here is the class:

```cpp
// Ch11Ex1Doc.h : interface of the CCh11Ex1Doc class
class CCh11Ex1Doc : public CDocument
{
protected: // create from serialization only
    CCh11Ex1Doc();
    DECLARE_DYNCREATE(CCh11Ex1Doc)

// Attributes
public:
    LPBYTE pData;
    DWORD cbDataSize;
    DWORD cbNumBytes;

// Operations
public:

// Overrides
    // ClassWizard generated virtual function overrides
    //{{AFX_VIRTUAL(CCh11Ex1Doc)
    public:
    virtual BOOL OnNewDocument();
    virtual void Serialize(CArchive& ar);
    //}}AFX_VIRTUAL

// Implementation
public:
    virtual ~CCh11Ex1Doc();

protected:

// Generated message map functions
protected:
    //{{AFX_MSG(CCh11Ex1Doc)
    //}}AFX_MSG
    DECLARE_MESSAGE_MAP()
};

// Ch11Ex1Doc.cpp : implementation of the CCh11Ex1Doc class
#include "stdafx.h"
#include "Ch11Ex1.h"

#include "Ch11Ex1Doc.h"
```

```
// CChllEx1Doc
IMPLEMENT_DYNCREATE(CChllEx1Doc, CDocument)

BEGIN_MESSAGE_MAP(CChllEx1Doc, CDocument)
     //{{AFX_MSG_MAP(CChllEx1Doc)
     //}}AFX_MSG_MAP
END_MESSAGE_MAP()

// CChllEx1Doc construction/destruction
CChllEx1Doc::CChllEx1Doc()
{
     pData = NULL;
     cbDataSize = 0;
     cbNumBytes = 0;
}


CChllEx1Doc::~CChllEx1Doc()
{
     // free any existing buffer
     if(pData)
             GlobalFree(GlobalHandle(pData));
}


BOOL CChllEx1Doc::OnNewDocument()
{
     if (!CDocument::OnNewDocument())
             return FALSE;

     // free any existing buffer
     if(pData)
             GlobalFree(GlobalHandle(pData));

     // allocate a starting buffer to receive the sysex data
     // this buffer will grow as needed, in 8K chunks
     cbDataSize = 8192;
     cbNumBytes = 0;
     pData = (LPBYTE)GlobalLock(GlobalAlloc(GHND, cbDataSize));

     return TRUE;
}

// CChllEx1Doc serialization
void CChllEx1Doc::Serialize(CArchive& ar)
{
     if (ar.IsStoring())
     {
     }
     else
     {
     }
}
```

When the program runs, an initial document is created and an 8-kbyte buffer is allocated. This buffer will hold any received sysex bytes. When a new document is created—by selecting New... from the File menu—any existing buffer is discarded and a new buffer is created in its place. When the document is destroyed (in the SDI case, when the application terminates), the buffer is freed.

The view class' implementation is very similar to that used in the other example programs. Both a MIDI input and MIDI output device are created, just as before. Although this program does not use the output device, it is used later. So, for the moment, the output device comes along for the ride.

A new menu item is added to the File menu: Receive Sysex. Two new functions are implemented to handle this menu selection: OnReceive() and OnUpdateReceive(). OnUpdateReceive() is called whenever the application is about to display the File menu. Here, the handler updates the menu text, depending on whether the program is currently receiving a sysex message. The application's response to OnReceive() also depends on its current state. If it is receiving—or waiting to receive—a sysex, it stops the receiving process. If it is not currently waiting for data, OnReceive() starts the receive process by calling the Receive() member function of the MyMidiIn class that maintains the MIDI input device. Here is the view class:

```
// Ch11Ex1View.h : interface of the CCh11Ex1View class
#include "MaxMidi.h"
#include "MyMidiIn.h"

class CCh11Ex1View : public CView
{
protected: // create from serialization only
    CCh11Ex1View();
    DECLARE_DYNCREATE(CCh11Ex1View)

// Attributes
public:
    CCh11Ex1Doc* GetDocument();

    CMaxMidiOut    MidiOut;
    MyMidiIn       MidiIn;

    // Input and Output Device Menus
    CMidiInDeviceMenu InMenu;
    CMidiOutDeviceMenu OutMenu;

    class definition continues...
};

// Ch11Ex1View.cpp : implementation of the CCh11Ex1View class
```

```
#include "stdafx.h"
#include "Ch11Ex1.h"

#include "Ch11Ex1Doc.h"
#include "Ch11Ex1View.h"

// CCh11Ex1View
IMPLEMENT_DYNCREATE(CCh11Ex1View, CView)

BEGIN_MESSAGE_MAP(CCh11Ex1View, CView)
    //{{AFX_MSG_MAP(CCh11Ex1View)
    ON_COMMAND(IDM_RECEIVE, OnReceive)
    ON_UPDATE_COMMAND_UI(IDM_RECEIVE, OnUpdateReceive)
    ON_WM_CREATE()
    //}}AFX_MSG_MAP
END_MESSAGE_MAP()

// CCh11Ex1View drawing
void CCh11Ex1View::OnDraw(CDC* pDC)
{
    CCh11Ex1Doc* pDoc = GetDocument();
    ASSERT_VALID(pDoc);
}

// CCh11Ex1View message handlers
int CCh11Ex1View::OnCreate(LPCREATESTRUCT lpCreateStruct)
{
    if (CView::OnCreate(lpCreateStruct) == -1)
            return -1;

    // attach the input and output devices to this window
    MidiOut.Attach(GetSafeHwnd());
    MidiIn.Attach(GetSafeHwnd());

    // get the parent menu
    CMenu* ParentMenu = GetParent()->GetMenu();

    // create the device menus and select the first devices
    InMenu.Create(ParentMenu->GetSafeHmenu(),
                  ParentMenu->GetMenuItemCount() - 1,
                  "&Input Device", IDM_INPUT);
    InMenu.Attach(&MidiIn);
    InMenu.SelectDevice(0);

    OutMenu.Create(ParentMenu->GetSafeHmenu(),
                   ParentMenu->GetMenuItemCount() - 1,
                   "&Output Device", IDM_OUTPUT);
    OutMenu.Attach(&MidiOut);
    OutMenu.SelectDevice(0);
    return 0;
}
```

```
BOOL CCh11Ex1View::OnCmdMsg(UINT nID, int nCode, void* pExtra,
AFX_CMDHANDLERINFO* pHandlerInfo)
{
    // check to see if one of the device menus has been selected
    if(nCode == 0)
    {
        InMenu.SelectDevice(nID);
        OutMenu.SelectDevice(nID);
    }

    return CView::OnCmdMsg(nID, nCode, pExtra, pHandlerInfo);
}

void CCh11Ex1View::OnReceive()
{
    CCh11Ex1Doc* pDoc = GetDocument();

    if(MidiIn.IsReceiving())
        MidiIn.StopRx();
    else
        MidiIn.Receive(&pDoc->pData, &pDoc->cbNumBytes,
                &pDoc->cbDataSize);
}

void CCh11Ex1View::OnUpdateReceive(CCmdUI* pCmdUI)
{
    if(MidiIn.IsReceiving())
        pCmdUI->SetText("Stop &Receiving");
    else
        pCmdUI->SetText("&Receive Sysex");
}
```

The MIDI input and output devices, and their selection menus, are opened the same way as the other example programs. However, OnCmdMsg() is implemented slightly differently from the *Ch10Ex3* example. The SetEchoOutput() function used in the other examples is eliminated, since this program does not echo any data from input to output.

The two new message handlers are added using the ClassWizard. To do this, modify the application's main menu by adding a Receive Sysex menu item to the File menu. Give this new item an ID of IDM_RECEIVE. Then, in the ClassWizard, add message handlers for the ON_COMMAND and UPDATE_COMMAND_UI messages. Edit these new handlers to add the implementations shown above. The new member functions for MyMidiIn— IsReceiving(), Receive(), and StopRx()—are discussed in the next section.

The most heavily modified class is the CMaxMidiIn-derived input class, MyMidiIn. It provides member functions to start and stop reception of sysex messages and store the received data in the document's buffer. Here is the modified class:

```cpp
#ifndef __MYMIDIIN__
#define __MYMIDIIN__
//=================================================================
//   MyMidiIn Class
//=================================================================
class MyMidiIn : public CMaxMidiIn
{
public:
     MyMidiIn();

public:
     LPBYTE* ppData;
     LPDWORD pNumBytes;
     LPDWORD pDataSize;
     BOOL fReceiving;

     void Receive(LPBYTE* ptr, LPDWORD pRxSize, LPDWORD pBufSize);
     void StopRx(void) { fReceiving = FALSE; };
     void StoreEvent(LPMIDIEVENT lpEvent);
     BOOL IsReceiving(void) { return fReceiving; };

// Overrides
     // ClassWizard generated virtual function overrides
     //{{AFX_VIRTUAL(MyMidiIn)
     virtual BOOL ProcessMidiData(LPMIDIEVENT lpEvent);
     //}}AFX_VIRTUAL

protected:
     //{{AFX_MSG(MyMidiIn)
     //}}AFX_MSG
     DECLARE_MESSAGE_MAP()
};
#endif //!__MYMIDIIN__

//=================================================================
//   MyMidiIn Class
//=================================================================
#include "stdafx.h"
#include "MaxMidi.h"
#include "MyMidiIn.h"

BEGIN_MESSAGE_MAP(MyMidiIn, CMaxMidiIn)
     //{{AFX_MSG_MAP(MyMidiIn)
     //}}AFX_MSG_MAP
END_MESSAGE_MAP()


//----------------------------------------
//   Constructor
//----------------------------------------
MyMidiIn::MyMidiIn()
{
     fReceiving = FALSE;
```

```
}

// MyMidiIn virtual functions
//─────────────────────────────
//    ProcessMidiData
//─────────────────────────────
BOOL MyMidiIn::ProcessMidiData(LPMIDIEVENT lpEvent)
{
    // store the sysex events in the doc buffer
    if(lpEvent->status == SYSEX)
            StoreEvent(lpEvent);

    return TRUE;
}


//─────────────────────────────
//    Receive
//─────────────────────────────
void MyMidiIn::Receive(LPBYTE* ptr, LPDWORD pRxSize, LPDWORD pBufSize)
{
    ppData = ptr;
    pNumBytes = pRxSize;
    pDataSize = pBufSize;
    fReceiving = TRUE;
    *pNumBytes = 0;
}


//─────────────────────────────
//    StoreEvent
//─────────────────────────────
void MyMidiIn::StoreEvent(LPMIDIEVENT lpEvent)
{
    // don't do anything if not receiving
    if(!fReceiving)
            return;

    // need to grow the buffer?
    if(*pNumBytes == *pDataSize)
    {
            // grow the buffer in 8K blocks
            *pDataSize += 8192;
            *ppData = (LPBYTE)GlobalLock( GlobalReAlloc(
                    GlobalHandle(*ppData), *pDataSize, GMEM_MOVEABLE));

            // did the realloc succeed?
            if(*ppData == NULL)
            {
                    // Very Bad News. Discard everything!
                    *pDataSize = *pNumBytes = 0;
            }
    }
```

```
// store the byte — which is always in data1 of the MidiEvent
// this will include the leading F0 and trailing F7
(*ppData)[*pNumBytes] = lpEvent->data1;

// next position in buffer
(*pNumBytes)++;

// stop if received the EOX
if(lpEvent->data1 == EOX)
        StopRx();
}
```

The receive process starts when the `Receive()` member function is called. The application passes the addresses of three variables that reside in the document class. The address of the pointer to the data buffer is passed in the `ptr` parameter. The class needs to be able to resize the buffer if the number of received bytes exceeds the original 8K allocation. A pointer to a pointer to the buffer allows the class to reallocate the buffer, while the document class still maintains "ownership." Similarly, a pointer to the count of bytes stored in the buffer (`cbNumBytes` in the document class) allows `MyMidiIn` to change the count as bytes are stored. And a pointer to the size of the buffer (`cbDataSize` in the document class) allows the variable in the document object to be modified when the buffer is resized. `Receive()` stores these pointers in the `MyMidiIn` class and sets the `fReceiving` flag. With the `fReceiving` flag set, `StoreEvent()` function will process received sysex bytes.

The `ProcessMidiData()` virtual function stores the bytes of the received sysex message by calling `StoreEvent()` for each `MidiEvent` whose status value is 0xF0 (SYSEX). `StoreEvent()` checks to see if the buffer needs to grow. If the buffer is too small to accept this newest byte, it is expanded by 8K by calling `GlobalReAlloc()`. During the reallocation process, the pointer to the head of the buffer might change (although none of the already saved values will be lost). This new pointer and the new buffer size are stored into the appropriate variables in the document object.

When there is enough room for the new byte, it is stored into the buffer and the count of stored bytes is updated. Reception stops when the trailing EOX is received, or when `StopRx()` is called (in response to user input).

To see this program in action, build a debug version of the application. Set a breakpoint on the second line of `CCh11Ex1View::OnReceive()`, or at some other point that can be triggered after a sysex is received. Be sure to choose a program line where the document pointer (`pDoc`) is valid. Run the program, select an appropriate MIDI input device and select Receive Sysex from the File menu. The breakpoint will be immediately hit. Click on the debugger's Go button to continue running the program. The menu item will change to Stop Receiving, indicating that the program is waiting for a sysex message.

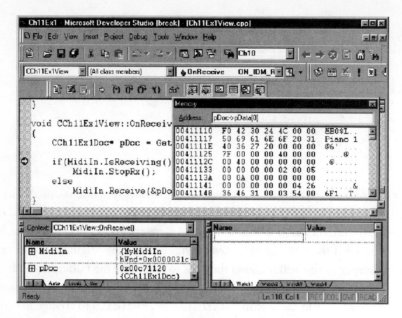

**Figure 11-1  The debugger screen**

Connect a MIDI device to the selected MIDI input and cause it to send a sysex message. When the sysex is completely transmitted, the Stop Receiving menu item will change back to Receive Sysex.

Hit the `OnReceive()` breakpoint by selecting Receive Sysex again. The debugger regains control at the breakpoint and displays the appropriate source code line in the editor. To view the data in the buffer, select Memory from the View menu. Type `pDoc->pData[0]` in the Address window and press Enter. The sysex data, beginning with the F0 byte, will be displayed in the Memory window.

# Sending Sysex Messages

Viewing sysex data in a debugger is interesting, but not very practical. It would be much more useful to be able to send the data back out. By adding a new class and modifying the view class, our example program can gain the chops to send sysex messages. A modified example program, *Ch11Ex2*, is supplied on the accompanying CDROM. Notice that as with the other examples, the project and file names have changed, so all of the application's classes have been renamed.

The new class, MyMidiOut, is derived from CMaxMidiOut. It is patterned after MyMidiIn and includes functions to start transmission and check sending status. It handles a single message, OUTBUFFER_READY, by overriding the ProcessOutBufferReady() virtual function. The OUTBUFFER_READY message is sent by the MaxMidi DLL while outputting a sysex message, whenever there are available sysex buffers. Here is the new class:

```
// from MyMidiOut.h — Class definition header
#ifndef __MYMIDIOUT__
#define __MYMIDIOUT__
//=================================================================
//   MyMidiOut Class
//=================================================================
class MyMidiOut : public CMaxMidiOut
{
public:
    MyMidiOut();
    void Send(LPBYTE ptr, DWORD size);
    BOOL IsSending(void) { return fSending; };
    DWORD NumSent(void) { return cbNumSent; };

public:
    BOOL fSending;
    DWORD cbNumSent;
    LPBYTE pData;
    DWORD cbDataSize;

// Overrides
    // ClassWizard generated virtual function overrides
    //{{AFX_VIRTUAL(MyMidiOut)
    virtual void ProcessOutBufferReady(void);
    //}}AFX_VIRTUAL

protected:
    //{{AFX_MSG(MyMidiOut)
    //}}AFX_MSG
    DECLARE_MESSAGE_MAP()
};
#endif //!__MYMIDIOUT__

// from MyMidiOut.cpp — Class implementation file
//=================================================================
//   MyMidiOut Class
//=================================================================
#include "stdafx.h"
#include "MaxMidi.h"
#include "MyMidiOut.h"
```

```
BEGIN_MESSAGE_MAP(MyMidiOut, CMaxMidiOut)
    //{{AFX_MSG_MAP(MyMidiOut)
    //}}AFX_MSG_MAP
END_MESSAGE_MAP()


//———————————————————————————
//    Constructor
//———————————————————————————
MyMidiOut::MyMidiOut()
{
    fSending = FALSE;
    cbNumSent = 0;
}


// MyMidiOut virtual functions
//———————————————————————————
//    ProcessOutBufferReady
//———————————————————————————
void MyMidiOut::ProcessOutBufferReady(void)
{
    MidiEvent evt;

    evt.status = SYSEX;

    do {
            evt.data1 = pData[cbNumSent];
    } while(Put(&evt) && cbNumSent++ < cbDataSize);

    fSending = (cbNumSent < cbDataSize);
}


//———————————————————————————
//    Send
//———————————————————————————
void MyMidiOut::Send(LPBYTE ptr, DWORD size)
{
    pData = ptr;
    cbDataSize = size;
    cbNumSent = 0;
    fSending = TRUE;

    // kick off the output process by "faking" an OUTBUFFER_READY
    ProcessOutBufferReady();
}
```

An instance of this class is created and opened to manage the MIDI output device. The application starts sending (an already received sysex) by calling `MyMidiOut::Send()` and passing a pointer to the buffer (located in the document object) and the number of significant bytes in the buffer. `Send()` saves these values and calls `ProcessOutBuffer-Ready()` to start the sending process. The `ProcessOutBufferReady()` member function puts each byte of the sysex into a `MidiEvent` structure and calls the MIDI output device's `Put()` function. It continues to output each byte until all of them are sent, or until the `Put()` function returns FALSE to indicate that its sysex buffers are full. Later, when one of the buffers is returned by the MIDI interface's device driver, the MaxMidi DLL will send an `OUTBUFFER_READY` message, triggering another call to `ProcessOutBufferReady()`. This process will pump an arbitrarily large sysex message out to the MIDI interface as fast as it is able to accept it.

The view class must be modified in two ways. First, the MIDI output device is changed to an instance of the `MyMidiOut` class. Then, message handlers are added to handle a new menu item. This menu item, Send Sysex, is added to the File menu with an ID of `IDM_SEND`. The two message handlers are added using the ClassWizard. Here are the modified portions of the view class:

```
// Ch11Ex2View.h : interface of the CCh11Ex2View class
#include "MaxMidi.h"
#include "MyMidiIn.h"
#include "MyMidiOut.h"

class CCh11Ex2View : public CView
{
protected: // create from serialization only
    CCh11Ex2View();
    DECLARE_DYNCREATE(CCh11Ex2View)

// Attributes
public:
    CCh11Ex2Doc* GetDocument();

    MyMidiOut       MidiOut;
    MyMidiIn        MidiIn;

    // Input and Output Device Menus
    CMidiInDeviceMenu InMenu;
    CMidiOutDeviceMenu OutMenu;

// Operations
public:

        class declaration continues...
};

// Ch11Ex2View.cpp : implementation of the CCh11Ex2View class
// CCh11Ex2View message handlers
void CCh11Ex2View::OnUpdateReceive(CCmdUI* pCmdUI)
{
    CCh11Ex2Doc* pDoc = GetDocument();
    pCmdUI->Enable(!MidiOut.IsSending());
```

```
            if(MidiIn.IsReceiving())
                   pCmdUI->SetText("Stop &Receiving");
            else
                   pCmdUI->SetText("&Receive Sysex");
      }

      void CCh11Ex2View::OnSend()
      {
            CCh11Ex2Doc* pDoc = GetDocument();
            MidiOut.Send(pDoc->pData, pDoc->cbNumBytes);
      }

      void CCh11Ex2View::OnUpdateSend(CCmdUI* pCmdUI)
      {
            CCh11Ex2Doc* pDoc = GetDocument();
            pCmdUI->Enable(!MidiIn.IsReceiving() && pDoc->cbNumBytes != 0);

            if(MidiOut.IsSending())
                   pCmdUI->SetText("Stop S&ending");
            else
                   pCmdUI->SetText("S&end Sysex");
      }
```

Since it does not make sense for the program to send and receive a sysex message at the same time, the two OnUpdate() functions check the state of sending and receiving, as needed, when enabling the two menu items. The Send Sysex menu item is disabled if there are no sysex bytes stored in the document's buffer. When the Send Sysex is selected, the menu name changes to Stop Sending and the MidiOut's Send() member function is called to start outputting the sysex message.

This example illustrates how to receive, store, and send sysex messages. But it is limited; it cannot save and load files from disk. That is the task for our next example.

# Loading and Saving Sysex Files

Our example program becomes much more useful when we add some simple file access capabilities. By storing the sysex messages in an unadorned binary format, the program is able to save and load any number of sysex messages. And since many commercial and shareware sysex handling programs use this format when storing sysex data, our example program can share data files with such applications. This example is an excellent starting point for a wide variety of System Exclusive projects.

This new program, called *SxLib*, is based on the previous example. In fact, other than the class name differences, the only changes needed are in the document class. Here they are:

```
// from SxLibDoc.cpp — document class implementation
// CSxLibDoc commands
BOOL CSxLibDoc::OnOpenDocument(LPCTSTR lpszPathName)
{
     HANDLE hFile;
     DWORD numRead;

     // open the specified file
     hFile = CreateFile(lpszPathName, GENERIC_READ, 0, NULL,
                          OPEN_EXISTING, FILE_ATTRIBUTE_NORMAL, NULL);

     if(hFile == NULL)
             return FALSE;

     // get the size of the data
     cbNumBytes = cbDataSize = GetFileSize(hFile, NULL);

     // allocate a buffer for the sysex
     pData = (LPBYTE)GlobalLock(GlobalAlloc(GHND, cbDataSize));

     // read the sysex
     if(!ReadFile(hFile, pData, cbDataSize, &numRead, NULL))
     {
             // error reading file — unwind the memory allocations
             GlobalFree(GlobalHandle(pData));
             pData = NULL;
             CloseHandle(hFile);
             return FALSE;
     }

     // sysex file successfully loaded
     CloseHandle(hFile);
     return TRUE;
}

BOOL CSxLibDoc::OnSaveDocument(LPCTSTR lpszPathName)
{
     HANDLE hFile;
     DWORD numWritten;

     // create the specified file
     hFile = CreateFile(lpszPathName, GENERIC_WRITE, 0, NULL,
                          CREATE_ALWAYS, FILE_ATTRIBUTE_NORMAL, NULL);

     if(hFile == NULL)
             return FALSE;

     // write the block out
     if(!WriteFile(hFile, pData, cbNumBytes, &numWritten, NULL))
     {
             // error writing file
             CloseHandle(hFile);
```

```
            return FALSE;
    }

    // file successfully written
    CloseHandle(hFile);
    return TRUE;
}
```

These two message handlers support the File menu's Open and Save menu items. To add these handlers, use the ClassWizard to edit the `CSxLibDoc` class. Select OnOpenDocument and click on the Add Function button to add a handler for this message. Likewise, select OnSaveDocument and add a handler for that message. Edit both function implementations and remove the `CDocument::OnOpenDocument()` and `CDocument::OnSaveDocument()` calls. This will disconnect these functions from the MFC `Serialize()` file handling, since these two functions directly handle file access. Alternatively, *SxLib*'s file handling could be implemented in `CDocument::Serialize()`. However, the implementations shown above provide the necessary file handling expertise needed to read and write these binary-format System Exclusive files.

Notice that in this example (as well as in the other two in this chapter), the implementation for `OnDraw()` does nothing. These examples do not display anything in their view classes. By modifying the view class to display the number of bytes received or to allow the user to edit the received data, the *SxLib* example can be made even more useful. The program could even become a sophisticated patch editor by interpreting the sysex data and displaying it—via the view class—in a set of controls for the particular originating MIDI device. By using these controls to change the values of the sysex data, and sending the edited message back to the device, the user-hostile front panels of many MIDI instruments can become just a bit friendlier.

# CHAPTER 12

# A Simple Sequencer

Musically speaking, MIDI is about performance. A musician plays notes, triggering MIDI events. Recording these events and playing them back with the same timing relationships reproduces the original performance. This process is called *sequencing*, since the sequence (and timing) of events is recorded. A *sequencer* is a program that records MIDI events, stores them, and plays them back. Sequencers are the most popular type of MIDI software. They are used for composition, education, music production, and good clean fun.

So far, we have seen the ToolKit's MIDI input and output classes, the sync class, and two convenient menu-handling classes. These classes provide enough functionality to write a wide range of sophisticated MIDI applications. For a sequencer, these classes are not enough. A sequencer handles MIDI events—recording, playing, and editing them along the way—so it needs a place to store these events. A new class, CMaxMidiTrack, comes to the rescue. This class encapsulates the MIDI data and all of the functions needed to manage these events, including the event editing and synchronization-related capabilities that a sequencer needs.

In this chapter, we'll develop a simple sequencer using the ToolKit classes. Using only a few lines of C++, this program will record a performance, store it in a special internal buffer called a track, and play that performance back exactly as received. This primordial example serves as a jumping off point for any program that records, plays, or edits MIDI performances.

# *Tracks*

In a sense, a sequencer is like a database program. Both databases and sequencers accept, store, and retrieve data. A database program might manage the employee records of a planet-spanning multinational corporation. On the other hand, our sequencer might hold a heartstring-tugging performance of *Feelings*. In either case, both programs store their data in some sort of container. A database uses a record to organize and manipulate its data. A sequencer uses a *track* to do the same job.

Tracks are similar to the staves or parts that make up sheet music. From a simplified viewpoint, each stave on the page corresponds to a part of the music that a particular instrument plays (e.g., a trumpet versus a French horn part in orchestral music). Likewise, each track in a sequence contains the notes for a particular instrument or sound. When there are multiple tracks in a sequence, all of the tracks play in parallel—just like the parallel staves in sheet music. Of course, as any musician knows, a single track—or stave—could hold notes for more than one instrument, and a single instrument's notes can be spread over several staves or tracks.

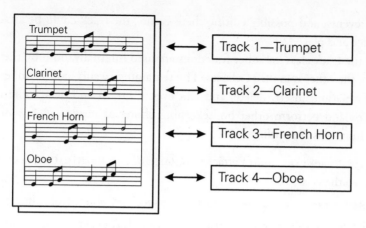

**Figure 12-1   Track assignment**

A track is a container for MIDI data. But a track is more than a repository. Any MIDI application needs to be able to access and manipulate the data in the track. Typical tasks include adding events to the buffer (recording), retrieving events for playback, combining events from multiple tracks during playback (to send to a single MIDI output), and modifying the events in the track (editing).

These requirements are a perfect match for a C++ track class. The MaxMidi ToolKit implements an extensive track class, called `CMaxMidiTrack`. Instances of this class can be attached to input devices for recording, output devices for playback, and, as we'll see in chapter 13, Standard MIDI File objects for reading and writing files. The track class provides over two dozen member functions that enable an application (and the other classes in the ToolKit) to manipulate the MIDI events contained in the track.

An instance of a track object, referred to here as a *track,* can be attached to instances of `CMaxMidiIn` and `CMaxMidiOut` classes. For example, to record data into a track in real time, attach the track to a MIDI input device that is derived from `CMaxMidiIn`. Data that is received by the input device will automatically be stored in the attached track. To play the same track back (assuming it was recorded using synchronization), attach it to a MIDI output device (which is also attached to a sync device) and start playback. The track will automatically feed its data to the output device and the track will play back exactly as recorded. If multiple tracks are attached to the same output device, all of the tracks will be combined automatically as they play.

Tracks can be attached to and detached from other ToolKit objects at any time. They can even be used as bachelors, unattached to anything else. For example, an application could create a track object and insert events directly into the track. After filling the track with MIDI events, and possibly editing these events, the track could be attached to an output device and played.

Some of the track class' member functions are used internally, both by the track class itself and by the other CMaxMidi classes. The remaining twenty-odd member functions provide information; insert, delete, and edit events; attach and detach the track from other objects; and perform other housekeeping chores as needed. A few of the more interesting functions are outlined here:

- CMaxMidiTrack::Attach() attaches a CMaxMidiIn, CMaxMidiOut, or CMaxMidiSMF object to the class.
- CMaxMidiTrack::Detach() detaches the specified object from the track.
- CMaxMidiTrack::InsertEvent() inserts a MIDI event at the specified location in the track.
- CMaxMidiTrack::DeleteEvent() removes the specified event from the track.
- CMaxMidiTrack::GetEvent() retrieves the specified event from the track.
- CMaxMidiTrack::SetEvent() replaces a specified event with a new one.
- CMaxMidiTrack::SlideTrack() moves events (in time) in the track. This is especially useful for correcting timing when events are inserted or deleted.
- CMaxMidiTrack::Read() retrieves the next event from the track.
- CMaxMidiTrack::Mute() enables or disables playback of the track without affecting the track's contents.
- CMaxMidiTrack::IsRecording() gets or sets the recording state for this track. Recording must be TRUE for events to be written to the track.

For more advanced applications, there are member functions that give direct access to the buffer that holds the MIDI events. A program might use these functions to quickly initialize or update the events in a track by directly replacing the track's buffer. These functions—along with the other internal functions—are also useful for applications that extend the track class by using it as a base class for an even more advanced track object. These advanced functions, along with all of the other CMaxMidiTrack functions, are documented in appendix A (as well as in the Windows help file included on the CDROM).

# Recording a Track

Let's design an application that will record a single track of MIDI events using synchronization. The three fundamental classes are logically arranged as shown below. A `CMaxMidiIn` object receives MIDI events from the MIDI interface. It timestamps those events based on the timing provided by the attached `CMaxMidiSync` sync object. These events are inserted into the attached `CMaxMidiTrack` track object. The track object maintains a buffer that grows as needed when events are inserted. Using instances of these three classes, and a little bit of MFC boilerplate, we can quickly implement a MIDI recording program.

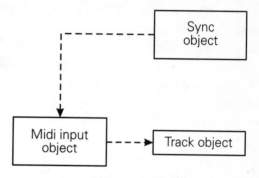

**Figure 12-2    Recording**

To implement the program using MFC, first create a minimal project using the same steps outlined in chapter 10. Call the program *Ch12Ex1*. The completed example is included on the CDROM. Then, follow these steps to flesh-out the project:

- Define `_MIDIIN`, `_MENUS`, `_SYNC`, and `_TRACK` in the Preprocessor definitions field of the Project Settings dialog.

- Add the following files to the project:

    MxMidi32.lib

    CMaxMidiIn.cpp

    CMaxMidiSync.cpp

    CMaxMidiTrack.cpp

    CMidiInDeviceMenu.cpp

- Add the `CMaxMidiIn`, `CMaxMidiSync`, and `CMaxMidiTrack` classes to the project using ClassWizard.

Now it's time to modify the four fundamental MFC classes. Although there is more than one way to organize the MIDI implementation in an MFC application, this example—and the examples that follow—distribute the MaxMidi classes and related tasks as shown below.

Much of this implementation is identical to the organization used in the other examples. These programs assume that different views might wish to access different MIDI devices, so instances of the MIDI input and output classes appear in the application's view class. But other organizations are possible, so feel free to rearrange these classes as you see fit. The application class still calls `GetMaxMidiVersion()` before any windows are created, to resize the window message queue. Likewise, the `CMainFrame` class enables all menu items, and the view class creates and opens the MIDI input device and manages device menu selections in the `OnCmdMsg()` handler.

But there are some differences. The `CMainFrame` class now creates and opens the sync device. The sync device could be put in any `CWnd` derived class, but here it is created in the `CMainFrame` class because the synchronization function is common to all possible views. In other words, even if there is more than one view of a given document, all of the views use the same synchronization to play or record.

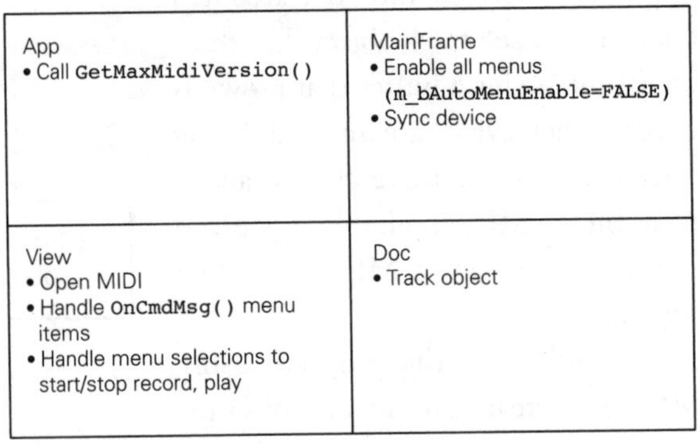

| App <br> • Call `GetMaxMidiVersion()` | MainFrame <br> • Enable all menus <br>   (m_bAutoMenuEnable=FALSE) <br> • Sync device |
| --- | --- |
| View <br> • Open MIDI <br> • Handle `OnCmdMsg()` menu <br>   items <br> • Handle menu selections to <br>   start/stop record, play | Doc <br> • Track object |

**Figure 12-3   MIDI organization**

The document class holds the track object, since the track contains the data that makes up the sequence. Logically, the sequence corresponds to a MIDI document. Therefore, if a sequence uses more than one track, all of the tracks are then contained in a single document. However, this example only contains a single track.

In addition to its usual tasks, the view class must attach all of the various MaxMidi objects together. Then, in response to menu item selections, it starts and stops recording by calling member functions of the proper classes. Here is the modified `CMainFrame` class, showing how the sync device is created:

```
// MainFrm.h : interface of the CMainFrame class
#include "MaxMidi.h"

class CMainFrame : public CFrameWnd
{
protected: // create from serialization only
    CMainFrame();
    DECLARE_DYNCREATE(CMainFrame)
```

```
// Attributes
public:
    CMaxMidiSync SyncDev;

    class definition continues...
};

// MainFrm.cpp : implementation of the CMainFrame class

// CMainFrame message handlers
int CMainFrame::OnCreate(LPCREATESTRUCT lpCreateStruct)
{
    // open the sync device with the default settings
    // open it before calling the base OnCreate, since the sync
    // device must be open before the view object is created.
    SyncDev.Attach(GetSafeHwnd());
    SyncDev.Open(S_INT, DEFAULT_TIMERPERIOD);

    if (CFrameWnd::OnCreate(lpCreateStruct) == -1)
            return -1;

    // since we don't have separate ON_UPDATE_COMMAND_UI handlers
    // or ON_COMMAND handlers for the device menu items we must
    // clear this flag so that the Input Device and Output Device
    // menu items are all enabled
    m_bAutoMenuEnable = FALSE;
    return 0;
}
```

Notice that the sync device is attached to the `CMainFrame` window and opened *before* the base class' `OnCreate()` function is called. This is because the view class is created during the `CFrameWnd::OnCreate()` call, and the sync device must exist for the view class to attach to the MIDI input device.

The document class is modified by adding the track object. The track is created when the document is created, and destroyed when the document is destroyed, or when New... is selected from the File menu. Here is the modified code for the document class:

```
// Ch12Ex1Doc.h : interface of the CCh12Ex1Doc class
#include "MaxMidi.h"

class CCh12Ex1Doc : public CDocument
{
protected: // create from serialization only
    CCh12Ex1Doc();
    DECLARE_DYNCREATE(CCh12Ex1Doc)

// Attributes
public:
```

```
        CMaxMidiTrack* pTrack;

// Operations
public:
    void CreateNewTrack(CString name);

    class definition continues...

};

// Ch12Ex1Doc.cpp : implementation of the CCh12Ex1Doc class
// CCh12Ex1Doc construction/destruction

CCh12Ex1Doc::CCh12Ex1Doc()
{
    pTrack = NULL;
}

CCh12Ex1Doc::~CCh12Ex1Doc()
{
    // free the track
    if(pTrack)
        delete pTrack;
}

BOOL CCh12Ex1Doc::OnNewDocument()
{
    if (!CDocument::OnNewDocument())
        return FALSE;

    // close any existing track
    if(pTrack)
    {
        delete pTrack;
        pTrack = NULL;
    }

    // create a new one
    CreateNewTrack("New Track");

    return TRUE;
}

void CCh12Ex1Doc::CreateNewTrack(CString name)
{
    // get the pointer to the view
    // (we only have one since this is SDI)
    POSITION pos = GetFirstViewPosition();
    CCh12Ex1View* pView = (CCh12Ex1View*)GetNextView(pos);
```

```
    // create a new track and attach it to the input device
    pTrack = new CMaxMidiTrack;
    pView->MidiIn.Attach(pTrack);

    // set the track name
    pTrack->SetName((LPSTR)(LPCTSTR)name);
}
```

Except for the code that deletes any existing track object, all of the action is in the `CreateNewTrack()` function. There, a new track is created, named, and attached to the MIDI input device that resides in the view-class object. There is no need to detach the track from the MIDI input device when the track is destroyed. It automatically detaches itself when its destructor is called.

Of the four MFC classes in our example, the view class requires the most extensive modifications. Some of this code is familiar: the MIDI input and menu handling code is the same as is used in the other examples. But there are two new menu items—with menu handlers to match—along with a few changes to the `OnCreate()` function to handle attaching the sync device to the MIDI input device. Here is the code:

```
// Ch12Ex1View.h : interface of the CCh12Ex1View class
#include "MaxMidi.h"

class CCh12Ex1View : public CView
{
protected: // create from serialization only
    CCh12Ex1View();
    DECLARE_DYNCREATE(CCh12Ex1View)

// Attributes
public:
    CCh12Ex1Doc* GetDocument();

    // MaxMidi Sync Device
    CMaxMidiSync* Sync;

    // MaxMidi Input Device Object
    CMaxMidiIn MidiIn;

    // Input Device Menu
    CMidiInDeviceMenu InMenu;
```

*class definition continues...*

```cpp
// Generated message map functions
protected:
    //{{AFX_MSG(CCh12Ex1View)
    afx_msg int OnCreate(LPCREATESTRUCT lpCreateStruct);
    afx_msg void OnRecordStart();
    afx_msg void OnRecordStop();
    //}}AFX_MSG
    DECLARE_MESSAGE_MAP()
};


// Ch12Ex1View.cpp : implementation of the CCh12Ex1View class
BEGIN_MESSAGE_MAP(CCh12Ex1View, CView)
    //{{AFX_MSG_MAP(CCh12Ex1View)
    ON_WM_CREATE()
    ON_COMMAND(IDM_RSTART, OnRecordStart)
    ON_COMMAND(IDM_RSTOP, OnRecordStop)
    //}}AFX_MSG_MAP
END_MESSAGE_MAP()

// CCh12Ex1View message handlers
int CCh12Ex1View::OnCreate(LPCREATESTRUCT lpCreateStruct)
{
    if (CView::OnCreate(lpCreateStruct) == -1)
            return -1;

    CCh12Ex1Doc* pDoc = GetDocument();

    // get a pointer to the sync device
    CFrameWnd* pMainFrm = GetParentFrame();
    Sync = &((CMainFrame*)pMainFrm)->SyncDev;

    // open the first input device
    MidiIn.Attach(GetSafeHwnd());

    // attach the sync device to the input device
    MidiIn.Attach(Sync);

    // get the parent menu
    CMenu* ParentMenu = GetParent()->GetMenu();

    // create the device menus and select the first device
    InMenu.Create(ParentMenu->GetSafeHmenu(),
            ParentMenu->GetMenuItemCount() - 1,
            "&Input Device", IDM_INPUT);
    InMenu.Attach(&MidiIn);
    InMenu.SelectDevice(0);
    return 0;
}
```

```
BOOL CCh12Ex1View::OnCmdMsg(UINT nID, int nCode, void* pExtra,
AFX_CMDHANDLERINFO* pHandlerInfo)
{
        // check to see if one of the device menus has been selected
        if(nCode == 0)
        {
                InMenu.SelectDevice(nID);
        }

        return CView::OnCmdMsg(nID, nCode, pExtra, pHandlerInfo);
}

void CCh12Ex1View::OnRecordStart()
{
        CCh12Ex1Doc* pDoc = GetDocument();

        // reset the timestamp for the input device since
        // input is always active
        MidiIn.Reset();

        // enable record for the selected track
        pDoc->pTrack->Flush();
        pDoc->pTrack->IsRecording(TRUE);

        // start input
        Sync->Start();
}

void CCh12Ex1View::OnRecordStop()
{
        CCh12Ex1Doc* pDoc = GetDocument();

        // stop recording
        pDoc->pTrack->IsRecording(FALSE);

        // stop input
        Sync->Stop();
}
```

This is where things come together. The OnCreate() function is called when the view
is created. There, the function retrieves a pointer to the sync device and tucks it away for
future use. It then attaches the sync device to the MIDI input device and continues to
open and initialize the device and its menu class.

The main menu must be modified to add a Record menu, with two items: Start and
Stop. The Record|Start selection is handled by OnRecordStart(), while Record|Stop is
handled by OnRecordStop(). Starting record requires only a few steps. The MIDI input
device is reset, since it was started when the view was first created. Remember, the
CMidiInDeviceMenu class starts newly-opened MIDI input devices in the SelectDevice()

function. The track is flushed in case any MIDI events were received before recording started. Then, sync is started and the recording process begins.

While recording, each received event is timestamped by the sync device and stored in the track. Recording is complete when the user selects Record|Stop, triggering a call to `OnRecordStop()`. This function disables recording into the track and stops the sync device. The track then contains the sequence of timestamped MIDI events.

To see what is happening inside of this example, set a breakpoint at the `Sync->Stop()` statement in the `OnRecordStop()` function. Run the program, select an appropriate MIDI input device, and record some MIDI data. Stop recording to trigger the breakpoint. Step over this statement to stop the sync device. Then, view the track buffer by selecting Memory from the View menu in the Developer Studio debugger. Specify the address to view by typing `pDoc->pTrack->lpBuffer[0]` in the Address field of the Memory window. The recorded MIDI events will be displayed, as an array of bytes that comprise the 8-byte `MidiEvent` structures.

This example shows the basic procedure for using the ToolKit classes to record MIDI events. Let's expand the example to add the ability to play back the recorded track. Then we'll really be able to make some noise and disturb the peace.

## Playing Back the Track

The necessary steps to play back the recorded track are: attach a MIDI output device to the sync device and to the track, and start the sync device. The track will play back from the beginning. The next example program, *Ch12Ex2*, takes the code of the previous example and adds the MIDI output device, along with the necessary code to start and stop playback. At the same time, we'll add a few nice touches to make the program friendlier and more professional.

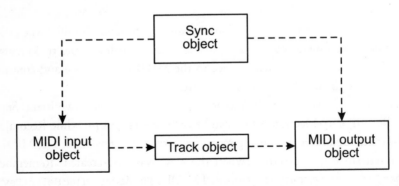

**Figure 12-4  Recording and playing**

Adding the CMaxMidiOut class and the support code to manage the output device is easy; we did that in chapter 10, so we won't dwell on it here. However, the document class needs a minor modification. The CreateNewTrack() function must attach the MIDI output device to the track so that it will play back. Here is the modified function:

```
void CCh12Ex2Doc::CreateNewTrack(CString name)
{
    // get the pointer to the view (we only have one since this is SDI)
    POSITION pos = GetFirstViewPosition();
    CCh12Ex2View* pView = (CCh12Ex2View*)GetNextView(pos);

    // create a new track and attach it to the input device
    pTrack = new CMaxMidiTrack;
    pView->MidiIn.Attach(pTrack);

    // attach the track to the output device
    pView->MidiOut.Attach(pTrack);

    // set the track name
    pTrack->SetName((LPSTR)(LPCTSTR)name);
}
```

The CMaxMidiSync-based sync device used in the earlier example works fine. But it would be nice to know whether the sequencer is recording or playing back the track and to be able to stop playback at the end of the sequence. We can enhance the sequencer by deriving a class from CMaxMidiSync and adding the necessary code to perform these functions. The new class, MySync, looks like this:

```
// from MySync.h — class definition
#include "MaxMidi.h"

//====================================================================
//    MySync Class
//====================================================================
#ifndef __MYSYNC__
#define __MYSYNC__
class MySync : public CMaxMidiSync
{
protected:
    BOOL    fRecord;                    // true if recording

public:
    MySync();

    void IsRecording(BOOL record) { fRecord = record; };
    BOOL IsRecording(void) { return fRecord; };
```

```
    // Overrides
        // ClassWizard generated virtual function overrides
        //{{AFX_VIRTUAL(MySync)
        virtual void ProcessSyncDone(void);
        //}}AFX_VIRTUAL

protected:
        //{{AFX_MSG(MySync)
        //}}AFX_MSG
        DECLARE_MESSAGE_MAP()
};
#endif //!__MYSYNC__


// from MySync.cpp — class implementation
//====================================================================
//    MySync Class
//====================================================================
#include "stdafx.h"
#include "Ch12Ex2Doc.h"
#include "Ch12Ex2View.h"

BEGIN_MESSAGE_MAP(MySync, CMaxMidiSync)
        //{{AFX_MSG_MAP(MySync)
        //}}AFX_MSG_MAP
END_MESSAGE_MAP()


//—————————————————————————
//    Constructor
//—————————————————————————
MySync::MySync()
{
        IsRecording(FALSE);
}


// MySync virtual functions
//—————————————————————————
//    ProcessSyncDone
//—————————————————————————
void MySync::ProcessSyncDone(void)
{
        // stop playback, but only if not recording
        if(!IsRecording())
                Stop();
}
```

In the example program, references to CMaxMidiSync are replaced by references to
MySync. The sync device now has a new function, IsRecording(), that sets or gets the
state of recording. This function is used in the view class when enabling menus. It is also
used by the sync device itself to know when to stop sync. The ProcessSyncDone()

virtual function is called when the sync device has no more MIDI events to send. If the sequencer is playing back a track, `ProcessSyncDone()`—as implemented in the `MySync` class—stops playback when all of the events have played. But it would not do to stop sync while recording, since the track is empty. If the sync device did not know the state of the sequencer, `ProcessSyncDone()` would stop recording before it got going.

The final changes to the *Ch12Ex2* sequencer example are in the view class. A new menu item, Play, and two new selections, Start and Stop, provide the user interface for the new functionality. These two menu selections connect to the message handlers `OnPlayStart()` and `OnPlayStop()`. Additionally, four new menu update handlers add some user-interface sanity to the program. These handlers determine whether Record|Start, Record|Stop, Play|Start, and Play|Stop menu items are enabled whenever they are displayed. For example, it does not make sense to be able to stop playback while recording. In this case, the update handlers disable both Play selections. It also doesn't make sense to be able to start recording while recording is already taking place. So, the update handlers also disable the Record|Start selection as well. Here are the modified portions of the view class:

```
// Ch12Ex2View.h : interface of the CCh12Ex2View class
#include "MaxMidi.h"
#include "MySync.h"

class CCh12Ex2View : public CView
{
protected: // create from serialization only
    CCh12Ex2View();
    DECLARE_DYNCREATE(CCh12Ex2View)

// Attributes
public:
    CCh12Ex2Doc* GetDocument();

    // MaxMidi Sync Device
    MySync* Sync;

    // MaxMidi Input and Output Device Objects
    CMaxMidiIn MidiIn;
    CMaxMidiOut MidiOut;

    // Device Menus
    CMidiInDeviceMenu InMenu;
    CMidiOutDeviceMenu OutMenu;

// Operations
public:
```

*class definition continues...*

```
// Generated message map functions
protected:
    //{{AFX_MSG(CCh12Ex2View)
    afx_msg int OnCreate(LPCREATESTRUCT lpCreateStruct);
    afx_msg void OnRecordStart();
    afx_msg void OnRecordStop();
    afx_msg void OnPlayStart();
    afx_msg void OnPlayStop();
    afx_msg void OnUpdateRecordStart(CCmdUI* pCmdUI);
    afx_msg void OnUpdateRecordStop(CCmdUI* pCmdUI);
    afx_msg void OnUpdatePlayStart(CCmdUI* pCmdUI);
    afx_msg void OnUpdatePlayStop(CCmdUI* pCmdUI);
    //}}AFX_MSG
    DECLARE_MESSAGE_MAP()
};


// Ch12Ex2View.cpp : implementation of the CCh12Ex2View class
IMPLEMENT_DYNCREATE(CCh12Ex2View, CView)


BEGIN_MESSAGE_MAP(CCh12Ex2View, CView)
    //{{AFX_MSG_MAP(CCh12Ex2View)
    ON_WM_CREATE()
    ON_COMMAND(IDM_RSTART, OnRecordStart)
    ON_COMMAND(IDM_RSTOP, OnRecordStop)
    ON_COMMAND(IDM_PSTART, OnPlayStart)
    ON_COMMAND(IDM_PSTOP, OnPlayStop)
    ON_UPDATE_COMMAND_UI(IDM_RSTART, OnUpdateRecordStart)
    ON_UPDATE_COMMAND_UI(IDM_RSTOP, OnUpdateRecordStop)
    ON_UPDATE_COMMAND_UI(IDM_PSTART, OnUpdatePlayStart)
    ON_UPDATE_COMMAND_UI(IDM_PSTOP, OnUpdatePlayStop)
    //}}AFX_MSG_MAP
END_MESSAGE_MAP()


// CCh12Ex2View message handlers
int CCh12Ex2View::OnCreate(LPCREATESTRUCT lpCreateStruct)
{
    if (CView::OnCreate(lpCreateStruct) == -1)
            return -1;

    CCh12Ex2Doc* pDoc = GetDocument();

    // get a pointer to the sync device
    CFrameWnd* pMainFrm = GetParentFrame();
    Sync = &((CMainFrame*)pMainFrm)->SyncDev;

    // open the first input and output devices
    MidiIn.Attach(GetSafeHwnd());
    MidiOut.Attach(GetSafeHwnd());
```

```
        // attach the sync device to the input and output devices
        MidiIn.Attach(Sync);
        MidiOut.Attach(Sync);

        // get the parent menu
        CMenu* ParentMenu = GetParent()->GetMenu();

        // create the device menus and select the first devices
        InMenu.Create(ParentMenu->GetSafeHmenu()
                        ParentMenu->GetMenuItemCount() - 1
                        "&Input Device", IDM_INPUT);
        InMenu.Attach(&MidiIn);
        InMenu.SelectDevice(0);

        OutMenu.Create(ParentMenu->GetSafeHmenu()
                        ParentMenu->GetMenuItemCount() - 1
                        "&Output Device", IDM_OUTPUT);
        OutMenu.Attach(&MidiOut);
        OutMenu.SelectDevice(0);
        return 0;
}

BOOL CCh12Ex2View::OnCmdMsg(UINT nID, int nCode, void* pExtra,
AFX_CMDHANDLERINFO* pHandlerInfo)
{
        // check to see if one of the device menus has been selected
        if(nCode == 0)
        {
                InMenu.SelectDevice(nID);
                OutMenu.SelectDevice(nID);
        }

        return CView::OnCmdMsg(nID, nCode, pExtra, pHandlerInfo);
}

void CCh12Ex2View::OnRecordStart()
{
        CCh12Ex2Doc* pDoc = GetDocument();

        // reset the timestamp for the input device since
        // input is always active
        MidiIn.Reset();

        // enable record for the selected track
        pDoc->pTrack->Flush();
        pDoc->pTrack->IsRecording(TRUE);

        // start input
        Sync->IsRecording(TRUE);
        Sync->Start();
}
```

```
void CCh12Ex2View::OnUpdateRecordStart(CCmdUI* pCmdUI)
{
    CCh12Ex2Doc* pDoc = GetDocument();

    // disable record start if already recording
    pCmdUI->Enable(!pDoc->pTrack->IsRecording());
}

void CCh12Ex2View::OnRecordStop()
{
    CCh12Ex2Doc* pDoc = GetDocument();

    // stop recording
    pDoc->pTrack->IsRecording(FALSE);

    // stop input
    Sync->IsRecording(FALSE);
    Sync->Stop();
}

void CCh12Ex2View::OnUpdateRecordStop(CCmdUI* pCmdUI)
{
    CCh12Ex2Doc* pDoc = GetDocument();

    // disable record stop if not recording
    pCmdUI->Enable(pDoc->pTrack->IsRecording());
}

void CCh12Ex2View::OnPlayStart()
{
    // sync must be started before any data is sent
    // to midi out so that data is sent with proper timing.
    Sync->Start();

    // start merging tracks into the output device
    MidiOut.StartOut();
}

void CCh12Ex2View::OnUpdatePlayStart(CCmdUI* pCmdUI)
{
    CCh12Ex2Doc* pDoc = GetDocument();

    // disable play start if track is empty or if it is already
    // playing or recording
    pCmdUI->Enable(!pDoc->pTrack->IsEmpty() && !Sync->IsRunning());
}

void CCh12Ex2View::OnPlayStop()
{
    // stop playback
    Sync->Stop();
}
```

```
void CCh12Ex2View::OnUpdatePlayStop(CCmdUI* pCmdUI)
{
     CCh12Ex2Doc* pDoc = GetDocument();

     // disable play stop if not playing or if recording
     pCmdUI->Enable(Sync->IsRunning() &&
                    !pDoc->pTrack->IsRecording());
}
```

Eagle-eyed readers may notice that both the sync device and the track have functions that indicate the state of recording. Why not use the track's IsRecording() function, instead of inventing a new, similar function in the MySync class? The answer is that the sync device does not know which track is recording. In fact, it does not know about tracks at all, since it attaches to MIDI input and output devices, but not to track objects. This distinction will become more important in chapter 14, when the sequencer adds support for multiple tracks.

The other aspects of the view class are straightforward. The OnCreate() function attaches the sync device to the output device (and to the input device, too). The usual code for handling the output device menu appears here as well. The four menu handlers, along with the four matching OnUpdate handlers, appear here. Study the implementation for all eight handlers to understand how record and playback are done.

Try recording and playing back sequences using this example. Notice how the menus behave in all the various states of the program. It's time to experiment and modify, and this example is a perfect guinea pig. For instance, the tempo and timing resolution are set to the ToolKit's default values: 120 bpm and 480 tpb. It's a simple matter to add menus or dialog boxes to modify these settings. Or, modify the view's OnDraw() function to display the recorded events as an event list. Use some of the track's editing functions to modify, add, and delete events. Go wild. No one will know but you and your compiler. Honest.

**CHAPTER 13**

# Standard MIDI Files

It's time to regress for a moment—back into the realm of C—and explore Standard MIDI Files (SMFs). The SMF specification defines a file format that contains timestamped MIDI data, along with nonplayable events in the form of Meta events. Standard MIDI Files are designed to be platform independent. Files created on one type of computer or program can be transferred to another system and read. For example, copying sequences between PCs and Macs, or between two different, unrelated MIDI programs on the same platform, are common tasks that SMFs do well. In fact, the Standard MIDI File format is intended to allow data to be exchanged between dissimilar systems.

But this is not its only use. Standard MIDI Files provide enough functionality to be used as the native file format for programs on any platform. But even if a program uses its own unique format for storing sequences, it is important to support the SMF format. Users expect to be able to trade sequences with their friends, download songs from the Internet, or move files between programs written by competing companies—all without hassle. Standard MIDI Files provide the conduit that makes these tasks possible.

Since SMF support is so important, the MaxMidi DLLs implement a set of routines that read and write Standard MIDI Files. These functions open, read, and write SMFs, and provide access to all of the features of this file format. Events are stored in SMF files using tracks. These tracks are similar in construction to the tracks used by the ToolKit classes. A Standard MIDI File might store all of the events in a single track, or in a number of tracks, depending on the type of file. Format 0 files contain a single track, while Format 1 files contain multiple tracks. Format 2 files, which are not supported by the ToolKit, contain one or more independent single-track patterns. Format 2 files are rarely used since many programs do not support this format.

This chapter covers Standard MIDI Files in three phases. First, we'll explore the basic file structure to gain an understanding of how data is stored. Next, we'll delve into the implementation of SMF support in the MaxMidi DLLs. Like all of the other routines contained in the DLLs, these routines are written in C. Finally, we'll return to the C++ world and learn about the SMF class, `CMaxMidiSMF`, that encapsulates the DLL functions for use with the other ToolKit classes.

# SMFs Use Chunks

A Standard MIDI File is organized into a series of blocks, called *chunks*. All chunks have the same structure. A four-character string identifies the type of a particular chunk. A 32-bit value—most significant byte first—specifies the number of bytes of data in the chunk. The chunk's data bytes follow. This format is similar to the RIFF file format used by

Windows when storing waveform and other multimedia files. However, unlike RIFF files, SMFs are not hierarchical. In a RIFF file, a chunk can contain another chunk, which can contain another chunk, *ad nauseam*. Chunks in an SMF are flat: each chunk follows the previous one, strung together like cars of a train.

A Standard MIDI File uses two types of chunks. A header chunk, whose type is MThd, specifies values that are true across the entire file. For example, the header chunk specifies the number of tracks in the file and the timing resolution used for the event timestamps in the tracks. Not surprisingly, a track chunk holds the data for a track of events. The track chunk uses a chunk type of MTrk. An SMF contains a header chunk followed by one or more track chunks, like this:

**Figure 13-1   SMF chunks**

A file may contain other types of chunks. But only the MThd and MTrk chunk types are currently valid in an SMF. Other chunk types may appear due to features added to future versions of the SMF spec, and to ensure compatibility, these extraneous chunk types must be ignored.

# Variable-Length Values

Each chunk contains the type and size values, occupying eight bytes, followed by a quantity of data. Some values in the data portion of a chunk—for example, MIDI event timestamps—are expressed using *variable-length values*. Encoding these values in a variable-length representation compacts the data by avoiding leading zeros.

A variable-length value contains one to four bytes. In each byte, only the lower seven bits are significant. The upper bit is used as a *continuation* bit. If this bit is set, seven more bits of the variable-length value are contained in the next byte in the data stream. Therefore, values that occupy seven bits fit into a single byte, while an 8-bit value requires two bytes.

At first, this might look like a step in the wrong direction since an 8-bit value requires two bytes. But variable-length encoding is used for data values that are often small but occasionally are large numbers. For example, MIDI event timestamps are often low, since they are delta values. But it's possible that a timestamp might be a high value—for example, as the first note in a track after a number of tacit measures. If all of the timestamps had to be 32 bits to account for the possibility of a large value, the more prevalent small values would waste space, since they would always be padded with leading 0s. Here are a few examples of numbers and their variable-length equivalents:

**Table 13-1   Variable-length Values**

| Hex value | Variable-length value |
|-----------|----------------------|
| 00 | 00 |
| 7F | 7F |
| 80 | 81 00 |
| 90 | 81 10 |
| FFFF | FF FF 03 |
| 100000 | C0 80 00 |
| 0FFFFFFF | FF FF FF 7F |

All of the values in an SMF are stored in Big-Endian format. That is, the most significant byte is first in the stream. For example, the 32-bit value 01234567 would appear in the file as four bytes, 01 23 45 67. But the Intel processors used in PCs are Little-Endian, with the least significant byte first. So, on a PC the proper representation of 01234567 would be 67 45 23 01. This does more than simply confuse the reader. Any 16-, 24-, or 32-bit values that are stored in an SMF must be byte-swapped when read or written using a PC. This means that variable-length values must also be byte-swapped when handling Standard MIDI Files on a PC.

Routines to read and write variable-length values and convert between Little-Endian and Big-Endian formats are included in the MaxMidi DLL. These functions are extensively used in the Standard MIDI File module. While they are closely tied to the buffering scheme used by the ToolKit's file-handling routines, they can be easily adapted to other uses. We'll see these functions later in this chapter.

# Format 0 and Format 1 Files

While the MIDI specification defines three different Standard MIDI File formats, the MaxMidi ToolKit supports only Format 0 and Format 1 files. The unsupported Format 2 type is rarely seen in captivity. Such a file contains a number of independent patterns, similar to the patterns available in a drum machine. If the MaxMidi routines encounter a

Format 2 file, it is handled as if it were a Format 0 type. In this case, only the first pattern is accessible.

A Format 0 file consists of a header, specifying the format type and other parameters, and a single track of data. All of the events in the file are contained in this single track: MIDI events, and Meta events—including starting tempo, time signature, and tempo changes. The starting tempo and time signature should appear at the beginning of the track. If these values are omitted, the tempo and time signature are assumed to be 120 bpm and 4/4 time, respectively.

Format 0 files serve as the lowest common denominator for Standard MIDI Files. Since all of the events in a sequence are lumped into a single track, programs that merely play or record events—and do not need to edit them—often use this format.

**Figure 13-2    A Format 0 SMF**

It's a good idea for more advanced multitrack programs to support Format 0 files, since this format is readable by even the simplest of MIDI file players. When writing a multitrack sequence as a Format 0 file, combine the tracks, sorting events by timestamp and correcting their values to maintain the proper timing relationships, and write them as a single track. For an example of combining tracks, see the `CMaxMidiOut::MergeOut()` function, discussed in chapter 14. While this code is not intended for SMF use, it is easily adapted to the purpose.

In contrast, Format 1 files are designed to contain two or more tracks. By convention, the first track contains the time signature and starting tempo Meta events, along with any tempo changes that occur during the sequence. No playable MIDI events should appear in this track. Each of the other tracks contains MIDI and Meta events corresponding to tracks in the original sequence. Normally, each track holds events directed to a single MIDI channel, although events for more than one channel may appear in a track.

**Figure 13-3    A Format 1 SMF**

Format 1 files are the *lingua franca* of multitrack sequencers. They maintain the organization of the sequence while allowing data to be transferred between dissimilar programs. These files can serve as the fundamental file format of a multitrack sequencer, since they can be read, edited in a multiple-track form, and written back out. However, Format 1 files may not be capable of handling all the features of a more advanced sequencing program. In that case, the program could use a native file format to hold its sequence data and provide SMF support for transferring data to other systems. Such a Standard MIDI File would lose some of the program's features—such as digital audio support—but would allow MIDI events to be processed by other applications.

## The SMF Header Chunk

All Standard MIDI Files begin with a header chunk. This chunk has a type value of MThd and contains three word-sized values. These three words specify the file format, the number of tracks in the file, and the timestamp units. A header chunk looks like this:

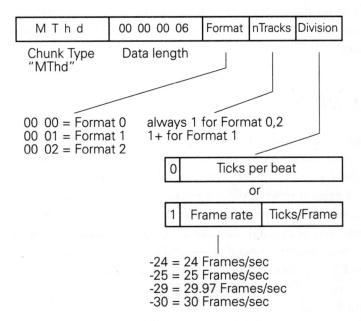

Figure 13-4   The header chunk

The four-byte chunk type, MThd, indicates that this is a header chunk. The size of the data portion of the header is specified by the 32-bit data length value. This is not a variable-length value. A header contains six bytes of data, organized as three 16-bit words, so the data length field is set to 00 00 00 06.

The first two of these data bytes indicate the format of the rest of the file. Valid values are 00 00 for Format 0, 00 01 for Format 1, and 00 02 for Format 2. The SMF routines in the MaxMidi DLLs will read a Format 2 file as a Format 0 file. The number of tracks in the file is specified by the next pair of data bytes in the header. This value will always be 00 01 for Format 0 and Format 2 files, while a Format 1 file can have one or more tracks.

The last two bytes specify the timing resolution used for timestamps in the file. There are two possible interpretations for this word value. If the upper bit is 0, the other 15 bits specify the resolution in ticks per beat. Things are more complicated if the upper bit of the word is set. In this case, the resolution is measured in terms of fractions of a second, using SMPTE frame rates as the timebase. The other 15 bits of the word are split into two fields. The upper field, bits 8 through 14, are encoded as the two's complement of the base frame rate, resulting in a negative number. The lower 8 bits specify the number of ticks that occur in each frame. For example, the frame rate field can be set to −25 and the number of ticks per frame set to 40 by using the E7 28 as the resolution value. Then, timestamps are measured in milliseconds, since 25 frames per second times 40 ticks per frame produces 1,000 ticks per second.

# *Track Chunks*

The actual data for a sequence is stored in one or more track chunks. The format of a track chunk is the same regardless of the format of the Standard MIDI File. A track chunk contains a 4-byte identifier, MTrk, a 32-bit data length, and one or more track events. A track event is either a MIDI event or a Meta event. In both cases the event is preceded by a variable-length timestamp that indicates when the event occurs in time.

MIDI events may be stored in the track using running status. System Exclusive messages include the length of the sysex data—stored as a variable-length value—immediately following the F0 status byte. This length value is not part of the sysex data; it merely indicates the number of bytes that follow. For example, a complete sysex message would appear in a track like this:

```
[timestamp] F0 [length] [sysex bytes following F0]
```

The F0 status byte is part of the sysex message. In a complete message, the trailing F7 is included in the packet of sysex data. But a long sysex message can be broken into multiple blocks, each with a timestamp. This is done by using an F7 byte as a continuation character. A continuation block looks like this:

```
[timestamp] F7 [length] [data bytes]
```

The F7 and the length value are not sent with the other data bytes. Notice that any data can be put into a track using this scheme, even illegal non-MIDI data or Real-Time MIDI events. Breaking up a large sysex message is useful for pacing the data when they are transmitted to a MIDI device, since each continuation block has its own timestamp.

# Meta Events

Meta events are timestamped non-MIDI events. Typical Meta events are tempo, track name, and time signature. Every track contains at least one Meta event—the End of Track event—which must occur as the last event in a track. A Meta event consists of a variable-length timestamp, followed by an FF byte that indicates that this is the start of a Meta event. This is followed by a single-byte type value, ranging from 0 to 127. The size of the data associated with the event is specified next using a variable-length value followed by the actual data. A Meta event has no data if the length value is 0. A prototypical Meta event looks like this:

```
[timestamp] FF [type] [length] [data]
```

There are 15 different Meta events defined in the MIDI specification. Let's look at a few of the more common events. The type value (in hexadecimal) of each event is shown in parenthesis.

A *Text Event* (01) allows freeform text to appear anywhere in a track. Any byte values can be used in the data portion of the event, although ASCII text is most common. The length value specifies the number of bytes in the text data.

A *Track Name* (03) event allows each track to have a unique text name. The track name of the track in a Format 0 file, and the track name of the first track of a Format 1 file is the name of the overall sequence. Like the Text Event, the length value specifies the number of bytes in the name.

A *Lyric* (05) is another type of text event. Typically, each syllable of a lyric is specified using a single Lyric event, with the timestamp of the event corresponding to its place in the song.

A *Marker* (06) is a text event that specifies the section name of a song, such as *Verse* or *Bridge*.

The *End of Track* (2F) event must occur at the end of each track in the file. It contains no data, so the length byte is always 0.

*Set Tempo* (51) specifies the current tempo in microseconds per beat. The 24-bit tempo value occupies three bytes. Set Tempo events should appear only in the first track of a Format 1 SMF. If there are no Set Tempo events in the sequence, the default tempo is 120 bpm.

Most sequences should include at least one *Time Signature* (58) event. The data portion of the event occupies 4 bytes. The first two bytes are the numerator and denominator of the time signature. The denominator is specified as a power of 2. Therefore, 4/4 time would be specified as 04 02, while 6/8 time is 06 03. The third byte indicates the number of MIDI clocks per metronome click. This byte is 18 hex (24 decimal) for a metronome click on every beat. The final byte of the event specifies the number of 32nd notes per 24 MIDI clocks. Normally, there are eight 32nd notes per beat, so this byte would be 08. Any number of Time Signature events may occur in a sequence, but at least one should appear at the beginning of the first track of a Format 1 file, or at the beginning of a Format 0 file. All Time Signature events should be in the first track of a Format 1 file. If the event is missing, the Time Signature is assumed to be 4/4.

A *Key Signature* (59) event specifies the number of sharps or flats in the sequence, and whether the key is major or minor. Two bytes are used. The first byte indicates the number of sharps (if the value is positive) or flats (if the value is negative). The second byte is 0 for a major key or 1 for a minor key.

Other Meta events are: *Copyright Notice* (02); *Instrument Name* (04); *Cue Point* (07); *MIDI Channel Prefix* (20); *SMPTE Offset* (54); and *Sequencer-Specific* (7F). These less-common events are documented in the MIDI specification.

# Reading an SMF in C

The MaxMidi DLL provides a menagerie of functions to open, read, and write Standard MIDI Files. It's time to take a look at how these functions are used to read events from an SMF.

The first step is to open the file using the OpenSMF() function. OpenSMF() will open the file, verify that it is a valid Standard MIDI File, and read the header chunk. The function returns three values. The function's return value is an opaque handle to the opened file. If there was an error opening the file, or the file could not be found, the handle will be NULL. The other two values are returned in parameters passed by the function call. The file format is returned in the integer variable pointed to by the Format parameter. Similarly, the number of tracks in the file is returned in the variable whose address is passed in the nTracks parameter. The file test.mid is opened for reading like this:

```
int NumOfTracks;
HSMF hSmf;
int format;

hSmf = OpenSMF("test.mid", &format, 'r', &NumOfTracks);
```

If the open call is successful, the handle will be nonzero and the format and the NumOfTracks variables will be set to the values found in the file's header chunk. Once the file is open, MIDI events can be read from the track. It is not necessary to read all of the events from one track before accessing a different one; events can be read from any track at any time.

MIDI events are read from the file a block at a time. A block can be as small as a single event, or as large as the entire track. The following example reads 512 events and sends them to an already opened MIDI output.

```
DWORD NumOfEvents;
int wTrack;
LPMIDIEVENT lpMidiBuff;
DWORD dwBuffLen;
DWORD eventCount;

// read the first track
wTrack = 0;

// use a 512 event buffer
wBuffLen = 512L;

// allocate memory for the buffer
lpMidiBuff = (LPMIDIEVENT)GlobalAlloc(GPTR,
                  dwBuffLen * sizeof(MidiEvent));

// read the SMF and send to Midi out
NumOfEvents = ReadSMF(hSmf, wTrack, lpMidiBuff, dwBuffLen);

while((eventCount < NumOfEvents) && (PutMidiOut(hMidiOut,
      (LPMIDIEVENT)(lpMidiBuff + eventCount)) == 0))
          eventCount++;
```

The `ReadSMF()` function reads the specified number of events from the file, storing them in the application's buffer. The `dwBuffLen` parameter indicates the size of the buffer in `MidiEvents`. Any track can be specified by changing the `wTrack` value, where track 0 corresponds to the first track in the file.

An application based on this example can read events from any track in any order and send those events to different MIDI outputs or combine the events into a single track for output to a single output device. It can then continue to read events, sending them to the proper device until there are no more events to read. Notice that this simple example reads events from the first track of the file, regardless of the SMF format. There may not be any playable MIDI events in the first track of a Format 1 file. In this case it may be more interesting to read events from another track in the file.

Meta events can be read from any track at any time. They are skipped when reading MIDI events, since `MidiEvent` structures can hold only MIDI messages. Instead, Meta events are retrieved using another function: `ReadMetaEvent()`. Here's the prototype for the function:

```
DWORD ReadMetaEvent(HSMF hSMF, int wTrack, BYTE MetaEvent, LPSTR
                    *EventValue, DWORD *EventSize);
```

Meta events are not playable MIDI events, so the MaxMidi DLL accesses them as a separate stream. Internally, the SMF reader keeps a table of the file pointers that locate each possible type of Meta event. When the next instance of a particular event is requested via a call to `ReadMetaEvent()`, the reader positions the file pointer to the proper location and returns the event. Future calls requesting the same type of event cause the reader to search for the next instance in the file, starting from the location of the last event. This allows any type of Meta event to be read at any time, as needed by the application. For example, if a program wishes to retrieve all of the lyric events in a track, it can do so without having to read and discard any other events.

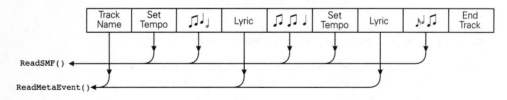

**Figure 13-5  Reading events**

The diagram above shows the two event streams used by the SMF reader. Calls to ReadSMF() will retrieve all of the playable MIDI events, either one at a time or as a block of events. Notice that Set Tempo Meta events are automatically returned as playable events, since the MaxMidi playback engine includes a mechanism for handling time-stamped tempo changes (i.e., MidiEvent.status set to 0, other MidiEvent bytes set to tempo in microseconds per beat). As the ReadSMF() function progresses through the track, it skips over all other Meta events.

The ReadMetaEvent() function, on the other hand, retrieves particular Meta events from the track. The diagram shows the Track Name event and all of the Lyric events being read. Although Set Tempo events are normally retrieved using the ReadSMF() function, they can also be accessed using ReadMetaEvent().

When ReadMetaEvent() locates the requested Meta event in the specified track, it returns a pointer to a buffer containing the event's data as an array of bytes. This pointer is passed back to the caller through the EventValue parameter. The returned pointer will be NULL if the event is not found. The EventSize variable contains the number of bytes in the data block. The size is 0 if the event exists but has no data. The calling application *must* copy the data from the temporary buffer returned by the function into its own memory if it wishes to retain the data. The ReadMetaEvent() function reuses (and reallocates) the buffer each time it is called. Disappointment awaits programs that rely on the existence of the returned buffer across calls. Here is an example code snippet that retrieves the track name (really the sequence name) of the first track.

```
LPSTR lpTName;
LPSTR lpTrackName;
DWORD NSize;
int wTrack;

// look for and read the track name for the first track
wTrack = 0;
if(ReadMetaEvent(hSmf, wTrack, META_NAME, &lpTName, &NSize) != -1)
{
    // allocate a buffer for the track name
    lpTrackName = (LPSTR)GlobalAlloc(GPTR, NSize));

    // copy the name into the new buffer
    lstrcpy(lpTrackName, lpTName);
}
```

Of course, all opened files must be closed when no longer needed. Do this by calling CloseSMF(), specifying the SMF handle assigned by the OpenSMF() call. Once the file is closed, the handle is invalid. It's a good idea to set the closed handle to 0 to prevent inadvertent use; NULL handles are always ignored by the MaxMidi DLLs.

```
CloseSMF(hSMF);
hSMF = 0;                        // safety first!
```

# *Writing an SMF in C*

Writing a Standard MIDI File is similar to reading one. The file must be opened by calling OpenSMF(). In the case of opening a file for writing, the application sets the format parameter to the desired SMF type. Valid types are 0 (for Format 0) and 1 (for Format 1). For example,

```
HSMF hSmf;
int format;
int nTracks;

// select the desired format for the file
format = 0;

hSmf = OpenSMF("test.mid", &format, 'w', &nTracks);
```

The function sets nTracks to 0, the number of tracks in the new file. If the open is successful, a file is created. If the file already exists, it is overwritten; a Standard MIDI File cannot be appended. As in the read case, OpenSMF() returns an opaque handle to the file. Remember, this handle is not related to a Windows file handle. The file can only be accessed through the MaxMidi SMF functions. If the open does not succeed, the returned handle will be NULL.

Tracks are added to the file as they are written, and the header chunk's count of tracks is automatically updated when the file is closed. Events are written to the file by calling WriteSMF(). Whenever WriteSMF() specifies a new track (i.e., the nTrack parameter is different from previous calls), it closes the current track, creates a new one, and increments the count of tracks in the header chunk. Once a new track is created, events cannot be added to earlier tracks, since they are already closed. Therefore, all of the events in a track—both MIDI events and Meta events—must be written before moving to the next track. Tracks are written in ascending order, with track 0 first, track 1 next, etc.

WriteSMF() accepts a block of events to write to a specified track. The function is prototyped like this:

```
DWORD WriteSMF(HSMF hSMF, int wTrack, LPMIDIEVENT lpMidiEventBuffer,
         DWORD dwBufferLen);
```

The function accepts the already opened handle, the track number, a pointer to the buffer containing an array of MidiEvents, and the number of events (not bytes) in the buffer. The function can write an entire track at once, a single event at a time, or any number of events in between. Notice that only playable MIDI events—along with tempo change events, which are automatically converted into Set Tempo Meta events—can be written to a track using WriteSMF(). Here is an example that writes an entire sequence to a track in the already opened SMF. The NumOfEvents variable is already set to the number of events contained in the lpMidiBuff buffer.

```
int NumOfEvents;
LPMIDIEVENT lpMidiBuff;

// write the SMF
WriteSMF(hSmf, wTrack, lpMidiBuff, NumOfEvents);
```

To write Meta events, use the WriteMetaEvent() function. This function accepts a single Meta event and inserts it into the specified track. Writing a Meta event to a new track will close the current track and open a new one, just as in the WriteSMF() case. The MetaEvent value specifies the particular event type. The format of the EventValue buffer is determined by the type of event. For text events, a null-terminated ASCII string is expected. Other events may require an array of binary values. All events in a Standard MIDI File, including Meta events, are timestamped. The timestamp for a new Meta event is specified using the dwTime parameter.

```
UINT WriteMetaEvent(HSMF hSMF, int wTrack, BYTE MetaEvent, LPSTR
           EventValue, DWORD dwTime);
```

An application should never attempt to write Set Tempo and End of Track events using WriteMetaEvent(). These events are automatically inserted as needed by the MaxMidi DLLs. However, the MaxMidi DLL routines do not automatically insert a Time Signature event into the first track. Applications should write this event manually. Likewise, an initial tempo event is not written unless a tempo event exists at the start of a track. Applications can add such an event to a track by calling SetTempo() when recording begins.

The file must be closed once all of the tracks are written. This is done by calling CloseSMF(), just as is done when reading an SMF. Closing the file ensures that all of the data is written to disk, and gives the ToolKit a chance to update the header chunk to reflect the actual number of tracks in the file.

# Other MaxMidi SMF Functions

An SMF's header chunk includes the timing resolution used by the timestamps in the file. The MaxMidi DLL includes two functions to access this value—one to set the resolution when writing an SMF, and one to retrieve the resolution when reading an SMF.

The default resolution for files created using the MaxMidi functions is 480 ticks per beat. The SetSMFResolution() function can be called any time before the file is closed (by calling CloseSMF()) to change the file's resolution. The Standard MIDI File specification includes support for SMPTE-based resolutions. An SMF can be created using SMPTE-based resolution by setting the resolution word to the proper value. SetSMFResolution() returns the resolution value if the call was successful. The function returns 0 if there was an error writing the new resolution. It is prototyped as

```
WORD SetSMFResolution(HSMF hSMF, WORD resolution);
```

GetSMFResolution() returns the resolution—as stored in the file's header chunk— as a word value. Normally, this value will be in ticks per quarter note (or beat). However, if the upper bit is set, the resolution is specified using SMPTE-based time. It is the responsibility of the application to properly handle the resolution format. It can refuse to process the file, convert the event timestamps to ticks per beat (corresponding to the SMPTE resolution), or handle the file and its fractional-second timestamps in some other way. GetSMFResolution() is prototyped as

```
WORD GetSMFResolution(HSMF hSMF);
```

There are occasions in handling Standard MIDI Files when it is useful to be able to read tracks from the beginning without closing and reopening the file. The RewindSMF() function does exactly that. It rewinds all of the tracks so that any subsequent call to ReadSMF() or ReadMetaEvent() returns events starting at the beginning of the file. Rewinding only makes sense when reading an SMF. The function returns TRUE if the rewind was successful. It returns FALSE if the file was originally opened for write.

# The CMaxMidiSMF Class

Now that we have a set of Standard MIDI File functions for reading and writing files, it's time to encapsulate them in a C++ class. Optimally, this class should enhance the building-block nature of the other CMaxMidi classes. Luckily, the CMaxMidiSMF class does exactly that. It allows track objects to be attached to SMF objects. All of the data in the tracks is then written or read using a single call. The best way to see how the class works is to look at some examples.

To open and read a Standard MIDI File, all we need do is to create the SMF object, create and attach the proper number of track objects, and call the CMaxMidiSMF::Load() member function. Here's an example that does the job:

```
CMaxMidiSMF SMF;                // the SMF object, allocated on the heap

// open the new SMF
SMF.Open("test.mid", READ);

// create a list of track objects (so we can delete them later)
int nTracks = SMF.NumTracks();
CMaxMidiTrack** pTrackList = (CMaxMidiTrack**)GlobalAlloc(GPTR,
                               sizeof(CMaxMidiTrack*) * nTracks);

// create and attach the tracks
for(i = 0; i < nTracks; i++)
{
    pTrackList[i] = new CMaxMidiTrack;
    SMF.Attach(pTrackList[i]);
}

// load 'em up
SMF.Load();
```

Here, the file test.mid is opened for reading. The SMF class provides an IsOpen() function that returns TRUE if the file is properly opened. Likewise, the Open() member function returns the state of the file. A more complete example could check the return value and behave accordingly. NumTracks() returns, not surprisingly, the number of tracks in the file. A Format 0 file always has a single track, while Format 1 files have one or more tracks. By checking the format of the file—returned by the GetFormat() member function—the application can interpret the tracks appropriately. For example, knowing the format of a file ensures that the proper format is used when later writing an updated version of the sequence.

This example creates a list of tracks—actually an array of pointers to track objects. Such a list is useful in two instances. Many of the CMaxMidiSMF functions take a pointer to a track to uniquely identify a particular track. Keeping a list of track pointers makes short work of retrieving such pointers. In addition, the application must destroy the track objects when they are no longer needed. While the tracks are destroyed when they are no longer in scope, having this list of pointers gives an application better control over the state of its objects.

The tracks are detached from the SMF when the object is destroyed or closed (by calling SMF.Close()). Of course, the tracks still retain their data after the SMF object is gone. They can be attached to a MIDI output object, ready to play, either before or after being filled with data by the SMF.Load() call.

If the attached tracks are themselves attached to a CMaxMidiSync object before the Load() function is called, the timing resolution will be automatically read from the file and set in the sync object. The resolution is available at any time by calling the SMF.Resolution() function.

Tracks are loaded from the file in the order in which they are attached. Thus, the first track to be attached corresponds to track 0, the second one corresponds to track 1, and so on. Tracks can be attached in any order. There are two forms of the Attach() function. The default form:

```
void CMaxMidiSMF::Attach(CMaxMidiTrack* pTrack);
```

attaches the specified track as the next track in the file. The track can be attached in a particular position using the function's second form:

```
void CMaxMidiSMF::Attach(CMaxMidiTrack* pTrack, int position);
```

where the position parameter specifies the position for the new track. Tracks are numbered sequentially, and the first track starts at 0. This feature is useful for inserting a new track into an existing SMF.

Tracks are uniquely identified to the CMaxMidiSMF object using their instance pointers. For example, a particular track can be detached from the SMF object by calling CMaxMidiSMF::Detach() and specifying the track's address, like this:

```
// detach the first track from the SMF object
// this works because pTrackList is an array of track pointers
SMF.Detach(pTrackList[0]);
```

Meta events are also supported when reading a file using the `CMaxMidiSMF` class. In fact, the `Load()` function reads the Track Name Meta event for each track in the file. The track name is retrieved from the track object using the `CMaxMidiTrack::GetName()` member function. Meta events are read from a particular track by calling the `CMaxMidiSMF::ReadMeta()` function. This function accepts a pointer to the desired track object (which must already be attached), along with the desired type of Meta event, the address of a variable that will hold a pointer to the returned data, and the address of a variable that will be set to the size of the data. Except for requiring a track pointer, this function is identical in operation to the `ReadNextMeta()` DLL function. The function looks like this:

```
DWORD CMaxMidiSMF::ReadMeta(CMaxMidiTrack* pTrack, BYTE type,
                            LPSTR* Value, DWORD* cbSize);
```

Writing a file using the SMF class is even easier than reading one. Here is an example:

```
CMaxMidiSMF wSMF;

// open a smf for writing and output the tracks
if(pTrackList)
{
    SMF.Close();    // just in case it was open for read
    SMF.Open("test.mid", WRITE);

    for(int i = 0; i < nTracks; i++)
            SMF.Attach(pTrackList[i]);

    SMF.Save();

    // gotta do this to make sure the file is completely written
    SMF.Close();
}
```

By default, the `Open()` member function creates the new SMF as a Format 1 file. To create a Format 0 file, use the alternative form of the function. The third parameter sets the format for the file.

```
SMF.Open("test.mid", WRITE, 0);
```

The `CMaxMidiSMF::Save()` function does all the work. It writes the tracks in the order they were attached. If a MIDI input device is attached to one of the attached tracks, and the input device is managed by a sync device, the `Save()` function automatically retrieves the timing resolution from this sync device and sets the file's resolution to this value. Alternatively, the application can set the resolution using the `CMaxMidiSMF::Resolution()` member function.

Writing Meta events is also supported by the `CMaxMidiSMF` class. As each track is saved, the track's name is written to the file as a Track Name event. The application sets the track name for each track by calling the `CMaxMidiTrack::SetName()` function. Additionally, tempo change events in any of the tracks are converted into Set Tempo Meta events by the MaxMidi DLLs.

Other Meta events are written to the file using the `CMaxMidiSMF::WriteMeta()` member function. However, each track is written to the file in its entirety. This precludes writing Meta events in the middle of a track. To write Meta events such as Time Signature, Lyric, or Marker, derive a new SMF class from `CMaxMidiSMF` and implement a modified `Write()` function.

The `CMaxMidiSMF` class provides two other member functions. `GetMode()` returns the mode of the opened file, either `'r'` (for read), or `'w'` (for write). This can be used to keep track of the state of a particular `CMaxMidiSMF` object, since a single object can be used for both reading and writing by closing and reopening the file. When reading a file, `Rewind()` will rewind the file to the beginning.

# Inside the MaxMidi DLL SMF Routines

As a source of entertainment and endless brain-teasers, the inner workings of the MaxMidi DLL SMF functions are hard to beat. This section provides an overview and roadmap of what awaits the adventurous seeker of truth when delving into these SMF routines.

All of the low-level Standard MIDI File functions are located in the smf.c file that is part of the 32-bit MxMidi32 DLL. Almost all of the other ToolKit DLL functions are in the MxMidi16 DLL. For those functions, the 32-bit DLL simply serves as a conduit between a 32-bit application and the desired 16-bit functions. The DLLs work this way because those functions are timing sensitive. Putting them in a 16-bit DLL and thunking to them from a 32-bit DLL solves the timing problems inherent in Windows 95 32-bit processes.

But the SMF functions are not timing sensitive. So, these functions can go into the 32-bit DLL. But why not be consistent and put all of the ToolKit functions in the 16-bit DLL and call them through the thunking mechanism? Two words: memory and speed. Any code located in a fixed 16-bit DLL exists in a limited-memory universe. Such DLLs are loaded into the low memory—the portion below 640K—and there is not much of that memory to go around. So it is important to minimize the amount of memory used by a fixed 16-bit DLL. Since the SMF routines don't *need* to be in the 16-bit portion, it is better to put them in the 32-bit DLL. As a side benefit, disk file access is faster for a 32-bit process, since in Windows 95 the file system is entirely 32-bit.

The organization of the major Standard MIDI File functions is outlined in the following hierarchical diagrams. These functions call other SMF functions, which in turn call other functions, and so on. The diagrams show the organization of these calls to make it easier to understand the source code. Only functions in the SMF source code are shown in the diagrams; calls to the normal Win32 API do not appear in the hierarchies.

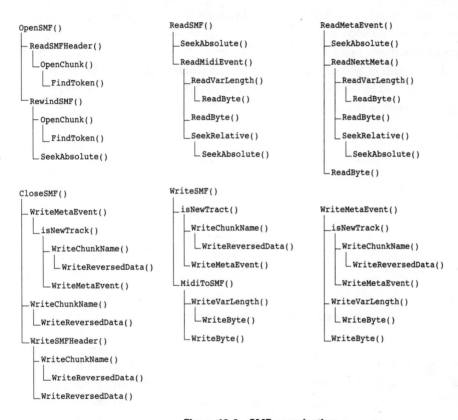

**Figure 13-6   SMF organization**

Calls to a few of the fundamental internal SMF functions appear throughout the source code. For example, `SeekAbsolute()` is called by all of the functions that read from Standard MIDI Files. For speed, data is not read from the SMF disk file a byte at a time. Instead, a buffer is maintained for each of the tracks in the file. Data is read in blocks from disk into these buffers. But the functions that process the track data need to access the data as a continuous stream, a byte at a time. The `SeekAbsolute()` function moves the internal buffer to the desired location if the requested byte is in the buffer, or it repositions the disk drive to the proper place in the file and reads an entire block, including the requested byte, into memory.

The `ReadByte()` function returns the next byte in the buffer. If all of the buffered bytes have been read, it reads another block of data from the disk drive. Handling track data using an intermediate buffer speeds access and allows the other functions to treat the tracks as byte-at-a-time streams.

On the writing side of the SMF functions, bytes are written directly to the disk file. This works without penalty, since disk writes are buffered by the system. Thus, the `WriteByte()` function writes directly to the file.

A daunting number of buffers and arrays are allocated and used by the SMF functions. All of them are created by the `OpenSMF()` function, and destroyed by `CloseSMF()`. The diagram shows how they interrelate.

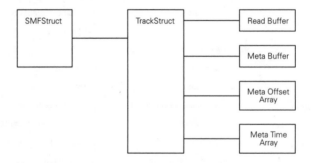

**Figure 13-7    SMF memory allocations**

The first memory allocated when opening an SMF is an `SMFStruct`. This structure holds the state of the file, along with pointers to all of the other memory blocks used by the SMF. The count of tracks in the file determines the size of the next memory allocation. This array of `TrackStructs` provides a set of structures, one per track, that manage the track data. A read buffer is used to store raw track data. This is the buffer that is read by the `ReadByte()` function.

The other memory allocations create buffers that manage Meta events. An initial one-byte buffer is allocated that will be resized later when reading Meta data. This buffer is returned to the calling application containing data from the requested Meta event. Two other arrays help the SMF functions properly locate Meta events in each of the tracks. An offset array holds the file offset for each of 128 possible Meta events. The offset values are updated as new events are found in response to `ReadMetaEvent()` calls. The file offsets are used as starting points when searching for other event instances. When an event is located, the proper timestamp—the elapsed time since the beginning of the track—must be returned with the event. The Meta time array holds the count of ticks since the last event, a count used to calculate the proper timestamp.

# CHAPTER 14

# *Enhancing the Sequencer*

Time slows to a crawl for a six-year-old child as Christmas day approaches. Long lists of acceptable toys sent early to the North Pole give Santa's elves plenty of time for shopping. For each child there is always a favorite toy, that Ultimate Avenger doll or Burp-Me Baby. But when the Big Day arrives, sometimes the Holy Grail of a child's desire turns into a disappointing ho-hum, soon relegated to the toy-heap and replaced with something more interesting.

So it goes with single-track sequencers. As a teaching example, a one-track sequencer is useful. As a sequencer, it leaves something to be desired. Multiple tracks, for example. In this chapter we will remedy that defect and add Standard MIDI File support along the way. When the surgery is through, our example sequencer will be able to record and play multiple tracks with various tempos and timing resolutions, and save and load these sequences as Standard MIDI Files. All that's needed to turn the program into a full-fledged commercial-grade sequencer is a user interface that allows viewing and editing the MIDI events.

## Playing Multiple Tracks

Playing a single track of events is a straightforward process. The events are written to the output device—attached to a sync device—one at a time. The sync device sees to it that each event is output by the MIDI interface at the proper time.

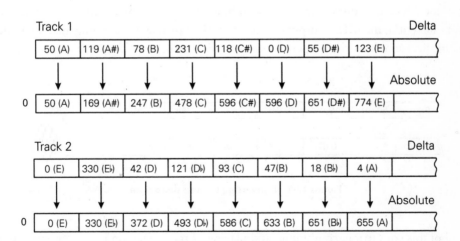

Figure 14-1 Converting delta time to absolute time

Playing multiple tracks through the same MIDI output device is a similar process, but it involves several extra steps. The timestamps of all of the events in each track are converted into absolute time. This means that the time at the start of the track is 0, and the timestamps accumulate through the track by adding up all of the event delta times.

The next step is to make a new, combined track of events from all of the original tracks. This new track is created by iterating through all of the tracks, and sorting and copying events in ascending order. Thus, the composite track contains the combination of the original tracks, with the event timestamps measured in absolute ticks.

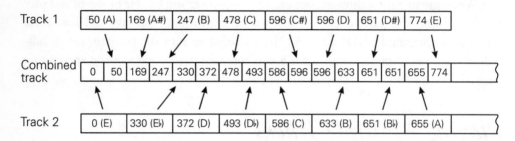

**Figure 14-2   Combining tracks**

The timestamps are converted back to delta times in the final step. The delta time for each event is the difference between the event's absolute time and the time of the preceding event. Once the timestamps in the combined track are converted to delta time, the events are sent to the MIDI output device where they are played, hopefully making beautiful music. Or at least the proper noises, as in the case of our example sequence.

| 0 (E) | 50 (A) | 119 (A#) | 78 (B) | 83 (E♭) | 42 (D) | 106 (C) | 15 (D♭) |
|---|---|---|---|---|---|---|---|

| 93 (C) | 10 (C#) | 0 (D) | 37 (B) | 18 (D#) | 0 (B♭) | 4 (A) | 119 (E) |
|---|---|---|---|---|---|---|---|

**Figure 14-3   Converting back to delta time**

All of this converting, combining, and playing of tracks goes on in the `CMaxMidiOut` class. Rather than attempt to combine all of the tracks at once, the `CMaxMidiOut` routines handle smaller sections of each track at a time. Since the buffer used by the MIDI output device is small (typically 512 events), it makes sense to process the tracks a bit at a time.

The class uses the `Put()` member function to send each event to the device. The return value of `Put()` indicates whether the event was accepted (i.e., if there was room in the buffer). When the output device is full, the `CMaxMidiOut` class remembers the current location in each of the tracks before moving on to other tasks.

When the MIDI output device's buffer falls below 25% full, an `OUTBUFFER_READY` message is sent to the `CMaxMidiOut` object. The message is handled by sending more track data to the output. The tracks are combined starting from exactly where they left off. This method of data pumping ensures that any number of tracks can be played while minimizing the amount of memory needed per track.

Most of the action happens in the `MergeTracks()` function. Applications call the `StartOut()` function to kick off the output process. `StartOut()` calls `MergeOut()`, as does the `OnOutBufferReady()` message handler. `MergeOut()` calls `MergeTracks()` to combine the tracks and then outputs events from the combined track to the MIDI output device. These functions, shown in all their glory in appendix C, make up the core of the multitrack MIDI output playback algorithm.

The `CMaxMidiTrack` class makes available two functions to aid `MergeTracks()` in its quest to combine tracks for playback. `CMaxMidiTrack::GetAbsBuffer()` returns a buffer containing track data, with the timestamps converted to absolute time. The number of events and starting location in the track are specified, so any "slice" of a track can be read using this function. The `CMaxMidiTrack::GetTime()` function returns the delta time for any particular event in a track. Each time `MergeTracks()` is called, it saves the event time of the first event it converts, as returned by `GetTime()`. Later, when converting the combined track's timestamps into delta time, `MergeTracks()` uses the saved timestamp for the first event in the combined track.

There is one potential snag to combining tracks: System Exclusive messages. There is no sensible way to combine or interleave sysex messages. When a sysex message is encountered in one of the tracks, all other tracks must be blocked until the message is finished. Otherwise, non-sysex events, or even sysex data from other tracks—if sysexes coincide in other tracks—will appear in the middle of a message. This is strictly *verboten*. This problem exists regardless of the algorithm used to merge the events.

The `CMaxMidiOut` class handles this issue by blocking all other tracks while a sysex message is being processed. Playable MIDI events may be delayed from their normal timing. Simply put, large System Exclusive messages clog the works. However, indigestion of this sort is inevitable when mixing sysex messages with other timestamped MIDI events. The impact of this problem is minimized by limiting the size of sysex messages in tracks, limiting the number of tracks containing sysexes, and accounting for the duration of sysex messages by adjusting timestamps of other surrounding MIDI events.

# The Multitrack Sequencer Revealed

Adding multitrack support to our single-track sequencer example involves little more than creating the tracks, keeping tabs on them via a list of pointers, and attaching them to the MIDI output device during playback. In the updated sequencer example, called *Ch14Ex1*, one particular track is designated as the record track; it will receive and store events during recording. New tracks are added to the list and named via a dialog box by selecting the Track|New... item in the main menu.

In the *Ch14Ex1* example program, the application, main frame, and MySync classes are identical to those used in the *Ch12Ex2* example, except for slight differences in class names. As usual, most of the modifications are in the document and view classes. In addition, there is a new dialog box class that enables the user to give each track a new name. The modified document class shows how the list of tracks is implemented.

```
// Ch14Ex1Doc.h : interface of the CCh14Ex1Doc class
#include "MaxMidi.h"

class CCh14Ex1Doc : public CDocument
{
protected: // create from serialization only
    CCh14Ex1Doc();
    DECLARE_DYNCREATE(CCh14Ex1Doc)

// Attributes
public:
    CMaxMidiTrack** pTrackList;
    intnTracks;
    CMaxMidiTrack* pRecTrack;

// Operations
public:
    void CreateNewTrack(CString name);

// Overrides
    // ClassWizard generated virtual function overrides
    //{{AFX_VIRTUAL(CCh14Ex1Doc)
    public:
    virtual BOOL OnNewDocument();
    virtual void Serialize(CArchive& ar);
    //}}AFX_VIRTUAL

// Implementation
public:
    virtual ~CCh14Ex1Doc();
```

```cpp
// Generated message map functions
protected:
    //{{AFX_MSG(CCh14Ex1Doc)
    afx_msg void OnNewTrack();
    //}}AFX_MSG
    DECLARE_MESSAGE_MAP()
};


// Ch14Ex1Doc.cpp : implementation of the CCh14Ex1Doc class
#include "stdafx.h"
#include "Ch14Ex1.h"

#include "Ch14Ex1Doc.h"
#include "Ch14Ex1View.h"

#include "NewTrackDialog.h"

// CCh14Ex1Doc
IMPLEMENT_DYNCREATE(CCh14Ex1Doc, CDocument)

BEGIN_MESSAGE_MAP(CCh14Ex1Doc, CDocument)
    //{{AFX_MSG_MAP(CCh14Ex1Doc)
    ON_COMMAND(IDM_NEWTRACK, OnNewTrack)
    //}}AFX_MSG_MAP
END_MESSAGE_MAP()

// CCh14Ex1Doc construction/destruction
CCh14Ex1Doc::CCh14Ex1Doc()
{
    pTrackList = NULL;
    nTracks = 0;
    pRecTrack = NULL;
}


CCh14Ex1Doc::~CCh14Ex1Doc()
{
    int i;

    // free the tracks
    if(pTrackList)
    {
        for(i = 0; i < nTracks; i++)
            delete pTrackList[i];

        GlobalFree(pTrackList);
        pTrackList = NULL;
    }
}
```

```
BOOL CCh14Ex1Doc::OnNewDocument()
{
    if (!CDocument::OnNewDocument())
        return FALSE;

    // close all existing tracks
    if(pTrackList)
    {
        for(int i = 0; i < nTracks; i++)
            delete pTrackList[i];

        GlobalFree(pTrackList);
        pTrackList = NULL;
    }

    // open an initial record track
    nTracks = 0;
    CreateNewTrack("New Track");

    return TRUE;
}


// CCh14Ex1Doc commands
void CCh14Ex1Doc::CreateNewTrack(CString name)
{
    // get the pointer to the view (we only have one since this is SDI)
    POSITION pos = GetFirstViewPosition();
    CCh14Ex1View* pView = (CCh14Ex1View*)GetNextView(pos);

    // create a new track
    nTracks++;
    if(pTrackList)
        pTrackList = (CMaxMidiTrack**)GlobalReAlloc(pTrackList,
            sizeof(CMaxMidiTrack*) * nTracks, GPTR | GMEM_MOVEABLE);
    else
        pTrackList = (CMaxMidiTrack**)GlobalAlloc(GPTR,
            sizeof(CMaxMidiTrack*));

    pTrackList[nTracks - 1] = new CMaxMidiTrack;
    pView->MidiOut.Attach(pTrackList[nTracks - 1]);
    pView->MidiIn.Attach(pTrackList[nTracks - 1]);

    // set the track name
    pTrackList[nTracks - 1]->SetName((LPSTR)(LPCTSTR)name);

    // the new track is the record track
    pRecTrack = pTrackList[nTracks - 1];
}

void CCh14Ex1Doc::OnNewTrack()
{
    NewTrackDialog NTDialog;
```

```
    // display the dialog
    NTDialog.m_Name.Format("New Track");
    if(NTDialog.DoModal() == IDOK)
        CreateNewTrack(NTDialog.m_Name);
}
```

Three variables appear in the class definition. A pointer to an array of track object pointers (pTrackList) maintains a list of tracks. This pointer is NULL, since no tracks exist when the document object is first created. Likewise, a count of tracks (nTracks) is cleared to 0 by the class' constructor, and the pointer to the record track (pRecTrack) is set to NULL.

When a new document is created, either in response to the File|New... menu item or when the document object is first created, any existing tracks are released and a new track is created by calling CreateNewTrack(). This function is similar to *Ch12Ex2's* function of the same name. The main difference is that the pointer to the new track object is stored in the list of tracks. This list—organized as an array of track pointers—grows as the number of tracks grows. The pRecTrack pointer is set to the address of the new track, making it the record track.

A user creates a new track and makes it the latest record track by selecting New... from the Track menu. This menu item has a message ID of IDM_NEWTRACK. Selecting the New... menu item triggers the OnNewTrack() message handler, which in turn creates a modal dialog box that accepts a name for the new track. When the dialog box returns, OnNewTrack() calls CreateNewTrack(), bringing the latest track into the world.

This dialog box class is contained in the NewTrackDialog.h and NewTrackDialog.cpp files in the project. The dialog template includes a single edit control, IDC_NAME, that is initialized to the default "New Track." The user can accept this name or modify it as necessary. Although this example program does not use the track name (i.e., it cannot be viewed or changed once entered), it will be used in later examples when reading and writing Standard MIDI Files. Here's the complete dialog class:

```
// NewTrackDialog.h : header file
class NewTrackDialog : public CDialog
{
// Construction
public:
    NewTrackDialog(CWnd* pParent = NULL); // standard constructor

// Dialog Data
    //{{AFX_DATA(NewTrackDialog)
    enum { IDD = IDD_NEWTRACK };
    CString   m_Name;
```

```
    //}}AFX_DATA


// Overrides
    // ClassWizard generated virtual function overrides
    //{{AFX_VIRTUAL(NewTrackDialog)
    protected:
    virtual void DoDataExchange(CDataExchange* pDX); // DDX/DDV support
    //}}AFX_VIRTUAL

// Implementation
protected:

    // Generated message map functions
    //{{AFX_MSG(NewTrackDialog)
    //}}AFX_MSG
    DECLARE_MESSAGE_MAP()
};


// NewTrackDialog.cpp : implementation file
#include "stdafx.h"
#include "Ch14Ex1.h"
#include "NewTrackDialog.h"

// NewTrackDialog dialog
NewTrackDialog::NewTrackDialog(CWnd* pParent /*=NULL*/)
    : CDialog(NewTrackDialog::IDD, pParent)
{
    //{{AFX_DATA_INIT(NewTrackDialog)
    m_Name = _T("");
    //}}AFX_DATA_INIT
}

void NewTrackDialog::DoDataExchange(CDataExchange* pDX)
{
    CDialog::DoDataExchange(pDX);
    //{{AFX_DATA_MAP(NewTrackDialog)
    DDX_Text(pDX, IDC_TRACKNAME, m_Name);
    //}}AFX_DATA_MAP
}

BEGIN_MESSAGE_MAP(NewTrackDialog, CDialog)
    //{{AFX_MSG_MAP(NewTrackDialog)
    //}}AFX_MSG_MAP
END_MESSAGE_MAP()
```

Only a few modifications are necessary in the view class. All of the MIDI input and output device creation code is identical to the *Ch12Ex2* example program. The rest of the code is similar. Only a few changes are needed to account for the multiple tracks. Here are the affected functions from the Ch14Ex1View.cpp file:

```
void CCh14Ex1View::OnRecordStart()
{
    CCh14Ex1Doc* pDoc = GetDocument();

    // reset the timestamp for the input device since
    // input is always active (for echo while idle)
    MidiIn.Reset();

    // enable record for the selected track
    pDoc->pRecTrack->Flush();
    pDoc->pRecTrack->IsRecording(TRUE);

    // start input
    Sync->IsRecording(TRUE);
    Sync->Start();

    // start merging (non-record) tracks into the output device
    MidiOut.StartOut();
}

void CCh14Ex1View::OnUpdateRecordStart(CCmdUI* pCmdUI)
{
    CCh14Ex1Doc* pDoc = GetDocument();

    BOOL rec = TRUE;

    // don't allow recording if record track does not exist
    if(pDoc->pRecTrack)
        rec = pDoc->pRecTrack->IsRecording();

    pCmdUI->Enable(!rec);
}

void CCh14Ex1View::OnUpdatePlayStart(CCmdUI* pCmdUI)
{
    CCh14Ex1Doc* pDoc = GetDocument();
    BOOL playable = FALSE;
    int i;

    for(i = 0; i < pDoc->nTracks; i++)
        playable |= !pDoc->pTrackList[i]->IsEmpty();

    pCmdUI->Enable(playable && !Sync->IsRunning());
}
```

The OnRecordStop(), OnUpdateRecordStop(), OnPlayStart(), OnPlayStop(), and OnUpdatePlayStop() functions are unchanged from the earlier example. OnRecord-Start() calls the MIDI output device's StartOut() function so that any previously recorded tracks are played while the new track is recorded. OnUpdateRecordStart() checks the record track to make sure it is not already recording before enabling the

Record|Start menu item. Similarly, the `OnUpdatePlayStart()` message handler checks all of the tracks to see if they contain any events. No tracks are playable if they are all empty, so the Play|Start menu item is enabled only when there are events in at least one of the tracks.

To test this example program, build it and run it. Select appropriate MIDI input and output devices. It's not necessary to create a new track; the program did that when it started. Select Record|Start to start recording and record a track of MIDI. Be sure to stop recording by choosing the Record|Stop menu item. The track can then be played by selecting Play|Start.

To add a new track to the sequence, select the New... menu item from the Track menu. A Create New Track dialog box will appear. Type in an appropriate track name or accept the default (but unoriginal) name of "New Track" and click OK to add a new track to the sequence. This new track is the designated record track. Record something into the new track and notice that the notes in the previous track play while the new track is recording. After recording, play both tracks by selecting Play|Start. Repeat this process until exhaustion.

## *Writing a Standard MIDI File*

Now that our sequencer is able to record and play multiple tracks, it's time to add support for Standard MIDI Files. First, let's flesh out the File|Save... menu and allow the user to save a recorded sequence in an SMF. Such files can be read and played by nearly any sequencer or MIDI file player.

The new program has the imaginative name of *Ch14Ex2*. The only changes needed are in the document class, since the program's disk-based document is an SMF. All of the rest of the program is the same as the *Ch14Ex1* example. Here's the code to do the deed:

```
// from Ch14Ex2Doc.cpp
BOOL CCh14Ex2Doc::OnSaveDocument(LPCTSTR lpszPathName)
{
    CMaxMidiSMF wSMF;
    int i;

    // open a smf for writing and output the recorded track
    if(pTrackList)
    {
        wSMF.Open(lpszPathName, WRITE);

        for(i = 0; i < nTracks; i++)
            wSMF.Attach(pTrackList[i]);
```

```
        wSMF.Save();
        wSMF.Close();
    }

    return TRUE;
}

void CCh14Ex2Doc::OnUpdateFileSave(CCmdUI* pCmdUI)
{
    BOOL saveable = FALSE;
    int i;

    for(i = 0; i < nTracks; i++)
        saveable |= !pTrackList[i]->IsEmpty();

    pCmdUI->Enable(saveable);
}

void CCh14Ex2Doc::OnUpdateFileSaveAs(CCmdUI* pCmdUI)
{
    OnUpdateFileSave(pCmdUI);
}
```

Selecting the File|Save... menu item on the application's main menu opens a Save As dialog box. The OnSaveDocument() function is called when the user selects a file and clicks the Save button. OnSaveDocument() opens a Standard MIDI File using the supplied filename, attaches the sequence's tracks, and saves the file. That's all there is to creating an SMF!

The `OnUpdateFileSave()` and `OnUpdateFileSaveAs()` menu item handlers make the program friendlier by disabling the File|Save... and File|Save As... menu items if all of the tracks in the sequence are empty. After all, what's the point of saving an empty sequence?

# Reading a Standard MIDI File

Our example program, which grew from modest beginnings, able only to store MIDI events in a single track, is now able to record any number of tracks and store the resulting sequence in a file that's readable by a wide variety of MIDI applications. But these files cannot be read back in and played. Not yet, anyway. For our last trick, let's add support for loading Standard MIDI Files.

This final example, called *MaxSeq*, can do more than just read and write SMFs. Menu items and dialog boxes that allow selection of nearly all of the features of the MaxMidi ToolKit round out the program. Dialog boxes that set the timing resolution and tempo complement menu items that select the sync mode (internal or MIDI Clock) and the timer period (10 milliseconds or 1 millisecond), and enable or disable MIDI echo. The view window displays a count of beats as the sequencer records or plays.

The changes needed to read a Standard MIDI File are minimal. Everything required is contained in the implementation of the OnOpenDocument() function.

```
BOOL CMaxSeqDoc::OnOpenDocument(LPCTSTR lpszPathName)
{
    int i;

    // get the pointer to the view (we only have one since this is SDI)
    POSITION pos = GetFirstViewPosition();
    CMaxSeqView* pView = (CMaxSeqView*)GetNextView(pos);

    // close any open tracks
    if(pTrackList)
    {
        for(i = 0; i < nTracks; i++)
            if(pTrackList[i])
                delete pTrackList[i];

        GlobalFree(pTrackList);
        pTrackList = NULL;
    }

    // open the new SMF
    SMF.Open(lpszPathName, READ);

    nTracks = SMF.NumTracks();
    pTrackList = (CMaxMidiTrack**)GlobalAlloc(GPTR,
            sizeof(CMaxMidiTrack*) * nTracks);

    for(i = 0; i < nTracks; i++)
    {
        pTrackList[i] = new CMaxMidiTrack;
        SMF.Attach(pTrackList[i]);
        pView->MidiOut.Attach(pTrackList[i]);
    }

    // load 'em up
    SMF.Load();

    return TRUE;
}
```

The OnOpenDocument() handler is called when the user selects a file from the *Open* dialog box that appears in response to the File|Open... menu selection. The function simply closes any open tracks, opens the requested file, attaches the required number of new tracks to the SMF object, and reads all of the track data via the Load() call.

That's all that is needed to implement file reading in our example program. But the other added features are spread throughout all of the files in the program. In addition, several new files are needed to add some features and support new dialog boxes.

To get a better idea of how the program's features are implemented throughout the program, look at the program organization diagram. This picture shows which features are implemented in which of the four main classes: CMaxSeqApp, CMainFrame, CMaxSeqDoc, and CMaxSeqView.

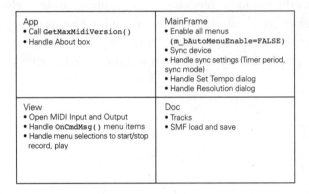

**Figure 14-4   MaxSeq program organization**

For example, the CMainFrame class contains the application's sync device. It also handles all of the sync-related user selections, such as the timer period (settable to either 1 millisecond or 10 milliseconds) and the sync mode (internal or MIDI sync). Two dialogs are managed in this class as well. The Set Tempo dialog appears in response to the Settings|Set Tempo... menu selections, while the Set Resolution dialog is created when Settings|Set Resolution... is selected.

The document class maintains the list of tracks along with the Standard MIDI File class objects used for reading and writing files. The tracks are accessed by the view class by retrieving a pointer to the document class. The view class itself is nearly identical to the *Ch14Ex2* example.

Two view class changes appear in MaxSeq: MIDI thru can be enabled and disabled, and the OnDraw() function displays a count of beats. These two new features force changes in two other program files. One of the files is new: the MyMidiIn class (similar to the

MyMidiIn class used in chapters 10 and 11) adds MIDI echo capability to the CMaxMidiIn class. In addition, the MySync class is modified to handle the ProcessMidiBeat() virtual function. The sync device sends a MIDI_BEAT message once per musical beat. This message triggers the ProcessMidiBeat() function. This modified implementation of ProcessMidiBeat() increments a beat counter and forces the view class to redraw its window, triggering a call to CMaxSeqView::OnDraw().

All of the source code for the *MaxSeq* example program appears in appendix D, so we won't repeat it here. Appendix D contains complete source code for *Maximum MIDI's* two other major examples: *MidiSpy* and *SxLib*. All of these programs—along with all of the other examples in this book—are also included on the accompanying CDROM. Take some time to study these example programs. These applications are useful by themselves, but they are even handier as starting points when writing your own programs. By understanding how these examples work and experimenting with them to see how they tick, you will be better prepared to write your own world-class MIDI applications.

**CHAPTER 15**

# Go Forth and Write

Having explored the example programs and dissected the low-level DLL source code, it's time to leave the nest and fly solo. But before you begin designing and writing your own MIDI programs, let's take stock of what we've seen and done so far.

Starting with the simplest of examples—sending a single MIDI event in a C program—we've progressed through more than a dozen programs. Each new example built on the previous ones, finally ending with a multitrack sequencer capable of reading and writing Standard MIDI Files.

Along the way we've used an extensive set of C++ classes that implement everything needed to add MIDI support to MFC-based applications. These classes cover MIDI input and output, synchronization for recording and playing back MIDI in musical time, tracks to store and manage MIDI events, a Standard MIDI File object that reads and writes tracks using a commonly supported format, and menu objects that handle user selection of input and output devices.

These classes implement a thorough set of tools that make the MIDI part of writing MIDI programs easy and painless. Because they are C++ classes, they are extendable by deriving classes from the originals and adding the desired functions.

# *Use the Source*

Every line of source discussed in the book or appearing in the MaxMidi DLLs and CMaxMidi classes is printed in appendices at the end of the book and is included on the accompanying CDROM. Install the files from the disk. Explore them, edit them, modify and tinker. There is no better way to learn how MIDI works than to stick your head in the code.

Hundreds of hours have gone into developing the ToolKit. The DLLs and C++ classes have a set of features that are designed to support a wide range of different types of MIDI programs and programming styles. But like any set of tools, the fit of tool to task may not be perfect in all cases. Sometimes a bigger wrench or smaller hammer is needed to do the job right. But unlike hand-tools, the ToolKit source is modifiable. Using the ToolKit as a starting place means that most of the work is already done. Only the new features need to be added or existing features changed to adapt the tools.

The source code is useful for at least one other purpose (other than propping up uneven table legs). There are numerous sources of documentation to help in using the ToolKit routines, including this book and two extensive Windows help files. But sometimes all that is not enough for understanding how to use the ToolKit or what it can do. The source serves as the ultimate documentation. Read it. Rely on it.

# Expanding the MIDI Horizon

The example programs provide excellent starting points when developing new MIDI applications. The three main programs, *MidiSpy*, *SxLib*, and *MaxSeq*, are especially useful. Here are a few ideas for additions to these programs that will make them more useful.

*MidiSpy*

- Store the received events in a buffer.
- Add a vertical scroll bar to scroll through previous events.
- Display MIDI Time Code in hours:minutes:seconds:frames format.
- Save received events in a disk file for later review.
- Add filters to get rid of unwanted events.
- Play a short sequence on demand to test connected MIDI instruments.

*SxLib*

- Make a patch editor by adding buttons, edit controls, sliders, etc. to edit settings for a particular MIDI device.
- Allow the user to build a patch editor for any instrument by dragging controls onto a window and connecting them to particular bytes of the device's documented System Exclusive message.
- Display a list of files available for an instrument along with the list of patches in each file.
- Download patches or files by double-clicking on them.
- Playback an SMF on demand to test changes to patches.

*MaxSeq*

- Display and edit track data in event list, piano roll, staff notation, and sysex views.
- Show tracks and settings in a track list.
- Write a pattern-based sequencer.
- Play lists of SMFs as a jukebox.
- Play SMFs by dragging and dropping.
- Combine all three programs into a super-sequencer that supports diagnostic, sysex librarian and patch editor, and sequence record, play, and edit functions.

These are just a few suggestions. Be creative. Adapt the example programs or start from scratch. Better yet, ignore these ideas and come up with your own. Using the ToolKit means you can concentrate on what the program is supposed to do instead of worrying about the MIDI implementation.

# Building An Even Better ToolKit

The ToolKit, including the C++ classes and MaxMidi DLLs, provides enough functionality to write most MIDI applications. But there are more advanced uses that the unmodified ToolKit may not support. Given the ToolKit source code and the information in this book, any features can be added. Here's an incomplete list of possibilities:

- Add support for SMPTE/MTC.
- Recompile everything in Windows NT.
- Port the ToolKit routines and C++ classes to the Macintosh O/S.
- Add event filtering on input and output.
- Echo received MIDI events to particular outputs at interrupt time.
- Allow applications to access the internal buffers in real time for modifying events during playback.
- Add support for non-MIDI events to synchronize animations or other application processes to sequence playback.
- Add an automatic MIDI metronome.
- Write an MFC-based DLL that calls MaxMidi and plays SMFs or does other MIDI functions.
- Call functions in the new DLL from other programs.
- Use this playback DLL to add SMF support to Microsoft Excel or Word (using WordBasic) to make office work less tedious.
- Adapt the DLLs to other languages, such as Visual Basic or Delphi.

By adding any or all of these features you can learn about the inner workings of the ToolKit, Windows, and MIDI. Your programming skills will skyrocket, the opposite sex will find you irresistible, and you may even increase your hat size. Anything is possible.

With all these tools and information at your disposal, writing MIDI applications in Windows is now easy and (dare we say it?) even fun. It's time to sit down at the computer and start working on the MIDI app you've always wanted to write. Get going!

# APPENDIX A

*The MIDI ToolKit APIs*

# MaxMidi Function Reference

## MIDI Output Functions

*GetNumOutDevices*
```
    UINT GetNumOutDevices(void);
```
This function returns the number of MIDI output devices installed in the system. It returns the same value as the MMSYSTEM API function midiOutGetNumDevs(). It is provided as a convenience by MaxMidi so that applications need not include the WINMM library when linking.

*GetMidiOutDescription*
```
    BOOL GetMidiOutDescription(WORD wDeviceID, LPSTR lpzDesc);
```
This function gets the text string description for the MIDI output device designated by wDeviceID.

**Parameters**      WORD wDevice ID
Specifies the device to be opened. The device ID value ranges from 0 to one less than the number of installed devices.

LPSTR lpzDesc
Specifies the long pointer to the string that will be filled with the description of the device. The description will be null terminated. The destination buffer must be at least MAXPNAMELEN bytes long.

**Return Value**      If there is no device by the requested ID, the function returns FALSE. Otherwise, it returns TRUE and sets the string lpzDesc to the device description.

*OpenMidiOut*
```
    HMOUT OpenMidiOut(HWND hWnd, WORD wDeviceID, HSYNC hSync,
                  DWORD dwFlags);
```
This function opens the specified device for MIDI output. Multiple MIDI output devices can be opened simultaneously, with or without synchronization. A handle to the structure is returned when the open is successful. This value is passed to all other MIDI output functions when specifying the MIDI output device. Zero is returned if the open request fails.

To open a device with playback synchronization, pass a handle to a previously opened sync device in hSync. Playback synchronization will then be handled by the specified sync device. To open the device as a simple output device without synchronization, pass 0 in place of hSync.

The dwFlags parameter further specifies the characteristics of the opened device. System Exclusive (sysex) messages may be optionally merged into the outgoing data stream by specifying ENABLE_SYSEX. If enabled, sysex data is handled as any other message, except that the status byte is always 0xF0 and data is passed in the data1 byte in the MidiEvent structure. The data2 byte is ignored. Additionally, the sysex and EOX status messages must be passed in the data1 byte of a MidiEvent structure. Therefore, a System Exclusive message occupies one MidiEvent structure per byte, including the leading sysex and terminating EOX status bytes.

If System Exclusive messages will not be sent by the application, DISABLE_SYSEX may be specified. This will minimize the memory requirements for the MIDI output device.

Internally, MaxMidi uses two user-specified buffers to handle MIDI output. The MIDI output queue is specified by the QUEUE_xxx flags. The MIDI output queue *must* be specified when opening the device. MIDI data is placed in this queue by calls to PutMidiOut(). MaxMidi takes messages that are in the queue and sends them out— immediately, if no sync device is specified, or when the sync device determines that it is time to send the message.

The second queue is used by MaxMidi to manage System Exclusive data. Since Microsoft Multimedia Windows handles System Exclusive messages separately from other ("short") messages, MaxMidi internally uses small queues to send sysex messages to the Windows driver. These queues are not visible to the application, but the size and number of queues must be specified when opening the device.

Finally, this output may be specified to be a sync output by setting SYNC_OUTPUT. A sync output automatically generates MIDI Start, Stop, Continue, and Timing Clock messages, depending on the settings of the hSync device. If no sync device is specified, this flag is ignored.

The hWnd window will receive MOM_CLOSE when the MIDI output device has been closed. OUTBUFFER_READY is sent when MIDI output is being performed during synchronization and the MIDI queue has fallen below 25% of its capacity, or when the output device is ready to accept more sysex data (while sending a System Exclusive message when not using sync). This allows the application to send more output data, if available, when the output device is ready.

**Parameters**   HWND hWnd

Specifies the handle to the application window that is to receive any messages from this device.

`WORD   wDeviceID`

Specifies the desired device to open. This value ranges from 0 to one less than the number of available devices.

`HSYNC hSync`

Specifies the handle to the previously opened sync device that will handle synchronization for this output. If no sync is to be used with this output, set hSync to 0.

`DWORD dwFlags`

Specifies flags that are used to affect the operation of this device and can be combined using the OR operator.

`ENABLE_SYSEX`

If this flag is specified, System Exclusive messages are merged into the normal MIDI stream that is sent to the device.

`DISABLE_SYSEX`

If this flag is specified, System Exclusive messages are ignored. This setting is the default.

`SYNC_OUTPUT`

If this flag is specified, this output serves as a sync output for MIDI messages for the hSync sync device. It is ignored if hSync is NULL or the sync mode has been set to `S_MIDI`. More than one output may be specified as a sync output.

*MIDI Queue and Sysex Queue Sizes*

| QUEUE_64 | SXBUF_64 | 64 messages |
|---|---|---|
| QUEUE_128 | SXBUF_128 | 128 messages |
| QUEUE_256 | SXBUF_256 | 256 messages |
| QUEUE_512 | SXBUF_512 | 512 messages |
| QUEUE_1K | SXBUF_1K | 1,024 messages |
| QUEUE_2K | SXBUF_2K | 2,048 messages |
| QUEUE_4K | SXBUF_4K | 4,096 messages |
| QUEUE_8K | SXBUF_8K | 8,192 messages |
| QUEUE_16K | SXBUF_16K | 16,384 messages |
| QUEUE_32K | SXBUF_32K | 32,768 messages |

Each message occupies 8 bytes of global memory. The number of sysex buffers of size `SXBUF_xxx` is ORed with the `dwFlags` parameter. The number may range from 0 to 255 buffers.

Typically, a moderate number of small buffers should be specified instead of one large buffer.

MIDIOUT_DEFAULT

This value specifies default settings that are appropriate for most applications. These settings are:

QUEUE_512 | SXBUF_512 | ENABLE_SYSEX | 32

**Return Value**    Returns the handle to the MIDI output if successful, or 0 if there was an error opening the device.

## CloseMidiOut

WORD ***CloseMidiOut***(HMOUT hMidiOut);

This function closes the MIDI output device. This function must be called before terminating the Windows application that opened the device. Call ResetMidiOut() for the device before closing it.

**Parameters**    HMOUT hMidiOut

Specifies the pointer to the previously opened MIDI output device.

**Return Value**    Returns 0 on success, nonzero on failure.

## PutMidiOut

WORD ***PutMidiOut***(HMOUT hMidiOut, LPMIDIEVENT lpMidiEvent);

This function sends the MIDI event, pointed to by lpMidiEvent, to the MIDI output specified by hMidiOut. If there is room, the message is placed in an internal queue. Otherwise, no action is taken and the function returns (WORD)-1. If no sync device was specified when the MIDI output device was opened, the message is output as soon as the Windows driver is ready to accept it. If synchronization is being performed, then the message is sent at the time corresponding to the timestamp associated with the message.

During synchronized record or playback, a message may be echoed to a MIDI output immediately by setting the MidiEvent.time parameter to –1 (0xFFFFFFFF). System Exclusive messages will be filtered and not echoed using this method since this immediate output mode is unbuffered.

**Parameters**    HMOUT hMidiOut

Specifies the handle to the previously opened MIDI output device.

LPMIDIEVENT lpMidiEvent

Specifies the pointer to the outgoing MidiEvent structure that contains the message and timestamp.

**Return Value**     Returns 0 if the message was accepted or filtered, −1 if the queue is full.

*ResetMidiOut*

> WORD ***ResetMidiOut***(HMOUT hMidiOut);

This function terminates MIDI output, sends Note Off messages for any notes that are still on, and flushes any pending sysex data from the output device. *Note:* when some Windows MIDI device drivers are reset, they send Note Off messages for all notes on all channels. This may take two seconds or more to complete. This function should be called before calling CloseMidiOut().

**Parameters**     HMOUT hMidiOut

> Specifies the handle to the previously opened MIDI output device.

**Return Value**     Returns 0 on success, nonzero on failure.

*FlushMidiOut*

> void ***FlushMidiOut***(HMOUT hMidiOut);

This function flushes any data that may be in the output buffer of this device.

**Parameters**     HMOUT hMidiOut

> Specifies the handle to the previously opened MIDI output device.

**Return Value**     None.

# MIDI Input Functions

*GetNumInDevices*

> UINT ***GetNumInDevices***(void);

This function returns the number of MIDI input devices installed on the system. It returns the same value as the MMSYSTEM API function midiInGetNumDevs(). It is provided as a convenience by MaxMidi so that applications need not include the WINMM library when linking.

*GetMidiInDescription*

> BOOL ***GetMidiInDescription***(WORD wDeviceID, LPSTR lpzDesc);

This function gets the text string description for the MIDI input device designated by wDeviceID.

**Parameters**     WORD wDevice ID

> Specifies the device to be retrieved. The device ID value ranges from 0 to one less than the number of installed devices.

```
LPSTR lpzDesc
```
Specifies the long pointer to the string that will be filled with the null terminated description of the device. The destination buffer must be at least `MAXPNAMELEN` bytes long.

**Return Value**    If there is no device corresponding to the requested ID, the function returns FALSE. Otherwise, it returns TRUE and sets the string `lpzDesc` to the device description.

## *OpenMidiIn*

```
HMIN OpenMidiIn(HWND hWnd, WORD wDeviceID, HSYNC hSync, DWORD
                dwFlags);
```

This function opens the specified device for MIDI input. Multiple MIDI input devices can be opened simultaneously, with or without synchronization. A handle to the opened device is returned if successful. This value is passed to all other MIDI input functions when specifying the device. Zero is returned if the open request fails.

To open a device with playback synchronization, pass a handle to a previously opened sync device in `hSync`. Record timestamping will then be handled by the specified sync device. To open the device as a simple input device without timestamping, pass a 0 in place of `hSync`. The `MidiEvent.time` parameter is in ticks if sync is enabled, and in milliseconds (since MIDI input was started) if not.

The `dwFlags` parameter further specifies the characteristics of the opened device. System Exclusive messages may optionally be merged into the incoming data stream by specifying `ENABLE_SYSEX`. If enabled, sysex data are handled as any other message, except that the status byte is always 0xF0 and data is passed in the `data1` byte in the `MidiEvent` structure. The `data2` byte is zero. Additionally, the sysex and EOX status messages are passed in the `data1` byte of a `MidiEvent` structure. Therefore, a System Exclusive message occupies one `MidiEvent` structure per byte, including the leading sysex and terminating EOX status bytes.

If System Exclusive messages will not be received by the application, `DISABLE_SYSEX` may be specified. This will minimize the memory requirements for the MIDI input device. Any inadvertently received sysex messages will be ignored.

Internally, MaxMidi uses two user-specified buffers to handle MIDI input. The MIDI input queue is specified by the `QUEUE_xxx` flags. The MIDI input queue *must* be specified when opening the device. MIDI data is placed in this queue as it is received. Data is retrieved from the queue by calls to `GetMidiIn()`.

The second queue is used by MaxMidi to manage System Exclusive data. Since Microsoft Multimedia Windows handles System Exclusive messages separately from other "short" messages, MaxMidi internally uses small queues to receive sysex messages from the Windows driver. These queues are not visible to the application, but the size and number of queues must be specified when opening the device.

This device may be specified to be a sync input by setting the SYNC_INPUT flag. Only one input may act as the sync input at a time. The sync input receives MIDI sync messages and passes them to the specified sync device, if the corresponding sync is enabled in the sync device. If no sync device is specified, this flag is ignored.

The hWnd window may receive two different messages from the MIDI input device. MIDI_DATA is sent when the device receives a MIDI message. The application may then retrieve the message by calling GetMidiIn(). MIM_CLOSE is sent when the MIDI input device has been closed.

**Parameters**       HWND hWnd

Specifies the handle to the application window that is to receive any messages from this device.

WORD wDeviceID

Specifies the desired device to open. This value ranges from 0 to one less than the number of available devices.

HSYNC hSync

Specifies the handle to the previously opened sync device that will handle synchronization for this input. If no sync is to be used with this input, set hSync to 0.

DWORD   dwFlags

Specifies flags that are used to affect the operation of this device that can be combined using the OR operator.

ENABLE_SYSEX

If this flag is specified, System Exclusive messages are merged into the normal MIDI stream that is sent to the application.

DISABLE_SYSEX

If this flag is specified, System Exclusive messages are filtered. This setting is the default.

SYNC_INPUT

This input serves as the sync input for MIDI sync for the previously opened sync device hSync. It is ignored if hSync is NULL or the sync mode has been set to S_INT.

*MIDI Queue and Sysex Queue Sizes*

| | | |
|---|---|---|
| QUEUE_64 | SXBUF_64 | 64 messages |
| QUEUE_128 | SXBUF_128 | 128 messages |
| QUEUE_256 | SXBUF_256 | 256 messages |
| QUEUE_512 | SXBUF_512 | 512 messages |
| QUEUE_1K | SXBUF_1K | 1,024 messages |
| QUEUE_2K | SXBUF_2K | 2,048 messages |
| QUEUE_4K | SXBUF_4K | 4,096 messages |
| QUEUE_8K | SXBUF_8K | 8,192 messages |
| QUEUE_16K | SXBUF_16K | 16,384 messages |
| QUEUE_32K | SXBUF_32K | 32,768 messages |

Each message occupies 8 bytes of global memory. The number of sysex buffers of size `SXBUF_xxx` is ORed with the `dwFlags` parameter. The number may range from 0 to 255 buffers. Typically, a moderate number of small buffers should be specified instead of one large buffer.

> **MIDIIN_DEFAULT**
>
> This value specifies default settings that are appropriate for most applications. These settings are:
>
> `QUEUE_512 | SXBUF_512 | ENABLE_SYSEX | 32`

**Return Value**     Returns the handle to the MIDI input device if successful, or 0 if there was an error opening the device.

*CloseMidiIn*

> WORD ***CloseMidiIn***(HMIN hMidiIn);

This function closes the MIDI input device. This function must be called before terminating the Windows application that opened the device. Call `StopMidiIn()` for the device before closing it.

**Parameters**     HMIN hMidiIn

> Specifies the handle to the previously opened MIDI input device that is to be closed.

**Return Value**     Returns 0 on success, nonzero on failure.

*GetMidiIn*

```
LPMIDIEVENT GetMidiIn(HMIN hMidiIn);
```

This function returns a pointer to an incoming MIDI event. If no messages are waiting, the function returns NULL.

**Parameters**       HMIN hMidiIn

Specifies the pointer to the desired previously opened MIDI input device structure.

**Return Value**    Returns a pointer to the `MidiEvent` structure containing the MIDI event if one is ready, or NULL if no messages are waiting.

*StartMidiIn*

```
WORD StartMidiIn(HMIN hMidiIn);
```

Starts MIDI input from the specified device. MIDI input must be started before MIDI messages or synchronization messages will be received.

**Parameters**       HMIN hMidiIn

Specifies the handle to the previously opened MIDI input device.

**Return Value**    Returns 0 on success, nonzero on failure.

*StopMidiIn*

```
WORD StopMidiIn(HMIN hMidiIn);
```

Stops MIDI input from the specified device.

**Parameters**       HMIN hMidiIn

Specifies the handle to the previously opened MIDI input device.

**Return Value**    Returns 0 on success, nonzero on failure.

## *Synchronization Functions*

*OpenSync*

```
HSYNC OpenSync(HSYNC hSync, HWND hWnd, WORD mode, WORD
              timerPeriod);
```

This function opens a sync device for timing MIDI input and/or MIDI output. A handle to the opened device is returned if successful. This value is passed to all other functions when specifying this sync device. Zero is returned if the open request fails. To open a sync device for the first time, pass 0 in the `hSync` parameter. To reopen a device with new settings, pass the already open `hSync` handle.

Timing is specified by setting the *resolution* (in ticks/beat) and *tempo* (in microseconds per beat.) The sync device then generates ticks at the specified rate. These ticks are used to timestamp incoming messages and play outgoing messages with the proper timing.

Message timestamping on input is performed by setting the `MidiEvent.time` value to the count of ticks since the last message. This same count of *delta* ticks is used during playback to compare with the generated tick count in the sync device. When the two tick counts are the same, the message is sent to the MIDI output device that is connected to this sync device.

The sync mode specifies the type of synchronization that will be performed. Two possible types of sync are available; *internal* and *MIDI sync*. The sync mode may be changed by reopening the sync device, and specifying the new mode.

When synchronizing to MIDI sync, MIDI input must be started by calling `StartMidiIn()` for the MIDI input device that will be providing sync messages. After stopping sync, stop MIDI input to prevent incorrectly timestamped messages from being added to the incoming MIDI buffer.

A synchronous Windows MMSYSTEM timer is used to provide a timebase for internal and MIDI sync modes. The timer period, in milliseconds (mS), may be specified when opening or reopening the device. The period must be 1 mS or greater. Faster (lower) values provide better timing accuracy (i.e., messages are sent closer to the exact time that they are expected) at a significant cost of system resources. With timer periods approaching 1 mS, Windows application response may be unacceptably slow. In this case, a more conservative timer period would be 10 mS.

Note that this timing accuracy is not related to the timing resolution. Resolution (in ticks/beat) specifies the number of ticks that elapse between each musical beat of time. Higher resolutions provide finer granularity in event timing, since there are more divisions between each beat. MaxMidi supports resolutions from 1 to 960 ticks per beat. It is recommended that the resolution be set to a multiple of 24, since there are 24 MIDI clocks per beat using MIDI sync. Odd resolutions may make synchronization difficult and prevent sequences from being played correctly on other timing systems. The default resolution is 480 bpm.

Tempo is specified in microseconds per beat, allowing fractional tempo settings. To convert from tempo in bpm to microseconds per beat, divide bpm into 60,000,000. MaxMidi supports tempos from 10 bpm to 250 bpm at all resolutions. The default tempo is 120 bpm.

The `hWnd` window receives two messages from the sync device. `MIDI_BEAT` is sent on every musical beat. The application can use this message to update a beats per measures display. `SYNC_DONE` is sent during playback when the sync device has no more data to send to any output device. Applications normally use this message to stop playback.

To change sync settings without closing the sync device first, reopen the device, passing the already opened hSync pointer and hWnd parameters. Set the mode and timer period to the desired settings. If USE_CURRENT is passed as the value for either mode or timer period, that setting will not be changed when the sync device is reopened. Thus, the application need not maintain a copy of these settings to reopen the device.

You may experience difficulty when embedding large sysex bulk dump messages in sequences intended for playback with synchronization. Such sequences play correctly with tempo settings equal to or slower than the original tempo. Playing back with tempos greater than the original tempo may cause events following the sysex message to be played back with incorrect timing. This is not a flaw of the ToolKit, but is the nature of System Exclusive messages. These messages take a fixed amount of time to send; increasing the tempo will not cause sysex dumps to be sent more quickly.

**Parameters**    HSYNC hSync

Specifies the handle to an already opened sync device when reopening the device to change settings. Pass 0 if not reopening an existing sync device.

HWND hWnd

Specifies the handle to the application window that is to receive messages from this device.

WORD mode

Specifies the sync mode. Possible modes are:

| | |
|---|---|
| S_INT | Internal sync |
| S_MIDI | MIDI sync |

WORD timerPeriod

Specifies the timer period in milliseconds. The timer period may be 1 milliseconds or greater. Note that if the requested timer period is unavailable from the Windows system, the fastest available period is used.

**Return Value**    Returns the handle to the sync device if successful, or 0 if there was an error opening the device.

*CloseSync*

```
WORD CloseSync(HSYNC hSync);
```

This function closes the sync device. This function must be called before terminating the Windows application that opened the device.

| Parameters | HSYNC hSync |
|---|---|

Specifies the handle to the previously opened sync device.

**Return Value**     Returns 0 on success, nonzero on failure.

## StartSync

> void **StartSync**(HSYNC hSync);

This function starts synchronization for the previously opened sync device. The count of ticks is cleared. When synchronizing to MIDI sync, MIDI input must be started by calling StartMidiIn() for the MIDI input device that will be providing sync messages.

**Parameters**     HSYNC hSync

Specifies the handle to the previously opened sync device.

**Return Value**     None.

## ReStartSync

> void **ReStartSync**(HSYNC hSync);

This function resumes sync from the last location after StopSync() was called. When synchronizing to MIDI sync, MIDI input must be started by calling StartMidiIn() for the MIDI input device that serves as the sync source.

**Parameters**     HSYNC hSync

Specifies the handle to the previously opened sync device.

**Return Value**     None.

## StopSync

> void **StopSync**(HSYNC hSync);

This function stops playback or record synchronization, if started. MIDI output buffers are flushed. StopSync() should be called before closing the sync device. Use PauseSync() and ReStartSync() instead of StopSync()/RestartSync() to pause playback.

**Parameters**     HSYNC hSync

Specifies the handle to the previously opened sync device.

**Return Value**     None.

## PauseSync

> void **PauseSync**(HSYNC hSync, BOOL reset);

This function stops playback or record synchronization, if started. Synchronization may be resumed by calling ReStartSync(). If reset is TRUE, then any currently playing notes will be stopped. If reset is FALSE, then any currently playing notes will continue to sound. In either case, MIDI output buffers are not flushed. Pausing sync with reset set to FALSE is intended for short, temporary pauses.

**Parameters**   `HSYNC hSync`

Specifies the handle to the previously opened sync device.

`BOOL reset`

If TRUE, Note Offs will be sent for any currently playing notes. If FALSE, no Note Offs will be sent.

**Return Value**   None.

*SetTempo*

        WORD ***SetTempo***(HSYNC hSync, DWORD uSPerBeat);

This function sets the tempo for synchronization in microseconds per beat. Tempo in microseconds/beat is calculated by dividing 60,000,000 by the tempo in beats per minute. This function supports fractional tempos, and may be called at any time by the application. If the tempo is not set by the application, a default tempo of 120 bpm is used.

In addition, tempo changes may be embedded in the outgoing MIDI data stream. To do this, set the `status` byte to 0. The 24-bit tempo is then stored in the three event bytes, starting at `MidiEvent.data1` with `MidiEvent.data1` as the MSB.

If tempo is changed by the application while sync is running during record, a change tempo event is inserted in the incoming data stream of the MIDI input device that is assigned as the sync input. Thus, application-created tempo changes are embedded into the sequence data.

**Parameters**   `HSYNC hSync`

Specifies the handle to the previously opened sync device.

`DWORD uSPerBeat`

Specifies the tempo in microseconds per beat. Tempos between 10 bpm (6,000,000) and 250 bpm (240,000) may be specified. Values outside of that range may produce unpredictable results. Attempts to change tempo to 0 microseconds per beat will be ignored.

**Return Value**   Returns 0 if successful, or `TIMERR_NOCANDO` if the `uSPerBeat` parameter is 0.

*GetTempo*

        DWORD ***GetTempo***(HSYNC hSync);

This function returns the current tempo in microseconds per beat.

**Parameters**      HSYNC hSync

                  Specifies the handle to the previously opened sync device.

**Return Value**    Returns the 24-bit tempo in microseconds per beat.

*SetResolution*
```
      void SetResolution(HSYNC hSync, WORD resolution);
```
This function sets the resolution of timing in ticks per beat. SetResolution() should be called after the sync device is opened and before playback or record is started. Higher values of resolution provide greater timing accuracy, though greater accuracy may not be realized above 240 tpb with a 1 millisecond timerPeriod at 250 bpm. The resolution may be set from 1 to 960 ticks per beat. It is recommended that the resolution be set to a multiple of 24, since there are 24 MIDI Clocks per beat. Odd resolutions may make synchronization too difficult and prevent sequences from being played correctly on other timing systems. The default resolution is 480 tpb.

Each musical beat at a given tempo is divided into resolution time slices, or ticks. Each MIDI event is timestamped with the duration in ticks since the last MIDI event. Ticks are generated more rapidly at higher tempos and more slowly at lower tempos. It is the generation of ticks that controls the synchronization of events by the MaxMidi DLL.

**Parameters**      HSYNC hSync

                  Specifies the handle to the previously opened sync device.

                  WORD resolution

                  Specifies the resolution in ticks per beat. The resolution may range from 1 to 960 tpb, and should normally be a multiple of 24.

**Return Value**    None.

*GetResolution*
```
      WORD GetResolution(HSYNC hSync);
```
This function returns the current resolution in ticks per beat.

**Parameters**      HSYNC hSync

                  Specifies the handle to the previously opened sync device.

**Return Value**    Returns the resolution in ticks per beat.

# Standard MIDI File Functions

*OpenSMF*

```
HSMF OpenSMF(LPSTR filename, int *Format, const char mode, int
             *nTracks);
```

This function opens a Standard MIDI File for either reading or writing. A handle to the SMF is returned. This value is passed to all other Standard MIDI File functions. This handle is *not* a Windows file handle and can only be used with the SMF functions documented here.

The `filename` parameter points to a partial or full path and filename, including extension, for the SMF to be opened. Format 0 (single track) and Format 1 (multiple track) files may be opened. When opened for reading, a Format 2 (multiple track, multiple sequence) file will be opened as a Format 0 file, and only the first sequence in the file will be available.

A Standard MIDI File is created by opening a file for writing. The file format should be determined by the number of tracks that are to be written to the file. The address of a variable that contains the desired format is passed in `Format`. If only one track will be written then the file should be a Format 0 file, while multiple track sequences should be written as a Format 1 Standard MIDI File. Format 2 files cannot be created by MaxMidi.

The number of tracks in the file is returned in `nTracks`. If the file is opened for write, `nTracks` is set to 0.

Once opened for writing, entire tracks are written to the file starting with the first track (track 0). All of the data for a particular track must be written before moving to the next track. Tempo changes, track 0 data, and certain other Meta events must be written to the first track. Other track data and Meta events may be written to any number of other tracks.

When opened for reading, each track in a Standard MIDI File can be accessed independently. That is, part or all of any track can be read without affecting any other track. Any remaining track data in partially read tracks is still available for subsequent reads. This means that very large Standard MIDI Files (larger than the available memory) can be read and processed, since the entire file does not need to be read to access any particular track.

The format of the file is returned at the address pointed to by `Format`. Track data is read or written on a block basis. Each block consists of a specified number of `MidiEvents` in an array. Meta events, other than tempo changes, are written or read using `WriteMetaEvent()` and `ReadMetaEvent()` respectively. Tempo change events are handled automatically by MaxMidi.

When writing to a file, timing resolution, in ticks per beat, must be set using the `SetSMFResolution()` function. Likewise, when reading a file, the timing resolution may be retrieved using `GetSMFResolution()`.

All tracks of a Standard MIDI File that is opened for reading may be rewound to the beginning by calling `RewindSMF()`. A file opened for writing cannot be rewound. When operations on a Standard MIDI File are complete, `CloseSMF()` will close the file and update file header chunks as necessary.

**Parameters**   `LPSTR filename`

Specifies a long pointer to an ASCIIZ filename, with extension, for the desired Standard MIDI File. The filename may optionally include a partial or full path.

`int *Format`

Specifies the address to an integer containing the format of this Standard MIDI File. The format variable should be set to the desired format (either 0 or 1) before opening a file for writing. Conversely, if opened for reading, this variable is set to the format of the read Standard MIDI File.

`const char mode`

Specifies the mode for the Standard MIDI File. Possible mode settings are 'r' to open the file for reading, or 'w' to open the file for writing. Opening an existing file for writing will cause it to be truncated to zero length and subsequently overwritten.

`int *nTracks`

Specifies the address to an integer that will be set to the number of tracks in the file, if opened for reading, or to 0 if opened for writing.

**Return Value**   Returns the handle to the SMF. Note that this is not a Windows file handle.

*CloseSMF*

        void ***CloseSMF***(HSMF hSMF);

This function closes the Standard MIDI File corresponding to the `hSMF` handle. If the file was opened for writing, the SMF header chunk is updated with the number of tracks and timing resolution.

**Parameters**   `HSMF hSMF`

Specifies the handle to the SMF that is to be closed.

**Return Value**   None.

*RewindSMF*

**BOOL RewindSMF**(HSMF hSMF);

This function rewinds all tracks of the Standard MIDI File corresponding to the hSMF handle to their beginning. If the file had been opened for writing, then this function returns an error and no rewind occurs.

**Parameters**    HSMF hSMF

Specifies the handle to the previously opened Standard MIDI File.

**Return Value**    Returns TRUE on success, or FALSE on error.


*ReadSMF*

DWORD **ReadSMF**(HSMF hSMF, int wTrack, LPMIDIEVENT
                    lpMidiEventBuffer, DWORD dwBufferLen);

This function reads a block of events from the previously opened Standard MIDI File. Up to dwBufferLen events from the specified track are read into the buffer pointed to by lpMidiEventBuffer.

Tracks range from 0 to one less than the number of available tracks returned from OpenSMF(). Attempts to read illegal tracks are ignored. There are no restrictions on the order of reading tracks. Once a track has been completely read, any subsequent reads of that track will result in an end of track return value.

ReadSMF() returns the number of events read, or 0 on end of track or error.

**Parameters**    HSMF hSMF

Specifies the handle to the previously opened Standard MIDI File.

int wTrack

Specifies the track number to read. Track numbers range from 0 to one less than the number of available tracks returned from OpenSMF().

LPMIDIEVENT lpMidiEventBuffer

Specifies a pointer to a buffer that will receive MidiEvents from the Standard MIDI File. The buffer must be at least dwBufferLen MidiEvents long (i.e., dwBufferLen * sizeof(MidiEvent)).

DWORD dwBufferLen

Specifies the length of the destination buffer in MidiEvents.

**Return Value**    Returns the number of events read, or 0 for end of track or error.


*WriteSMF*

DWORD **WriteSMF**(HSMF hSMF, int wTrack, LPMIDIEVENT
                    lpMidiEventBuffer, DWORD dwBufferLen);

This function writes a block of events to the previously opened Standard MIDI File. Up to `dwBufferLen` events from the specified track may be written to the file from the buffer pointed to by `lpMidiEventBuffer`.

Tracks range from 0 to one less than the number of tracks to be written. All of the events for a specific track must be written before attempting to write another track, since specifying a new track number will permanently close the current track. Tracks must be written in numerical order, beginning with 0, without skipping any track numbers.

`dwBufferLen` must specify the actual number of valid events in the buffer to be written. `WriteSMF()` returns the number of events written, or 0 on error.

**Parameters**     `HSMF hSMF`

Specifies the handle to the previously opened Standard MIDI File.

`int wTrack`

Specifies the track number to write. Track numbers range from 0 to one less than the number of tracks to be written.

`LPMIDIEVENT lpMidiEventBuffer`

Specifies a pointer to a buffer that contains `MidiEvents` to be written to the Standard MIDI File. The buffer must be at least `dwBufferLen` `MidiEvents` long (i.e., `dwBufferLen * sizeof(MidiEvent)`).

`DWORD dwBufferLen`

Specifies the number of valid `MidiEvents` in the source buffer that will be written to the file.

**Return Value**     Returns the number of events written, or 0 on error.

## GetSMFResolution

    `UINT GetSMFResolution(HSMF hSMF);`

This function returns the resolution in ticks per beat for the previously opened (for reading) Standard MIDI File. If the SMF was opened for writing, this function returns 0.

**Parameters**     `HSMF hSMF`

Specifies the handle to the previously opened Standard MIDI File.

**Return Value**     Returns the resolution in ticks per beat, or 0 on error.

## SetSMFResolution

    `UINT SetSMFResolution(HSMF hSMF, UINT resolution);`

This function sets the resolution in ticks per beat for the previously opened (for writing) Standard MIDI File. If the SMF was opened for reading, this function returns 0, otherwise it return the resolution.

**Parameters**      HSMF hSMF

Specifies the handle to the previously opened Standard MIDI File.

UINT resolution

Specifies the resolution in ticks per beat for the Standard MIDI File.

**Return Value**    Returns the resolution in ticks per beat, or zero on error.

*ReadMetaEvent*

```
DWORD ReadMetaEvent(HSMF hSMF, int wTrack, BYTE MetaEvent,
                    LPSTR *EventValue, DWORD *EventSize);
```

This function reads the next Meta event of the specified type, if present, from the specified track of the previously opened (for reading) Standard MIDI File. If the Meta event is found, EventValue points to a buffer that contains the data for the Meta event. This string should be copied into an application buffer before calling ReadMetaEvent() again, or the previous value will be lost. The function returns the event timestamp, or -1 on error.

**Parameters**    HSMF hSMF

Specifies the handle to the previously opened (for reading) Standard MIDI File.

int wTrack

Specifies the track number from which to read the Meta event. Track numbers range from 0 to one less than the number of tracks returned by OpenSMF().

BYTE MetaEvent

Specifies the Meta event to retrieve from the Standard MIDI File. Possible Meta events are:

> META_SEQUENCE_NUMBER
> Specifies a sequence number for this file.
>
> META_TEXT
> Specifies a general purpose text string.
>
> META_COPYRIGHT
> Specifies a copyright notice for the Standard MIDI File sequence.
>
> META_NAME
> Specifies the name of the sequence if read from track zero, or the name of the track if read from other tracks.

`META_INST_NAME`

Specifies the name of the instrumentation used for the specified track.

`META_LYRIC`

Specifies a lyric to be sung.

`META_MARKER`

Specifies a marker name for a particular point in a sequence.

`META_CUE_POINT`

Specifies a description of cue events in a sequence.

`META_CHAN_PREFIX`

Specifies the MIDI channel that will apply to all events to follow, until the next MIDI event that specifies a channel.

`META_SMPTE_OFFSET`

Specifies the SMPTE offset for the specified track.

`META_TIME_SIG`

Specifies the current Time Signature.

`META_KEY_SIG`

Specifies the current Key Signature.

`LPSTR *EventValue`

Specifies the pointer to a string that contains the value of the found Meta event, or NULL if not found.

`DWORD *EventSize`

Specifies the pointer to a `DWORD` that contains the size in bytes of the Meta event value string, or 0 if not found.

**Return Value**    Returns the timestamp of the event, or -1 if not found or error.

*WriteMetaEvent*

```
UINT WriteMetaEvent(HSMF hSMF, int wTrack, BYTE MetaEvent,
                    LPSTR EventValue, DWORD dwTime);
```

This function writes a Meta event to the desired track of the previously opened Standard MIDI File. All of the Meta events for a specific track must be written before attempting to write another track, since specifing a new track number will permanently close the current track. Meta events are normally interleaved with MIDI events that are written using `WriteSMF()`. Tracks must be written in numerical order, beginning with 0, without skipping any track numbers.

**Parameters**    `HSMF hSMF`

Specifies the handle to the previously opened (for writing) Standard MIDI File.

`int wTrack`

Specifies the track number to which to write the Meta event. Track numbers range from 0 to one less than the number of tracks.

`BYTE MetaEvent`

Specifies the Meta event to write to the Standard MIDI File. Possible Meta events are:

`META_SEQUENCE_NUMBER`

Specifies a sequence number for this file. If used, this event must precede any playable MIDI events.

`META_TEXT`

Specifies a general purpose text string.

`META_COPYRIGHT`

Specifies a copyright notice for the Standard MIDI File sequence. This should be the first Meta event of track 0, preceding any playable MIDI events.

`META_NAME`

Specifies the name of the sequence if written to track 0, or the name of the track if written to other tracks.

`META_INST_NAME`

Specifies the name of the instrumentation used for the specified track.

`META_LYRIC`

Specifies a lyric or syllable to be sung.

`META_MARKER`

Specifies a marker name for a particular point in a sequence.

`META_CUE_POINT`

Specifies a description of cue events in a sequence.

**META_CHAN_PREFIX**

Specifies the MIDI channel that will apply to all events to follow, until the next MIDI event that specifies a channel.

**META_SMPTE_OFFSET**

Specifies the SMPTE offset for the specified track.

**META_TIME_SIG**

Specifies the current Time Signature.

**META_KEY_SIG**

Specifies the current Key Signature.

**META_EOT**

Specifies an end of track. Used internally by MaxMidi. An application must not attempt to write this Meta event.

**META_TEMPO**

Specifies a tempo change event. Used internally by MaxMidi. An application must not attempt to write this Meta event.

**LPSTR *EventValue**

Specifies the pointer to a string that contains the value of the Meta event.

**DWORD dwTime**

Specifies the timestamp for the Meta event.

**Return Value**    Returns 0 if the requested Meta event is written, nonzero on error.

## System Functions

### GetMaxMidiVersion

```
WORD GetMaxMidiVersion(void);
```

This function returns the version number of the MaxMidi DLL and adjusts Windows parameters for MaxMidi to operate properly. This function *must* be called by the application before any windows are created and before any calls are made to MaxMidi, or the application performance may be unpredictable. Normally, this function should be called in the WinMain() function of the application before the Windows message loop is started.

**Parameters**    None.

**Return Value**    Returns the version number of the MaxMidi DLL as a word with the major version in the high byte and the minor version in the low byte.

# Error Codes

These error codes are returned by MaxMidi, as documented for the functions that return handles or other return codes.

- `MXMIDIERR_NOERROR`   No error occurred.
- `MXMIDIERR_BADDEVICEID`   Specified device does not exist.
- `MXMIDIERR_NOMEM`   Out of memory.
- `MXMIDIERR_BADHANDLE`   An illegal handle was passed.
- `MXMIDIERR_BADTEMPO`   An illegal tempo was passed.
- `MMSYSERR_ALLOCATED`   The specified device is already in use.
- `MXMIDIERR_MAXERR`   Error codes are guaranteed to be less than this value. Valid handles will always be greater than `MXMIDIERR_MAXERR`.

# MaxMidi Messages

## MIDI_BEAT

This message is sent to the `hWnd` window passed to the `OpenSync()` function on each musical beat during synchronization.

**Parameters**    `WPARAM wParam`

Always 0.

`LPARAMlParam`

Specifies the handle to the originating sync device.

## MIM_CLOSE

This message is sent to the `hWnd` window passed to the `OpenMidiIn()` function when the MIDI input device is closed as a result of calling `CloseMidiIn()`.

**Parameters**    `WPARAM wParam`

Always 0.

`LPARAM lParam`

Always 0.

## MIDI_DATA

This message is sent to the hWnd window passed to the OpenMidiIn() function when MIDI messages are received by the MIDI input device. The application can then retrieve the data by calling GetMidiIn().

**Parameters**    WPARAM wParam

Always 0.

LPARAM lParam

Specifies the handle to the originating MIDI input device.

## MOM_CLOSE

This message is sent to the hWnd window passed to the OpenMidiOut() function when the MIDI output device is closed as a result of calling CloseMidiOut().

**Parameters**    WPARAM wParam

Always 0.

LPARAM lParam

Always 0.

## OUTBUFFER_READY

This message is sent to the hWnd window passed to the OpenMidiOut() function when the MIDI output device is ready to accept more data. Normally, an application sends data to the MIDI output device until PutMidiOut() returns −1 to indicate that the buffer is full or until the application runs out of messages. OUTBUFFER_READY signals the application that the device can accept more data.

There are two conditions under which the output device will post an OUTBUFFER_READY. When using sync with an output device, this message is posted when the output buffer falls below 25% full. Otherwise, when no synchronization is used, the message is posted, while sending a System Exclusive message, when the device is ready to accept more sysex data. Sending non-sysex MIDI events without synchronization will never generate an OUTBUFFER_READY message, since such events are sent synchronously during the PutMidiOut() function call.

**Parameters**    WPARAM wParam

Always 0.

LPARAM lParam

Specifies the handle to the originating MIDI output device.

## SYNC_DONE

This message is sent to the hWnd window passed to the OpenSync() function. It is sent during playback when the sync device has no more data to send to any output device. Applications normally use this message to stop playback.

**Parameters**     WPARAM wParam

Always 0.

LPARAM lParam

Specifies the handle to the originating Sync device.

# MaxMidi Structures

## MidiEvent

The MidiEvent structure holds a complete MIDI event. An LPMIDIEVENT is a long pointer to the event.

```
struct MidiEvent {
        DWORD   time;
        BYTE            status;
        BYTE            data1;
        BYTE            data2;
        BYTE            data3;
};
```

**Fields**     DWORD time

Specifies event time in ticks since the last event. If MIDI input is received without opening sync first, this field contains the time in milliseconds since MIDI input was started.

BYTE status

Specifies the status byte for the message. All messages must have a status byte, even if running status is to be used. Running status compression is handled by the Windows MIDI driver. If status is 0, this event is a tempo change and the three data bytes make a 24-bit tempo.

BYTE data1

Specifies a status-specific optional first data byte.

BYTE data2

Specifies a status-specific optional second data byte.

BYTE data3

Specifies a third byte of tempo data for tempo change events. It is ignored for all non-tempo change events.

# MaxMidi C++ Classes

## MIDI Output Class — CMaxMidiOut

This class encapsulates the behavior of a MIDI output device. It is derived from `CWnd` and provides all of the functionality necessary to open, send MIDI data, and close a device. Informational member functions provide device status and device description values.

To use this class, use one of the constructor members to create an instance of the class, or create a derived class and implement the virtual callback function, `ProcessOutBuffer-Ready()`.

The default implementation of `ProcessOutBufferReady()` does nothing. However, if one or more tracks are attached and the `StartOut()` function has been called, tracks will be automatically merged in response to this message. In this case it is neither necessary nor desirable for an application to send data using the `Put()` function unless the data is for immediate output. If `ProcessOutBufferReady()` is overridden in a derived class, this function will be called whenever the `OUTBUFFER_READY` message is received. Your implementation may perform further processing in response to this message. In either case, any attached tracks will continue to be merged and sent to the MIDI output.

If no tracks are attached to the output device, an application sends data to the device using the `Put()` member function until it runs out of messages to send, or until `Put()` returns FALSE (to indicate that the buffer is full). In the latter case, `ProcessOutBuffer-Ready()` is called when the buffer falls below 25% full (when using synchronization) or when the output device is ready to accept more sysex data (when sending a System Exclusive message). More data can then be sent to the device.

Tracks are attached by calling the `Attach()` member function. See the `CMaxMidiTrack` class for more information.

Your derived class can be viewed and modified using ClassWizard if you implement the *AFX* message map and virtual function macros in your source. To do this, add the following to the bottom of your derived class' class declaration:

```
public:
// Overrides
    // ClassWizard generated virtual function overrides
```

```
        //{{AFX_VIRTUAL(MyMaxMidiOut)
        virtual void ProcessOutBufferReady(void);
        //}}AFX_VIRTUAL

protected:
        //{{AFX_MSG(MyMaxMidiOut)
        //}}AFX_MSG
        DECLARE_MESSAGE_MAP()
```

Change `MyMaxMidiOut` to your derived class' name. Then, add this to your class' implementation .cpp file:

```
BEGIN_MESSAGE_MAP(MyMaxMidiOut, CMaxMidiOut)
        //{{AFX_MSG_MAP(MyMaxMidiOut)
        //}}AFX_MSG_MAP
END_MESSAGE_MAP()
```

Again, change `MyMaxMidiOut` to the name of your derived class. Finally, add the new class to ClassWizard by selecting Add Class…|From a file… .

### *CMaxMidiOut::CMaxMidiOut() Constructor*

> **CMaxMidiOut**();
>
> **CMaxMidiOut**(HWND hParentWnd, WORD wDeviceID = 0);
>
> **CMaxMidiOut**(HWND hParentWnd, WORD wDeviceID, CMaxMidiSync*
>        pSync,= 0, DWORD dwFlags = MIDIOUT_DEFAULT);

**Parameters**    HWND hParentWnd

Specifies the window handle of the parent window for the hidden window that will handle device messages.

WORD wDeviceID

Specifies the desired device to open. This value ranges from 0 to one less than the number of available devices.

CMaxMidiSync* pSync

Specifies a pointer to a sync device that will handle synchronization for this device. If no sync is to be used with this input set `pSync` to NULL.

DWORD dwFlags

Specifies flags that are used to affect the operation of this device. These flags are the same as the ones defined for the `Open()` member function.

The default constructor creates the device object, but does not open a device or attach a parent window to the device object. The parent window and, optionally, a sync device can be attached later by calling the `Attach()` member function, and the device can be opened using the `Open()` member function.

By specifying the parent window and device ID the constructor will create a hidden window that will handle the output device and the device will be opened. This constructor is normally called using the `new` operator.

The final constructor allows the device to be opened and all of its characteristics to be specified in a single call. Note that if this constructor is used, the sync device must be constructed in advance and cannot be attached later without closing the device and re-opening it. This constructor is normally called using the `new` operator.

## CMaxMidiOut::~CMaxMidiOut() Destructor

```
~CMaxMidiOut();
```

The destructor is called automatically when the object is destroyed. It closes the device, if it is still open, and detaches any attached tracks.

## CMaxMidiOut::Attach()

```
void Attach(CMaxMidiTrack* pTrack);
```

**Parameters**    HWND hParentWnd

Specifies the window handle of the parent window for the hidden window that will handle device messages.

CMaxMidiSync* pSync

Specifies a pointer to a sync device that will handle synchronization for this device.

CMaxMidiTrack* pTrack

Specifies a pointer to a track that is to be attached to this device for merged output.

This overloaded member function can be used to attach a track, parent window or sync device to the MIDI output device.

A parent window must be attached to the device before the `Open()` member function is called. This can be done using one of the constructors that specifies `hParentWnd` as a parameter, or by using the `Attach()` member function.

If this output device is to be opened using synchronization, a pointer to a `CMaxMidiSync` sync object must be attached, either using `Attach()` or using the proper constructor. If no sync device is attached, MIDI output will be performed without synchronization.

Any number of `CMaxMidiTrack` track objects can be attached. By attaching a sync device, starting synchronization, and calling the `StartOut()` member function, all of the attached tracks will be merged during playback and output to a single MIDI output. Note that System Exclusive messages in a track may block data from other tracks until the sysex message is complete. This is because sysex messages cannot be interleaved with other MIDI messages; they must be sent as a single, uninterrupted block of data.

### CMaxMidiOut::Close()

```
void Close(void);
```

This member function will close the hardware device, without destroying the CMaxMidiOut object. Use this member function to close a device in order to reopen it with different settings. It is not necessary to call this function before destroying the object. Note that any tracks that are attached will remain attached when the device is closed.

### CMaxMidiOut::Detach()

```
void Detach(CMaxMidiSync* pSync);
void Detach(CMaxMidiTrack* pTrack);
```

Detaches the specified object, if attached, from the output object. The detached object is not affected.

**Parameters**     CMaxMidiSync* pSync

Specifies a pointer to a sync device that is to be detached.

CMaxMidiTrack* pTrack

Specifies a pointer to a track that is to be detached.

### CMaxMidiOut::Flush()

```
void Flush(void);
```

Flushes any data that may be in the output buffer queue of this device.

### CMaxMidiOut::GetDescription()

```
LPSTR GetDescription(void);
```

This member function returns a pointer to an ASCIIZ string description for this device. This string is valid once a particular device has been selected, either by specifying wDeviceID in the constructor or calling the Open() member function.

### CMaxMidiOut::GetNumDevices()

```
int GetNumDevices(void);
```

This member function returns the number of MIDI output devices that are installed on the system. The return value for this function is valid at all times, even if no device is currently open or attached to this object.

### CMaxMidiOut::GetSync()

```
CMaxMidiSync* GetSync(void);
```

This function returns a pointer to the attached sync object, or NULL if no sync object is attached.

### CMaxMidiOut::IsOpen()

```
BOOL IsOpen(void);
```

This function returns TRUE if a MIDI output device is currently attached and open.

### CMaxMidiOut::MergeOut()

```
void MergeOut(void);
```

Processes tracks during playback and outputs merged events to the output device. This function is used internally by the class and should not be called by applications. Doing so may cause interruptions or skipped events in the output stream.

### CMaxMidiOut::MergeTracks()

```
void MergeTracks(void);
```

This function iterates through all of the attached tracks and merges them, a block at a time, into a single track. This function is used internally by the class and should not be called by applications. Doing so may cause interruptions or skipped events in the output stream.

### CMaxMidiOut::Open()

```
BOOL Open(WORD wDeviceID = 0, DWORD dwFlags =
MIDIOUT_DEFAULT);
```

This member function opens the specified device using the specified settings. It returns TRUE if the open was successful, or FALSE if the device could not be opened. To open the Midi Mapper, if present, set wDeviceID to MIDI_MAPPER. Multiple MIDI output devices can be opened simultaneously, with or without synchronization.

To open a device with playback synchronization, attach a sync device using the Attach() member function. Playback of events will then proceed, based on the timestamp of each event as interpreted by the sync device.

The dwFlags parameter further specifies the characteristics of the opened device. System Exclusive messages may be optionally merged into the outgoing data stream by specifying ENABLE_SYSEX. If enabled, sysex data is handled as any other message, except that the status byte is always 0xF0 and data is passed in the data1 byte in the MidiEvent structure. The data2 byte is 0. Additionally, the sysex and EOX status messages are passed in the data1 byte of a MidiEvent structure. Therefore, a System Exclusive message occupies one `MidiEvent` structure per byte, including the leading sysex and terminating EOX status bytes.

If System Exclusive messages will not be sent by the application, `DISABLE_SYSEX` may be specified. This will minimize the memory requirements for the MIDI output device. Any inadvertently sent sysex messages will be ignored.

Internally, MaxMidi uses two user-specified buffers to handle MIDI output. The MIDI output queue is specified by the `QUEUE_xxx` flags. The MIDI output queue *must* be specified when opening the device. MIDI data is placed in this queue by calls to the member function `Put()`. The MaxMidi DLL retrieves queued messages and sends them out immediately if no sync device is specified, or when the sync device determines it is time to send them.

The second queue is used by MaxMidi to manage System Exclusive data. Since Microsoft Multimedia Windows handles System Exclusive messages separately from other ("short") messages, MaxMidi internally uses small queues to send sysex messages to the Windows device driver. These queues are not visible to the application, but the size and number of queues must be specified when opening the device.

This device may be specified to be a sync output by setting the `SYNC_OUTPUT` flag. A sync output automatically generates MIDI Start, Stop, Continue, and MIDI Clock messages, depending on the settings of the attached sync device. If no sync device is attached, this flag is ignored.

**Parameters**      WORD wDeviceID

Specifies the desired device to open. This value ranges from 0 to one less than the number of available devices.

DWORD dwFlags

Specifies flags that are used to affect the operation of this device that can be combined using the OR operator.

ENABLE_SYSEX

If this flag is specified, System Exclusive messages are merged into the normal MIDI stream that is sent to the Windows device driver. This setting is the default.

DISABLE_SYSEX

If this flag is specified, System Exclusive messages are filtered.

SYNC_OUTPUT

If this flag is specified, this output serves as a sync output for MIDI sync messages from the attached sync device. It is ignored if no sync device is attached or the sync mode has been set to S_MIDI. More than one output device can be specified as a sync output.

*MIDI Queue and Sysex Queue Sizes*

| | | |
|---|---|---|
| QUEUE_64 | SXBUF_64 | 64 messages |
| QUEUE_128 | SXBUF_128 | 128 messages |
| QUEUE_256 | SXBUF_256 | 256 messages |
| QUEUE_512 | SXBUF_512 | 512 messages |
| QUEUE_1K | SXBUF_1K | 1,024 messages |
| QUEUE_2K | SXBUF_2K | 2,048 messages |
| QUEUE_4K | SXBUF_4K | 4,096 messages |
| QUEUE_8K | SXBUF_8K | 8,192 messages |
| QUEUE_16K | SXBUF_16K | 16,384 messages |
| QUEUE_32K | SXBUF_32K | 32,768 messages |

Each message occupies 8 bytes of global memory. The number of sysex buffers of size SXBUF_xxx is ORed with the dwFlags parameter. The number may range from 0 to 255 buffers. Typically, a moderate number of small buffers should be specified instead of one large buffer.

**MIDIOUT_DEFAULT**

This value specifies default settings that are appropriate for most applications. These settings are:

QUEUE_512 | SXBUF_512 | ENABLE_SYSEX | 32

*CMaxMidiOut::Put()*

```
BOOL Put(LPMIDIEVENT lpEvent);
```

This member function sends the MIDI event pointed to by lpEvent to the device. If there is room, the message is placed in an internal queue and the function returns TRUE; otherwise, no action is taken and the function returns FALSE.

If no sync device is attached, the message is output as soon as the Windows driver for this output is ready to accept it. If synchronization is active, the message is sent according to the timestamp associated with the message.

During synchronized record or playback, a message may be echoed to a MIDI output immediately by setting the MidiEvent.time parameter to -1L (0xFFFFFFFF). System Exclusive messages will be filtered and not echoed using this method since this immediate output mode is unbuffered.

A `MidiEvent` is an eight-byte structure that specifies a single, complete MIDI message. The structure is defined as follows:

```
struct {
    DWORD   time;
    BYTE            status;
    BYTE            data1;
    BYTE            data2;
    BYTE            data3;
} MidiEvent;
```

**Fields**

DWORD time

Specifies event time in ticks since the last event. If MIDI is received without attaching a sync device this field contains the time in milliseconds since `Start()` was called.

BYTE status

Specifies the status byte for the message. All received messages will contain a valid status byte.

BYTE data1

Specifies a status-specific optional first data byte.

BYTE data2

Specifies a status-specific optional second data byte.

BYTE data3

Specifies a third byte of tempo data for tempo change events. It will always be 0 for received MIDI messages.

## CMaxMidiOut::Reset()

```
void Reset(void);
```

This member function terminates MIDI output, sends Note Off messages for notes that are still sounding, and flushes pending sysex data from the device. Note that some Windows MIDI drivers, when reset, send Note Off messages for all notes on all channels; this may take quite some time.

## CMaxMidiOut::StartOut()

```
void StartOut(void);
```

This function causes all attached tracks to be merged into a single stream for output. Once the merging process has been started it will continue until the attached sync device is stopped or all of the tracks have played. Events are merged by converting their timestamps to absolute time (time in ticks since the beginning of the track) and sorting the events in ascending order into an output buffer. The timestamps in the output buffer are converted back into delta time (time since the last event) and sent to the MIDI output device.

### CMaxMidiOut::ProcessOutBufferReady() Virtual Member Function

```
virtual void ProcessOutBufferReady(void);
```

Your application may derive a class from CMaxMidiOut and override this virtual callback function to perform processing in addition to the default implementation. It is called whenever the output device is ready to receive more data during synchronization.

If one or more tracks are attached and the StartOut() function has been called, tracks will continue to be automatically merged in response to this message. In this case it is neither necessary nor desirable for an application to send data using the Put() function unless the data is for immediate output.

Otherwise, an application sends data to the device using the Put() member function until it runs out of messages to send, or until Put() returns FALSE (to indicate that the buffer is full). In the latter case, ProcessOutBufferReady() is called when the buffer falls below 25% full. More data can then be sent to the device.

## MIDI Input Class – CMaxMidiIn

This class encapsulates the behavior of a MIDI input device. It is derived from CWnd and provides all of the functionality necessary to open, receive MIDI data, and close a device. Informational member functions provide device status and device description values.

To use this class, use one of the constructor members to create an instance of the class, or create a derived class and implement the virtual callback function, ProcessMidiData().

The default implementation of ProcessMidiData() does not modify or change the received events in any way. If a track is attached and the Start() function has been called, all received data will be inserted into the track. If no receive track is used, the virtual function should be overridden in a derived class to have access to the received events.

A track is attached by calling the Attach() member function. The attached track will receive and store MIDI events if input is started and the track is set to record. See the CMaxMidiTrack class for more information.

Your implementation of ProcessMidiData() is called whenever the input device receives MIDI data. The MIDI event that was received is passed as a parameter to the function. If a track is attached and set to record, it will receive and store the event if `ProcessMidiData( )` returns TRUE. Otherwise, the event will be ignored. Any changes to the event made by `ProcessMidiData( )` will appear in the stored data.

```
void MyMaxMidiIn::ProcessMidiData(LPMIDIEVENT lpEvent)
{
    // process the data as needed
}
```

Your derived class can be viewed and modified using ClassWizard if you implement the *AFX* message map and virtual function macros in your source. To do this, add the following to the bottom of your derived class' class declaration:

```
public:
// Overrides
    // ClassWizard generated virtual function overrides
    //{{AFX_VIRTUAL(MyMaxMidiIn)
    virtual void ProcessMidiData(LPMIDIEVENT lpEvent);
    //}}AFX_VIRTUAL

protected:
    //{{AFX_MSG(MyMaxMidiIn)
    //}}AFX_MSG
    DECLARE_MESSAGE_MAP()
```

Change `MyMaxMidiIn` to your derived class' name. Then, add this to your class' implementation .cpp file:

```
BEGIN_MESSAGE_MAP(MyMaxMidiIn, CMaxMidiIn)
    //{{AFX_MSG_MAP(MyMaxMidiIn)
    //}}AFX_MSG_MAP
END_MESSAGE_MAP()
```

Again, change `MyMaxMidiIn` to the name of your derived class. Finally, add the new class to ClassWizard by selecting Add Class…|From a file… .

*CMaxMidiIn::CMaxMidiIn() Constructor*

```
CMaxMidiIn();
CMaxMidiIn(HWND hParentWnd, WORD wDeviceID = 0);
CMaxMidiIn(HWND hParentWnd, WORD wDeviceID, CMaxMidiSync*
            pSync = 0, DWORD dwFlags = MIDIIN_DEFAULT);
```

| Parameters | HWND hParentWnd |
|---|---|

HWND hParentWnd

Specifies the window handle of the parent window for the hidden window that will handle device messages.

WORD wDeviceID

Specifies the desired device to open. This value ranges from 0 to one less than the number of available devices.

CMaxMidiSync* pSync

Specifies a pointer to a sync device that will handle synchronization for this input device. If no sync is to be used with this input set pSync to NULL.

DWORD dwFlags

Specifies flags that are used to affect the operation of this device. These flags are the same as the ones defined for the Open() member function.

The default constructor creates the device object, but does not open a device or attach a parent window to the device object. The parent window and, optionally, a sync device can be attached later by calling the Attach() member function and the device can be opened using the Open() member function.

By specifying the parent window and device ID, the constructor will create a hidden window that will handle the input device and open the device. This constructor is normally called using the new operator.

The final constructor allows the device to be opened and all of its characteristics to be specified in a single call. Note that if this constructor is used the sync device must be constructed in advance and cannot be attached later without closing the device and re-opening it. This constructor is normally called using the new operator.

*CMaxMidiIn::~CMaxMidiIn() Destructor*

```
~CMaxMidiIn();
```

The destructor is called automatically when the object is destroyed. It closes the device, if it is still open.

*CMaxMidiIn::Attach()*

```
void Attach(HWND hParentWnd);
void Attach(CMaxMidiSync* pSync);
void Attach(CMaxMidiTrack* pTrack);
```

**Parameters**  HWND hParentWnd

Specifies the window handle of the parent window for the hidden window that will handle device messages.

CMaxMidiSync* pSync

Specifies a pointer to a sync device that will handle synchronization for this input device.

CMaxMidiTrack* pTrack

Specifies the track object that is to be attached.

This overloaded member function can be used to attach a track, parent window or sync device to the MIDI input device.

A parent window must be attached to the device before the Open() member function is called. This can be done using one of the constructors that specifies hParentWnd as a parameter, or by using the Attach() member function.

If this input device is to be opened using synchronization, a pointer to a CMaxMidiSync sync object must be attached, either using Attach() or using the proper constructor. If no sync device is attached, MIDI input will be performed without synchronization, and the timestamps for the received MIDI events will be in milliseconds since the Start() member function was called.

A single CMaxMidiTrack track object can be attached. Attaching another track will automatically detach the original track object. By attaching a sync device, starting synchronization, and calling the IsRecording() member function to enable recording for one or more tracks, received events will be stored in the tracks.

*CMaxMidiIn::Close()*

```
void Close(void);
```

This member function will close the hardware device, without destroying the CMaxMidiIn object. Use this member function to close a device in order to reopen it with different settings. It is not necessary to call this function before destroying the object.

*CMaxMidiIn::Detach()*

```
void Detach(CMaxMidiSync* pSync);

void Detach(CMaxMidiTrack* pTrack);
```

This function detaches the specified object, if attached, from the input object. The detached object is not affected.

**Parameters**     CMaxMidiSync* pSync

Specifies a pointer to a sync device that is to be detached.

CMaxMidiTrack* pTrack

Specifies a pointer to a track that is to be detached.

*CMaxMidiIn::Get()*

```
LPMIDIEVENT Get(void);
```

This member function returns a pointer to the next MidiEvent in the received event queue for this device. If no events are waiting in the queue it returns NULL.

A MidiEvent is an eight-byte structure that specifies a single, complete MIDI message. The structure is defined as follows:

```
struct {
    DWORD     time;
    BYTE              status;
    BYTE              data1;
    BYTE              data2;
    BYTE              data3;
} MidiEvent;
```

**Fields**     DWORD time

Specifies event time in ticks since the last event. If MIDI is received without attaching a sync device this field contains the time in milliseconds since Start() was called.

BYTE status

Specifies the status byte for the message. All received messages will contain a valid status byte.

BYTE data1

Specifies a status-specific optional first data byte.

BYTE data2

Specifies a status-specific optional second data byte.

BYTE data3

Specifies a third byte of tempo data for tempo change events. It will always be 0 for received MIDI messages.

### *CMaxMidiIn::GetDescription()*

```
LPSTR GetDescription(void);
```

This member function returns a pointer to an ASCIIZ string description for this device. This string is valid once a particular device has been selected, either by specifying `wDeviceID` in the constructor or calling the `Open()` member function.

### *CMaxMidiIn::GetNumDevices()*

```
int GetNumDevices(void);
```

This member function returns the number of MIDI input devices that are installed on the system. The return value for this function is valid at all times, even if no device is currently open or attached to this object.

### *CMaxMidiIn::GetSync()*

```
CMaxMidiSync* GetSync(void);
```

This function returns a pointer to the attached sync object, or NULL if no sync object is attached.

### *CMaxMidiIn::IsOpen()*

```
BOOL IsOpen(void);
```

This function returns TRUE if a MIDI input device is currently attached and open.

### *CMaxMidiIn::Open()*

```
BOOL Open(WORD wDeviceID = 0, DWORD dwFlags = MIDIIN_DEFAULT);
```

This member function opens the specified device using the specified settings. It returns TRUE if the open was successful, or FALSE if the device could not be opened.

To open a device with record synchronization, attach a sync device using the `Attach()` member function. Record timestamping will then be handled by the specified sync device. The `MidiEvent.time` parameter is in ticks if a sync device is attached, and in milliseconds since MIDI input was started if a sync device is not attached.

The `dwFlags` parameter further specifies the characteristics of the opened device. System Exclusive messages may optionally be merged into the incoming data stream by specifying `ENABLE_SYSEX`. If enabled, sysex data is handled as any other message, except that the `status` byte is always 0xF0 and data is passed in the `data1` byte in the `MidiEvent` structure. The `data2` byte is 0. Additionally, the sysex and EOX status messages are passed in the `data1` byte of a `MidiEvent` structure. Therefore, a System Exclusive message occupies one `MidiEvent` structure per byte, including the leading sysex and terminating EOX status bytes.

If System Exclusive messages will not be received by the application, `DISABLE_SYSEX` may be specified. This will minimize the memory requirements for the MIDI input device. Any inadvertently received sysex messages will be ignored.

Internally, MaxMidi uses two user-specified buffers to handle MIDI input. The MIDI input queue is specified by the `QUEUE_xxx` flags. The MIDI input queue *must* be specified when opening the device. MIDI data are placed in this queue as it is received. Data is retrieved from the queue by calls to the `Get()` member function.

The second queue is used by MaxMidi to manage System Exclusive data. Since Microsoft Multimedia Windows handles System Exclusive messages separately from other ("short") messages, MaxMidi internally uses small queues to receive sysex messages from the Windows driver. These queues are not visible to the application, but the size and number of queues must be specified when opening the device.

This device may be specified to be a sync input by setting the `SYNC_INPUT` flag. Only one input may act as the sync input at a time. The sync input receives MIDI sync messages and passes them to the specified sync device, if the corresponding sync is enabled in the sync device. If no sync device is specified, this flag is ignored.

**Parameters**     WORD wDeviceID

Specifies the desired device to open. This value ranges from 0 to one less than the number of available devices.

DWORD dwFlags

Specifies flags that are used to affect the operation of this device that can be combined using the OR operator.

ENABLE_SYSEX

If this flag is specified, System Exclusive messages are merged into the normal MIDI stream that is sent to the application. This setting is the default.

DISABLE_SYSEX

If this flag is specified, System Exclusive messages are filtered.

SYNC_INPUT

This input serves as the sync input for MIDI sync for the previously opened and attached sync device. It is ignored if no sync device is attached or the sync mode has been set to `S_INT`.

*MIDI Queue and Sysex Queue Sizes*

| | | |
|---|---|---|
| QUEUE_64 | SXBUF_64 | 64 messages |
| QUEUE_128 | SXBUF_128 | 128 messages |
| QUEUE_256 | SXBUF_256 | 256 messages |
| QUEUE_512 | SXBUF_512 | 512 messages |
| QUEUE_1K | SXBUF_1K | 1,024 messages |
| QUEUE_2K | SXBUF_2K | 2,048 messages |
| QUEUE_4K | SXBUF_4K | 4,096 messages |
| QUEUE_8K | SXBUF_8K | 8,192 messages |
| QUEUE_16K | SXBUF_16K | 16,384 messages |
| QUEUE_32K | SXBUF_32K | 32,768 messages |

Each message occupies 8 bytes of global memory. The number of sysex buffers of size SXBUF_xxx is ORed with the dwFlags parameter. The number may range from 0 to 255 buffers. Typically, a moderate number of small buffers should be specified instead of one large buffer.

MIDIIN_DEFAULT

This value specifies default settings that are appropriate for most applications. These settings are:

QUEUE_512 | SXBUF_512 | ENABLE_SYSEX | 32

## *CMaxMidiIn::Start()*

```
void Start(void);
```

Once an input device has been opened, call this function to allow MIDI to be received by the device. Until this member is called no data will be received from the input device.

## *CMaxMidiIn::Stop()*

```
void Stop(void);
```

Call this member function to stop receiving MIDI messages from the open device, without closing the device. By using Start() and Stop() an application can control which input device is active.

## *CMaxMidiIn::ProcessMidiData() Virtual Member Function*

```
virtual BOOL ProcessMidiData(LPMIDIEVENT lpEvent);
```

Your application may derive a class from CMaxMidiIn and override this virtual callback function to perform processing in addition to the default implementation. It is called each time a complete MIDI event is received by the input device.

If a track is not attached, you should override this virtual function by deriving a class from `CMaxMidiIn` and process the MIDI event in this callback function, as required for your application. The return value is ignored in this case.

If a track is attached and enabled for record, each event is processed in this callback before it is stored by the track. Your function can modify the timestamp or any of the bytes of the event. If the function returns TRUE, the event is stored in the attached track. If FALSE is returned, the event is ignored and is not stored in the attached track object. Note that the timestamp of the next event will be relative to this event.

## MIDI Sync Class — CMaxMidiSync

This class encapsulates the behavior of a synchronization device. It is derived from `CWnd` and provides all of the functionality necessary to open, synchronize `CMaxMidiIn` and `CMaxMidiOut` devices, and close the device. Informational member functions provide device status.

To use this class, use one of the constructor members to create an instance of the class, or create a derived class and implement the virtual callback functions, `ProcessMidiBeat()` and `ProcessSyncDone()`. The default implementations for both functions do nothing.

Your implementation of `ProcessMidiBeat()` is called on each beat while synchronization is running. `ProcessSyncDone()` is called when the sync device finds that there are no events left to send from any attached MIDI output devices.

Your derived class can be viewed and modified using ClassWizard if you implement the *AFX* message map and virtual function macros in your source. To do this, add the following to the bottom of your derived class' class declaration:

```
public:
// Overrides
    // ClassWizard generated virtual function overrides
    //{{AFX_VIRTUAL(MyMaxMidiSync)
    virtual void ProcessMidiBeat(void);
    virtual void ProcessSyncDone(void);
    //}}AFX_VIRTUAL

protected:
    //{{AFX_MSG(MyMaxMidiSync)
    //}}AFX_MSG
    DECLARE_MESSAGE_MAP()
```

Change `MyMaxMidiSync` to your derived class' name. Then, add this to your class' implementation .cpp file:

```
BEGIN_MESSAGE_MAP(MyMaxMidiSync, CMaxMidiSync)
    //{{AFX_MSG_MAP(MyMaxMidiSync)
    //}}AFX_MSG_MAP
END_MESSAGE_MAP()
```

Again, change `MyMaxMidiSync` to the name of your derived class. Finally, add the new class to ClassWizard by selecting Add Class…|From a file… .

### CMaxMidiSync::CMaxMidiSync() Constructor

**CMaxMidiSync**();

**CMaxMidiSync**(HWND hParentWnd);

**CMaxMidiSync**(HWND hParentWnd, WORD mode = S_INT, WORD
            timerPeriod = 10);

**Parameters**    HWND hParentWnd

Specifies the window handle of the parent window for the hidden window that will handle device messages.

WORD mode

Specifies the sync mode. Possible modes are:

| | |
|---|---|
| S_INT | Internal sync |
| S_MIDI | MIDI sync |

WORD timerPeriod

Specifies the timer period in milliseconds. The timer period may be 1 millisecond or greater. Note that if the requested timer period is not available from Windows, the fastest available period is used.

The default constructor creates the device object, but does not open a device or attach a parent window to the device object. The parent window can be attached later by calling the `Attach()` member function and the device can be opened using the `Open()` member function.

By specifying the parent window the constructor will create a hidden window that will handle the output device. The device is not opened, however. The device can then be opened by calling `Open()`. This constructor is normally called using the `new` operator.

The final constructor allows the device to be opened and all of its characteristics to be specified in a single call. This constructor is normally called using the `new` operator.

### CMaxMidiSync::~CMaxMidiSync() Destructor

**~CMaxMidiSync**();

The destructor is called automatically when the object is destroyed. It closes the device, if it is still open.

*CMaxMidiSync::Attach()*

        void **Attach**(HWND hParentWnd);

**Parameters**     HWND hParentWnd

             Specifies the window handle of the parent window for the hidden window that will handle device messages.

This member function can be used to attach a parent window to the sync device.

A parent window must be attached to the device before the Open() member function is called. This can be done using one of the constructors that specifies hParentWnd as a parameter, or by using the Attach() member function.

*CMaxMidiSync::Close()*

        void **Close**(void);

This member function will close the sync device, without destroying the CMaxMidiSync object. Use this member function to close a device in order to reopen it with different settings. It is not necessary to call this function before destroying the object.

*CMaxMidiSync::Convert()*

        DWORD **Convert**(double tempo);

        double **Convert**(DWORD tempo);

This overloaded member function converts between tempo in beats per minute (as a double) and microseconds per beat (as a DWORD).

**Parameters**     double tempo

             Specifies the tempo in beats per minute. Tempo can range from 10.000 to 250.000 or greater, depending on the current resolution.

             DWORD tempo

             Specifies the tempo in microseconds per beat. This is the representation that is used internally by the MaxMidi DLL in order to allow fractional tempos to be specified.

*CMaxMidiSync::IsOpen()*

        BOOL **IsOpen**(void);

This function returns TRUE if the sync device is currently open.

*CMaxMidiSync::IsRunning()*

        BOOL **IsRunning**(void);

This function returns TRUE if the sync device is actively synchronizing. It returns FALSE if synchronization is stopped or paused.

*CMaxMidiSync::GetHSync()*

```
HSYNC GetHSync(void);
```

This member function returns the handle to the attached sync device. It is used internally by `CMaxMidiSync`, but can also be used when calling MaxMidi DLL functions directly.

*CMaxMidiSync::GetPosition()*

```
DWORD GetPosition(WORD units = POS_MS);
```

This member function returns the current position since the start of sync in either milliseconds or ticks. The default units are milliseconds.

**Parameters**     WORD     units

Specifies the desired units. Possible values are:

POS_MS          Position specified in milliseconds.

POS_TICKS       Position specified in ticks.

*CMaxMidiSync::Mode()*

```
BOOL Mode(WORD mode);
```
```
WORD Mode(void);
```

This overloaded member function selects a new sync mode for the already opened sync device or returns the current mode. If setting a new mode, it returns TRUE if the change was successful, or FALSE if the device was not open or the mode change was not successful.

**Parameters**     WORD mode

Specifies the sync mode. Possible modes are:

S_INT           Internal sync

S_MIDI          MIDI sync

*CMaxMidiSync::Open()*

```
BOOL Open(WORD mode = S_INT, WORD timerPeriod = 10);
```

This member function opens the sync device using the specified settings. It returns TRUE if the open was successful, or FALSE if the device could not be opened.

Timing is specified by setting the resolution (in ticks per beat) and tempo (in µS per beat.) The sync device then generates ticks at the specified rate. These ticks are used to timestamp incoming messages and play outgoing messages with the proper timing.

Message timestamping on output is performed by setting the `MidiEvent.time` value to the count of ticks since the last message. This same count of delta ticks is used during playback to compare with the generated tick count in the sync device. When the two tick counts are the same, the message is sent to the MIDI output device that is connected to this sync device.

The sync mode specifies the type of synchronization that will be performed. Two possible types of sync are available: internal and MIDI sync. The sync mode may be changed by calling the `Mode()` member function.

When synchronizing to MIDI sync, MIDI input must be started by calling `Start()` for the MIDI input device that will be providing sync messages. After stopping sync, stop MIDI input to prevent incorrectly timestamped messages from being added to the incoming MIDI buffer.

A synchronous Windows MMSYSTEM timer is used to provide a timebase for internal and MIDI sync modes. The timer period, in milliseconds (mS), may be specified when opening. The period must be 1 mS or greater. Faster (lower) values provide better timing accuracy (i.e., messages are sent closer to the exact time that they are expected) at a significant cost of system resources. With timer periods approaching 1 mS, Windows application response may be unacceptably slow. In this case, a more conservative timer period would be 10 mS. The timer period may be changed by calling the `Period()` member function.

Note that this timing accuracy is not related to the timing resolution. Resolution (in ticks per beat) specifies the number of ticks that elapse between each musical beat of time. Higher resolutions provide finer granularity in event timing, since there are more divisions between each beat. MaxMidi supports resolutions from 1 to 960 ticks per beat. It is recommended that the resolution be set to a multiple of 24, since there are 24 MIDI clocks per beat using MIDI sync. Odd resolutions may make synchronization difficult and prevent sequences from being played correctly on other timing systems. The default resolution is 480 tpb.

Tempo is specified in μS per beat, allowing fractional tempo settings. To convert from tempo in beats per min to μS per beat or vice versa use the `Convert()` member function. The sync device supports tempos from 10 bpm to 250 bpm at all resolutions. The default tempo is 120 bpm.

You may experience difficulty when embedding large sysex bulk dump messages in sequences intended for playback with synchronization. Such sequences will play correctly with tempo settings equal to or slower than the original tempo. Playing back with tempos greater than the original tempo may cause events following the sysex message to be played back with incorrect timing. This is not a flaw of the ToolKit, but rather it is a function of the nature of System Exclusive messages. These messages take a fixed amount of time to send; increasing the tempo will not cause sysex dumps to be sent more quickly.

**Parameters**       WORD mode

Specifies the sync mode. Possible modes are:

| | |
|---|---|
| S_INT | Internal sync |
| S_MIDI | MIDI sync |

WORD timerPeriod

Specifies the timer period in milliseconds. The timer period may be 1 millisecond or greater. Note that if the requested timer period is not available from Windows, the fastest available period is used.

### CMaxMidiSync::Pause()

```
void Pause(BOOL reset = FALSE);
```

This function stops playback or record synchronization, if started. Synchronization may be resumed by calling ReStart(). If reset is TRUE then any currently playing notes will be stopped. If reset is FALSE, then any currently playing notes will continue to sound. In either case, MIDI output buffers are not flushed. Pausing sync with reset set to FALSE is intended for short, temporary pauses.

**Parameters**       BOOL reset

If TRUE, Note Offs will be sent for any currently playing notes. If FALSE, no Note Offs will be sent.

### CMaxMidiSync::Period()

```
BOOL Period(WORD period);
WORD Period(void);
```

This overloaded member function selects a new timer period or returns the current value. The specified period must be 1 mS or greater. Faster (lower) values provide better timing accuracy (i.e., messages are sent closer to the exact time that they are expected) at a significant cost of system resources. With timer periods approaching 1 mS, Windows application response may be unacceptably slow. In this case, a more conservative timer period would be 10 mS.

When setting the period the function returns TRUE if the change was successful, or FALSE if the device was not open or the period change was not successful.

**Parameters**       WORD timerPeriod

Specifies the timer period in milliseconds. The timer period may be 1 millisecond or greater. Note that if the requested timer period is not available from Windows, the fastest available period is used.

*CMaxMidiSync::Resolution()*

```
WORD Resolution(void);
void Resolution(WORD res);
```

This overloaded member function gets or sets the current resolution, in ticks per beat. See `Open()` for more information.

*CMaxMidiSync::ReStart()*

```
void ReStart(void);
```

This function restarts synchronization, if it was paused by `Pause()`.

*CMaxMidiSync::Start()*

```
void Start(void);
```

This member function starts synchronization for the previously opened device. The count of ticks is cleared. When syncing to MIDI sync, MIDI input must be started by calling `Start()` for the input device that will provide sync messages.

*CMaxMidiSync::Stop()*

```
void Stop(void);
```

This member function stops playback or record synchronization, if started. MIDI output buffers are not flushed. Synchronization may be resumed by calling `ReStart()`.

*CMaxMidiSync::Tempo()*

```
BOOL Tempo(DWORD tempo);
BOOL Tempo(double tempo);
DWORD Tempo(void);
```

This overloaded member function sets or gets the current tempo. It can be called at any time, either before or during synchronization. If the tempo is not set by the application, a default tempo of 120 bpm is used.

In addition, tempo changes may be embedded in the outgoing MIDI data stream that is sent by the application to any `CMaxMidiOut` device attached to this sync device. To do this, set the `MidiEvent` status byte to 0. The 24-bit tempo is then stored in the three event bytes, starting at `MidiEvent.data1` with `MidiEvent.data1` as the MSB.

If tempo is changed by the application while sync is running during record, a change tempo event is inserted in the incoming data stream of the MIDI input device that is assigned as the sync input. Thus, application-created tempo changes are embedded into the sequence data.

**Parameters**     `double tempo`

Specifies the tempo in beats per minute. Tempo can range from 10.000 to 250.000 or greater, depending on the current resolution.

`DWORD tempo`

Specifies the tempo in microseconds per beat. This is the representation that is used internally by the MaxMidi DLL to allow fractional tempos to be specified.

*CMaxMidiSync::ProcessMidiBeat() Virtual Member Function*

```
virtual void ProcessMidiBeat(void);
```

The default implementation of this function does nothing. To implement a custom version, derive a new class from `CMaxMidiSync` and override the virtual function. Your implementation will be called by the sync device on each MIDI beat.

*CMaxMidiSync::ProcessSyncDone() Virtual Member Function*

```
virtual void ProcessSyncDone(void);
```

The default implementation of this function does nothing. To implement a custom version, derive a new class from `CMaxMidiSync` and override the virtual function. Your implementation is called when the sync device finds that there are no events left to send from any attached MIDI output devices.

## MIDI Input Menu Class — CMidiInDeviceMenu

This class manages a pop-up menu of MIDI input devices. It automatically creates the menu and fills it with the list of device names. A `CMaxMidiIn` device is then attached. Then, whenever the `SelectDevice()` member function is called by the application, the MIDI input device will be closed and re-opened using the new device ID. This allows an application to easily manage the selection of a single MIDI input device.

The `_MENUS` conditional must be defined if the `CMidiInDeviceMenu` class is used in an application.

*CMidiInDeviceMenu::CMidiInDeviceMenu() Constructor*

```
CMidiInDeviceMenu();

CMidiInDeviceMenu(HMENU hMenu, UINT position, LPSTR name, UINT
                  baseMsg);
```

The default constructor creates the object but does not attach the application menu or create the popup menu.

By specifying the application menu handle, desired position for the pop-up menu, name, and starting base message number, the pop-up menu will be created. It is inserted at the specified location, and filled with the list of MIDI input devices that are present on the system.

**Parameters**     HMENU hMenu

Specifies the handle to the parent menu that will contain the new pop-up menu item.

UINT position

Specifies the position in the parent menu for the new pop-up menu. The left-most position is 0. This is the same value as used in the InsertMenu() function.

LPSTR name

Specifies the name of the pop-up menu. This name will appear in the parent menu.

UINT baseMsg

Specifies the ID of the first item in the pop-up menu. This message ID is passed as nID to the OnCmdMsg() handler of the window that receives and processes command messages from this menu.

## *CMidiInDeviceMenu::Attach()*

```
void Attach(CMaxMidiIn* Device);
```

This member function attaches the specified MIDI input device to the pop-up menu. Device selections made by calling SelectDevice() will be made to this attached device.

**Parameters**     CMaxMidiIn* Device

Specifies the pointer to a CMaxMidiIn device.

## *CMidiInDeviceMenu::Create()*

```
void Create(HMENU hMenu, UINT position, LPSTR name, UINT
           baseMsg);
```

This member function creates the pop-up menu and fills it with the list of devices available on the system. Create() should be used if the object is instantiated using the default constructor.

**Parameters**     HMENU hMenu

Specifies the handle to the parent menu that will contain the new pop-up menu item.

```
UINT position
```

Specifies the position in the parent menu for the new pop-up menu. The left-most position is 0. This is the same value as used in the `InsertMenu()` function.

```
LPSTR name
```

Specifies the name of the pop-up menu. This name will appear in the parent menu.

```
UINT baseMsg
```

Specifies the ID of the first item in the pop-up menu. This message ID is passed as `nID` to the `OnCmdMsg()` handler of the window that receives and processes command messages from this menu.

### *CMidiInDeviceMenu::GetDeviceCount()*

```
int GetDeviceCount(void);
```

This function returns the number of MIDI input devices available on the system (and in the pop-up menu).

### *CMidiInDeviceMenu::GetDeviceName()*

```
virtual BOOL GetDeviceName(WORD wDeviceID, LPSTR name);
```

This virtual function retrieves the name of the specified input device, if it exists. If the device exists the function returns TRUE, if the `wDeviceID` is not valid it returns FALSE.

This function is used internally by the `CMidiInDeviceMenu` object and is not normally called by the application.

**Parameters**
```
WORD wDeviceID
```

Specifies the desired device. This value ranges from 0 to one less than the number of available devices.

```
LPSTR name
```

The name of the device is returned as an ASCIIZ string. The returned name is invalid if the device does not exist.

### *CMidiInDeviceMenu::GetMenu()*

```
HMENU GetMenu(void);
```

This function returns the menu handle for the pop-up menu. Returns NULL if the menu has not been created.

```
virtual BOOL SelectDevice(UINT id);
```

This virtual member function selects a new MIDI input device, corresponding to the specified ID. If the menu exists and the ID is within the valid range of menu items, then the MIDI input device is closed and reopened for the new device and the function returns TRUE. If the menu does not exist, or the ID is not within the valid range of devices then the function returns FALSE.

Device IDs can be specified two different ways. A logical ID can be used to directly open a device. Logical IDs range from 0 to one less than the number of devices present on the system. This is identical to the wDeviceID values used by the CMaxMidiIn class for specifying devices.

A command message-based ID can be used to select devices as well. These IDs begin at the baseMsg value (as specified when the menu is created) for the first device and progress to baseMsg + GetDeviceCount() - 1 for the last device in the menu.

**Parameters**     UINT id

Specifies the device to select, either as wDeviceID or as offsets from baseMsg.

Use the following as a guide to make the handling of the device menu easy and transparent in MFC-derived applications.

In the OnCreate() member of your MainFrm.cpp implementation, set

```
m_bAutoMenuEnable = FALSE;
```

so that the pop-up menu items will be enabled. This must be done since the number of devices, and thus the number of items in the menu, is not known until run-time. There will not be OnCommand() handlers for these menu items, and normally MFC would disable those menu items.

Then, handle all of the command messages for this menu by overriding OnCmdMsg() in your view or MainFrm window class using ClassWizard. Implement OnCmdMsg() like this:

```
BOOL CMyView::OnCmdMsg(UINT nID, int nCode, void* pExtra,
AFX_CMDHANDLERINFO* pHandlerInfo)
{
    // check to see if one of the device menus
    // has been selected
    if(nCode == 0)
    {
```

```
                    // this works because SelectDevice will ignore
                    // all out of range ID's
                    InMenu.SelectDevice(nID);
            }

        return CView::OnCmdMsg(nID, nCode, pExtra, pHandlerInfo);
    }
```

If you have both an input device menu and an output device menu you can call
`SelectDevice()` for both menus in the same `OnCmdMsg()` handler, since `SelectDevice()`
ignores message IDs that are outside of its range.

## MIDI Output Menu Class — CMidiOutDeviceMenu

This class manages a pop-up menu of MIDI output devices. It automatically creates the
menu and fills it with the list of device names. A `CMaxMidiOut` device is then attached.
Then, whenever the `SelectDevice()` member function is called by the application the
MIDI output device will be closed and reopened using the new device ID. This allows an
application to easily manage the selection of a single MIDI output device.

The `_MENUS` conditional must be defined if the `CMidiOutDeviceMenu` class is used in
an application.

### CMidiOutDeviceMenu::CMidiOutDeviceMenu() Constructor

```
CMidiOutDeviceMenu();

CMidiOutDeviceMenu(HMENU hMenu, UINT position, LPSTR name,
                    UINT baseMsg);
```

The default constructor creates the object but does not attach the application menu or
create the popup menu.

By specifying the application menu handle, desired position for the pop-up menu,
name, and starting base message number, the pop-up menu will be created. It is inserted
at the specified location, and filled with the list of MIDI output devices that are present
on the system.

**Parameters**     HMENU hMenu

Specifies the handle to the parent menu that will contain the new pop-up menu item.

UINT position

Specifies the position in the parent menu for the new pop-up menu.
The leftmost position is 0. This is the same value as used in the
`InsertMenu()` function.

```
LPSTR name
```

Specifies the name of the pop-up menu. This name will appear in the parent menu.

```
UINT baseMsg
```

Specifies the ID of the first item in the pop-up menu. This message ID is passed as `nID` to the `OnCmdMsg()` handler of the window that receives and processes command messages from this menu.

## *CMidiOutDeviceMenu::Attach()*

```
void Attach(CMaxMidiOut* Device);
```

This member function attaches the specified MIDI output device to the pop-up menu. Device selections made by calling `SelectDevice()` will be made to this attached device.

**Parameters**        `CMaxMidiOut* Device`

Specifies the pointer to a `CMaxMidiOut` device.

## *CMidiOutDeviceMenu::Create()*

```
void Create(HMENU hMenu, UINT position, LPSTR name, UINT
            baseMsg);
```

This member function creates the pop-up menu and fills it with the list of devices available on the system. `Create()` should be used if the object is instantiated using the default constructor.

**Parameters**        `HMENU hMenu`

Specifies the handle to the parent menu that will contain the new pop-up menu item.

```
UINT position
```

Specifies the position in the parent menu for the new pop-up menu. The leftmost position is 0. This is the same value as used in the `InsertMenu()` function.

```
LPSTR name
```

Specifies the name of the pop-up menu. This name will appear in the parent menu.

```
UINT baseMsg
```

Specifies the ID of the first item in the pop-up menu. This message ID is passed as `nID` to the `OnCmdMsg()` handler of the window that receives and processes command messages from this menu.

*CMidiOutDeviceMenu::GetDeviceCount()*

```
int GetDeviceCount(void);
```

Returns the number of MIDI output devices available on the system (and in the pop-up menu).

*CMidiOutDeviceMenu::GetDeviceName()*

```
virtual BOOL GetDeviceName(WORD wDeviceID, LPSTR name);
```

This virtual function retrieves the name of the specified output device, if it exists. If the device exists the function returns TRUE, if the `wDeviceID` is not valid it returns FALSE.

This function is used internally by the `CMidiOutDeviceMenu` object and is not normally called by the application.

**Parameters**    WORD wDeviceID

Specifies the desired device. This value ranges from 0 to one less than the number of available devices.

LPSTR name

The name of the device is returned as an ASCIIZ string. The returned name is invalid if the device does not exist.

*CMidiOutDeviceMenu::GetMenu()*

```
HMENU GetMenu(void);
```

This function returns the menu handle for the pop-up menu. Returns NULL if the menu has not been created.

*CMidiOutDeviceMenu::SelectDevice()*

```
virtual BOOL SelectDevice(UINT id);
```

This virtual member function selects a new MIDI output device, corresponding to the specified ID. If the menu exists and the ID is within the valid range of menu items, then the MIDI output device is closed and reopened for the new device and the function returns TRUE. If the menu does not exist, or if the ID is not within the valid range of devices then the function returns FALSE.

Device IDs can be specified two different ways. A logical ID can be used to directly open a device. Logical IDs range from 0 to one less than the number of devices present on the system. This is identical to the `wDeviceID` values used by the `CMaxMidiOut` class for specifying devices.

A command message-based ID can be used to select devices as well. These IDs begin at the `baseMsg` value (as specified when the menu is created) for the first device and progress to `baseMsg + GetDeviceCount() - 1` for the last device in the menu.

**Parameters**     UINT id

Specifies the device to select, either as `wDeviceID` or as offsets from `baseMsg`.

Use the following as a guide to make the handling of the device menu easy and transparent in MFC-derived applications.

In the `OnCreate()` member of your MainFrm.cpp implementation, set

```
m_bAutoMenuEnable = FALSE;
```

so that the pop-up menu items will be enabled. This must be done since the number of devices, and thus the number of items in the menu, is not known until run-time. There will not be `OnCommand()` handlers for these menu items, and normally MFC would disable those menu items.

Then, handle all of the command messages for this menu by overriding `OnCmdMsg()` in your view or `MainFrm` window class using ClassWizard. Implement `OnCmdMsg()` like this:

```
BOOL CMyView::OnCmdMsg(UINT nID, int nCode, void* pExtra,
AFX_CMDHANDLERINFO* pHandlerInfo)
{
    // check to see if one of the device menus
    // has been selected
    if(nCode == 0)
    {
        // this works because SelectDevice will ignore
        // all out of range ID's
        OutMenu.SelectDevice(nID);
    }

    return CView::OnCmdMsg(nID, nCode, pExtra,
                        pHandlerInfo);
}
```

If you have both an input device menu and an output device menu you can call `SelectDevice()` for both menus in the same `OnCmdMsg()` handler, since `SelectDevice()` ignores message IDs that are outside of its range.

# Track Class — CMaxMidiTrack

This class serves as a container of MIDI data that can be connected to Standard MIDI File classes (CMaxMidiSMF), MIDI Input classes (CMaxMidiIn), and MIDI Output classes (CMaxMidiOut).

Tracks can be filled with events in several ways. Events can be recorded into a track by attaching it to a CMaxMidiIn object. Events can also be directly written into a track, edited, or removed using various member functions. They can then be attached to CMaxMidiOut devices to play the data back, either with or without synchronization. Likewise, tracks can also be attached to CMaxMidiSMF objects in order to read, playback, or write multitrack Standard MIDI Files.

## CMaxMidiTrack::CMaxMidiTrack() Constructor

**CMaxMidiTrack**();

This function creates and initializes the track object. The track may be filled with events or attached to other objects for input or output.

## CMaxMidiTrack::AbsNow()

DWORD **AbsNow**(DWORD eventNum);

This is not an exercise aid that is advertised on late-night television. Instead, it returns the absolute time, in ticks since the beginning of the track, for the specified event.

**Parameters**     DWORD eventNum

Specifies the index of the event in the track, beginning at 0.

## CMaxMidiTrack::AbsToDelta()

void **AbsToDelta**(LPMIDIEVENT lpBuf, DWORD startEvent, DWORD numEvents);

This function converts the buffer from absolute time to relative (delta) time. startEvent indicates the event in the track to which the first event in lpBuf corresponds. This function is used internally in support of track merging (see CMaxMidiOut::Merge()) and is not normally called by applications.

**Parameters**     LPMIDIEVENT lpBuf

Specifies the buffer of events that will be converted from absolute time to delta time.

DWORD startEvent

Specifies the index of the event in the track to which the first event in the buffer corresponds. This is used to locate the buffer relative to the track data in order to find the delta time for the first event in the buffer.

```
DWORD numEvents
```
Specifies the number of events in the buffer that are to be converted.

## *CMaxMidiTrack::Attach()*

```
void Attach(CMaxMidiSMF* pSMF);
void Attach(CMaxMidiOut* pMidiOut);
void Attach(CMaxMidiIn* pMidiIn);
```

Normally, a track is created and attached to another (target) object by calling the target object's `Attach()` member. For example, to attach a track to a MIDI input, call its `Attach()` member like this:

```
MyMaxMidiIn MyMidiIn;
CMaxMidiTrack ThisTrack;

MyMidiIn.Attach(&ThisTrack);
```

These member functions attach the corresponding object to the track object and are used internally by the `CMaxMidi` classes. They are automatically called when the `Attach()` members of the target classes are called.

**Parameters**      `CMaxMidiSMF* pSMF`

Specifies a pointer to an already created Standard MIDI File object.

`CMaxMidiMidiOut* pMidiOut`

Specifies a pointer to an already created MIDI output object.

`CMaxMidiIn* pMidiIn`

Specifies a pointer to an already created MIDI input object.

## *CMaxMidiTrack::DeleteEvent()*

```
void DeleteEvent(DWORD eventNum);
```

This function deletes the specified event from the track. Event timestamps are not changed; deleting an event may move following events earlier in time. You may need to call `SlideTrack()` on the event following the deleted event to correct for a nonzero timestamp.

**Parameters**      `DWORD eventNum`

Specifies the event that will be deleted from the track. Setting this value to –1 will remove the event at the end of the track.

## CMaxMidiTrack::DeltaToAbs()

```
void DeltaToAbs(LPMIDIEVENT lpBuf, DWORD startEvent, DWORD
numEvents);
```

This function converts the buffer from delta time to absolute time. `startEvent` indicates the event in the track to which the first event in `lpBuf` corresponds. This function is used internally in support of track merging (see `CMaxMidiOut::Merge()`) and is not normally called by applications.

**Parameters**

LPMIDIEVENT lpBuf

Specifies the buffer of events that will be converted from delta time to absolute time.

DWORD startEvent

Specifies the index of the event in the track to which the first event in the buffer corresponds. This is used to locate the buffer relative to the track data in order to find the delta time for the first event in the buffer.

DWORD numEvents

Specifies the number of events in the buffer that are to be converted.

## CMaxMidiTrack::Detach()

```
void Detach(void);
void Detach(CMaxMidiSMF* pSMF);
void Detach(CMaxMidiOut* pMidiOut);
void Detach(CMaxMidiIn* pMidiIn);
```

This function detaches the specified device from the track. When a track is destroyed it is automatically detached from any objects to which it is attached. Calling the `Detach()` function without any parameters will detach the track without destroying it.

**Parameters**

CMaxMidiSMF* pSMF

Specifies a pointer to an already created Standard MIDI File object.

CMaxMidiMidiOut* pMidiOut

Specifies a pointer to an already created MIDI output object.

CMaxMidiIn* pMidiIn

Specifies a pointer to an already created MIDI input object.

## CMaxMidiTrack::Flush()

```
void Flush(void);
```

This function flushes the events from the track. Subsequent calls to `Write()` will insert events, starting at the beginning of the track. Calls to `Read()` will return NULL until one or more events have been written to the track. Note that the data in the track has not been lost and can still be accessed using `GetEvent()`. If the number of events is reset to a valid number using `SetNumEvents()`, the track can be read again using `Read()`.

## CMaxMidiTrack::GetAbsBuffer()

```
LPMIDIEVENT GetAbsBuffer(DWORD startEvent, DWORD* numEvents);
```

This function returns a pointer to a buffer that contains track data, starting at `start-Event`, that has been converted to absolute time. Each track begins at time 0, and event timestamps are normally specified in delta ticks since the last event or from the beginning of the track for the first event. This function converts a requested number of events, starting at `startEvent`, into absolute ticks since the beginning of the track. This function is used internally in support of track merging (see `CMaxMidiOut::Merge()`) and is not normally called by applications.

**Parameters**　　`DWORD startEvent`

Specifies the index of the event, beginning at 0, in the track that will appear as the first event in the returned buffer.

`DWORD* numEvents`

Specifies a pointer to the requested number of events to convert to absolute time. If there are fewer events in the track to be converted, `numEvents` will be set to the actual number of events in the returned buffer.

## CMaxMidiTrack::GetBuffer()

```
LPMIDIEVENT GetBuffer(void);
```

This function returns the address of the first event in the track. This function can be used to directly access the track buffer, though its use is discouraged. It is used internally by the track object and is not normally called by applications.

## CMaxMidiTrack::GetBufferSize()

```
DWORD GetBufferSize(void);
```

This function returns the size of the buffer, in events. Note that this is not the number of events in the track. This function is used internally by the track object and is not normally called by applications.

*CMaxMidiTrack::GetEvent()*

```
LPMIDIEVENT GetEvent(DWORD eventNum);
```

This function returns a pointer to the specified event in the track, or NULL if the event does not exist. Events can be accessed randomly using this function. `eventNum` zero is at the beginning of the track.

**Parameters**    DWORD eventNum

Specifies the index of the event in the track, beginning at 0.

*CMaxMidiTrack::GetMidiIn()*

```
CMaxMidiIn* GetMidiIn(void);
```

This function returns the pointer to the attached `CMaxMidiIn` object, or NULL if no object is attached.

*CMaxMidiTrack::GetMidiOut()*

```
CMaxMidiOut* GetMidiOut(void);
```

This function returns the pointer to the attached `CMaxMidiOut` object, or NULL if no object is attached.

*CMaxMidiTrack::GetName()*

```
LPSTR GetName(void);
```

This function returns the name of the track, or NULL if the track has no name. The name of the first track of a Format 1 Standard MIDI File will be the name of the sequence. All other tracks in an SMF will have names corresponding to the individual tracks. For more information, see the `CMaxMidiSMF` class.

*CMaxMidiTrack::GetNumEvents()*

```
DWORD GetNumEvents(void);
```

This function returns the number of MIDI events that are in the track.

*CMaxMidiTrack::GetSMF()*

```
CMaxMidiSMF* GetSMF(void);
```

This function returns the pointer to the attached `CMaxMidiSMF` object, or NULL if no object is attached.

## CMaxMidiTrack::GetTime()

> DWORD **GetTime**(DWORD eventNum);

This function returns the time, in ticks since the last event in the track, of the specified event. The function will return 0 if an event index greater than the number of events in the track is specified.

**Parameters**  DWORD eventNum

Specifies the index of the event in the track, beginning at 0.

## CMaxMidiTrack::InsertEvent()

> void **InsertEvent**(LPMIDIEVENT lpEvent, DWORD beforeEvent);

This function inserts the event immediately before the specified event. The first event in the track is always event 0. Event timestamps are not changed; inserting an event may move following events later in time. You may need to call SlideTrack() on the event following the new event in order to correct for a nonzero timestamp.

**Parameters**  LPMIDIEVENT lpEvent

Specifies a pointer to the event that will be inserted in the track.

DWORD beforeEvent

The new event will be inserted just before the specified event. Setting this value to −1 will add the event to the end of the track, growing the track buffer, if necessary.

## CMaxMidiTrack::IsEmpty()

> BOOL **IsEmpty**(void);

This function returns TRUE if the track does not contain any events.

## CMaxMidiTrack::IsRecording()

> BOOL **IsRecording**(void);

> void **IsRecording**(BOOL record);

This function sets or retrieves the record state of the track. When connected to a MIDI input object, events will not be recorded to a track if it is not in record mode. This serves as a record mute function; tracks can be attached to input objects that have been started without recording events until desired.

**Parameters**  BOOL record

TRUE if the track is enabled for record, FALSE if record is disabled. Tracks cannot record and play at the same time.

## CMaxMidiTrack::Load()

```
BOOL Load(void);
```

This function loads the track with data from the Standard MIDI File, if attached and opened for read. Returns TRUE if the track was successfully loaded, FALSE if there was an error or no SMF is attached. Normally, applications should load all of the tracks of an SMF at once by calling the `Load()` member of `CMaxMidiSMF`.

## CMaxMidiTrack::Mute()

```
BOOL Mute(void);
```

```
void Mute(BOOL mute);
```

This function sets or retrieves the mute state of the track. A track that is muted will not play, and the `Read()` member function will always return NULL. Likewise, a muted track will not be written to a Standard Midi File when the `Save()` member is called.

**Parameters**     `BOOL mute`

TRUE if the track is muted, FALSE if the track is enabled for playback.

## CMaxMidiTrack::Read()

```
LPMIDIEVENT Read(void);
```

This function returns a pointer to the next event in the track, or NULL if there are no more events to read. The track can be rewound to the beginning by calling `Rewind()`. Subsequent calls to `Read()` will return sequential events from the track. The events in the track can be discarded by calling `Flush()`.

## CMaxMidiTrack::Rewind()

```
void Rewind(void);
```

This function rewinds the track to the beginning. Subsequent calls to `Read()` will return events, starting at the first event in the track.

## CMaxMidiTrack::Save()

```
BOOL Save(void);
```

This function saves the track into the Standard MIDI File, if attached and opened for writing. Tracks must be written in the order in which you wish them to appear. That is, the first track written is track 0, the next track is track 1, and so on. Returns TRUE if the track was saved, FALSE if there was an error or no SMF is attached. Normally, applications should save all of the tracks of to an SMF at once by calling the `Save()` member of `CMaxMidiSMF`.

*CMaxMidiTrack::SetBuffer()*

    void **SetBuffer**(LPMIDIEVENT lpBuf);

This function replaces the buffer in the track with the specified buffer. Note that the existing buffer is not freed, you must free it by getting its pointer using GetBuffer() and calling GlobalFree() before attaching a new buffer using this function. You should also set the size of the buffer using SetBufferSize() before using the track.

**Parameters**     LPMIDIEVENT lpBuf

             Specifies a pointer to the buffer that will be attached to the track.


*CMaxMidiTrack::SetBufferSize()*

    void **SetBufferSize**(DWORD numEvents);

This function sets the current size of the buffer. Note that this is not the number of events in the track. This function does not resize the buffer, and improper use can cause track corruption and instability. It is used internally by the track object and is not normally called by applications.

**Parameters**     DWORD numEvents

             Specifies the size of the buffer in events. Specifying an incorrect size may
             cause instability.


*CMaxMidiTrack::SetEvent()*

    void **SetEvent**(LPMIDIEVENT lpEvent, DWORD eventNum);

This function sets the specified event in the track to the MidiEvent structure pointed to by lpEvent. Attempts to set event numbers that are greater than the size of the track are ignored.

**Parameters**     LPMIDIEVENT lpEvent

             Specifies a pointer to the event that will be copied into the track.

             DWORD eventNum

             Specifies the index of the event in the track, beginning at 0.


*CMaxMidiTrack::SetName()*

    void **SetName**(LPSTR name);

This function sets the name for this track to the specified string. This name can be read using GetName(). It will be written to the Standard MIDI File if the track is attached to an SMF object and the Save() member function is called.

**Parameters**     LPSTR name

             Specifies a pointer to the new track name, as an ASCIIZ string.

## CMaxMidiTrack::SetNumEvents()

        void **SetNumEvents**(DWORD nEvents);

This function sets the number of events that are in the track. Subsequent reads from the track will begin at the start of the track. This function is used internally by the track object and is not normally called by applications.

**Parameters**      DWORD nEvents

Specifies the number of valid events that are in the track. Setting this value to a number greater than the size of the track buffer may cause loss of data or instability.

## CMaxMidiTrack::SlideTrack()

        void **SlideTrack**(DWORD eventNum, int delta);

This function slides the track, starting at the specified event, by the signed delta value. Note that it is not possible to slide a track such that an event delta time will become negative. That is, specifying a negative delta value that, when added to the event time for the specified event, would cause the delta time to become negative will force the time to 0. Thus, the event will be coincident with the preceding event.

**Parameters**      DWORD eventNum

Specifies the event whose time will be changed, thus moving all the following events in the track.

int delta

Specifies the signed amount to slide the track, in ticks.

## CMaxMidiTrack::Write()

        void **Write**(LPMIDIEVENT lpEvent);

This function appends the event to the end of the track. If there is not enough room for the event, the track buffer is grown before adding the event. The events in the track can be discarded by calling `Flush()`.

**Parameters**      LPMIDIEVENT lpEvent

Specifies a pointer to the event that will be written to the end of the track.

# Standard MIDI File Class—CMaxMidiSMF

This class provides all of the behavior necessary in order to read and write Standard MIDI Files. Files may be opened for reading or for writing. Events in an SMF are accessed by attaching one or more `CMaxMidiTrack` objects to a `CMaxMidiSMF` object. Calling the `Load()` or `Save()` member function will then read or write the tracks.

### CMaxMidiSMF::CMaxMidiSMF() Constructor

```
CMaxMidiSMF();
CMaxMidiSMF(LPSTR filename, const char Mode);
CMaxMidiSMF(LPCTSTR filename, const char Mode);
```

These constructors will initialize the SMF object, and optionally open the specified file in the desired mode. For more information on opening Standard MIDI Files, see the `Open()` member function.

### CMaxMidiSMF::Attach()

```
void Attach(CMaxMidiTrack* pTrack);
void Attach(CMaxMidiTrack* pTrack, int position);
```

This function attaches the track object to the SMF object. SMF tracks are assigned to attached track objects in the order in which they are attached. That is, the first track that is attached corresponds to track 0, the second track corresponds to track 1, and so on.

A track can be attached at a particular position by specifying its position, thus moving all higher tracks up in the list of attached tracks.

**Parameters**    `CMaxMidiTrack* pTrack`

Specifies a pointer to the track object that will be attached.

`int position;`

Specifies the position of the new track in the track list. The first track position is 0. Specifying –1 will append the track to the end of the list.

### CMaxMidiSMF::Close()

```
void Close(void);
```

This function closes an open Standard MIDI File, updating its header and flushing any buffers. The attached tracks are not detached or changed. Deleting the `CMaxMidiSMF` object will also close the file.

*CMaxMidiSMF::Detach()*

```
void Detach(CMaxMidiTrack* pTrack);
```

This function removes the specified track from the list, moving all the remaining higher-numbered tracks down in the list of attached tracks.

**Parameters**     `CMaxMidiTrack* pTrack`

Specifies a pointer to the track object that will be attached.


*CMaxMidiSMF::GetFormat()*

```
int GetFormat(void);
```

This function returns the format of the opened SMF. Two formats are supported: Format 0 (single track file), and Format 1 (multiple track file). If the file is opened for writing and more than one track is attached, the format is automatically set to Format 1.


*CMaxMidiSMF::GetMode()*

```
char GetMode(void);
```

This function returns READ ('r') if the SMF was opened for reading, or WRITE ('w') if the file was opened for writing.


*CMaxMidiSMF::IsOpen()*

```
BOOL IsOpen(void);
```

This function returns TRUE if a Standard MIDI File is open for reading or writing, or FALSE if no file is open.


*CMaxMidiSMF::Load()*

```
BOOL Load(void);
```

This function loads all of the attached tracks from the Standard MIDI File, if opened for read. It returns TRUE if the tracks were read properly, or FALSE if the file was not opened for reading.


*CMaxMidiSMF::NumTracks()*

```
int NumTracks(void);
```

This function returns the number of tracks in the opened SMF. Use this member function to determine how many CMaxMidiTrack objects to create and attach to the SMF object. If the file is opened for write, this function returns 0.

*CMaxMidiSMF::Open()*

```
BOOL Open(LPSTR filename, const char Mode, int Format = 0);

BOOL Open(LPCTSTR filename, const char Mode, int Format = 0);
```

This function opens the specified Standard MIDI File for reading or writing. Format 0 (single track) and Format 1 (multiple track) files can be read or written. When opened for reading, a Format 2 (multiple track, multiple sequence) file will be opened as a Format 0 file, but only the first sequence in the file will be available.

When opening a file for reading, the Format parameter is ignored. The format type of the file can be retrieved using `GetFormat()`. When a file is opened for writing, the format can be explicitly set, or the default Format 0 setting can be used. If more than one track is written to a Format 0 file, it is automatically converted to Format 1.

The filename is a long filename that can include an optional path. Normally, a Standard MIDI File has a .mid or .mff extension, but any extension can be used.

Once a file is opened for reading, the resolution (in ticks per beat) can be retrieved using the `Resolution()` member function. The number of tracks in the file is returned by `NumTracks()`. When a file is opened for writing, the default resolution is 480 ticks per beat. Other resolutions can be set by calling `Resolution()` before saving the file.

To read an SMF, open the file, setting Mode to READ. Get the number of tracks by calling `NumTracks()`. Create that number of CMaxMidiTrack objects and call the `CMaxMidiSMF::Attach()` member function to attach each track. Tracks in the file are assigned to the track objects in the order in which they are attached. Calling the `Load()` member function will load all of the data for each of the tracks into the track objects. The SMF object can be left attached to the track objects or it can be detached and discarded.

To write an SMF, open the file, setting Mode to WRITE. If the file already exists it is overwritten. Attach any track objects for tracks you wish to appear in the file, in ascending order. Normally, the first track (track 0) of a Format 1 file contains tempo events, track 0 events, the sequence name (as a META_NAME Meta event) and certain other Meta events. See `WriteMeta()` for more information.

The function returns TRUE if the file was opened properly, or FALSE if the file could not be found or there was an error opening the file.

**Parameters**   `LPSTR filename`

Specifies the long filename for the file to read or write, with optional path. Normally SMFs have a .mid or .mff extension.

`LPCSTR filename`

Specifies the long filename for the file to read or write as a constant char string, with optional path. Normally SMFs have a .mid or .mff extension.

```
const char Mode
```
Specifies the read or write mode for the file. Possible values for Mode are:

    `READ`    Opens the file for read ('r')

    `WRITE`  Opens the file for write ('w')

```
int Format
```
Specifies the format of the file. Format 0 files have a single track that contains all of the data in the file. Format 1 files contain multiple tracks.

## *CMaxMidiSMF::Read()*

```
BOOL Read(CMaxMidiTrack* pTrack);
```

This function reads all of the data for the specified track into the track object. The track must first be attached using the `Attach()` member function. Normally, you should use the `Load()` function instead, since it reads the data for all of the attached tracks automatically. This function returns TRUE if the track was read correctly, or FALSE if the file is not open or is not opened for reading.

**Parameters**    `CMaxMidiTrack* pTrack`

Specifies a pointer to the track object that will be read.

## *CMaxMidiSMF::ReadMeta()*

```
DWORD ReadMeta(CMaxMidiTrack* pTrack, BYTE MetaEvent, LPSTR*
               Value, DWORD* cbSize);
```

This function reads the next Meta event of the specified type, if present, from the specified track of the previously opened (for reading) Standard MIDI File. The track must be attached to the SMF object. If the Meta event is found, `Value` points to a buffer that contains the data for the Meta event. The function returns the event timestamp, or −1 on error.

**Parameters**    `CMaxMidiTrack* pTrack`

Specifies a pointer to the track object that will be read.

`BYTE MetaEvent`

Specifies the Meta event to retrieve from the Standard MIDI File. Possible Meta events are:

    `META_SEQUENCE_NUMBER`

    Specifies a sequence number for this file.

    `META_TEXT`

    Specifies a general-purpose text string.

**META_COPYRIGHT**

Specifies a copyright notice for the Standard MIDI File sequence.

**META_NAME**

Specifies the name of the sequence if read from track 0, or the name of the track if read from other tracks.

**META_INST_NAME**

Specifies the name of the instrumentation used for the specified track.

**META_LYRIC**

Specifies a lyric to be sung.

**META_MARKER**

Specifies a marker name for a particular point in a sequence.

**META_CUE_POINT**

Specifies a description of cue events in a sequence.

**META_CHAN_PREFIX**

Specifies the MIDI channel that will apply to all events to follow, until the next MIDI event that specifies a channel.

**META_SMPTE_OFFSET**

Specifies the SMPTE offset for the specified track.

**META_TIME_SIG**

Specifies the current Time Signature.

**META_KEY_SIG**

Specifies the current Key Signature.

**LPSTR* Value**

Specifies the pointer to a string that contains the value of the found Meta event, or NULL if not found.

**DWORD* cbSize**

Specifies the pointer to a DWORD that contains the size in bytes of the Meta event value string, or 0 if not found.

**Return Value**    Returns the timestamp of the event, or –1 if not found or error.

### CMaxMidiSMF::Resolution()

```
WORD Resolution(void);
WORD Resolution(WORD res);
```

This function gets or sets the resolution of the timestamps used in the file, in ticks per beat. The function returns the current resolution, or 0 if there was an error. For more information on resolution, see the `CMaxMidiSync::Resolution()` function.

### CMaxMidiSMF::Rewind()

```
BOOL Rewind(void);
```

This function rewinds the Standard MIDI File to the beginning, if opened for reading. Subsequent calls to `Load()` will then reload the tracks from the file. It returns TRUE if the rewind was successful, or FALSE if the file was not opened for reading.

### CMaxMidiSMF::Save()

```
BOOL Save(void);
```

This function saves all of the attached tracks to the Standard MIDI File, if opened for writing. It returns TRUE if the tracks were written properly, or FALSE if the file was not opened for writing.

### CMaxMidiSMF::Write()

```
BOOL Write(CMaxMidiTrack* pTrack);
```

This function writes all of the data for the specified track to the track object. The track must first be attached with the `Attach()` member function. Normally, you should use the `Save()` function instead, since it writes the data for all of the attached tracks automatically. This function returns TRUE if the track was written correctly, or FALSE if the file is not open or is not opened for write.

**Parameters**   CMaxMidiTrack* pTrack

Specifies a pointer to the track object that will be written.

### CMaxMidiSMF::WriteMeta()

```
UINT WriteMeta(CMaxMidiTrack* pTrack, BYTE MetaEvent, LPSTR
              Value, DWORD time);
```

This function writes a Meta event to the desired track of the previously opened Standard MIDI File. All of the Meta events for a specific track must be written before attempting to write another track, since specifying a new track will permanently close the current track.

**Parameters**      `CMaxMidiTrack* pTrack`

Specifies a pointer to the track object that will be written.

`BYTE MetaEvent`

Specifies the Meta event to write to the Standard MIDI File. Possible Meta events are:

`META_SEQUENCE_NUMBER`

Specifies a sequence number for this file. If used, this event must precede any playable MIDI events.

`META_TEXT`

Specifies a general-purpose text string.

`META_COPYRIGHT`

Specifies a copyright notice for the Standard MIDI File sequence. This should be the first Meta Event of track 0, preceding any playable MIDI events.

`META_NAME`

Specifies the name of the sequence if written to track 0, or the name of the track if written to other tracks.

`META_INST_NAME`

Specifies the name of the instrumentation used for the specified track.

`META_LYRIC`

Specifies a lyric or syllable to be sung.

`META_MARKER`

Specifies a marker name for a particular point in a sequence.

`META_CUE_POINT`

Specifies a description of cue events in a sequence.

`META_CHAN_PREFIX`

Specifies the MIDI channel that will apply to all events to follow, until the next MIDI event that specifies a channel.

`META_SMPTE_OFFSET`

Specifies the SMPTE offset for the specified track.

**META_TIME_SIG**

Specifies the current Time Signature.

**META_KEY_SIG**

Specifies the current Key Signature.

**META_EOT**

Specifies an end of track. Used internally by MaxMidi. An application must not attempt to write this Meta event.

**META_TEMPO**

Specifies a tempo change event. Used internally by MaxMidi. An application must not attempt to write this Meta event.

`LPSTR *EventValue`

Specifies the pointer to a string that contains the value of the Meta event.

`DWORD dwTime`

Specifies the timestamp for the Meta event.

**Return Value**   Returns 0 if the requested Meta event is written, nonzero on error.

# APPENDIX B

# *MaxMidi DLL Source Code*

# MaxMidi Header Files

## MaxMidi.h

```
//-------------------------------------------------------------------------------
// Maximum MIDI Programmer's ToolKit
// 32-bit App Header File
//
// Copyright (c) Paul A. Messick, 1994-1996
//
// Written by Paul A. Messick
//-------------------------------------------------------------------------------
//-------------------------------------------------------------------------------
//   Definitions
//-------------------------------------------------------------------------------
#ifndef __MAXMIDI__
#define __MAXMIDI__       // include header only once per file

#include <mmsystem.h>

#ifdef __cplusplus
extern "C" {              // Assume C declarations for C++
#endif

#ifndef __WIN32__
    #ifdef _WIN32
        #define __WIN32__
    #else
        #ifdef WIN32
            #define __WIN32__
        #endif
    #endif
#endif

#ifdef __WIN32__
    #define PREFIX __declspec(dllexport)
    #define EXPORT
#else
    #define PREFIX
    #define EXPORT __export
#endif

//   midi buffer sizes
#define QUEUE_64 (0 << 12)
#define QUEUE_128(1 << 12)
#define QUEUE_256(2 << 12)
#define QUEUE_512(3 << 12)
#define QUEUE_1K (4 << 12)
#define QUEUE_2K (5 << 12)
#define QUEUE_4K (6 << 12)
#define QUEUE_8K (7 << 12)
#define QUEUE_16K(8 << 12)
#define QUEUE_32K(9 << 12)

#define SXBUF_64 (0 << 8)
#define SXBUF_128(1 << 8)
#define SXBUF_256(2 << 8)
#define SXBUF_512(3 << 8)
#define SXBUF_1K (4 << 8)
#define SXBUF_2K (5 << 8)
#define SXBUF_4K (6 << 8)
#define SXBUF_8K (7 << 8)
#define SXBUF_16K(8 << 8)
#define SXBUF_32K(9 << 8)

//   midi sync status messages
#define NOTEOFF       0x80
#define NOTEON        0x90
#define SYSEX         0xF0
#define MTC_QFRAME    0xF1
#define EOX           0xF7
#define MIDI_CLOCK    0xF8
#define MIDI_START    0xFA
#define MIDI_CONTINUE 0xFB
```

```
#define MIDI_STOP          0xFC

// maxmidi messages
#define WM_MAXMIDI                 (WM_USER + 0x504D)    // 'PM'
#define MOM_LONGDATA       (WM_MAXMIDI+3)
#define MIDI_BEAT          (WM_MAXMIDI+5)
#define OUTBUFFER_READY    (WM_MAXMIDI+6)
#define SYNC_DONE          (WM_MAXMIDI+10)
#define MIDI_DATA          MIM_DATA

// external (user settable) flags
#define ENABLE_SYSEX       0x00010000L
#define DISABLE_SYSEX      (~ENABLE_SYSEX)
#define SYNC_INPUT               0x00020000L
#define SYNC_OUTPUT        0x00020000L

// MxMidi DLL error values
#define MXMIDIERR_NOERROR        0
#define MXMIDIERR_BADDEVICEID    MMSYSERR_BADDEVICEID
#define MXMIDIERR_NOMEM          MMSYSERR_NOMEM
#define MXMIDIERR_BADHANDLE      MMSYSERR_ALLOCATED
#define MXMIDIERR_BADTEMPO       30
#define MXMIDIERR_MAXERR         32
#define ERR_NOMATCH              0xFFF0

//------------------------------------------------------------------------
//  Event structures
//------------------------------------------------------------------------
#pragma pack(1)
typedef struct {
    DWORD   time;      // time in ticks since last event
    BYTE status;       // status byte of this midi message
    BYTE data1;        // first data byte of message
    BYTE data2;        // second data byte of message
    BYTE data3;        // third data byte, used for tempo changes
} MidiEvent;
#pragma pack()

typedef MidiEvent* LPMIDIEVENT;

//------------------------------------------------------------------------
//  Midi In Definitions
//------------------------------------------------------------------------
#define MIDIIN_DEFAULT (QUEUE_512|SXBUF_512|ENABLE_SYSEX|32)
typedef DWORD HMIN;

//------------------------------------------------------------------------
//  MIDI Out Definitions
//------------------------------------------------------------------------
#define MIDIOUT_DEFAULT (QUEUE_512|SXBUF_512|ENABLE_SYSEX|32)
typedef DWORD HMOUT;

//------------------------------------------------------------------------
//  Sync Timer definitions
//------------------------------------------------------------------------
#define USE_CURRENT 0xFFFF
#define DEFAULT_TIMERPERIOD 10
#define MAX_RESOLUTION 960
#define S_INT         0
#define S_MIDI        1
#define POS_TICKS     0
#define POS_MS        1
typedef DWORD HSYNC;

//------------------------------------------------------------------------
//  Standard MIDI File definitions
//------------------------------------------------------------------------
#define META                     0xFF
#define META_SEQUENCE_NUMBER     0x00
#define META_TEXT                0x01
#define META_COPYRIGHT           0x02
#define META_NAME                0x03
#define META_INST_NAME           0x04
#define META_LYRIC               0x05
#define META_MARKER              0x06
#define META_CUE_POINT           0x07
#define META_CHAN_PREFIX         0x20
#define META_EOT                 0x2F
```

```
#define META_TEMPO            0x51
#define META_SMPTE_OFFSET     0x54
#define META_TIME_SIG         0x58
#define META_KEY_SIG          0x59
#define META_SEQ_SPECIFIC     0x7F
#define MAX_META_EVENT        0x80

typedef DWORD HSMF;
//----------------------------------------------------------------------
//   Exported MaxMidi DLL entry point function prototypes
//----------------------------------------------------------------------
PREFIX WORD WINAPI EXPORT GetMaxMidiVersion(void);

PREFIX UINT WINAPI EXPORT GetNumOutDevices(void);
PREFIX BOOL WINAPI EXPORT GetMidiOutDescription(WORD wDeviceID, LPSTR lpzDesc);
PREFIX HMOUT WINAPI EXPORT OpenMidiOut(HWND hWnd, WORD wDeviceID, HSYNC hSync, DWORD
dwFlags);
PREFIX WORD WINAPI EXPORT ResetMidiOut(HMOUT hMidiOut);
PREFIX void WINAPI EXPORT FlushMidiOut(HMOUT hMidiOut);
PREFIX WORD WINAPI EXPORT CloseMidiOut(HMOUT hMidiOut);
PREFIX WORD WINAPI EXPORT PutMidiOut(HMOUT hMidiOut, LPMIDIEVENT lpMidiEvent);

PREFIX UINT WINAPI EXPORT GetNumInDevices(void);
PREFIX BOOL WINAPI EXPORT GetMidiInDescription(WORD wDeviceID, LPSTR lpzDesc);
PREFIX HMIN WINAPI EXPORT OpenMidiIn(HWND hWnd, WORD wDeviceID, HSYNC hSync, DWORD
dwFlags);
PREFIX WORD WINAPI EXPORT StartMidiIn(HMIN lpMidiIn);
PREFIX WORD WINAPI EXPORT StopMidiIn(HMIN lpMidiIn);
PREFIX WORD WINAPI EXPORT CloseMidiIn(HMIN lpMidiIn);
PREFIX LPMIDIEVENT WINAPI EXPORT GetMidiIn(HMIN lpMidiIn);

PREFIX HSYNC WINAPI EXPORT OpenSync(HSYNC hSync, HWND hWnd, WORD mode, WORD
timerPeriod);
PREFIX WORD WINAPI EXPORT CloseSync(HSYNC hSync);
PREFIX void WINAPI EXPORT StopSync(HSYNC hSync);
PREFIX void WINAPI EXPORT StartSync(HSYNC hSync);
PREFIX void WINAPI EXPORT PauseSync(HSYNC hSync, BOOL reset);
PREFIX void WINAPI EXPORT ReStartSync(HSYNC hSync);
PREFIX WORD WINAPI EXPORT SetTempo(HSYNC hSync, DWORD uSPerBeat);
PREFIX void WINAPI EXPORT SetResolution(HSYNC hSync, WORD resolution);
PREFIX DWORD WINAPI EXPORT GetTempo(HSYNC hSync);
PREFIX WORD WINAPI EXPORT GetResolution(HSYNC hSync);
PREFIX DWORD WINAPI EXPORT GetPosition(HSYNC hSync, WORD units);

PREFIX HSMF WINAPI EXPORT OpenSMF(LPSTR filename, int *Format, const char mode, int
*nTracks);
PREFIX void WINAPI EXPORT CloseSMF(HSMF hSMF);
PREFIX BOOL WINAPI EXPORT RewindSMF(HSMF hSMF);
PREFIX DWORD WINAPI EXPORT ReadSMF(HSMF hSMF, int wTrack, LPMIDIEVENT lpMidiEventBuffer,
DWORD dwBufferLen);
PREFIX DWORD WINAPI EXPORT WriteSMF(HSMF hSMF, int wTrack, LPMIDIEVENT
lpMidiEventBuffer, DWORD dwBufferLen);
PREFIX WORD WINAPI EXPORT GetSMFResolution(HSMF hSMF);
PREFIX WORD WINAPI EXPORT SetSMFResolution(HSMF hSMF, WORD resolution);
PREFIX DWORD WINAPI EXPORT ReadMetaEvent(HSMF hSMF, int wTrack, BYTE MetaEvent, LPSTR
*EventValue, DWORD *EventSize);
PREFIX int WINAPI EXPORT WriteMetaEvent(HSMF hSMF, int wTrack, BYTE MetaEvent, LPSTR
EventValue, DWORD dwTime);

#ifdef __cplusplus
}    // End of extern "C" {
#endif

#ifdef __cplusplus         // Include MaxMidi Classes
#ifdef __AFX_H__      // MFC Only!
#ifdef _SMF
    #ifndef _TRACK          // SMF requires TRACK
        #define _TRACK
    #endif
#endif
#ifdef _TRACK
    class CMaxMidiTrack;
#endif
#ifdef _SMF
    #include "CMaxMidiSMF.h"
#endif
#ifdef _SYNC
    #include "CMaxMidiSync.h"
#endif
```

```
#ifdef _MIDIIN
    #include "CMaxMidiIn.h"
    #ifdef _MENUS
        #include "CMidiInDeviceMenu.h"
    #endif
#endif
#ifdef _MIDIOUT
    #include "CMaxMidiOut.h"
    #ifdef _MENUS
        #include "CMidiOutDeviceMenu.h"
    #endif
#endif
#ifdef _TRACK
    #include "CMaxMidiTrack.h"
#endif
#endif //__AFX_H__
#endif
#endif //!__MAXMIDI__
```

# MxDll.h

```
//--------------------------------------------------------------------------------
// Maximum MIDI Programmer's ToolKit
// 32-bit App Header File
//
// Copyright (c) Paul A. Messick, 1994-1996
//
// Written by Paul A. Messick
//--------------------------------------------------------------------------------
//--------------------------------------------------------------------------------
//   Definitions
//--------------------------------------------------------------------------------
#include <mmsystem.h>
#include "MaxMidi.h"

#ifdef _WIN32
#define PREFIX   __declspec(dllexport)
#define EXPORT
#else
#define PREFIX
#define EXPORT   __export
#endif

#ifdef __cplusplus
extern "C" {            // Assume C declarations for C++
#endif

#define MIDIINCLASS "MaxMidiInClass"
#define MIDIOUTCLASS "MaxMidiOutClass"
#define WINDOWS_QUEUE_SIZE 64
#define SCALE 256L

#define QMASK   0x0000F000L
#define SXMASK  0x00000F00L
#define NMASK   0x000000FFL

//   flag bit definations
//   internal flags
#define MIDI_IN_INTERNAL   0x000FFFFFL
#define MIDI_IN_STARTED    0x00100000L
#define MIDI_OUT_INTERNAL  0x000FFFFFL
#define SENDING_SYSEX      0x00200000L
#define SYNC_ENABLED       0x0001
#define SYNC_RUNNING       0x0002
#define IN_SYNC            0x0008
#define MC_HOLD            0x0010
#define MC_RESYNC          0x0020
#define SENT_SYNCDONE      0x0040
#define RUNNING_STATUS     0x0080

// smf internals
#define META_SEQUENCE_NUMBER_LENGTH     2
#define META_CHAN_PREFIX_LENGTH         1
#define META_EOT_LENGTH                 0
#define META_TEMPO_LENGTH               3
#define META_SMPTE_OFFSET_LENGTH        5
#define META_TIME_SIG_LENGTH            4
#define META_KEY_SIG_LENGTH             2
```

```c
#define SMF_HEADER_SIZE            6L
#pragma pack(1)
//---------------------------------------------------------------------------
//   Midi In Definitions
//---------------------------------------------------------------------------
typedef struct {
     HWND      hWnd;                // handle to the window that will receive MIM_... messages
     HMIDIIN     hMidiIn;           // handle to the opened midi in device
     WORD      wDeviceID;           // the device ID corresponding to this device
     void FAR*    lpSync;           // pointer to sync device for midi in
     DWORD      dwFlags;            // internal flags used to manage midi in
     MidiEvent      sysexEvent;     // expanded sysex event for MidiIn
     HWND      hMWnd;               // handle to the window that is to process messages
     WORD      nSysexBufSize;       // size, in bytes, of each sysex buffer
     DWORD         pMidiInDataIn;   // pointer to location to receive next message
     DWORD         pMidiInDataOut;  // pointer to location to retrieve this message
     WORD      nMidiInSize;         // size of the midi in buffer
     LPMIDIEVENT lpMidiInDataHead;  // address of start of queue
     DWORD         lpSysexData;     // offset pointer to sysex data in current buffer
     DWORD         dwLastEventTicks;// time of the last event to calculate delta times
     LPDWORD* lpHeaderList;         // start of list of midiin headers in round-robin
     WORD      nSysexBuffs;         // number of sysex buffers allocated
     WORD      nHeaderIn;           // index to next header to insert into the list
     WORD      nHeaderOut;          // index to this header to retreive data from
} MidiInStruct;

typedef MidiInStruct FAR* LPMIDIIN;

//---------------------------------------------------------------------------
//   MIDI Out Definitions
//---------------------------------------------------------------------------
typedef struct {
     HWND      hWnd;                // handle to the window that receives MOM_... messages
     HMIDIOUT hMidiOut;             // handle to the opened midi out device
     void FAR*    lpSync;           // pointer to sync device for midi out
     WORD      wDeviceID;           // the device ID corresponding to this device
     DWORD         dwFlags;         // flags used to manage midi out
     HWND      hMWnd;               // handle to the window that is to receive midi out
process msgs
     WORD      nSysexBufSize;       // size, in bytes, of each sysex buffer
     DWORD         pMidiOutDataIn;  // pointer to location to receive next message
     DWORD         pMidiOutDataOut; // pointer to location to retrieve this message
     LPMIDIEVENT lpMidiOutDataHead; // address of start of queue
     WORD      nMidiOutSize;        // size, in events, of the out buffer
     WORD      wSpan;               // distance in events between in and out buffer pointers
     WORD      wNotes[128];         // tracking array for note on/offs
     LPDWORD* lpHeaderList;         // start of list of midiout headers in round-robin
     WORD      nThisHeader;         // index of next header to use for sysex output
     WORD      nAvailableBuffs;     // count of queue-able sysex buffers left
     WORD      nSysexBuffsAllowed;  // max number of active sysex buffers
     DWORD         dwLastEventTicks;// time of the last event to calculate delta times
} MidiOutStruct;

typedef MidiOutStruct FAR* LPMIDIOUT;

//---------------------------------------------------------------------------
//   Sync Timer definitions
//---------------------------------------------------------------------------
typedef struct {
     HWND      hWnd;                // handle to the window that will receive messages
     WORD      wSyncMode;           // sync mode, S_INT, S_CLOCK...
     WORD      wTimerPeriod;        // period of timer in ms
     LPMIDIIN lpSyncIn;             // input device for sync--tempo events go to this device's
queue
     WORD      wFlags;              // flags used to manage sync
     WORD      wTimerID;            // ID of the timer, NULL if not in use
     DWORD         dwTicks;         // current tick value for sync
     WORD      nTicksSinceBeat;     // number of ticks since last beat
     DWORD         dwTempo;         // current tempo in uS/midi beat
     WORD      wResolution;         // sync resolution in ticks/midi beat
     DWORD         dwTRtime;        // set to resolution*ticktime[syncMode]
     DWORD         dwFticks;        // remaining fraction of a tick in (resolution*time)
     LPMIDIOUT FAR*  lpMidiOutList; // pointer to head of list of midi outs that
                                    // are serviced by this sync device
     WORD      nTicksPerClock;      // number of ticks per midi beat for clocks
     WORD      nTicksSinceClock;    // number of ticks since last clock
     WORD      wTempoTicks;         // count of elaspsed ticks for midi sync tempo calc
```

```c
        DWORD           dwLastTicks;          // tick count at last midi clock for midi sync
        WORD            nSysexBuffsActive;    // count of active sysex buffers
        DWORD           msPosition;           // current position in sequence, in milliseconds
} SyncStruct;

typedef SyncStruct FAR* LPSYNC;

//------------------------------------------------------------------------------
// Standard Midi File Structures
//------------------------------------------------------------------------------
#define IN_SYSEX 0x0001          // true if currently reading a sysex

typedef struct {
        DWORD           dwLength;             // length of track in bytes
        BYTE            bStatus;              // running status for this track
        LPSTR           lpReadBuf;            // buffer for data to read
        DWORD           dwRBsize;             // size of the read buffer
        DWORD           dwBuffOfs;            // current offset into buffer
        DWORD           dwFileOfs;            // file offset for start of buffer
        DWORD           dwBytesRemaining;     // number of bytes in buffer
        DWORD           dwSysexLen;           // length of sysex block
        BYTE            bMetaStatus;          // running status for ReadMeta...
        LPDWORD         lpMetaOfs;            // pointer to array of offsets
                                              // to meta events for ReadMeta...
        BOOL            fEndOfTrack;          // true if reading has reached EOT
        WORD            wFlags;               // flags used by this track
        DWORD           dwMetaDeltaTime;      // accumulated delta time for skipped meta events
        LPDWORD         lpMetaTime;           // pointer to array of elapsed times
                                              // for each meta event for ReadMeta...
} TrackStruct;
typedef TrackStruct* LPTRACK;

typedef struct {
        char     mode;                        // mode for read 'r' or write 'w'
        HANDLE          hsmf;                 // file handle for smf
        short           wFormat;              // smf file format
        short           wTracks;              // number of tracks in file
        short           resolution;           // timing resolution in tpb
        LPTRACK         lpTrack;              // pointer to array of track structures
        short           wCurTrack;            // current working track number
        LPSTR           lpMetaBuff;           // buffer for meta strings
        DWORD           dwCurFileOfs;         // actual offset into file
        DWORD           dwChunkStart;         // start position of chunk for WriteSMF
        DWORD           dwChunkLen;           // length of chunk for WriteSMF
        BYTE            bStatus;              // current status for WriteSMF
        DWORD           dwSxLen;              // length of sysex for WriteSMF
        DWORD           dwSxBuffSize;         // size of buffer for sysex write
        LPSTR           lpSxBuff;             // pointer to sysex write buffer
} SMFStruct;

typedef SMFStruct* LPSMF;
#pragma pack()
//------------------------------------------------------------------------------
//    Internal Function Prototypes
//------------------------------------------------------------------------------
PREFIX void CALLBACK WINAPI EXPORT MidiInCallback(HMIDIIN hMI, UINT wMsg, DWORD
dwInstance, DWORD dwParam1, DWORD dwParam2);
PREFIX LRESULT CALLBACK WINAPI EXPORT MidiInProc(HWND hWnd, UINT iMessage, WPARAM
wParam, LPARAM lpMidiIn);
PREFIX LRESULT CALLBACK WINAPI EXPORT MidiOutProc(HWND hWnd, UINT iMessage, WPARAM
wParam, LPARAM lParam);
PREFIX void CALLBACK WINAPI EXPORT MidiOutCallback(HMIDIIN hMI, UINT wMsg, DWORD
dwInstance, DWORD dwParam1, DWORD dwParam2);
PREFIX LRESULT CALLBACK WINAPI EXPORT MidiOutProc(HWND hWnd, UINT iMessage, WPARAM
wParam, LPARAM lParam);
PREFIX void CALLBACK WINAPI EXPORT syncTimer(UINT wTimerID, UINT wMsg, DWORD dwUser,
DWORD dw1, DWORD dw2);
void PostUserMessage(HWND hWnd, LPMIDIEVENT lpEvent);

//------------------------------------------------------------------------------
// MxMidi16 16-bit API
//------------------------------------------------------------------------------
PREFIX WORD WINAPI EXPORT GetMaxMidiVersion16(void);
PREFIX void WINAPI EXPORT FreeGlobalMem16(void FAR* gMem);

PREFIX BOOL WINAPI EXPORT GetMidiOutDescription16(WORD wDeviceID, LPSTR lpzDesc);
PREFIX HMOUT WINAPI EXPORT OpenMidiOut16(HWND hWnd, WORD wDeviceID, HSYNC hSync, DWORD
dwFlags);
PREFIX WORD WINAPI EXPORT ResetMidiOut16(HMOUT hMidiOut);
```

```
PREFIX void WINAPI EXPORT FlushMidiOut16(HMOUT hMidiOut);
PREFIX WORD WINAPI EXPORT CloseMidiOut16(HMOUT hMidiOut);
PREFIX WORD WINAPI EXPORT PutMidiOut16(HMOUT hMidiOut, LPMIDIEVENT lpMidiEvent);

PREFIX BOOL WINAPI EXPORT GetMidiInDescription16(WORD wDeviceID, LPSTR lpzDesc);
PREFIX HMIN WINAPI EXPORT OpenMidiIn16(HWND hWnd, WORD wDeviceID, HSYNC hSync, DWORD
    dwFlags);
PREFIX WORD WINAPI EXPORT StartMidiIn16(HMIN lpMidiIn);
PREFIX WORD WINAPI EXPORT StopMidiIn16(HMIN lpMidiIn);
PREFIX WORD WINAPI EXPORT CloseMidiIn16(HMIN lpMidiIn);
PREFIX LPMIDIEVENT WINAPI EXPORT GetMidiIn16(HMIN lpMidiIn);

PREFIX HSYNC WINAPI EXPORT OpenSync16(HSYNC hSync, HWND hWnd, WORD mode, WORD
    timerPeriod);
PREFIX WORD WINAPI EXPORT CloseSync16(HSYNC hSync);
PREFIX void WINAPI EXPORT StopSync16(HSYNC hSync);
PREFIX void WINAPI EXPORT StartSync16(HSYNC hSync);
PREFIX void WINAPI EXPORT PauseSync16(HSYNC hSync, BOOL reset);
PREFIX void WINAPI EXPORT ReStartSync16(HSYNC hSync);
PREFIX WORD WINAPI EXPORT SetTempo16(HSYNC hSync, DWORD uSPerBeat);
PREFIX void WINAPI EXPORT SetResolution16(HSYNC hSync, WORD resolution);
PREFIX DWORD WINAPI EXPORT GetTempo16(HSYNC hSync);
PREFIX WORD WINAPI EXPORT GetResolution16(HSYNC hSync);
PREFIX DWORD WINAPI EXPORT GetPosition16(HSYNC hSync, WORD units);

#ifdef __cplusplus
}                        // End of extern "C" {
#endif
```

# MxMidi16 DLL Source

## MidiIn.c

```
// Maximum MIDI Programmer's ToolKit - MxMidi16.DLL
// MIDI Input Module
//
// Copyright (c) Paul A. Messick, 1994-1996
//
// Written by Paul A. Messick
//
// Provides a 16-bit API to open, close, and receive midi messages,
// with system exclusive messages merged into the normal midi stream.
//----------------------------------------------------------------------------
#include <windows.h>
#include "MxDLL.h"
//----------------------------------------------------------------------------
//   DllEntryPoint definitions
//----------------------------------------------------------------------------
#define DLL_PROCESS_DETACH 0
#define DLL_PROCESS_ATTACH 1
BOOL FAR PASCAL _export MxMidi_ThunkConnect16(LPSTR pszDll16, LPSTR pszDll32,
        HINSTANCE hInst, DWORD dwReason);

//----------------------------------------------------------------------------
// Function Prototypes used in this DLL module
//----------------------------------------------------------------------------
WORD AllocateMidiInQueue(LPMIDIIN lpMidiIn, DWORD dwEvents);
HWND CreateMidiInWindow(LPMIDIIN lpMidiIn);
LPMIDIHDR AllocateMidiInSysexBuffer(LPMIDIIN lpMidiIn, WORD wSize);
void MidiClock(LPSYNC lpSync);
//----------------------------------------------------------------------------
// Global Variables
//----------------------------------------------------------------------------
HINSTANCE ghInstance; // global instance handle for this dll
                    // buffer size table
WORD bufSize[10] = { 64, 128, 256, 512, 1024, 2048, 4096, 8192, 16384, 32768 };
WORD wQueueSize = 8; // the size of the windows message queue

#define MSHORT 0
#define MSYSEX 1
```

```
//-----------------------------------------------------------------------------
//   DllEntryPoint
//
//   Connects this 16-bit Windows 4.0 (Windows 95) DLL to its 32-bit counterpart
//   through the flat thunk layer.  This entry point is called (in addition to
//   LibMain) for DLLs that are tagged as version 4.0 (using the special rc.exe
//   resource compiler in the Win95 SDK: 'rc -40 mxmidi16.dll mxmidi16.res').
//-----------------------------------------------------------------------------
BOOL FAR PASCAL _export DllEntryPoint(DWORD dwReason, HINSTANCE hInst, WORD wDS,
        WORD wHeapSize, DWORD dwReserved1, WORD wReserved2)
{
    if(!(MxMidi_ThunkConnect16("MXMIDI16.DLL", "MXMIDI32.DLL", hInst, dwReason)))
        return FALSE;

    switch(dwReason)
    {
        // DLL is attaching to the address space of the current process.
        case DLL_PROCESS_ATTACH:
            break;

        // The calling process is detaching the DLL from its address space.
        case DLL_PROCESS_DETACH:
            break;
    }

    return TRUE;
}

//-----------------------------------------------------------------------------
// LibMain
//
// Only one LibMain may exist in a dll, so it appears only in midiin.cpp.
// This function registers the window classes used in this DLL.
//-----------------------------------------------------------------------------
int WINAPI _export LibMain(HINSTANCE hInst, WORD wDS, WORD cbHeapSize,
        LPSTR lpCmdLine)
{
    WNDCLASS wndclass;        // Structure used to register class

    ghInstance = hInst;       // the instance handle for this dll

    // setup window class parameters. Notice that this window is NEVER
    // displayed, so the display-specific parameters are set to NULL.
    wndclass.style         = CS_GLOBALCLASS;
    wndclass.lpfnWndProc   = MidiInProc;
    wndclass.cbClsExtra    = 0;
    wndclass.cbWndExtra    = 0;
    wndclass.hInstance     = ghInstance;
    wndclass.hIcon         = NULL;
    wndclass.hCursor       = NULL;
    wndclass.hbrBackground = NULL;
    wndclass.lpszMenuName  = NULL;
    wndclass.lpszClassName = MIDIINCLASS;
    RegisterClass(&wndclass);

    // setup hidden midi out window class parameters.  Notice that
    // this window is NEVER displayed, so the display-specific
    // parameters are set to NULL.
    wndclass.style         = CS_GLOBALCLASS;
    wndclass.lpfnWndProc   = MidiOutProc;
    wndclass.cbClsExtra    = 0;
    wndclass.cbWndExtra    = 0;
    wndclass.hInstance     = ghInstance;
    wndclass.hIcon         = NULL;
    wndclass.hCursor       = NULL;
    wndclass.hbrBackground = NULL;
    wndclass.lpszMenuName  = NULL;
    wndclass.lpszClassName = MIDIOUTCLASS;
    RegisterClass(&wndclass);
    return 1;
}

//-----------------------------------------------------------------------------
// Windows Exit Procedure
//
// Unregister the hidden windows that are used by this DLL.
//-----------------------------------------------------------------------------
int WINAPI _export WEP(int nParameter)
{
    UnregisterClass(MIDIINCLASS, ghInstance);
```

```
                UnregisterClass(MIDIOUTCLASS, ghInstance);
                return 0;
        }
        //------------------------------------------------------------------------------
        // GetMxMidiVersion
        //
        // Returns the current dll version number as a word with the major version
        // number in the high byte and the minor version number in the low byte.
        // This function must be called before the message loop of the
        // application that is to use midi can begin to use functions in this dll,
        // since the dll must set the message queue list size.
        //------------------------------------------------------------------------------
        WORD WINAPI _export GetMaxMidiVersion16(void)
        {
                // the queue size determines the upper limit on the number
                // of queue-able sysex buffers. If this function is not called
                // the QueueSize is the default 8 messages.
                wQueueSize = WINDOWS_QUEUE_SIZE;
                SetMessageQueue(wQueueSize);
                return (1 << 8) | 0;
        }

        //------------------------------------------------------------------------------
        // GetMidiInDescription
        //
        // Gets the text string description for the midi in device designated by
        // wDeviceID. If there is no device by that ID the function returns FALSE
        // Otherwise, it returns TRUE and sets the string lpzDesc to the device
        // description.
        //------------------------------------------------------------------------------
        BOOL WINAPI _export GetMidiInDescription16(WORD wDeviceID, LPSTR lpzDesc)
        {
                MIDIINCAPS Caps;

                if(midiInGetDevCaps(wDeviceID, (LPMIDIINCAPS) &Caps, sizeof(Caps)) ==
                        MMSYSERR_BADDEVICEID)
                    return FALSE;

                lstrcpy(lpzDesc, (LPSTR)Caps.szPname);
                return TRUE;
        }
        //------------------------------------------------------------------------------
        // OpenMidiIn
        //
        // Opens the device wDevice for midi input.
        //
        // hWnd is the handle to the window that is to receive any messages from
        //   this device.
        //
        // wDeviceID ranges from 0 to one less than the number of available
        //   devices and indicates which device is to be opened.
        //
        // hSync is the handle to the previously opened sync device that will
        //   handle syncronization for this input. If no sync is to be used
        //   with this input, hSync must be zero.
        //
        // dwFlags are used to affect the particular operation of the midi in
        //   device and can be combined using the OR operator.
        //
        // Current flags are:
        //   SYSEX_ENABLED     if set, system exclusive messages are merged into
        //                     the normal midi stream that is sent to the app
        //  *SYSEX_DISABLED    if set, system exclusive messages are filtered (default)
        //   SYNC_INPUT    this input serves as the sync input for MTC or
        //                 CLOCK sync for the previously opened sync
        //                 device lpSync. It is ignored if lpSync
        //                 is NULL or the sync mode has been set to
        //                 S_STOPPED or S_INT.
        //
        // The function returns the handle to the device if midi in was correctly
        // opened, or an error value (that is less than MXMIDIERR_MAXERR) if there
        // was an error opening the device.
        //------------------------------------------------------------------------------
        HMIN WINAPI _export OpenMidiIn16(HWND hWnd, WORD wDeviceID, HSYNC hSync,
                DWORD dwFlags)
        {
                LPMIDIIN lpMI;        // local pointer to allocated MidiIn structure
```

```
WORD i;                    // loop counter
LPSYNC lpSync = (LPSYNC)hSync;
WORD wLastError;

// if an attempt to open more than then max number of devices return bad
// ID error
if(midiInGetNumDevs() <= wDeviceID)
    return MXMIDIERR_BADDEVICEID;

// attempt to allocate memory for this device
lpMI = (LPMIDIIN)GlobalLock(GlobalAlloc(GPTR, sizeof(MidiInStruct)));

// check for an allocation error
if(lpMI == NULL)
    return MXMIDIERR_NOMEM;

// this is the handle to the window that is to receive messages
lpMI->hWnd = hWnd;

// the device id associated with this device
lpMI->wDeviceID = wDeviceID;

// attempt to open the device
wLastError = midiInOpen(&lpMI->hMidiIn, wDeviceID, (DWORD)MidiInCallback,
        (DWORD)lpMI, CALLBACK_FUNCTION);

// if there is an error opening midi in, return a null handle and
// free the allocated structure
if(wLastError != 0)
{
    FreeGlobalMem16(lpMI);
    return wLastError;
}

// setup the necessary flags and default values
lpMI->dwFlags = (dwFlags & MIDI_IN_INTERNAL);   // set external flags only
lpMI->nSysexBufSize = bufSize[(dwFlags & SXMASK) >> 8];

// if this is the sync input device, adjust the pointer in lpSync
// and insert this device into lpSync as the sync in device
lpMI->lpSync = lpSync;

if((dwFlags & SYNC_INPUT) && (lpSync != NULL))
    lpSync->lpSyncIn = lpMI;

// allocate the queue for non-sysex messages
if(AllocateMidiInQueue(lpMI, bufSize[(dwFlags & QMASK) >> 12]) != 0)
{
    FreeGlobalMem16(lpMI);            // delete structure
    return MXMIDIERR_NOMEM;
}

// initialize the pointer to the round-robin list of sysex buffers
lpMI->lpHeaderList = NULL;

// if ENABLE_SYSEX flag is set, setup driver to process sysex messages
if(dwFlags & ENABLE_SYSEX)
{
    // sysex buffer offset starts at zero
    lpMI->lpSysexData = 0;

    // get the number of sysex buffers that will be allocated
    lpMI->nSysexBuffs = (int)(dwFlags & NMASK);

    // allocate buffer for round-robin sysex header list
    if( (lpMI->lpHeaderList = (LPDWORD*)GlobalLock(GlobalAlloc(GMEM_MOVEABLE
            | GMEM_SHARE | GMEM_ZEROINIT, (DWORD)(sizeof(DWORD) *
            (lpMI->nSysexBuffs)) )))  != NULL)
    {
        // allocate the actual sysex buffers
        for(i = 0; i < lpMI->nSysexBuffs; i++)
            AllocateMidiInSysexBuffer(lpMI, lpMI->nSysexBufSize);
    }
    else
        lpMI->dwFlags &= DISABLE_SYSEX;

    // point to the first header in the list
    lpMI->nHeaderIn = lpMI->nHeaderOut = 0;
}
// create the (invisible) window that processes midi-in action messages
CreateMidiInWindow(lpMI);

return (HMIN)lpMI;
```

```
}
//-----------------------------------------------------------------------
// StartMidiIn
//
// Must be called after the device is opened in order to enable receiving
// midi messages.
//-----------------------------------------------------------------------
WORD WINAPI _export StartMidiIn16(HMIN hMidiIn)
{
    LPMIDIIN lpMidiIn = (LPMIDIIN)hMidiIn;
    WORD wLastError;

    // check for null pointer
    if(hMidiIn < MXMIDIERR_MAXERR)
        return 1;

    // if midi in was already started, do nothing
    if(lpMidiIn->dwFlags & MIDI_IN_STARTED)
        return 0;

    // reset the pointers to the queue
    lpMidiIn->pMidiInDataIn = lpMidiIn->pMidiInDataOut = 0;

    // start the midi in
    wLastError = midiInStart(lpMidiIn->hMidiIn);
    if(wLastError == 0)
        lpMidiIn->dwFlags |= MIDI_IN_STARTED;

    // clear the last event time to calculate delta times
    lpMidiIn->dwLastEventTicks = 0L;

    return wLastError;
}

//-----------------------------------------------------------------------
// StopMidiIn
//
// Must be called before closing a device in order to stop midi messages
// from being sent by the midi driver.
//-----------------------------------------------------------------------
WORD WINAPI _export StopMidiIn16(HMIN hMidiIn)
{
    LPMIDIIN lpMidiIn = (LPMIDIIN)hMidiIn;
    WORD wLastError;

    // check for null pointer
    if(hMidiIn < MXMIDIERR_MAXERR)
        return 1;

    // try to stop the midi in
    wLastError = midiInStop(lpMidiIn->hMidiIn);

    // if stopped, adjust flag
    if(wLastError == 0)
        lpMidiIn->dwFlags &= ~MIDI_IN_STARTED;

    return wLastError;
}

//-----------------------------------------------------------------------
// CloseMidiIn
//
// Closes the midi device lpMidiIn.
//-----------------------------------------------------------------------
WORD WINAPI _export CloseMidiIn16(HMIN hMidiIn)
{
    LPMIDIHDR lpMidiHdr;
    LPMIDIIN lpMidiIn = (LPMIDIIN)hMidiIn;

    // just in case the user didn't follow directions
    if(hMidiIn < MXMIDIERR_MAXERR)
        return 0;

    if(lpMidiIn->dwFlags & MIDI_IN_STARTED)
        StopMidiIn16(hMidiIn);

    // reset midi in
    midiInReset(lpMidiIn->hMidiIn);

    // if sysex was enabled, go through the list of sysex buffer
    // headers and unprepare and free each one.
    if(lpMidiIn->dwFlags & ENABLE_SYSEX)
    {
```

```
        while(lpMidiIn->nHeaderIn != lpMidiIn->nHeaderOut)
        {
            // get the header
            lpMidiHdr = (LPMIDIHDR)lpMidiIn->lpHeaderList[lpMidiIn->nHeaderOut];

            // this sysex buffer is to be removed: unprepare it
            midiInUnprepareHeader(lpMidiIn->hMidiIn, (LPMIDIHDR)lpMidiHdr,
                (WORD)sizeof(MIDIHDR));

            // free the memory associated with this item
            FreeGlobalMem16(lpMidiHdr->lpData);
            FreeGlobalMem16(lpMidiHdr);

            // point to next header, wrap if necessary
            if(++lpMidiIn->nHeaderOut == lpMidiIn->nSysexBuffs)
                lpMidiIn->nHeaderOut = 0;
        }

        // free the buffer list
        FreeGlobalMem16(lpMidiIn->lpHeaderList);
    }

    // now that all the buffers are removed and the driver is reset
    // we can close the device for midi in
    midiInClose(lpMidiIn->hMidiIn);
    return 1;
}
//-----------------------------------------------------------------------------
// GetMidiIn
//
// Returns a pointer to a midi event, if one is available.
//-----------------------------------------------------------------------------
LPMIDIEVENT WINAPI _export GetMidiIn16(HMIN hMidiIn)
{
    LPMIDIEVENT rc;
    LPMIDIHDR lpMidiHdr;        // local pointer to MidiHdr
    LPMIDIIN lpMidiIn = (LPMIDIIN)hMidiIn;

    // check for null pointer
    if(hMidiIn < MXMIDIERR_MAXERR)
        return NULL;

    // are we receiving a sysex? (i.e. any buffers in the list?)
    if(lpMidiIn->nHeaderOut != lpMidiIn->nHeaderIn)
    {
        // yes, point to the event (that will be in the lpMidiIn header)
        rc = (LPMIDIEVENT) &(lpMidiIn->sysexEvent);
        lpMidiHdr = (LPMIDIHDR)lpMidiIn->lpHeaderList[lpMidiIn->nHeaderOut];

        // setup the event values
        lpMidiIn->sysexEvent.status = SYSEX;
        lpMidiIn->sysexEvent.data1 = *(lpMidiHdr->lpData + lpMidiIn->lpSysexData);
        // time is only valid for sysex message status, data gets zero timestamp
        // time is in dwUser of the MidiHdr structure
        if(lpMidiIn->sysexEvent.data1 == SYSEX)
            lpMidiIn->sysexEvent.time = lpMidiHdr->dwUser;
        else
            lpMidiIn->sysexEvent.time = 0L;

        lpMidiIn->sysexEvent.data2 = 0;
        lpMidiIn->lpSysexData++;

        // are we at the end of the buffer?
        if(lpMidiHdr->dwBytesRecorded == lpMidiIn->lpSysexData)
        {
            // one less buffer in the sysex queue
            lpMidiIn->lpSysexData = 0L;

            // this sysex buffer is empty: re-prepare it
            // setup midihdr structure
            lpMidiHdr->dwBytesRecorded = 0L;    // number of bytes in this buffer
            lpMidiHdr->dwFlags = 0L;            // initialize flags
            lpMidiHdr->dwUser = 0L;             // user data - will be used for
                                                // sysex time

            // prepare the header
            midiInPrepareHeader(lpMidiIn->hMidiIn, (LPMIDIHDR)lpMidiHdr,
                (WORD)sizeof(MIDIHDR));

            // add the sysex buffer to the driver
            midiInAddBuffer(lpMidiIn->hMidiIn, lpMidiHdr, sizeof(MIDIHDR));
```

```
                        // point to next output buffer
                        if(++lpMidiIn->nHeaderOut == lpMidiIn->nSysexBuffs)
                            lpMidiIn->nHeaderOut = 0;
                }

                return rc;
        }

        // else its normal midi data
        // any data to get?
        if(lpMidiIn->pMidiInDataOut == lpMidiIn->pMidiInDataIn)
            return NULL;

        // get the address from the buffer
        rc = lpMidiIn->lpMidiInDataHead + lpMidiIn->pMidiInDataOut;

        // if necessary wrap the pointer
        if(lpMidiIn->pMidiInDataOut++ == lpMidiIn->nMidiInSize)
            lpMidiIn->pMidiInDataOut = 0;

        return rc;
}
//-------------------------------------------------------------------------------
// AllocateMidiInQueue
//
// Allocates a queue of dwEvents size to midi-in device lpMidiIn.
// Returns 0 if successful, MXMIDIERR_NOMEM if there is not enough global
// memory to allocate the queue.
//-------------------------------------------------------------------------------
WORD AllocateMidiInQueue(LPMIDIIN lpMidiIn, DWORD dwEvents)
{
        LPMIDIEVENT lpQueue;  // pointer to the newly allocated queue
        DWORD dwBytes;        // number of bytes to allocate

        // calculate number of bytes to allocate
        dwBytes = (dwEvents + 1) * sizeof(MidiEvent);

        // abort if not enough memory
        if((lpQueue = (LPMIDIEVENT) GlobalLock(GlobalAlloc(GPTR, dwBytes))) == NULL)
            return MXMIDIERR_NOMEM;

        // queue exists, setup pointers
        lpMidiIn->lpMidiInDataHead = lpQueue;
        lpMidiIn->pMidiInDataIn = lpMidiIn->pMidiInDataOut = 0;
        lpMidiIn->nMidiInSize = (int)dwEvents;
        return 0;
}
//-------------------------------------------------------------------------------
// AllocateMidiInSysexBuffer
//
// Adds a buffer of wSize bytes to the previously opened midi in, pointed
// to by lpMidiIn.  Returns the LPMIDIHDR for the new buffer, or NULL
// if not successful.
//-------------------------------------------------------------------------------
LPMIDIHDR AllocateMidiInSysexBuffer(LPMIDIIN lpMidiIn, WORD wSize)
{
        LPMIDIHDR lpMidiHdr;  // pointer to header structure for this buffer
        LPSTR lpData;         // pointer to sysex buffer
        WORD wLastError;

        // allocate MIDIHDR structure
        // it will be fixed and pagelocked by the midiInPrepareHeader call
        lpMidiHdr = (LPMIDIHDR)GlobalLock(GlobalAlloc(GMEM_MOVEABLE | GMEM_SHARE,
sizeof(MIDIHDR)));

        if(lpMidiHdr == NULL)
            return NULL;

        // allocate buffer
        // it will be fixed and pagelocked by the midiInPrepareHeader call
        lpData = (LPSTR)GlobalLock(GlobalAlloc(GMEM_MOVEABLE | GMEM_SHARE, (DWORD)wSize));

        // if not enough memory for buffer, free header memory
        if(lpData == NULL)
        {
                FreeGlobalMem16(lpMidiHdr);
                return NULL;
        }

        // setup midihdr structure
        lpMidiHdr->lpData = lpData;                // pointer to start of buffer
```

```c
        lpMidiHdr->dwBufferLength = wSize;       // buffer size
        lpMidiHdr->dwBytesRecorded = 0L;         // number of bytes in this buffer
        lpMidiHdr->dwFlags = 0L;                 // initialize flags
        lpMidiHdr->dwUser = 0L;                  // user data - will be used for sysex time

        // prepare the header
        wLastError = midiInPrepareHeader(lpMidiIn->hMidiIn, lpMidiHdr, sizeof(MIDIHDR));

        if(wLastError != 0)
        {
            FreeGlobalMem16(lpMidiHdr->lpData);
            FreeGlobalMem16(lpMidiHdr);
            return NULL;
        }

        // add the sysex buffer to the driver
        wLastError = midiInAddBuffer(lpMidiIn->hMidiIn, lpMidiHdr, sizeof(MIDIHDR));

        if(wLastError != 0)
        {
            FreeGlobalMem16(lpMidiHdr->lpData);
            FreeGlobalMem16(lpMidiHdr);
            return NULL;
        }

        return lpMidiHdr;
}
//-----------------------------------------------------------------------------
// CreateMidiInWindow
//
// Creates a window that will receive notification messages from the
// MidiInCallback function.  Returns a handle to the new window, or NULL
// on error.
//-----------------------------------------------------------------------------
HWND CreateMidiInWindow(LPMIDIIN lpMidiIn)
{
        HWND hWnd;         // handle to the new window

        // create the (invisible) window
        hWnd = CreateWindow( MIDIINCLASS,        // lpClassName
            MIDIINCLASS,                          // lpWindowName
            WS_DISABLED,                          // dwStyle
            CW_USEDEFAULT,                        // X position
            CW_USEDEFAULT,                        // Y position
            CW_USEDEFAULT,                        // nWidth
            CW_USEDEFAULT,                        // nHeight
            NULL,                                 // hWinParent
            NULL,                                 // hMenu
            ghInstance,                           // hInstance
            NULL );

        // this is the handle to the sysex window now
        lpMidiIn->hMWnd = hWnd;
        return hWnd;
}
//-----------------------------------------------------------------------------
// GetIndex
//
// Returns the index corresponding to the message status
// index = 0 for 0x80, 1 for 0x90 ... 8 for 0xF0, 9 for 0xF1 ... 21
// for 0xFF.  index is -1 for EOX.
//-----------------------------------------------------------------------------
WORD GetIndex(BYTE msg)
{
        WORD index;

        if(msg == EOX)
            return (WORD)-1;                 // skip eox

        if((msg & 0xF0) < SYSEX)             // is it a channel message?
            index = ((msg & 0xF0) >> 4) - 8;
        else                                 // or a system message?
        {
            if(msg > EOX)
                index = (msg & 0x0F) + 6;
            else
                index = (msg & 0x0F) + 7;
        }

        return index;
```

```
}
//-----------------------------------------------------------------------------
// GetEventTimeInTicks
//
// Returns the event time in ticks at the current tempo and resolution.
//-----------------------------------------------------------------------------
DWORD GetEventTimeInTicks(LPMIDIIN lpMidiIn, DWORD time, LPMIDIHDR lpMidiHdr, WORD type)
{
    DWORD rt;              // returned time in ticks
    LPSYNC lpSync;         // local pointer to sync device
    DWORD tmpo;            // tempo in uS/beat
    DWORD dur;             // sysex buffer duration in ticks

    // if sync is enabled, calculate time in ticks, else return time in mS
    if(lpMidiIn->lpSync == NULL)
        return time;

    lpSync = (LPSYNC)lpMidiIn->lpSync;

    if(type == MSYSEX)
    {
        // get tempo in uS/beat
        tmpo = lpSync->dwTempo / SCALE;

        // since sysex notification occurs at the end of a buffer calculate the
        // duration of the buffer in ticks and subtract from elaspsed ticks.
        // This works for buffers up to 4.473 seconds long at 960 bpm, or about
        // 13K long.
        dur = (320L * lpMidiHdr->dwBytesRecorded * (DWORD)lpSync->wResolution)/tmpo;
    }
    else
        dur = 0L;

    // calculate the elaspsed ticks
    rt = lpSync->dwTicks - lpMidiIn->dwLastEventTicks - dur;
    lpMidiIn->dwLastEventTicks = lpSync->dwTicks - dur;
    return rt;
}

//-----------------------------------------------------------------------------
// MidiInCallback
//
// This function is called at interrupt time.  It saves the message in the
// queue, or if a sysex, it puts the sysex header in the list and posts a
// MIDI_DATA message to the client window.
//
// dwInstance is the lpMidiIn
//
// For MIM_DATA
//    dwParam1 is the midi event with status in the low byte
//    dwParam2 is the event time in ms since the start of midi in
//
// For MIM_LONGDATA
//    dwParam1 is the lpMidiHdr
//    dwParam2 is the event time in ms since the start of midi in
//         Note that this time is for the last byte in the buffer _not_ the first.
//-----------------------------------------------------------------------------
void CALLBACK _export MidiInCallback(HMIDIIN hMI, UINT wMsg, DWORD dwInstance,
        DWORD dwParam1, DWORD dwParam2)
{
    LPMIDIIN lpMidiIn;        // pointer to MidiIn structure
    LPMIDIHDR lpMidiHdr;      // pointer to MidiHdr structure
    DWORD FAR* lpB;           // pointer to buffer event as dwords

    // the pointer to the midi in structure is passed in the instance data
    lpMidiIn = (LPMIDIIN) dwInstance;

    // don't process this message if the queue is not initialized yet
    // this is necessary in case midi-in occurs while the output device
    // is being opened
    if(lpMidiIn->lpMidiInDataHead == NULL)
        return;

    if(wMsg == MIM_DATA)
    {
        // if this is the sync in device, is this an mtc or midi
        // clock message?  If so, call the corresponding function
        // to process the sync
        if(lpMidiIn->dwFlags & SYNC_INPUT)
            switch(LOBYTE(LOWORD(dwParam1)))
```

```
            {
                case MIDI_CLOCK:
                    if(((LPSYNC)lpMidiIn->lpSync)->wSyncMode == S_MIDI)
                        if(((LPSYNC)lpMidiIn->lpSync)->wFlags & SYNC_ENABLED)
                        {
                            MidiClock((LPSYNC)lpMidiIn->lpSync);
                            return;
                        }
                    break;

                case MIDI_START:
                case MIDI_CONTINUE:
                    if(((LPSYNC)lpMidiIn->lpSync)->wSyncMode == S_MIDI)
                        if(((LPSYNC)lpMidiIn->lpSync)->wFlags & SYNC_ENABLED)
                        {
                            ((LPSYNC)lpMidiIn->lpSync)->wFlags |= SYNC_RUNNING;
                            return;
                        }
                    break;

                case MIDI_STOP:
                    if(((LPSYNC)lpMidiIn->lpSync)->wSyncMode == S_MIDI)
                        if(((LPSYNC)lpMidiIn->lpSync)->wFlags & SYNC_ENABLED)
                        {
                            ((LPSYNC)lpMidiIn->lpSync)->wFlags &= ~SYNC_RUNNING;
                            return;
                        }
                    break;
            }
        // get the address of the start of the queue
        lpB = (DWORD FAR*)(lpMidiIn->lpMidiInDataHead + lpMidiIn->pMidiInDataIn);

        // store the data in the buffer
        // first, get the delta time for this event
        *lpB = GetEventTimeInTicks(lpMidiIn, dwParam2, NULL, MSHORT);
        *(lpB + 1) = dwParam1;

        // if necessary wrap the pointer
        if(++lpMidiIn->pMidiInDataIn == lpMidiIn->nMidiInSize)
            lpMidiIn->pMidiInDataIn = 0;

        // send a message to the application
        PostMessage(lpMidiIn->hWnd, MIDI_DATA, 0, (DWORD)lpMidiIn);
        return;
    }

    if((wMsg == MIM_LONGDATA) || (wMsg == MIM_LONGERROR))
    {
        // for MIM_LONG... dwParam1 is lpMidiHdr
        lpMidiHdr = (LPMIDIHDR)dwParam1;

        // add the buffer to the header list
        lpMidiIn->lpHeaderList[lpMidiIn->nHeaderIn] = (LPDWORD)lpMidiHdr;

        // point to the next slot in the list
        if(++lpMidiIn->nHeaderIn == lpMidiIn->nSysexBuffs)
            lpMidiIn->nHeaderIn = 0;

        if(lpMidiHdr->dwBytesRecorded != 0)
        {
            // get the time for this message -- this is stored in
            // dwUser in the MidiHdr structure
            if((BYTE)*(lpMidiHdr->lpData) == SYSEX)
                lpMidiHdr->dwUser = GetEventTimeInTicks(lpMidiIn, timeGetTime(),
lpMidiHdr, MSYSEX);
            else
                lpMidiHdr->dwUser = 0L;

            // send MIDI_DATA to the app in there was any data in the
            // buffer (it will be of zero length if returned as a result
            // of a call to midiInClose
            PostMessage(lpMidiIn->hWnd, MIDI_DATA, 0, (DWORD)lpMidiIn);
        }

        return;
    }

    if(wMsg == MIM_CLOSE)
    {
        // send a message to the sysex proc indicating that the
        // device is closed and to free any remaining memory
```

```
            PostMessage(lpMidiIn->hMWnd, MIM_CLOSE, 0, (DWORD)MAKELONG(HIWORD(lpMidiHdr),
                    HIWORD(lpMidiIn)));
    }
}
//------------------------------------------------------------------------------
// MidiInProc
//
// Processes the notification messages for MidiIn window.  lpMidiIn (in
// the lParam parameter) is a pointer to the midi in header that is
// receiving this sysex.
//------------------------------------------------------------------------------
LRESULT CALLBACK _export MidiInProc(HWND hWnd, UINT iMessage, WPARAM wParam,
        LPARAM lParam)
{
    LPMIDIIN lpMidiIn;          // pointer to MidiIn structure

    lpMidiIn = (LPMIDIIN) MAKELONG(0, HIWORD(lParam));

    if(iMessage == MIM_CLOSE)
    {
        // destroy the sysex window
        DestroyWindow(lpMidiIn->hMWnd);

        // free the midi in queue
        FreeGlobalMem16(lpMidiIn->lpMidiInDataHead);

        // send a close message to the application
        SendMessage(lpMidiIn->hWnd, MIM_CLOSE, 0, 0L);

        // and the rest of the MidiIn structure
        FreeGlobalMem16(lpMidiIn);

        return 0;
    }

    // all messages that are not completely processed above must be processed here.
    return DefWindowProc( hWnd, iMessage, wParam, lParam );
}
//------------------------------------------------------------------------------
// FreeGlobalMem
//
// Frees the global memory, gMem, that was previously allocated.
// This function expects a pointer to previously allocated global memory.
//------------------------------------------------------------------------------
void WINAPI _export FreeGlobalMem16(void FAR* gMem)
{
    HANDLE hMem;

    hMem = (HANDLE)LOWORD(GlobalHandle(SELECTOROF(gMem)));
    if(hMem != NULL)
    {
        GlobalUnlock(hMem);
        GlobalFree(hMem);
    }
}
```

## MidiOut.c

```
//------------------------------------------------------------------------------
// Maximum MIDI Programmer's ToolKit - MxMidi16.DLL
// MIDI Output Module
//
// Copyright (c) Paul A. Messick, 1994-1996
//
// Written by Paul A. Messick
//
// Provides a 16-bit API to open, close, and send midi messages,
// with system exclusive messages merged into the normal midi stream.
//------------------------------------------------------------------------------
#include <windows.h>
#include "MxDLL.h"

//------------------------------------------------------------------------------
// Function Prototypes used in this DLL
//------------------------------------------------------------------------------
WORD AllocateMidiOutQueue(LPMIDIOUT lpMidiOut, DWORD dwEvents);
LPMIDIHDR AllocateMidiOutSysexBuffer(LPMIDIOUT lpMidiOut, WORD wSize);
HWND CreateMidiOutWindow(LPMIDIOUT lpMidiOut);
```

```
WORD TurnNotesOff(LPMIDIOUT lpMidiOut);
//----------------------------------------------------------------------------
// Global Variables
//----------------------------------------------------------------------------
extern HINSTANCE ghInstance;    // global instance handle for this dll
extern UINT bufSize[10];        // buffer size table
extern UINT wQueueSize;         // the size of the windows message queue

// note on masks for each channel
UINT NtOn[16] = { 0x0001, 0x0002, 0x0004, 0x0008,
                  0x0010, 0x0020, 0x0040, 0x0080,
                  0x0100, 0x0200, 0x0400, 0x0800,
                  0x1000, 0x2000, 0x4000, 0x8000 };

// note off masks for each channel
UINT NtOff[16] = { 0xFFFE, 0xFFFD, 0xFFFB, 0xFFF7,
                   0xFFEF, 0xFFDF, 0xFFBF, 0xFF7F,
                   0xFEFF, 0xFDFF, 0xFBFF, 0xF7FF,
                   0xEFFF, 0xDFFF, 0xBFFF, 0x7FFF };

//----------------------------------------------------------------------------
// GetMidiOutDescription
//
// Gets the text string description for the midi out device designated by
// wDeviceID.  If there is no device by that ID the function returns FALSE
// Otherwise, it returns TRUE and sets the string lpzDesc to the device
// description.
//----------------------------------------------------------------------------
BOOL WINAPI _export GetMidiOutDescription16(WORD wDeviceID, LPSTR lpzDesc)
{
    MIDIOUTCAPS Caps;

    if(midiOutGetDevCaps(wDeviceID, (LPMIDIOUTCAPS) &Caps, sizeof(Caps)) ==
                         MMSYSERR_BADDEVICEID)
        return FALSE;

    lstrcpy(lpzDesc, (LPSTR)Caps.szPname);
    return TRUE;
}
//----------------------------------------------------------------------------
// OpenMidiOut
//
// Opens the device wDevice for midi output.
//
// hWnd is the handle to the window that is to receive any messages from
//   this device.
//
// wDeviceID ranges from 0 to one less than the number of available
//   devices and indicates which device is to be opened.
//
// hSync is the handle to the previously opened sync device that will
//   handle synchronization for this output.  If no sync is to be used
//   with this output, hSync must be zero.
//
// dwFlags are used to affect the operation of this particular midi out
//   device and can be combined using the OR operator.
//
// Current flags are:
//   ENABLE_SYSEX if set, system exclusive messages are merged
//                into the normal midi stream that is sent
//                to the device.
//
// *DISABLE_SYSEXif set, system exclusive messages are ignored
//
//   SYNC_OUTPUT  this output serves as a sync output for midi clock
//                sync messages for the previously opened
//                sync device lpSync.  It is ignored if
//                lpSync is NULL or the sync mode has been
//                set to S_STOPPED or S_MIDI (clock output
//                messages are not sent when receiving clock
//                sync.)
//
// The function returns the handle to the device if midi out was correctly
// opened, or an error value (less than MXMIDIERR_MAXERR) if there was an
// error opening the device.
//----------------------------------------------------------------------------
HMOUT WINAPI _export OpenMidiOut16(HWND hWnd, WORD wDeviceID, HSYNC hSync,
        DWORD dwFlags)
```

```c
{
    LPMIDIOUT lpMO;         // pointer to allocated MidiOut structure
    WORD i;                 // loop counter
    LPMIDIOUT FAR* newlpMidiOutList;  // pointer to new (larger) midi out device list
    HGLOBAL hg;             // handle to global memory
    LPSYNC lpSync = (LPSYNC)hSync;
    WORD wLastError;

    // if an attempt to open more than then max number of devices,
    // return bad ID error
    if((midiOutGetNumDevs() <= wDeviceID) && ((int)wDeviceID != MIDI_MAPPER))
        return MXMIDIERR_BADDEVICEID;

    // attempt to allocate memory for this device
    lpMO = (LPMIDIOUT)GlobalLock(GlobalAlloc(GPTR, sizeof(MidiOutStruct)));

    // check for an allocation error
    if(lpMO == NULL)
        return MXMIDIERR_NOMEM;

    // this is the handle to client window that is to receive messages
    lpMO->hWnd = hWnd;

    // the device id associated with this device
    lpMO->wDeviceID = wDeviceID;

    // is there a sync device specified?
    if(lpSync != NULL)
    {
        // yes, is this device ID already open?
        i = 0;
        while(*(lpSync->lpMidiOutList + i) != NULL)
        {
            if( ((LPMIDIOUT)*(lpSync->lpMidiOutList + i))->wDeviceID == wDeviceID)
            {
                // its already open, don't open it again
                lpMO->hMidiOut = ((LPMIDIOUT)*(lpSync->lpMidiOutList + i))->hMidiOut;
            }
        }
    }

    // attempt to open the device
    wLastError = midiOutOpen(&lpMO->hMidiOut, wDeviceID, (DWORD)MidiOutCallback,
            (DWORD)lpMO, CALLBACK_FUNCTION);

    // if there is an error opening midi out, return a null handle and
    // free the allocated structure
    if(wLastError != 0)
    {
        FreeGlobalMem16(lpMO);
        return MXMIDIERR_BADDEVICEID;
    }

    // get the queue sizes from dwFlags
    lpMO->nSysexBufSize = bufSize[(dwFlags & SXMASK) >> 8];

    // the number of (possibly) available sysex buffers that can be queued
    // at a time is equal to the size of the windows message queue/2
    lpMO->nSysexBuffsAllowed = lpMO->nAvailableBuffs = min(wQueueSize/2, (WORD)(dwFlags
                                                        & NMASK));

    // allocate the queue for non-sysex messages
    if(AllocateMidiOutQueue(lpMO, bufSize[(dwFlags & QMASK) >> 12]) != 0)
    {
        FreeGlobalMem16(lpMO);
        return MXMIDIERR_NOMEM;
    }

    // setup the necessary flags and internal values
    lpMO->dwFlags = (dwFlags & MIDI_OUT_INTERNAL); // set external flags only
    lpMO->lpSync = lpSync;                          // sync device, if not NULL

    // allocate an extra slot for a pointer to this midi out device in
    // the list of devices held in the lpSync device
    if(lpSync != NULL)
    {
        hg = (HGLOBAL)GlobalHandle(SELECTOROF(lpSync->lpMidiOutList));

        newlpMidiOutList = (LPMIDIOUT FAR*)GlobalLock(GlobalReAlloc(hg,
                        GlobalSize(hg) + sizeof(LPMIDIOUT),   GMEM_MOVEABLE |
                        GMEM_ZEROINIT));
```

```
        if(newlpMidiOutList != NULL)
        {
            lpSync->lpMidiOutList = newlpMidiOutList;

            // find the last entry (before the last terminating null)
            while(*newlpMidiOutList != NULL)
                newlpMidiOutList++;

            // insert new entry
            *newlpMidiOutList = lpMO;
        }
    }

    // initialize the pointers to the round-robin list of sysex
    // buffers that will be removed later (on close)
    lpMO->lpHeaderList = NULL;

    // if ENABLE_SYSEX flag is set, setup driver to process sysex messages
    if(dwFlags & ENABLE_SYSEX)
    {
        // allocate buffer for round-robin sysex header list
        // with an extra null end-of-list entry
        if((lpMO->lpHeaderList = (LPDWORD*)GlobalLock(GlobalAlloc(GMEM_MOVEABLE |
                GMEM_SHARE | GMEM_ZEROINIT, (DWORD)(sizeof(DWORD) *
                ( (dwFlags & NMASK) + 1 )) ))) != NULL)
        {
            // allocate the actual sysex buffers
            for(i = 0; i < (WORD)(dwFlags & NMASK); i++)
                lpMO->lpHeaderList[i] = (LPDWORD)AllocateMidiOutSysexBuffer(lpMO,
                        lpMO->nSysexBufSize);

            // point to the first header in the list
            lpMO->nThisHeader = 0;
        }
        else
            lpMO->dwFlags &= DISABLE_SYSEX;
    }

    // create the (invisible) window that processes midi-out action messages
    CreateMidiOutWindow(lpMO);

    return (HMOUT)lpMO;
}
//-----------------------------------------------------------------------------
// FlushMidiOut
//
// Flushes any data that may be in the midiOut buffer for this device.
//-----------------------------------------------------------------------------
void WINAPI _export FlushMidiOut16(HMOUT hMidiOut)
{
    LPMIDIOUT lpMidiOut = (LPMIDIOUT)hMidiOut;

    // check for null pointer
    if(hMidiOut < MXMIDIERR_MAXERR)
        return;

    // flush any pending messages in the buffer
    lpMidiOut->pMidiOutDataOut = lpMidiOut->pMidiOutDataIn = lpMidiOut->wSpan = 0;
}
//-----------------------------------------------------------------------------
// ResetMidiOut
//
// Sends all notes off to midi device and releases any pending sysex
// buffers.  Flushes the output buffer.
// Returns 0 if successful, non-zero on error.
//-----------------------------------------------------------------------------
WORD WINAPI _export ResetMidiOut16(HMOUT hMidiOut)
{
    LPMIDIOUT lpMidiOut = (LPMIDIOUT)hMidiOut;

    // check for null pointer
    if(hMidiOut < MXMIDIERR_MAXERR)
        return 1;

    // flush the output buffer
    FlushMidiOut16(hMidiOut);

    // turn off any playing notes
    return TurnNotesOff(lpMidiOut);
}
```

```
//-----------------------------------------------------------------------
// TurnNotesOff
//
// Sends all notes off to midi device and releases any pending sysex
// buffers.
//-----------------------------------------------------------------------
WORD TurnNotesOff(LPMIDIOUT lpMidiOut)
{
    int n;              // note number
    int chan;           // channel number
    WORD mask;          // channel mask
    DWORD note;         // note off message

    // send note offs for any notes that are currently on
    for(n = 0; n < 128; n++)
        if(lpMidiOut->wNotes[n] != 0)
        {
            // search through all channels to see if this note is on
            mask = 1;
            for(chan = 0; chan < 16; chan++)
            {
                if(lpMidiOut->wNotes[n] & mask)
                {
                    // build and send the note off
                    note = 0x00000090 | (n << 8) | chan;
                    midiOutShortMsg(lpMidiOut->hMidiOut, note);
                }

                // next channel
                mask <<= 1;
            }

            // clear the value in the array so it is not sent again if reset
            // is called again
            lpMidiOut->wNotes[n] = 0;
        }

    // send all notes off messages in case the above didn't do it for all notes
    // i.e. some synths require exact pairing of note on/offs
    for(n = 0; n < 16; n++)
        midiOutShortMsg(lpMidiOut->hMidiOut, 0x00007BB0 | (DWORD)n);

    // have driver send note-offs for any notes that are currently on
    // and flush any pending sysex blocks
    return midiOutReset(lpMidiOut->hMidiOut);
}
//-----------------------------------------------------------------------
// TrackMidiOut
//
// Tracks note ons and note offs in the Note[] array of the MidiOutStruc
// structure.  This array is used to turn any still-sounding note off when
// ResetMidiOut() is called.  The array is organized as 128 words, one
// word per note number.  Each bit of the words corresponds to the channel
// of the note, with the lsb corresponding to channel 1.  A one in a bit
// position indicates that that note on that channel is currently on.
//-----------------------------------------------------------------------
void TrackMidiOut(LPMIDIOUT lpMidiOut, DWORD dwMsg)
{
    void FAR *n;            // pointer to the note data
    BYTE FAR *status;       // status byte
    BYTE FAR *note;         // note number
    BYTE FAR *vel;          // velocity
    BYTE noChanStatus;      // status with channel masked

    // cast pointers to the double word message to access the message as bytes
    n = &dwMsg;
    status = (BYTE FAR*)n;
    note = (BYTE FAR*)n + 1;
    vel = (BYTE FAR*)n + 2;
    noChanStatus = *status & 0xF0;

    // set the bit in the array if this is a note on or clear it if a note off
    // make sure that the two data bytes are valid data by forcing
    // the upper bits of each byte to a zero
    if((noChanStatus == NOTEON) && (*vel != 0))
        lpMidiOut->wNotes[0x7f & *note] |= NtOn[*status & 0x0F];
    else
        if((noChanStatus == NOTEOFF) || (noChanStatus == NOTEON))
            lpMidiOut->wNotes[0x7f & *note] &= NtOff[*status & 0x0F];
```

```
}
//-----------------------------------------------------------------------------
// CloseMidiOut
//
// Closes the midi device lpMidiOut and frees the lpMidiOut structure.
// Returns 0 if successful, non-zero on error.
//-----------------------------------------------------------------------------
WORD WINAPI _export CloseMidiOut16(HMOUT hMidiOut)
{
    LPMIDIOUT FAR* newlpMidiOutList;    // pointer to midi out device list
    HGLOBAL hg;                         // handle to global memory
    WORD nDev;                          // device counter
    LPSYNC lpS;                         // local pointer to sync device
    int i;                              // loop counter
    LPMIDIOUT lpMidiOut = (LPMIDIOUT)hMidiOut;

    // if not open, ignore request
    if(hMidiOut < MXMIDIERR_MAXERR)
        return 0;

    // reset the output device, forcing it to return any pending buffers
    ResetMidiOut16(hMidiOut);

    // if sysex was enabled, remove sysex buffers from list and free memory
    if(lpMidiOut->dwFlags & ENABLE_SYSEX)
    {
        // the list is terminated by a null entry
        i = 0;
        while(lpMidiOut->lpHeaderList[i] != NULL)
        {
            // this sysex buffer is to be removed: unprepare it
            midiOutUnprepareHeader(lpMidiOut->hMidiOut,
                (LPMIDIHDR)lpMidiOut->lpHeaderList[i], (WORD)sizeof(MIDIHDR));

            // free the memory
            FreeGlobalMem16(((LPMIDIHDR)lpMidiOut->lpHeaderList[i])->lpData);
            FreeGlobalMem16(lpMidiOut->lpHeaderList[i]);

            // next item in list
            i++;
        }

        // free the (empty) list
        FreeGlobalMem16(lpMidiOut->lpHeaderList);
    }

    // close midi out
    midiOutClose(lpMidiOut->hMidiOut);

    // if sync is enabled, remove the device from the sync device list
    if(lpMidiOut->lpSync != NULL)
    {
        // create a convenient pointer to lpSync
        lpS = (LPSYNC)(lpMidiOut->lpSync);

        // search through the list to find this device pointer
        nDev = 0;
        while((*(lpS->lpMidiOutList + nDev) != NULL) && (*(lpS->lpMidiOutList +
                nDev) != lpMidiOut))
            nDev++;

        // remove it from the list by copying all of the other
        // pointers up one slot
        while(*(lpS->lpMidiOutList + nDev) != NULL)
        {
            *(lpS->lpMidiOutList + nDev) = *(lpS->lpMidiOutList + nDev + 1);
            nDev++;
        }

        // resize the memory block
        hg = (HGLOBAL)GlobalHandle(SELECTOROF(lpS->lpMidiOutList));

        newlpMidiOutList = (LPMIDIOUT FAR*)GlobalLock(GlobalReAlloc(hg,
                    GlobalSize(hg) - sizeof(LPMIDIOUT),   GMEM_MOVEABLE |
                    GMEM_SHARE));

        if(newlpMidiOutList != NULL)
            lpS->lpMidiOutList = newlpMidiOutList;
    }

    return 1;
}
```

```
//-------------------------------------------------------------------------------
// InsertInSysexBuffer
//
// Insert this midi event into the sysex buffer.  If the buffer is full
// send a message to have it sent to the driver, then find the next buffer.
//-------------------------------------------------------------------------------
void InsertInSysexBuffer(LPMIDIOUT lpMidiOut, LPMIDIEVENT thisEvent)
{
    LPMIDIHDR lpMidiHdr;

    // insert the event into the sysex buffer
    lpMidiHdr = (LPMIDIHDR)lpMidiOut->lpHeaderList[lpMidiOut->nThisHeader];
    *(lpMidiHdr->lpData) = thisEvent->data1;
    lpMidiHdr->lpData++;

    // if buffer is full, send a message to have it sent to the driver
    if((++lpMidiHdr->dwBytesRecorded == lpMidiHdr->dwBufferLength) ||
            (thisEvent->data1 == EOX))
    {
        // point to the next buffer in the list
        // if this is the end of the list (i.e. a null entry) then wrap around
        // to the head of the list
        lpMidiOut->nThisHeader++;
        if(lpMidiOut->lpHeaderList[lpMidiOut->nThisHeader] == NULL)
            lpMidiOut->nThisHeader = 0;

        // one less buffer is available now
        lpMidiOut->nAvailableBuffs--;

        // we are now sending a sysex message
        lpMidiOut->dwFlags |= SENDING_SYSEX;

        // one more buffer is active
        if(lpMidiOut->lpSync != NULL)
            ((LPSYNC)lpMidiOut->lpSync)->nSysexBuffsActive++;

        // post a message so that the header will be sent to the driver.
        // This has to be done since the driver may not return before the buffer
        // has been sent.
        PostMessage(lpMidiOut->hMWnd, MOM_LONGDATA, 0, (LPARAM)MAKELONG(
                HIWORD(lpMidiHdr), HIWORD(lpMidiOut)));
    }
}
//-------------------------------------------------------------------------------
// PutMidiOut
//
// Puts a midi event into the outgoing queue.  If no sync device is attached,
// the event is then removed from the queue and sent to the MIDI output driver.
// For sysex data, the event is added to the the current buffer; when the buffer
// is full, it is sent to the driver as a long message.
//
// If sync is being used, the event, sysex or short, is always queued.  It will
// then be output at the proper time by the sync engine.
//
// Returns 0 if event accepted, -1 if queue is full.
//-------------------------------------------------------------------------------
WORD WINAPI _export PutMidiOut16(HMOUT hMidiOut, LPMIDIEVENT lpMidiEvent)
{
    DWORD dwMsg;                // echo message
    DWORD FAR* lpE;             // pointer to event structure
    DWORD FAR* lpB;             // pointer to buffer event
    LPMIDIOUT lpMidiOut = (LPMIDIOUT)hMidiOut;

    // check for null pointer
    if(hMidiOut < MXMIDIERR_MAXERR)
        return (WORD)-1;

        // get pointer to event for access as dword
    lpE = (DWORD FAR*)lpMidiEvent;

    // The message can be sent out immediately, without buffering,
    // by setting the time to -1L and calling MidiOut().
    // This can be used during syncronized record or playback to echo
    // incoming midi data to a particular output.  Since this is
    // unbuffered output, system exclusive messages are filtered and
    // cannot be echoed through this method.
    if(lpMidiEvent->time == (DWORD)-1L)
    {
```

```
                // filter sysex from echo out
                if(lpMidiEvent->status == SYSEX)
                    return 0;

                // build the event as a dword
                dwMsg = (DWORD)*(lpE + 1);

                // send the message to the driver
                // the driver could return MIDIERR_NOTREADY here, but no
                // credible drivers will do so.  If desired, this return
                // value could be handled here.
                midiOutShortMsg(lpMidiOut->hMidiOut, dwMsg);
                TrackMidiOut(lpMidiOut, dwMsg);
                return 0;
        }
        // if this is a sysex message and no more buffers are available for
        // queueing (because the "windows messaging queue size - 1" worth
        // of buffers have been sent) then refuse the message
        if((lpMidiEvent->status == SYSEX) && (lpMidiOut->nAvailableBuffs == 0))
            return (WORD)-1;

        // is this part of a sysex message?
        // if sync is enabled, treat the sysex as a regular midi message
        // Otherwise, insert the sysex in an outgoing buffer
        if(lpMidiEvent->status == SYSEX)
            if(lpMidiOut->dwFlags & ENABLE_SYSEX)
                if((lpMidiOut->lpSync == NULL) || (((LPSYNC)lpMidiOut->lpSync)->wFlags
                        & SYNC_ENABLED) == 0)
                {
                    // if sync not enabled, insert the event in the
                    // outgoing sysex buffer
                    InsertInSysexBuffer(lpMidiOut, lpMidiEvent);
                    return 0;
                }
        // just a normal midi event
        // check the wSpan to see if queue is full
        if(lpMidiOut->wSpan == lpMidiOut->nMidiOutSize)
            return (WORD)-1;

        // save event in the queue - 1st dword is time, 2nd dword is event
        lpB = (DWORD FAR*)(lpMidiOut->pMidiOutDataIn + lpMidiOut->lpMidiOutDataHead);
        *lpB = *lpE;
        *(lpB + 1) = *(lpE + 1);

        // if necessary, wrap the pointer
        if(lpMidiOut->pMidiOutDataIn++ == lpMidiOut->nMidiOutSize)
            lpMidiOut->pMidiOutDataIn = 0;

        // one more in the wSpan
        lpMidiOut->wSpan++;

        // send any queued messages to the driver
        if((LPSYNC)lpMidiOut->lpSync == NULL)
            while(lpMidiOut->wSpan != 0)
            {
                // read the next event - 2nd dword is event data
                lpE = (DWORD FAR*)(lpMidiOut->lpMidiOutDataHead +
                        lpMidiOut->pMidiOutDataOut);
                dwMsg = *(lpE + 1);

                // increment the out pointer, wrapping if necessary
                if(lpMidiOut->pMidiOutDataOut++ == lpMidiOut->nMidiOutSize)
                    lpMidiOut->pMidiOutDataOut = 0;

                lpMidiOut->wSpan--;

                // send the event to the driver
                midiOutShortMsg(lpMidiOut->hMidiOut, dwMsg);
                TrackMidiOut(lpMidiOut, dwMsg);
            }

    return 0;
}
//-----------------------------------------------------------------------
// AllocateMidiOutQueue
//
// allocates a queue of dwEvents size to midi-out device lpMidiOut.
// Returns 0 if successful, MXMIDIERR_NOMEM if there is not enough global
// memory to allocate the queue.
//-----------------------------------------------------------------------
```

```
WORD AllocateMidiOutQueue(LPMIDIOUT lpMidiOut, DWORD dwEvents)
{
    LPMIDIEVENT lpQueue;            // pointer to the newly allocated queue
    DWORD dwBytes;                  // number of bytes to allocate

    // calculate number of bytes to allocate
    dwBytes = (dwEvents + 1) * sizeof(MidiEvent);

    // abort if not enough memory
    if((lpQueue = (LPMIDIEVENT)GlobalLock(GlobalAlloc(GPTR | GMEM_SHARE, dwBytes))) ==
NULL)
        return MXMIDIERR_NOMEM;

    // queue exists, setup pointers
    lpMidiOut->lpMidiOutDataHead = lpQueue;
    lpMidiOut->pMidiOutDataIn = lpMidiOut->pMidiOutDataOut = 0;
    lpMidiOut->nMidiOutSize = (int)dwEvents;
    lpMidiOut->wSpan = 0;

    return 0;
}
//-----------------------------------------------------------------------------
// AllocateMidiOutSysexBuffer
//
// Adds a buffer of wSize bytes to the previously opened midi out, pointed
// to by lpMidiOut.  Returns a pointer to the midi header structure on
// success or NULL on failure.
//-----------------------------------------------------------------------------
LPMIDIHDR AllocateMidiOutSysexBuffer(LPMIDIOUT lpMidiOut, WORD wSize)
{
    LPMIDIHDR lpMidiHdr;        // pointer to header structure for this buffer
    LPSTR lpData;               // pointer to sysex buffer

    // allocate MIDIHDR structure
    lpMidiHdr = (LPMIDIHDR)GlobalLock(GlobalAlloc(GMEM_MOVEABLE | GMEM_SHARE,
                                            sizeof(MIDIHDR)));

    if(lpMidiHdr == NULL)
        return NULL;

    // allocate buffer
    lpData = (LPSTR)GlobalLock(GlobalAlloc(GMEM_MOVEABLE | GMEM_SHARE, (DWORD)wSize));

    // if not enough memory for buffer, free header memory
    if(lpData == NULL)
    {
        FreeGlobalMem16(lpMidiHdr);
        return NULL;
    }

    // setup midihdr structure
    lpMidiHdr->lpData = lpData;             // pointer to start of buffer
    lpMidiHdr->dwBytesRecorded = 0L;        // number of bytes in buffer
    lpMidiHdr->dwBufferLength = wSize;      // buffer size
    lpMidiHdr->dwFlags = 0L;                // initialize flags
    lpMidiHdr->dwUser = 0L;                 // user data

    // prepare the header
    if(midiOutPrepareHeader(lpMidiOut->hMidiOut, lpMidiHdr, sizeof(MIDIHDR)) != 0)
    {
        FreeGlobalMem16(lpMidiHdr->lpData);
        FreeGlobalMem16(lpMidiHdr);
        return NULL;
    }

    return lpMidiHdr;
}
//-----------------------------------------------------------------------------
// CreateMidiOutWindow
//
// Registers and creates a window that will receive messages from the
// MidiOutCallback function.  Returns a handle to the new window,
// or NULL on error.
//-----------------------------------------------------------------------------
HWND CreateMidiOutWindow(LPMIDIOUT lpMidiOut)
{
    HWND hWnd;      // handle to the new window

    // create the (invisible) window
    hWnd = CreateWindow(MIDIOUTCLASS, // lpClassName
        MIDIOUTCLASS,                 // lpWindowName
```

```
                WS_DISABLED,                    // dwStyle
                CW_USEDEFAULT,                  // X position
                CW_USEDEFAULT,          ¦       // Y position
                CW_USEDEFAULT,                  // nWidth
                CW_USEDEFAULT,                  // nHeight
                NULL,                           // hWinParent
                NULL,                           // hMenu
                ghInstance,                     // hInstance
                NULL);

        // this is the handle to the sysex window now
        lpMidiOut->hMWnd = hWnd;
        return hWnd;
}
//------------------------------------------------------------------------------
// MidiOutCallback
//
// This function is called at interrupt time.  It processes MOM_DONE and
// MOM_CLOSE messages from the driver.  MOM_DONE indicates that the driver
// has finished sending the last sysex block and is ready for another one.
// MOM_CLOSE is sent by the driver when it has finished any cleanup that
// resulted from a midiOutClose().
//------------------------------------------------------------------------------
void CALLBACK _export MidiOutCallback(HMIDIOUT hMO, UINT wMsg, DWORD dwInstance,
        DWORD dwParam1, DWORD dwParam2)
{
    LPMIDIOUT lpMidiOut;        // pointer to MidiOut structure
    LPMIDIHDR lpMidiHdr;        // pointer to MidiHdr structure

    lpMidiOut = (LPMIDIOUT)dwInstance;

    if(wMsg == MOM_DONE)
    {
        // for MOM_DONE dwParam1 is lpMidiHdr
        lpMidiHdr = (LPMIDIHDR)dwParam1;

        // Some drivers send spurious MOM_DONE messages with dwParam1 == NULL
        // don't process these...
        if(lpMidiHdr == NULL || lpMidiOut == NULL)
            return;

        // prepare the header again for reuse
        // The block will remain in the lpHeaderList list to be reused later.
        midiOutPrepareHeader(lpMidiOut->hMidiOut, lpMidiHdr, sizeof(MIDIHDR));

        lpMidiHdr->dwBytesRecorded = 0L;
        lpMidiHdr->dwBufferLength = lpMidiOut->nSysexBufSize;

        // one less buffer is active
        if(lpMidiOut->lpSync != NULL)
            ((LPSYNC)lpMidiOut->lpSync)->nSysexBuffsActive--;

        // one more buffer is available
        lpMidiOut->nAvailableBuffs++;

        // are we done sending this sysex?
        if(lpMidiOut->nAvailableBuffs == lpMidiOut->nSysexBuffsAllowed)
            lpMidiOut->dwFlags &= ~SENDING_SYSEX;

        // if no sync device, post a message to let the client know there is
        // more room for sysex data -- otherwise this is handled by the sync device
        if(lpMidiOut->lpSync == NULL)
            PostMessage(lpMidiOut->hWnd, OUTBUFFER_READY, 0, (DWORD)lpMidiOut);
    }

    if(wMsg == MOM_CLOSE)
    {
        // send a message to the sysex proc indicating that the
        // device is closed and to free any remaining memory
        PostMessage(lpMidiOut->hMWnd, MOM_CLOSE, 0, (DWORD)MAKELONG(
                HIWORD(lpMidiHdr), HIWORD(lpMidiOut)));
    }
}
//------------------------------------------------------------------------------
// MidiOutProc
//
// Processes the messages for the Midi Out window.
// If the message is MOM_CLOSE, then cleanup the hidden window and memory
// allocations and alert the app that the driver is closed.
//------------------------------------------------------------------------------
```

```
LRESULT CALLBACK _export MidiOutProc(HWND hWnd, UINT iMessage, WPARAM wParam,
    LPARAM lParam)
{
    LPMIDIOUT lpMidiOut;  // pointer to MidiOut structure
    LPMIDIHDR lpMidiHdr;  // pointer to MidiHdr structure

    lpMidiOut = (LPMIDIOUT) MAKELONG(0, HIWORD(lParam));
    lpMidiHdr = (LPMIDIHDR) MAKELONG(0, LOWORD(lParam));

    if(iMessage == MOM_CLOSE)
    {
        // destroy the sysex window
        DestroyWindow(lpMidiOut->hMWnd);

        // free the midi out queue
        FreeGlobalMem16(lpMidiOut->lpMidiOutDataHead);

        // send a close message to the application
        SendMessage(lpMidiOut->hWnd, MOM_CLOSE, 0, 0L);

        // and the rest of the MidiOut structure
        FreeGlobalMem16(lpMidiOut);
    }

    if(iMessage == MOM_LONGDATA)
    {
        // reset data pointer to start of buffer
        lpMidiHdr->lpData -= lpMidiHdr->dwBytesRecorded;
        lpMidiHdr->dwBufferLength = lpMidiHdr->dwBytesRecorded;

        // send the midi header to the driver
        midiOutLongMsg(lpMidiOut->hMidiOut, lpMidiHdr, sizeof(MIDIHDR));
    }

    // all messages that are not completely processed above must be processed here.
    return DefWindowProc(hWnd, iMessage, wParam, lParam);
}
```

# Sync.c

```
//--------------------------------------------------------------------------------
// Maximum MIDI Programmer's ToolKit - MxMidi16.DLL
// MIDI Event Synchronization Module
//
// Copyright (c) Paul A. Messick, 1994-1996
//
// Written by Paul A. Messick
//
// Provides functions to play and time midi events.
//
// The algorithm used here provides timing of midi events that is
// independent of the available timer interrupt rate.  Resolutions of up
// to 960 ticks/beat at tempos between 10 and 250 beats/min are
// effectively handled.
//
// The maximum error in timing when syncing to tape is approximately
// 1.3 ns per smpte quarter frame, or more than 26 minutes per tick at
// 960 tpb.
//
// The error calculation is as follows:
//   error = 1/3 uS per qF / 256 = 1.3 nS/qF
//   error = 1.3nS/qF * 4qF/fr * 30fr/sec = 156 nS/sec
//   960t/b * 250b/min * 1min/60sec * 1sec/1e9nS = 4e-6 ticks/nS
//
//   error = 156 nS/sec * 4e-6 ticks/nS = 624e-6 ticks/sec
//         = 1602 sec/tick
//   error = 1602 sec/tick * 1min/60sec = 26.7 min/tick
//--------------------------------------------------------------------------------

#include <windows.h>
#include "MxDLL.h"

//--------------------------------------------------------------------------------
// Function Prototypes used in this DLL module
//--------------------------------------------------------------------------------
void InsertInSysexBuffer(LPMIDIOUT lpMidiOut, LPMIDIEVENT thisEvent);
void TrackMidiOut(LPMIDIOUT lpMidiOut, DWORD dwMsg);
WORD TurnNotesOff(LPMIDIOUT lpMidiOut);
//--------------------------------------------------------------------------------
```

```
// OpenSync
//
// Enables sync for playback and record for the sync mode selected.
// To change the sync mode of a previously opened sync device, open the
// device again, passing the old hSync handle.  Reopening can be used
// to change hWnd, mode, and/or wTimerPeriod.  Any previous sync input
// setting is preserved.
//
// On reopen, the mode and/or wTimerPeriod parameters can be set to
// USE_CURRENT to preserve previous settings.
//
// hSync is the handle to the already opened sync device, if reopening in order
//   to change settings, or zero if initially opening a device.
//
//  hWnd is the handle to the window that will receive sync messages
//      MIDI_BEAT is sent on every beat at the current tempo
//      OUTBUFFER_READY is sent when a particular output is below
//          25% full and is ready for more data
//
// mode can be set to:
//   S_INT        internal sync
//   S_MIDI       midi clock sync
//
// wTimerPeriod is the requested timer period in mS.  The final actual
// period may be greater than the requested period, depending on the
// capabilities of the installed Windows timer driver.
//
// the function returns a handle to the sync device if sync was correctly opened,
// or an error value (less than MXMIDIERR_MAXERR) if there was an error opening.
//-----------------------------------------------------------------------
HSYNC WINAPI _export OpenSync16(HSYNC hSync, HWND hWnd, WORD mode, WORD wTimerPeriod)
{
    TIMECAPS timeCaps;          // timer capabilities structure
    LPSYNC lpSY;                // pointer to sync structure
    LPSYNC lpSync = (LPSYNC)hSync;

    // check to see if already open
    // open is defined as lpSync having a corresponding valid handle
    // the assumption here is that lpSync might have garbage in it and
    // that that garbage is not accidentally a valid pointer
    if((hSync > MXMIDIERR_MAXERR) && (GlobalHandle(SELECTOROF(lpSync)) != NULL))
    {
        // already open, use the old pointer
        lpSY = lpSync;

        // if timer was active, kill the timer
        if(lpSY->wTimerID != NULL)
        {
            // stop the timer
            timeKillEvent(lpSync->wTimerID);

            // release the timer
            timeEndPeriod(lpSync->wTimerPeriod);
        }
    }
    else
    {
        // attempt to allocate memory for this device
        lpSY = (LPSYNC)GlobalLock(GlobalAlloc(GMEM_MOVEABLE | GMEM_SHARE |
                                              GMEM_ZEROINIT,
                  sizeof(SyncStruct)));

        // check for an allocation error
        if(lpSY == NULL)
            return MXMIDIERR_NOMEM;

        // allocate memory for start of list of midi out devices
        // that will be serviced by this sync device
        lpSY->lpMidiOutList = (LPMIDIOUT FAR*)GlobalLock(GlobalAlloc(GMEM_MOVEABLE |
                GMEM_SHARE | GMEM_ZEROINIT, sizeof(LPMIDIOUT)));
    }

    // this is the handle to the window that is to receive messages
    lpSY->hWnd = hWnd;

    // set the new sync mode
    if(mode != USE_CURRENT)
        lpSY->wSyncMode = mode;

    // sync starts out disabled
```

```
        lpSY->wFlags = 0;

        // no sysex buffers are currently active
        lpSY->nSysexBuffsActive = 0;

        // setup timer settings
        if(wTimerPeriod != USE_CURRENT)
            lpSY->wTimerPeriod = wTimerPeriod;

        lpSY->wTimerID = NULL;

        // set the default resolution and tempo for midi playback
        SetResolution16((HSYNC)lpSY, 480);    // 480 ticks per beat
        SetTempo16((HSYNC)lpSY, 500000L);      // 120 bpm

        // enable the timer
        // get the capabilities of the timer driver
        if(timeGetDevCaps((LPTIMECAPS)&timeCaps, sizeof(timeCaps)) != 0)
        {
            FreeGlobalMem16(lpSY);
            return MMSYSERR_ALLOCATED;
        }

        // set the timer to the desired period
        if(timeCaps.wPeriodMin <= lpSY->wTimerPeriod)
            lpSY->wTimerPeriod = lpSY->wTimerPeriod;
        else
            lpSY->wTimerPeriod = timeCaps.wPeriodMin;

        if(timeBeginPeriod(lpSY->wTimerPeriod) != 0)
        {
            FreeGlobalMem16(lpSY);
            return MMSYSERR_ALLOCATED;
        }

        // start the timer
        if((lpSY->wTimerID = timeSetEvent(lpSY->wTimerPeriod, lpSY->wTimerPeriod,
            (LPTIMECALLBACK)syncTimer, (DWORD)lpSY, TIME_PERIODIC)) == NULL)
        {
            FreeGlobalMem16(lpSY);
            return MMSYSERR_ALLOCATED;
        }

        return (HSYNC)lpSY;
}
//------------------------------------------------------------------------------
// CloseSync
//
// Closes the sync device and frees the Sync structure.
// Returns 0 if successful, non-zero on error.
//------------------------------------------------------------------------------
WORD WINAPI _export CloseSync16(HSYNC hSync)
{
        LPMIDIOUT FAR* lpMOL; // pointer to item in midiout list
        LPSYNC lpSync = (LPSYNC)hSync;

        // if not open, ignore request
        if(hSync < MXMIDIERR_MAXERR)
            return 0;

        // was internal sync enabled?
        if(lpSync->wTimerID != NULL)
        {
            // stop the timer
            timeKillEvent(lpSync->wTimerID);

            // release the timer
            timeEndPeriod(lpSync->wTimerPeriod);
        }
        // disconnect all attached midi out devices from this sync device
        lpMOL = lpSync->lpMidiOutList;
        while(*lpMOL != NULL)
        {
            ((*lpMOL)->lpSync) = NULL;
            lpMOL++;
        }

        // free the lpMidiOutList structure
        FreeGlobalMem16(lpSync->lpMidiOutList);

        // free the Sync structure
        FreeGlobalMem16(lpSync);
```

```
        return 1;
}
//-----------------------------------------------------------------------------
// StopSync
//
// Disables the sync device, but does not remove the timer, if enabled.
// In contrast to the printed documentation, this function does flush
// the output buffers.
//-----------------------------------------------------------------------------
void WINAPI _export StopSync16(HSYNC hSync)
{
    LPMIDIOUT FAR* lpMOL;       // pointer to item in midiout list
    LPMIDIOUT lpMO;             // pointer to this midi out
    LPSYNC lpSync = (LPSYNC)hSync;

    // if not open, ignore request
    if(hSync < MXMIDIERR_MAXERR)
        return;

    // disable the timer
    lpSync->wFlags = 0;

    // reset midi out for each output
    lpMOL = lpSync->lpMidiOutList;
    while(*lpMOL != NULL)
    {
        // send midi stop if not in midi clock sync mode
        if(lpSync->wSyncMode != S_MIDI)
        {
            // send start if not midi sync
            lpMO = ((LPMIDIOUT)(*lpMOL));

            if(lpMO->dwFlags & SYNC_OUTPUT)
                midiOutShortMsg(lpMO->hMidiOut, (DWORD)MIDI_STOP);
        }

        // reset the output
        ResetMidiOut16((HMOUT)(*lpMOL));
        lpMOL++;
    }
}

//-----------------------------------------------------------------------------
// PauseSync
//
// Disables the sync device, but does not remove the timer, if enabled.
// This function does not flush the midi output buffers.  If reset is TRUE
// then MidiOutReset is called, turning off any currently playing notes and
// flushing the sysex buffers.  If reset is FALSE then MidiOutReset is
// not called.  Pausing sync without resetting Midi out is intended for
// short duration pauses, since "stuck notes" may result from prolonged
// pauses without resetting the outputs.
//-----------------------------------------------------------------------------
void WINAPI _export PauseSync16(HSYNC hSync, BOOL reset)
{
    LPMIDIOUT FAR* lpMOL;       // pointer to item in midiout list
    LPMIDIOUT lpMO;             // pointer to this midi out
    LPSYNC lpSync = (LPSYNC)hSync;

    // if not open, ignore request
    if(hSync < MXMIDIERR_MAXERR)
        return;
    // save the state of the SYNC_RUNNING flag for later
    lpSync->wFlags &= ~RUNNING_STATUS;
    lpSync->wFlags |= (lpSync->wFlags & SYNC_RUNNING ? RUNNING_STATUS : 0);

    // disable the timer
    lpSync->wFlags &= ~SYNC_RUNNING;
        lpSync->wFlags &= ~SYNC_ENABLED;

    // if the reset parameter is TRUE, reset midi out for each output
    if(reset)
    {
        lpMOL = lpSync->lpMidiOutList;
        while(*lpMOL != NULL)
        {
            // send midi stop if not in midi clock sync mode
            if(lpSync->wSyncMode != S_MIDI)
            {
```

```
                  // send start if not midi sync
                  lpMO = ((LPMIDIOUT)(*lpMOL));

                  if(lpMO->dwFlags & SYNC_OUTPUT)
                       midiOutShortMsg(lpMO->hMidiOut, (DWORD)MIDI_STOP);
             }

             // turn off any currently playing notes
             TurnNotesOff((LPMIDIOUT)(*lpMOL));

             lpMOL++;
         }
     }
}

//-------------------------------------------------------------------------------
// StartSync
//
// Enables the sync device and clears the ticks count.
//-------------------------------------------------------------------------------
void WINAPI _export StartSync16(HSYNC hSync)
{
    LPMIDIOUT FAR* lpMOL;
    LPSYNC lpSync = (LPSYNC)hSync;

    // if not open, ignore request
    if(hSync < MXMIDIERR_MAXERR)
        return;

    // reset sync
    lpSync->dwFticks = 0L;
    lpSync->dwTicks = 0L;
    lpSync->nTicksSinceClock = 0;
    lpSync->nTicksSinceBeat = 0;
    lpSync->wTempoTicks = 0;
    lpSync->dwLastTicks = 0L;
    lpSync->msPosition = 0L;

    // clear the time of the last event
    lpMOL = lpSync->lpMidiOutList;
    while(*lpMOL != NULL)
    {
        ((LPMIDIOUT)(*lpMOL))->dwLastEventTicks = 0L;
        lpMOL++;
    }

    ReStartSync16(hSync);
}

//-------------------------------------------------------------------------------
// ReStartSync
//
// Enables the sync device from the current ticks position.
//-------------------------------------------------------------------------------
void WINAPI _export ReStartSync16(HSYNC hSync)
{
    LPMIDIOUT FAR* lpMOL;      // pointer to item in midiout list
    LPMIDIOUT lpMO;            // pointer to this midi out
    LPSYNC lpSync = (LPSYNC)hSync;

    // if not open, ignore request
    if(hSync < MXMIDIERR_MAXERR)
        return;

    // enable the timer
    lpSync->wFlags |= SYNC_ENABLED;

    // allow a sync_done to be sent
    lpSync->wFlags &= ~SENT_SYNCDONE;

    // if its not S_MIDI sync...
    if(lpSync->wSyncMode != S_MIDI)
    {
        // start the timer running (if S_MIDI it will be
        // started by reception of MIDI_START message)
        lpSync->wFlags |= SYNC_RUNNING;

        // send start if not midi sync
        lpMOL = lpSync->lpMidiOutList;
        while(*lpMOL != NULL)
        {
            lpMO = ((LPMIDIOUT)(*lpMOL));
            if(lpMO->dwFlags & SYNC_OUTPUT)
```

```
                    midiOutShortMsg(lpMO->hMidiOut, (DWORD)MIDI_START);

                lpMOL++;
            }
    }
    else
    // restore the status of the SYNC_RUNNING flag
    // for the S_MIDI sync mode
    if(lpSync->wFlags & RUNNING_STATUS)
    {
            lpSync->wFlags &= ~RUNNING_STATUS;
            lpSync->wFlags |= SYNC_RUNNING;
    }
}
//-----------------------------------------------------------------------
// SetTempo
//
// Sets the current tempo.  This function may be called at
// any time to change the tempo.  The tempo is set in micro-
// seconds per midi beat so that tempo may be set fractionally.
//
// Returns 0 if successful, TIMERR_NOCANDO if the uSPerBeat parameter is
// zero.
//-----------------------------------------------------------------------
WORD WINAPI _export SetTempo16(HSYNC hSync, DWORD uSPerBeat)
{
    LPMIDIIN lpMidiIn;      // local pointer to midi in structure
    DWORD dwTicks;          // num of elaspsed ticks for tempo event
    LPMIDIEVENT Qptr;       // pointer to buffer event
    LPSYNC lpSync = (LPSYNC)hSync;

    // if not open, ignore request
    if(hSync < MXMIDIERR_MAXERR)
        return MXMIDIERR_BADHANDLE;

    // tempo must be greater than zero
    if(uSPerBeat == 0)
        return MXMIDIERR_BADTEMPO;

    lpSync->dwTempo = uSPerBeat * SCALE;

    // Test for uninitialized lpSyncIn -- without a sync input
    // device there is no valid destination for (sync) tempo changes
    // if sync is running, insert the tempo change in the buffer
    if((lpSync->wFlags & SYNC_RUNNING) && (lpSync->lpSyncIn != NULL))
    {
            lpMidiIn = lpSync->lpSyncIn;

            // calculate the elaspsed ticks
            dwTicks = lpSync->dwTicks - lpMidiIn->dwLastEventTicks;
            lpMidiIn->dwLastEventTicks = lpSync->dwTicks;

            // get a pointer to the buffer
            Qptr = (LPMIDIEVENT)(lpMidiIn->lpMidiInDataHead + lpMidiIn->pMidiInDataIn);

            // store the data in the buffer
            // make sure status is zero.
            Qptr->time = dwTicks;
            Qptr->status = 0;
            Qptr->data1 = LOBYTE(HIWORD(uSPerBeat));
            Qptr->data2 = HIBYTE(LOWORD(uSPerBeat));
            Qptr->data3 = LOBYTE(LOWORD(uSPerBeat));

            // if necessary wrap the pointer
            if(lpMidiIn->pMidiInDataIn++ == lpMidiIn->nMidiInSize)
                    lpMidiIn->pMidiInDataIn = 0;

            // send a message to the application
            PostMessage(lpMidiIn->hWnd, MIDI_DATA, 0, (DWORD)lpMidiIn);
    }

    return 0;
}
//-----------------------------------------------------------------------
// SetResolution
//
// Sets the resolution in ticks per midi beat.  Higher values
// of resolution provide greater timing accuracy.  This function should
// be called after the device is opened and before playback or record
// starts.
```

```
//-------------------------------------------------------------------------------
void WINAPI _export SetResolution16(HSYNC hSync, WORD resolution)
{
    LPSYNC lpSync = (LPSYNC)hSync;

    // if not open, ignore request
    if(hSync < MXMIDIERR_MAXERR)
        return;

    if(resolution > MAX_RESOLUTION)
        return;

    lpSync->wResolution = resolution;
    lpSync->nTicksPerClock = resolution/24;
    lpSync->dwTRtime = resolution * lpSync->wTimerPeriod * 256000L;
}
//-------------------------------------------------------------------------------
// GetTempo
//
// Gets the current tempo.  The tempo is set in microseconds
// per midi beat so that tempo may be set fractionally.
//-------------------------------------------------------------------------------
DWORD WINAPI _export GetTempo16(HSYNC hSync)
{
    LPSYNC lpSync = (LPSYNC)hSync;

    // if not open, ignore request
    if(hSync < MXMIDIERR_MAXERR)
        return 0L;
    else
        return lpSync->dwTempo / SCALE;
}
//-------------------------------------------------------------------------------
// GetResolution
//
// Gets the resolution in ticks per midi beat.  Higher values
// of resolution provide greater timing accuracy.
//-------------------------------------------------------------------------------
WORD WINAPI _export GetResolution16(HSYNC hSync)
{
    LPSYNC lpSync = (LPSYNC)hSync;

    // if not open, ignore request
    if(hSync < MXMIDIERR_MAXERR)
        return 0;
    else
        return lpSync->wResolution;
}
//-------------------------------------------------------------------------------
//  GetPosition
//
//  Returns the current playback position in either milliseconds since the
//  last time StartSync() was called (by specifying POS_MS for units) or in
//  elapsed ticks since the last time StartSync() was called (by specifying
//  POS_TICKS for units).
//-------------------------------------------------------------------------------
DWORD WINAPI _export GetPosition16(HSYNC hSync, WORD units)
{
    LPSYNC lpSync = (LPSYNC)hSync;
    DWORD rc;

    // if not open, ignore request
    if(hSync < MXMIDIERR_MAXERR)
        return 0L;

    switch(units)
    {
        case POS_MS:
            rc = lpSync->msPosition;
            break;

        case POS_TICKS:
            rc = lpSync->dwTicks;
            break;

        default:
            rc = 0;
            break;
```

```
        }
        return rc;
}
//------------------------------------------------------------------------
// sync handler
//
// This function calculates the number of ticks since last message sent,
// based on the current sync mode.  If it is time, it sends the next midi
// message.
//
//    The algorithm used for timing is outlined below:
//
// given:
//    resolution in ticks/beat, tempo in uS/beat, and thistime in
//         nS/interrupt
// and
//    time in nS, corresponding to accumulated fractions of a tick
//
// then,
//    nticks = ((resolution * time) + (resolution * thistime)) / tempo
// and,
//    fticks = (thistime * resolution) - (nticks * tempo)
//
// since:
//    (resolution * thistime) is known in advance it is calculated
//    outside of this routine and stored in lpSync->dwTRtime.  It need
//    only be changed if the sync mode or resolution are changed.
//
// therefore:
//    nticks = (fticks + trtime)/tempo
//    fticks += trtime - nticks*tempo
//    elasped ticks += nticks
//------------------------------------------------------------------------
void sync(LPSYNC lpSync)
{
    LPMIDIEVENT thisEvent;     // pointer to current event to (possibly) send
    DWORD FAR* lpE;            // pointer to event structure as dwords
    DWORD dwMsg;               // outgoing packed midi message
    WORD nticks;               // number of ticks elasped since last call
    LPMIDIOUT FAR* lpMOL;      // pointer to item in midiout list
    LPMIDIOUT lpMO;            // pointer to this midi out
    WORD nclocks;              // number of midi clocks to send
    WORD nc;                   // midi clock sent counter
    DWORD newTempo;            // tempo value for tempo changes
    BOOL fDone;                // true if no messages are left in queue

    // if sync enabled, calculate number of elasped ticks since last call
    if((lpSync->wFlags & SYNC_RUNNING) != SYNC_RUNNING)
        return;

    lpSync->wFlags |= IN_SYNC;

    // add time to the position accumulator for millisecond postion
    lpSync->msPosition += lpSync->wTimerPeriod;

    // if sync is Midi clock, ticks may be handled differently
    // if sync is being re-synchronized to a clock boundary or
    // the tick count is being held at nTicksPerClock-1
    if(lpSync->wSyncMode == S_MIDI)
    {
        // only interpolate up to the tick before the next clock
        // but keep counting new ticks for later tempo calculation
        if(lpSync->wFlags & MC_HOLD)
        {
            nticks = (WORD)((lpSync->dwFticks + lpSync->dwTRtime) / lpSync->dwTempo);
            lpSync->dwFticks += lpSync->dwTRtime - ((DWORD)nticks * lpSync->dwTempo);
            lpSync->wTempoTicks += nticks;
            lpSync->wFlags &= ~IN_SYNC;
            return;
        }

        // re-synchronize midi clock ticks
        if(lpSync->wFlags & MC_RESYNC)
        {
            // clear fractional ticks to re-synchronize tick interpolation
            lpSync->dwFticks = 0L;

            // calculate any extra ticks needed
```

```
                nticks = (WORD)(lpSync->nTicksPerClock -
                        (lpSync->dwTicks - lpSync->dwLastTicks));

                // save new last ticks count
                lpSync->dwLastTicks = lpSync->dwTicks + nticks;

                // done re-syncing
                lpSync->wFlags &= ~MC_RESYNC;
            }
            else
            {
                // interpolate ticks between midi clocks
                nticks = (WORD)((lpSync->dwFticks + lpSync->dwTRtime) / lpSync->dwTempo);
                lpSync->dwFticks += lpSync->dwTRtime - ((DWORD)nticks * lpSync->dwTempo);

                // add ticks to value used to calculate tempo
                lpSync->wTempoTicks += nticks;

                // the number of elaspsed ticks cannot be greater than the number
                // of ticks per clock - 1 until the next midi clock arrives (and
                // the ticks get re-synced.)  Hold the number of ticks, if necessary.
                if((lpSync->dwTicks - lpSync->dwLastTicks + nticks) >=
                        lpSync->nTicksPerClock)
                {
                    nticks = (WORD)(lpSync->nTicksPerClock - 1 -
                            (lpSync->dwTicks - lpSync->dwLastTicks));
                    lpSync->wFlags |= MC_HOLD;
                }
            }
        }
        else
        {
            // calculate the number of new ticks
            nticks = (WORD)((lpSync->dwFticks + lpSync->dwTRtime) / lpSync->dwTempo);
            lpSync->dwFticks += lpSync->dwTRtime - ((DWORD)nticks * lpSync->dwTempo);
            lpSync->nTicksSinceClock += nticks;
        }

        // calculate final tick counts
        lpSync->dwTicks += (DWORD)nticks;
        lpSync->nTicksSinceBeat += nticks;

        // time to send a beat message to the app?
        if(lpSync->nTicksSinceBeat >= lpSync->wResolution)
        {
            PostMessage(lpSync->hWnd, MIDI_BEAT, 0, (DWORD)lpSync);
            lpSync->nTicksSinceBeat -= lpSync->wResolution;
        }

        // calculate how many clocks need to be sent, if any
        if(lpSync->wSyncMode != S_MIDI)
        {
            nclocks = 0;
            while(lpSync->nTicksSinceClock >= lpSync->nTicksPerClock)
            {
                nclocks++;
                lpSync->nTicksSinceClock -= lpSync->nTicksPerClock;
            }
        }

        // time to output midi event?
        // search through all attached midi out devices for any that
        // have messages waiting to go out
        lpMOL = lpSync->lpMidiOutList;

        // assume that nothing is waiting to be sent
        fDone = TRUE;

        while(*lpMOL != NULL)
        {
            lpMO = ((LPMIDIOUT)(*lpMOL));

            // time to send midi clock(s)?
            nc = nclocks;
            if((lpMO->dwFlags & SYNC_OUTPUT) && (lpSync->wSyncMode != S_MIDI))
                while(nc > 0)
                {
                    midiOutShortMsg(lpMO->hMidiOut, (DWORD)MIDI_CLOCK);
                    nc--;
                }

            thisEvent = (LPMIDIEVENT)(lpMO->pMidiOutDataOut + lpMO->lpMidiOutDataHead);
```

```
        // any messages to send?
        if(lpMO->wSpan != 0)
        {
            // there is at least one message to be sent
            fDone = FALSE;

            // if this output is currently sending a sysex make no
            // attempt to send any short data, to prevent short messages
            // and long message from being sent out of order
            // last event time is on per midi output basis
            while((thisEvent->time <= lpSync->dwTicks - lpMO->dwLastEventTicks) &&
                  (lpMO->wSpan != 0) && (((lpMO->dwFlags & SENDING_SYSEX) == 0) ||
                  (thisEvent->status == SYSEX)))
            {
                // time to send this one
                lpMO->dwLastEventTicks += thisEvent->time;

                // is this a tempo change event?
                if(thisEvent->status == 0)
                {
                    newTempo = MAKELONG((thisEvent->data2 << 8) + thisEvent->data3,
                              thisEvent->data1);
                    if(newTempo != 0L)
                        lpSync->dwTempo = newTempo * SCALE;
                }
                // no, it's a MIDI event
                else
                {
                    // if this is a sysex message, insert it into a sysex buffer
                    // where it will eventually be sent out.
                    if(thisEvent->status == SYSEX)
                        InsertInSysexBuffer(lpMO, thisEvent);
                    else
                    {
                        // it's a short midi message, build the message to send
                        lpE = (DWORD FAR*)thisEvent;
                        dwMsg = (DWORD)*(lpE + 1);

                        midiOutShortMsg(lpMO->hMidiOut, dwMsg);
                        TrackMidiOut(lpMO, dwMsg);
                    }
                }

                // increment the out pointer, wrapping if necessary
                if(lpMO->pMidiOutDataOut++ == lpMO->nMidiOutSize)
                    lpMO->pMidiOutDataOut = 0;

                // if number of events left in the buffer
                // has fallen below the threshold, send
                // the OUTBUFFER_READY message to the app
                // requesting more data.
                // The threshold is 25% of the buffer size
                if(lpMO->wSpan == (lpMO->nMidiOutSize >> 2))
                    PostMessage(lpMO->hWnd, OUTBUFFER_READY, 0, (DWORD)lpMO);

                // one less message in the buffer
                lpMO->wSpan--;

                // reset thisEvent to the next (possible) event and look again
                thisEvent = (LPMIDIEVENT)(lpMO->pMidiOutDataOut +
                            lpMO->lpMidiOutDataHead);
            }
        }

        // next device in list -- last one will be null
        lpMOL++;
    }

    // were there any messages in the queue or is sysex still busy?
    // send only one message
    if(fDone && (lpSync->nSysexBuffsActive == 0) &&
          ((lpSync->wFlags & SENT_SYNCDONE) == 0))
    {
        // send a SYNC_DONE to the app
        PostMessage(lpSync->hWnd, SYNC_DONE, 0, (DWORD)lpSync);
        lpSync->wFlags |= SENT_SYNCDONE;
    }

    lpSync->wFlags &= ~IN_SYNC;
}
```

```
//------------------------------------------------------------------------
// syncTimer callback function
//
// This callback processes the periodic timer events for internal sync
// and serves as a timebase for midi sync.
//
// Parameter dwUser is lpSync.  Other parameters are unused.
//------------------------------------------------------------------------
void CALLBACK _export syncTimer(UINT wTimerID, UINT wMsg, DWORD dwUser,
        DWORD dw1, DWORD dw2)
{
    // don't call sync if already servicing a midi clock event
    if((((LPSYNC)dwUser)->wFlags & IN_SYNC) == 0)
        sync((LPSYNC)dwUser);
}

//------------------------------------------------------------------------
// midi sync handler
//
// This function is called when the sync in device receives a midi clock
// message.  It calculates a new tempo based on the number of ticks since
// the last clock.
//------------------------------------------------------------------------
void MidiClock(LPSYNC lpSync)
{
    // next sync() will be a re-sync
    lpSync->wFlags |= MC_RESYNC;

    // we are no longer holding the count
    lpSync->wFlags &= ~MC_HOLD;

    // generate these ticks
    sync(lpSync);

    // calculate new tempo
    lpSync->dwTempo -= ((long)lpSync->nTicksPerClock - (long)lpSync->wTempoTicks) *
            (lpSync->dwTempo / (long)lpSync->wResolution);

    // clear tempo tick count
    lpSync->wTempoTicks = 0;
}
```

## MxMidi.def

```
LIBRARY         MXMIDI16
DESCRIPTION     'Maximum MIDI ToolKit 16-bit DLL'
EXETYPE         WINDOWS
CODE            PRELOAD FIXED
DATA            PRELOAD FIXED SINGLE
HEAPSIZE        5120
EXPORTS
    DLLENTRYPOINT               @1  RESIDENTNAME
    MXMIDI_THUNKDATA16          @2  RESIDENTNAME

IMPORTS
    C16THKSL01                  =   KERNEL.631
    THUNKCONNECT16              =   KERNEL.651
```

# MxMidi32 DLL Source

## MxMidi32.c

```
//------------------------------------------------------------------------
// Maximum MIDI Programmer's ToolKit - MxMidi32.DLL
// MaxMidi Flat Thunk Module
//
// Copyright (c) Paul A. Messick, 1994-1996
//
```

```
// Written by Paul A. Messick
//
// Thunks between 32-bit applications and the 16-bit MaxMidi DLL.  Also provides
// 32-bit SMF read and write functions.
//------------------------------------------------------------------------
#include <windows.h>
#include "MxDLL.h"

__declspec(dllexport) BOOL WINAPI MxMidi_ThunkConnect32(LPSTR pszDll16, LPSTR pszDll32,
HINSTANCE hInst, DWORD dwReason);
//========================================================================
//   Internal Functions
//========================================================================
//------------------------------------------------------------------------
//   DllMain
//
//   This is the 32-bit equivalent to "LibMain".  It connects with the 16-bit
//   DLL through the thunk layer.
//------------------------------------------------------------------------
__declspec(dllexport) BOOL WINAPI DllMain(HINSTANCE hDLL, DWORD dwReason,
        LPVOID lpReserved)
{
    // call the entry point for the thunk layer
    if(!(MxMidi_ThunkConnect32("MXMIDI16.DLL", "MXMIDI32.DLL", hDLL, dwReason)))
        return FALSE;

    switch(dwReason)
    {
        // DLL is attaching to the address space of the current process.
        case DLL_PROCESS_ATTACH:
            break;

        // The calling process is detaching the DLL from its address space.
        case DLL_PROCESS_DETACH:
            break;

        // A new thread is being created in the current process.
        case DLL_THREAD_ATTACH:
            break;

        // A thread is exiting cleanly.
        case DLL_THREAD_DETACH:
            break;
    }

    return TRUE;
}
//------------------------------------------------------------------------
//   GetMaxMidiVersion
//------------------------------------------------------------------------
__declspec(dllexport) WORD WINAPI GetMaxMidiVersion(void)
{
    return GetMaxMidiVersion16();
}
//------------------------------------------------------------------------
//   GetNumInDevices
//
//   For convenience: use in place of midiInGetNumDevs to avoid dealing with
//   MMSYSTEM directly.
//------------------------------------------------------------------------
_declspec(dllexport) UINT WINAPI GetNumInDevices(void)
{
    return midiInGetNumDevs();
}
//------------------------------------------------------------------------
//   GetNumOutDevices
//
//   For convenience: use in place of midiOutGetNumDevs to avoid dealing with
//   MMSYSTEM directly.
//------------------------------------------------------------------------
_declspec(dllexport) UINT WINAPI GetNumOutDevices(void)
{
    return midiOutGetNumDevs();
}
//------------------------------------------------------------------------
//   GetMidiOutDescription
```

```
//-------------------------------------------------------------------
__declspec(dllexport) BOOL WINAPI GetMidiOutDescription(WORD wDeviceID,
    LPSTR lpzDesc)
{
    return GetMidiOutDescription16(wDeviceID, lpzDesc);
}
//-------------------------------------------------------------------
//  OpenMidiOut
//-------------------------------------------------------------------
__declspec(dllexport) HMOUT WINAPI OpenMidiOut(HWND hWnd, WORD wDeviceID,
    HSYNC hSync, DWORD dwFlags)
{
    return OpenMidiOut16(hWnd, wDeviceID, hSync, dwFlags);
}
//-------------------------------------------------------------------
//  ResetMidiOut
//-------------------------------------------------------------------
__declspec(dllexport) WORD WINAPI ResetMidiOut(HMOUT hMidiOut)
{
    return ResetMidiOut16(hMidiOut);
}
//-------------------------------------------------------------------
//  FlushMidiout
//-------------------------------------------------------------------
__declspec(dllexport) void WINAPI FlushMidiOut(HMOUT hMidiOut)
{
    FlushMidiOut16(hMidiOut);
}
//-------------------------------------------------------------------
//  CloseMidiOut
//-------------------------------------------------------------------
__declspec(dllexport) WORD WINAPI CloseMidiOut(HMOUT hMidiOut)
{
    return CloseMidiOut16(hMidiOut);
}
//-------------------------------------------------------------------
//  PutMidiOut
//-------------------------------------------------------------------
__declspec(dllexport) WORD WINAPI PutMidiOut(HMOUT hMidiOut, LPMIDIEVENT lpMidiEvent)
{
    return PutMidiOut16(hMidiOut, lpMidiEvent);
}
//-------------------------------------------------------------------
// GetMidiInDescription
//-------------------------------------------------------------------
__declspec(dllexport) BOOL WINAPI GetMidiInDescription(WORD wDeviceID,
    LPSTR lpzDesc)
{
    return GetMidiInDescription16(wDeviceID, lpzDesc);
}
//-------------------------------------------------------------------
//  OpenMidiIn
//-------------------------------------------------------------------
__declspec(dllexport) HMIN WINAPI OpenMidiIn(HWND hWnd, WORD wDeviceID,
    HSYNC hSync, DWORD dwFlags)
{
    return OpenMidiIn16(hWnd, wDeviceID, hSync, dwFlags);
}
//-------------------------------------------------------------------
//  StartMidiIn
//-------------------------------------------------------------------
__declspec(dllexport) WORD WINAPI StartMidiIn(HMIN hMidiIn)
{
    return StartMidiIn16(hMidiIn);
}
//-------------------------------------------------------------------
//  StopMidiIn
//-------------------------------------------------------------------
__declspec(dllexport) WORD WINAPI StopMidiIn(HMIN hMidiIn)
{
    return StopMidiIn16(hMidiIn);
}
```

```
//-------------------------------------------------------------------
//   CloseMidiIn
//-------------------------------------------------------------------
__declspec(dllexport) WORD WINAPI CloseMidiIn(HMIN hMidiIn)
{
    return CloseMidiIn16(hMidiIn);
}
//-------------------------------------------------------------------
//   GetMidiIn
//-------------------------------------------------------------------
__declspec(dllexport) LPMIDIEVENT WINAPI GetMidiIn(HMIN hMidiIn)
{
    return GetMidiIn16(hMidiIn);
}
//-------------------------------------------------------------------
//   OpenSync
//-------------------------------------------------------------------
__declspec(dllexport) HSYNC WINAPI OpenSync(HSYNC hSync, HWND hWnd, WORD mode,
        WORD timerPeriod)
{
    return OpenSync16(hSync, hWnd, mode, timerPeriod);
}
//-------------------------------------------------------------------
//   CloseSync
//-------------------------------------------------------------------
__declspec(dllexport) WORD WINAPI CloseSync(HSYNC hSync)
{
    return CloseSync16(hSync);
}
//-------------------------------------------------------------------
//   StopSync
//-------------------------------------------------------------------
__declspec(dllexport) void WINAPI StopSync(HSYNC hSync)
{
    StopSync16(hSync);
}
//-------------------------------------------------------------------
//   StartSync
//-------------------------------------------------------------------
__declspec(dllexport) void WINAPI StartSync(HSYNC hSync)
{
    StartSync16(hSync);
}
//-------------------------------------------------------------------
//   PauseSync
//-------------------------------------------------------------------
__declspec(dllexport) void WINAPI PauseSync(HSYNC hSync, BOOL reset)
{
    PauseSync16(hSync, reset);
}
//-------------------------------------------------------------------
//   ReStartSync
//-------------------------------------------------------------------
__declspec(dllexport) void WINAPI ReStartSync(HSYNC hSync)
{
    ReStartSync16(hSync);
}
//-------------------------------------------------------------------
//   SetTempo
//-------------------------------------------------------------------
__declspec(dllexport) WORD WINAPI SetTempo(HSYNC hSync, DWORD uSPerBeat)
{
    return SetTempo16(hSync, uSPerBeat);
}
//-------------------------------------------------------------------
//   SetResolution
//-------------------------------------------------------------------
__declspec(dllexport) void WINAPI SetResolution(HSYNC hSync, WORD resolution)
{
    SetResolution16(hSync, resolution);
}
```

```
//------------------------------------------------------------------------
//  GetTempo
//------------------------------------------------------------------------
__declspec(dllexport) DWORD WINAPI GetTempo(HSYNC hSync)
{
    return GetTempo16(hSync);
}
//------------------------------------------------------------------------
//  GetResolution
//------------------------------------------------------------------------
__declspec(dllexport) WORD WINAPI GetResolution(HSYNC hSync)
{
    return GetResolution16(hSync);
}
//------------------------------------------------------------------------
//  GetPosition
//------------------------------------------------------------------------
__declspec(dllexport) DWORD WINAPI GetPosition(HSYNC hSync, WORD units)
{
    return GetPosition16(hSync, units);
}
```

## SMF.c

```
//-------------------------------------------------------------------
// MaxMidi MIDI Programmer's ToolKit
// Standard Midi File Module
//
// Copyright (c) Paul A. Messick, 1994-1996
//
// Written by Paul A. Messick
//
// Provides functions to open, close, read and write Standard Midi Files
// of Format 0 and 1.
//-------------------------------------------------------------------
#include <windows.h>
#include <string.h>
#include "MxDLL.h"

//-------------------------------------------------------------------
// Function Prototypes used in this DLL module
//-------------------------------------------------------------------
#define CurFilePos(lpsmf) SetFilePointer(lpsmf->hsmf, 0, NULL, FILE_CURRENT)
#define SeekTo(lpsmf, ofs) SetFilePointer(lpsmf->hsmf, ofs, NULL, FILE_BEGIN)
#define GetMsgLength(b)    (b < 0xF0 ? CMsgLen[(b >> 4) - 8] : SMsgLen[b & 0x0F]);

int ReadSMFHeader(LPSMF lpSMF);
int OpenChunk(LPSMF lpSMF, LPSTR ChunkName, DWORD *offset, DWORD *len);
int ReadChunk(HFILE hsmf, DWORD len, LPSTR lpBuffer);
void SeekAbsolute(LPSMF lpSMF, DWORD offset);
void SeekRelative(LPSMF lpSMF, DWORD offset);
DWORD ReadVarLength(LPSMF lpSMF);
BOOL ReadMidiEvent(LPSMF lpSMF, LPMIDIEVENT lpOutBuf);
DWORD ReadNextMeta(LPSMF lpSMF, LPTRACK lpCurTrack, BYTE MetaEvent, DWORD *time);
BYTE ReadByte(LPSMF lpSMF);

void WriteChunkName(LPSMF lpSMF, LPSTR ChunkName, DWORD offset, DWORD len);
void WriteSMFHeader(LPSMF lpSMF);
DWORD MidiToSMF(LPSMF lpSMF, LPMIDIEVENT lpMidiEvent);
DWORD WriteVarLength(LPSMF lpSMF, DWORD value);
void isNewTrack(LPSMF lpSMF, int wTrack);
void WriteReversedData(LPSMF lpSMF, LPVOID lpData, int wSize);
void WriteByte(LPSMF lpSMF, BYTE val);

//-------------------------------------------------------------------
// Local Data
//-------------------------------------------------------------------
// midi message length arrays
static int CMsgLen[] = { 2, 2, 2, 2, 1, 1, 2 };
static int SMsgLen[] = { 0, 1, 2, 1, 0, 0, 0, 0, 0, 0, 0, 0, 0, 0, 0, 0 };

// time in uS/Frame for each frame rate
DWORD usPerFrame[7] = {33333, 33367, 0, 0, 0, 40000, 41667};

//-------------------------------------------------------------------
// OpenSMF
```

```
//
// This function opens an SMF for read or write.
// hSMF is the handle to the opened SMF, though not an actual file handle.
//
// filename is an asciiz string, including optional path, for the SMF
// to be opened.
//
// *Format is the address of a UINT that contains the SMF format for the
// opened file.  If the file is opened for read, Format is set to the
// format read from the file.  Format 2 files are read as Format 1 files.
// If the file is opened for write, Format must be set to the desired
// value.
//
// mode is a constant character that determines the mode in which the
// file is opened.  mode can be either 'r' for read, or 'w' for write.
//
// OpenSMF returns the number of tracks in the SMF if opened for read,
// zero if the file is successfully opened for write, or -1 if there is
// an error.
//--------------------------------------------------------------------------
PREFIX HSMF WINAPI EXPORT OpenSMF(LPSTR filename, int *Format, const char mode,
        int *nTracks)
{
    LPSMF lpS;          // local pointer to SMF struct
    int track;          // track counter

    // attempt to allocate memory for this SMF structure
    if((lpS = (LPSMF)GlobalLock(GlobalAlloc(GHND, sizeof(SMFStruct)))) == NULL)
        return 0;

    // check for a valid mode
    if((mode != 'r') && (mode != 'w'))
        return 0;

    // setup the mode to open the file
    lpS->mode = mode;

    // Open the file in the requested mode
    lpS->hsmf = CreateFile(filename,
                           (mode == 'r' ? GENERIC_READ : GENERIC_WRITE),
                           FILE_SHARE_READ,(LPSECURITY_ATTRIBUTES)NULL,
                           (mode == 'r' ? OPEN_EXISTING : CREATE_ALWAYS),
                           FILE_ATTRIBUTE_NORMAL | FILE_FLAG_RANDOM_ACCESS,
                           (HANDLE)NULL);

    // was the open ok?
    if(lpS->hsmf == INVALID_HANDLE_VALUE)
    {
        // on error, unwind the memory allocations
        GlobalFree(lpS);
        return 0;
    }

    if(lpS->mode == 'r')
    {
        // read the smf header
        if(ReadSMFHeader(lpS) == -1)
        {
            // on error, unwind the memory allocations
            GlobalFree(lpS);
            return 0;
        }

        // if format is 2, force it to one
        if(lpS->wFormat == 2)
            lpS->wFormat = 1;

        *Format = lpS->wFormat;

        // allocate an array of structures to manage each track
        if((lpS->lpTrack = (LPTRACK)GlobalLock(GlobalAlloc(GHND, lpS->wTracks *
                sizeof(TrackStruct)))) == NULL)
        {
            // on error, unwind the memory allocations
            GlobalFree(lpS);
            return 0;
        }

        // allocate a buffer for each track that is used to
        // read track data from the file
        for(track = 0; track < lpS->wTracks; track++)
```

```
        {
            lpS->lpTrack[track].dwRBsize = 8192;
            if((lpS->lpTrack[track].lpReadBuf = (LPSTR)GlobalAlloc(GPTR,
                    lpS->lpTrack[track].dwRBsize)) == NULL)
            {
                // on error, unwind the memory allocations
                for(track = 0; track < lpS->wTracks; track++)
                    GlobalFree(lpS->lpTrack[track].lpReadBuf);

                GlobalFree(lpS->lpTrack);
                GlobalFree(lpS);
                return 0;
            }

            lpS->lpTrack[track].dwBytesRemaining = 0;
        }

        // allocate buffers for each track to manage meta event
        // offsets and elapsed time in the file (used for ReadMetaEvent())
        for(track = 0; track < lpS->wTracks; track++)
        {
            if((lpS->lpTrack[track].lpMetaOfs = (LPDWORD)GlobalAlloc(GPTR,
                    MAX_META_EVENT * sizeof(DWORD))) == NULL)
            {
                // on error, unwind the memory allocations
                for(track = 0; track < lpS->wTracks; track++)
                {
                    GlobalFree(lpS->lpTrack[track].lpMetaOfs);
                    GlobalFree(lpS->lpTrack[track].lpReadBuf);
                }

                GlobalFree(lpS->lpTrack);
                GlobalFree(lpS);
                return 0;
            }

            // this buffer holds elapsed time in ticks from the start
            // of the track for each meta event
            if((lpS->lpTrack[track].lpMetaTime = (LPDWORD)GlobalAlloc(GPTR,
                    MAX_META_EVENT * sizeof(DWORD))) == NULL)
            {
                // on error, unwind the memory allocations
                for(track = 0; track < lpS->wTracks; track++)
                {
                    GlobalFree(lpS->lpTrack[track].lpMetaOfs);
                    GlobalFree(lpS->lpTrack[track].lpReadBuf);
                }

                GlobalFree(lpS->lpTrack);
                GlobalFree(lpS);
                return 0;
            }
        }

        // allocate a one byte long buffer for reading Meta Events
        // this buffer will be reallocated as needed
        for(track = 0; track < lpS->wTracks; track++)
            lpS->lpMetaBuff = (LPSTR)GlobalAlloc(GPTR, 1);

        // find the beginning offsets for each track by rewinding the file
        RewindSMF((HSMF)lpS);

        // smf successfully opened, return number of tracks
        *nTracks = lpS->wTracks;
        return (HSMF)lpS;
    }

    // else it is opened for write
    // setup the format and division values
    lpS->wFormat = *Format;
    lpS->resolution = 480;

    // initially, no tracks have been written to
    lpS->wCurTrack = -1;

    // write the header - this will be overwritten later
    WriteSMFHeader(lpS);

    // return zero tracks for write
    *nTracks = lpS->wTracks = 0;
    return (HSMF)lpS;
}
```

```
//--------------------------------------------------------------------------
// CloseSMF
//
// This function closes a previously opened SMF, frees the SMFStruct
// memory and sets the lpSMF pointer to NULL to prevent further attempts
// to accesses the file.
//--------------------------------------------------------------------------
PREFIX void WINAPI EXPORT CloseSMF(HSMF hSMF)
{
    int track;                    // track counter
    LPSMF lpSMF = (LPSMF)hSMF;

    // don't try to close a null device
    if(lpSMF == NULL)
        return;

    // free the track structures and buffers
    if(lpSMF->mode == 'r')
    {
        for(track = 0; track < lpSMF->wTracks; track++)
        {
            GlobalFree(lpSMF->lpTrack[track].lpMetaTime);

            GlobalFree(lpSMF->lpTrack[track].lpMetaOfs);
            GlobalFree(lpSMF->lpTrack[track].lpReadBuf);
            GlobalFree(lpSMF->lpMetaBuff);
        }

        GlobalFree(lpSMF->lpTrack);

    }
    else
        if(lpSMF->dwChunkStart != 0) // make sure a track was started
    {
        // write the end of track meta event
        WriteMetaEvent(hSMF, lpSMF->wCurTrack, META_EOT, NULL, 0);

        // seek to the start of the track chunk and
        // update the chunk with the correct length
        WriteChunkName(lpSMF, "MTrk", lpSMF->dwChunkStart, lpSMF->dwChunkLen);

        // update the header with number of tracks, format, etc.
        WriteSMFHeader(lpSMF);
    }

    // close the file
    if(lpSMF->hsmf != 0)
        CloseHandle(lpSMF->hsmf);

    // free the smf structure
    GlobalFree(lpSMF);
}

//--------------------------------------------------------------------------
// RewindSMF
//
// If the SMF was opened for read this function rewinds the tracks of
// the SMF to the beginning and returns TRUE.  If the file was opened for
// write, no action is taken and the function returns FALSE.
//--------------------------------------------------------------------------
PREFIX BOOL WINAPI EXPORT RewindSMF(HSMF hSMF)
{
    DWORD dwTrkOfs;           // offset into file for this track
    int track;                // track counter
    DWORD dwLen;              // length of track in bytes
    int meta;                 // meta event loop counter
    LPSMF lpSMF = (LPSMF)hSMF;

    // if the file is opened for write, nothing to rewind
    if(lpSMF->mode == 'w')
        return FALSE;

    // start at the beginning of the file to rewind
    dwTrkOfs = 0;

    // locate and save file offset and length for each track
    for(track = 0; track < lpSMF->wTracks; track++)
    {
        OpenChunk(lpSMF, "MTrk", &dwTrkOfs, &dwLen);
        lpSMF->lpTrack[track].dwFileOfs = dwTrkOfs;
        lpSMF->lpTrack[track].dwBuffOfs = 0;
        lpSMF->lpTrack[track].dwLength = dwLen;
```

```
                    lpSMF->lpTrack[track].fEndOfTrack = FALSE;

                    // all meta event offsets are at start of track and elapsed times are zero
                    for(meta = 0; meta < MAX_META_EVENT; meta++)
                    {
                        lpSMF->lpTrack[track].lpMetaOfs[meta] = dwTrkOfs;
                        lpSMF->lpTrack[track].lpMetaTime[meta] = 0;
                    }

                    // not in a SYSEX
                    lpSMF->lpTrack[track].wFlags &= ~IN_SYSEX;

                    // clear the meta event delta time for this track
                    lpSMF->lpTrack[track].dwMetaDeltaTime = 0;
                }

        // seek to the first track's data
        lpSMF->wCurTrack = 0;
        SeekAbsolute(lpSMF, lpSMF->lpTrack[0].dwFileOfs);

        return TRUE;
}
//----------------------------------------------------------------------------
// Standard Midi File Read Functions
//----------------------------------------------------------------------------
//----------------------------------------------------------------------------
// ReadSMF
//
// This function reads a block of events from the previously opened SMF.
//----------------------------------------------------------------------------
PREFIX DWORD WINAPI EXPORT ReadSMF(HSMF hSMF, int wTrack, LPMIDIEVENT lpMidiEventBuffer,
DWORD dwBufferLen)
{
        DWORD dwNumEvents = 0;              // number of events read
        LPSMF lpSMF = (LPSMF)hSMF;

        // if the file is opened for write, nothing to read
        if(lpSMF->mode == 'w')
                return 0;

        // save which track we are reading
        lpSMF->wCurTrack = wTrack;

        // seek to the proper location for this track
        SeekAbsolute(lpSMF, lpSMF->lpTrack[wTrack].dwFileOfs);

        // read the track, filling the lpMidiEventBuffer with events
        while((dwNumEvents < dwBufferLen) && (ReadMidiEvent(lpSMF, lpMidiEventBuffer)
                != TRUE))
        {
                // another event read
                lpMidiEventBuffer++;
                dwNumEvents++;
        }

        return dwNumEvents;
}
//----------------------------------------------------------------------------
// GetSMFResolution
//
// This function returns the timing resolution for the SMF in ticks/beat.
//----------------------------------------------------------------------------
PREFIX WORD WINAPI EXPORT GetSMFResolution(HSMF hSMF)
{
        LPSMF lpSMF = (LPSMF)hSMF;

        if(lpSMF->mode == 'r')
                return lpSMF->resolution;

        // not valid for write mode
        return 0;
}
//----------------------------------------------------------------------------
// SetSMFResolution
//
// This function sets the timing resolution for the SMF in ticks/beat.
// It returns 0 if the file was opened for read, or the resolution if
// opened for write.
//----------------------------------------------------------------------------
PREFIX WORD WINAPI EXPORT SetSMFResolution(HSMF hSMF, WORD resolution)
```

```
{
    LPSMF lpSMF = (LPSMF)hSMF;

    if(lpSMF->mode == 'w')
    {
        lpSMF->resolution = resolution;
        return resolution;
    }
    return 0;
}
//-------------------------------------------------------------------------
// ReadMetaEvent
//
// This function reads a Meta Event from the selected track.
// It returns the time of the event, if found, or -1 if not.  The value
// is in a string of length *EventSize pointed to by *EventValue.
// If the event is not found in the track, further attempts to find the
// same event will also return not found.  *EventSize is set to zero and
// *EventValue is set to NULL if the event is not found.
//-------------------------------------------------------------------------
PREFIX DWORD WINAPI EXPORT ReadMetaEvent(HSMF hSMF, int wTrack, BYTE MetaEvent,
        LPSTR* EventValue, DWORD* EventSize)
{
    LPSMF lpSMF = (LPSMF)hSMF;
    DWORD dwOldFilePos;        // starting file position
    LPTRACK lpCurTrack;        // current track to read
    DWORD time;                // event time
    DWORD dwEvents;            // event counter
    LPSTR lpDestBuff;          // destination buffer pointer

    // save the current file offset
    dwOldFilePos = lpSMF->dwCurFileOfs;

    // which track are we reading?
    lpCurTrack = (LPTRACK)&(lpSMF->lpTrack[wTrack]);

    // if this track contains no more of these meta events, return
    if(lpCurTrack->lpMetaOfs[MetaEvent] == (DWORD)-1)
        return (DWORD)-1;

    // seek to the location of the end of the last one of these
    // meta events
    SeekAbsolute(lpSMF, lpCurTrack->lpMetaOfs[MetaEvent]);

    // look for the next one
    *EventSize = ReadNextMeta(lpSMF, lpCurTrack, MetaEvent, &time);

    // if one was found, return it to app
    if(*EventSize != (DWORD)-1)
    {
        // update the location of next meta event
        lpCurTrack->lpMetaOfs[MetaEvent] = lpSMF->dwCurFileOfs + *EventSize;

        // if the event length is zero, just return pointing to an empty string
        if(*EventSize == 0)
        {
            *EventValue = NULL;

            // restore original file position
            SeekAbsolute(lpSMF, dwOldFilePos);
            return time;
        }

        // else re-allocate the internal buffer for the new event
        lpSMF->lpMetaBuff = (LPSTR)GlobalReAlloc(lpSMF->lpMetaBuff, *EventSize, GPTR |
                                                 GMEM_MOVEABLE);

        if(lpSMF->lpMetaBuff == NULL)
        {
            // on error, return not found
            // restore original file position
            SeekAbsolute(lpSMF, dwOldFilePos);
            return (DWORD)-1;
        }

        // read the event data into the application buffer
        dwEvents = *EventSize;
        lpDestBuff = lpSMF->lpMetaBuff;

        while(dwEvents--)
            *(lpDestBuff++) = ReadByte(lpSMF);
```

```
                // return success, pointing to buffer
                *EventValue = lpSMF->lpMetaBuff;

                // restore original file position
                SeekAbsolute(lpSMF, dwOldFilePos);

                // return the elapsed time since the start of the track
                time += lpCurTrack->lpMetaTime[MetaEvent];
                lpCurTrack->lpMetaTime[MetaEvent] = time;
                return time;
        }

        // else, meta event not found
        // tag this as the last one of these meta events
        lpCurTrack->lpMetaOfs[MetaEvent] = (DWORD)-1;

        // restore original file position
        SeekAbsolute(lpSMF, dwOldFilePos);
        return (DWORD)-1;
}
//----------------------------------------------------------------------------
// FindToken
//
// This function searches buffer s1 for the first occurrence of token s2,
// for up to len bytes.  It returns zero if the token is found, non-zero
// if token does not appear in s1.
// If s2 is found in s1, *offset is set to the count of bytes from the
// beginning of s1 to the first byte after the token found in s1.  If the
// token is not found, offset is undefined.
//----------------------------------------------------------------------------
int FindToken(LPSTR s1, LPSTR s2, DWORD len, DWORD *offset)
{
        HPSTR sx;               // search string pointer
        HPSTR hpStart;          // start of buffer
        DWORD s2len;

        // setup pointers to the strings
        sx = (HPSTR)s1;
        hpStart = sx;
        s2len = lstrlen(s2);

        do {
                // search for first character in string
                if((sx = (LPSTR)memchr((LPSTR)sx, s2[0], (size_t)len)) == NULL)
                        return -1;

                // calculate remaining buffer length
                len -= (DWORD)(sx - (HPSTR)s1) + 1L;
                s1 = (LPSTR)sx;

                // find rest of token
        } while(strncmp((LPSTR)(sx++), s2, (size_t)s2len) != 0 );

        *offset = (DWORD)(sx - hpStart) + s2len - 1L;

        return 0;
}
//----------------------------------------------------------------------------
// OpenChunk
//
// This function opens the specified chunk, if found, and sets offset to
// the number of bytes from the start of the file where chunk data begins
// and sets len to the number of bytes of data in the chunk.
// It returns 0 if the chunk was found and read correctly, or -1 on error
//----------------------------------------------------------------------------
int OpenChunk(LPSMF lpSMF, LPSTR ChunkName, DWORD *offset, DWORD *len)
{
        DWORD dwBufferSize;     // buffer size in bytes
        DWORD wBytesRead;       // number of bytes read from file
        DWORD ofs;              // offset into this block
        DWORD fptr;             // final file pointer offset
        LPSTR lpRawData;        // raw file data buffer
        DWORD n;

        // allocate a buffer to read file data into
        dwBufferSize = 8192;
        if((lpRawData = (LPSTR)GlobalAlloc(GPTR, dwBufferSize)) == NULL)
                return -1;

        // read a block of data
```

```
        SeekTo(lpSMF, *offset);
        fptr = *offset;

        ReadFile(lpSMF->hsmf, lpRawData, dwBufferSize, &wBytesRead, NULL);
        while(wBytesRead != 0)
        {
            // look for occurrence of ChunkName in buffer
            if(FindToken(lpRawData, ChunkName, (DWORD)wBytesRead, &ofs) == 0)
            {
                // found it, now set the file pointer to the start of chunk data
                fptr += ofs;
                SeekTo(lpSMF, fptr);

                // read the chunk length
                ReadFile(lpSMF->hsmf, lpRawData, sizeof(DWORD), &n, NULL);
                if(n == 0)
                {
                    // on error, unwind the memory allocations
                    GlobalFree(lpRawData);
                    return -1;
                }

                // offset is the start of chunk data, after len
                *offset = CurFilePos(lpSMF);

                // length is 4 bytes, msb first
                *len = MAKELONG((lpRawData[2] << 8) + lpRawData[3],
                        (lpRawData[0] << 8) + lpRawData[1]);

                // done with the buffer now
                GlobalFree(lpRawData);

                // return success
                return 0;
            }
            else
                fptr += wBytesRead;

            ReadFile(lpSMF->hsmf, lpRawData, dwBufferSize, &wBytesRead, NULL);
        }

        // done with the buffer now
        GlobalFree(lpRawData);

        // chunk never found, return error
        return -1;
}
//--------------------------------------------------------------------------
// ReadSMFHeader
//
// This function reads the smf header information and stores the values
// in the lpSMF structure for later use.
// It returns 0 on success and -1 if the file is not a SMF or other error.
//--------------------------------------------------------------------------
int ReadSMFHeader(LPSMF lpSMF)
{
    DWORD FileOffset = 0;    // offset into file for header
    DWORD length;            // length of header chunk
    UINT division;           // timing resolution
    LPSTR lpHeader;          // header buffer pointer
    DWORD dwBytesRead;
    DWORD sig = 0;

    // read the first DWORD of the file
    // if it is not "MThd", this is not a valid SMF
    ReadFile(lpSMF->hsmf, &sig, sizeof(DWORD), &dwBytesRead, NULL);
    if(sig != mmioFOURCC('M', 'T', 'h', 'd'))
        return -1;
    else// rewind the file
        SeekTo(lpSMF, 0);

    // locate and open the chunk
    // offset to the start of chunk data is returned in FileOffset
    // length of chunk data is returned in length
    if(OpenChunk(lpSMF, "MThd", &FileOffset, &length) == -1)
        return -1;

    // allocate the header buffer
    if((lpHeader = (LPSTR)GlobalAlloc(GPTR, length)) == NULL)
        return -1;

    // read the data into the header buffer
```

```
        ReadFile(lpSMF->hsmf, lpHeader, length, &dwBytesRead, NULL);
        if(dwBytesRead != length)
        {
            // on error, unwind the memory allocations
            GlobalFree(lpHeader);
            return -1;
        }

        // parse the buffer to get the three word parameters
        // format, ntrks, and division
        lpSMF->wFormat = (lpHeader[0] << 8) + (BYTE)lpHeader[1];
        lpSMF->wTracks = (lpHeader[2] << 8) + (BYTE)lpHeader[3];
        division = (lpHeader[4] << 8) + (BYTE)lpHeader[5];
        lpSMF->resolution = division;

        // free the header buffer
        GlobalFree(lpHeader);
        return 0;
}

//----------------------------------------------------------------------------
// SeekAbsolute
//
// This function moves the read buffer pointer to the specified offset,
// reading new buffers as necessary.
//----------------------------------------------------------------------------
void SeekAbsolute(LPSMF lpSMF, DWORD offset)
{
        LPTRACK lpCurTrack;         // current track structure
        DWORD dwRelOffset;          // relative offset

        // which track are we reading?
        lpCurTrack = (LPTRACK)&(lpSMF->lpTrack[lpSMF->wCurTrack]);

        // if offset is before the start of buffer or after remaining
        // bytes count (end of buffer) seek to new location and read a buffer full
        if((offset < lpCurTrack->dwFileOfs - lpCurTrack->dwBuffOfs) ||
           (offset > lpCurTrack->dwFileOfs + lpCurTrack->dwBytesRemaining) ||
           (lpSMF->dwCurFileOfs != lpCurTrack->dwFileOfs))
        {
            // seek to new location and read a buffer full
            SeekTo(lpSMF, offset);

            // read the new block
            ReadFile(lpSMF->hsmf, lpCurTrack->lpReadBuf, lpCurTrack->dwRBsize,
                     &lpCurTrack->dwBytesRemaining, NULL);

            // update the track offset and remaining length
            lpCurTrack->dwFileOfs = offset;
            lpSMF->dwCurFileOfs = offset;
            lpCurTrack->dwBuffOfs = 0;

            return;
        }

        // else offset is within current buffer, update pointers only
        dwRelOffset = offset - lpCurTrack->dwFileOfs;
        lpCurTrack->dwBytesRemaining -= dwRelOffset;
        lpCurTrack->dwBuffOfs += dwRelOffset;
        lpCurTrack->dwFileOfs += dwRelOffset;
        lpSMF->dwCurFileOfs += dwRelOffset;
}

//----------------------------------------------------------------------------
// SeekRelative
//
// This function moves the read buffer pointer by the specified number
// of bytes, reading new buffers as necessary.
//----------------------------------------------------------------------------
void SeekRelative(LPSMF lpSMF, DWORD offset)
{
        LPTRACK lpCurTrack;         // current track structure

        // if offset is zero, do nothing
        if(offset == 0)
            return;

        // which track are we reading?
        lpCurTrack = (LPTRACK)&(lpSMF->lpTrack[lpSMF->wCurTrack]);

        // convert to absolute address and seek
        SeekAbsolute(lpSMF, offset + lpCurTrack->dwFileOfs);
```

```
}
//---------------------------------------------------------------------------
// ReadByte
//
// This function returns a single byte of data read from the file.
// The data is read from the file in blocks, but is passed to the caller
// as single bytes.
//---------------------------------------------------------------------------
BYTE ReadByte(LPSMF lpSMF)
{
    LPTRACK lpCurTrack;          // current track structure

    // which track are we reading?
    lpCurTrack = (LPTRACK)&(lpSMF->lpTrack[lpSMF->wCurTrack]);

    // anything in the buffer?
    if(lpCurTrack->dwBytesRemaining == 0)
    {
        // file offset is at start of buffer
        lpSMF->dwCurFileOfs = lpCurTrack->dwFileOfs;
        SeekTo(lpSMF, lpCurTrack->dwFileOfs);

        // read the new block
        ReadFile(lpSMF->hsmf, lpCurTrack->lpReadBuf, lpCurTrack->dwRBsize,
                 &lpCurTrack->dwBytesRemaining, NULL);

        // update buffer offset
        lpCurTrack->dwBuffOfs = 0;

        if(lpCurTrack->dwBytesRemaining == 0)
            return 0;
    }

    // one less in the buffer
    lpCurTrack->dwBytesRemaining--;

    // get a byte from the buffer and return it to the caller
    lpCurTrack->dwFileOfs++;
    lpSMF->dwCurFileOfs++;
    return *(lpCurTrack->lpReadBuf + lpCurTrack->dwBuffOfs++);
}
//---------------------------------------------------------------------------
// ReadVarLength
//
// This function reads the variable length value from the buffer.
// The value is returned as a DWORD and the buffer pointer is updated to
// point to the byte following the value.
//
// A variable-length value is made up of one to four bytes.  Each byte
// contains seven significant bits.  Bit eight serves as a continuation
// bit; if it is set then at least one more byte follows.  The bytes are
// stored most significant first.
//---------------------------------------------------------------------------
DWORD ReadVarLength(LPSMF lpSMF)
{
    DWORD v = 0;      // result
    BYTE b;           // current byte from file

    // add up all of the byte values
    do {
        v = (v << 7) | ((b = ReadByte(lpSMF)) & 0x7F);
    } while(b & 0x80);

    return v;
}

//---------------------------------------------------------------------------
// ReadMidiEvent
//
// This function reads the next Midi event from the file and places it
// in the next location in the lpOutBuffer.  Meta Events are
// skipped, except for META_TEMPO which is merged into the Midi Events
// as a tempo change event.
// Returns TRUE if end of track, FALSE otherwise.
//---------------------------------------------------------------------------
BOOL ReadMidiEvent(LPSMF lpSMF, LPMIDIEVENT lpOutBuf)
{
    BYTE event;        // event byte read from file
    DWORD dwLen;       // length of event data
    UINT nDataBytes;   // count of remaining data bytes
```

```
    // don't read anything if already at end of track
    if(lpSMF->lpTrack[lpSMF->wCurTrack].fEndOfTrack == TRUE)
        return TRUE;

    while(TRUE)      // read through file until an event is found
    {
        // don't read timestamp if reading sysex data block
        if(lpSMF->lpTrack[lpSMF->wCurTrack].dwSysexLen == 0)
        {
            // read the leading delta time value
            // add any accumulated time from skipped meta events
            lpOutBuf->time = ReadVarLength(lpSMF) +
                    lpSMF->lpTrack[lpSMF->wCurTrack].dwMetaDeltaTime;

            // now clear the delta time, since it has been added to the event time
            lpSMF->lpTrack[lpSMF->wCurTrack].dwMetaDeltaTime = 0;
        }

        // read the first event byte
        // process it according to the event type
        // if it is a status (other than sysex or eox)
        //      read the following bytes
        //   if it is a data byte for a midi message
        //      read the following bytes - use running status
        //   if it is a 0xFF - its a meta event
        //      skip the entire event
        //   if it is a sysex or eox
        //      read a single byte and return as a sysex
        event = ReadByte(lpSMF);

        // is it a meta event?
        if(event == META)
        {
            // read meta event type
            event = ReadByte(lpSMF);

            // length of the meta event
            dwLen = ReadVarLength(lpSMF);

            // is it end of track?
            if(event == META_EOT)
            {
                // read and discard the dummy length byte
                ReadVarLength(lpSMF);

                // return EOT
                lpSMF->lpTrack[lpSMF->wCurTrack].fEndOfTrack = TRUE;
                return TRUE;
            }

            // is it a tempo change?
            if(event == META_TEMPO)
            {
                // read the tempo value
                lpOutBuf->data1 = ReadByte(lpSMF);
                lpOutBuf->data2 = ReadByte(lpSMF);
                lpOutBuf->data3 = ReadByte(lpSMF);

                // status is zero on tempo change events
                lpOutBuf->status = 0;

                // we have read three, skip any others
                SeekRelative(lpSMF, dwLen - 3L);

                // found an event
                return FALSE;
            }

            // save the delta time of the meta event so that the
            // timestamp of the _next_ event is correct, since
            // the meta event will be filtered out
            lpSMF->lpTrack[lpSMF->wCurTrack].dwMetaDeltaTime = lpOutBuf->time;

            // skip over any meta data we don't want
            SeekRelative(lpSMF, dwLen);
        }
        else
        {
            // is it a sysex?
            if(event == SYSEX)
            {
                // it's a sysex, leave the status alone
```

```
                    // set the IN_SYSEX flag
                    lpSMF->lpTrack[lpSMF->wCurTrack].wFlags |= IN_SYSEX;
                    lpOutBuf->status = event;

                    // get the length of sysex block
                    lpSMF->lpTrack[lpSMF->wCurTrack].dwSysexLen = ReadVarLength(lpSMF);

                    // build the first MidiEvent
                    lpOutBuf->data1 = event;
                    lpOutBuf->data2 = 0;
                    lpOutBuf->data3 = 0;

                    // found an event
                    return FALSE;
            }
            else
            // is it an eox?
            if(event == EOX)
            {
                    // is this the termination of a current sysex?
                    if(lpSMF->lpTrack[lpSMF->wCurTrack].wFlags & IN_SYSEX)
                    {
                            // yes, return the eox to the client
                            lpOutBuf->status = SYSEX;

                            // build the MidiEvent
                            lpOutBuf->data1 = event;
                            lpOutBuf->data2 = 0;
                            lpOutBuf->data3 = 0;

                            // timestamp is zero
                            lpOutBuf->time = 0;

                            // done with this sysex
                            lpSMF->lpTrack[lpSMF->wCurTrack].wFlags &= ~IN_SYSEX;
                            lpSMF->lpTrack[lpSMF->wCurTrack].dwSysexLen = 0;

                            // found an event
                            return FALSE;
                    }

                    // it's a sysex "escape", set the IN_SYSEX flag
                    lpSMF->lpTrack[lpSMF->wCurTrack].wFlags |= IN_SYSEX;
                    lpOutBuf->status = SYSEX;

                    // get the length of sysex block
                    lpSMF->lpTrack[lpSMF->wCurTrack].dwSysexLen = ReadVarLength(lpSMF);

                    // build the first MidiEvent
                    lpOutBuf->data1 = ReadByte(lpSMF);
                    lpOutBuf->data2 = 0;
                    lpOutBuf->data3 = 0;

                    // read one of the bytes in block
                    lpSMF->lpTrack[lpSMF->wCurTrack].dwSysexLen--;

                    // found an event
                    return FALSE;
            }
            else
            // is it a data byte for a running status message?
            if((event & 0x80) == 0)
            {
                    // if we are in a sysex block, return a single byte from the buffer
                    if(lpSMF->lpTrack[lpSMF->wCurTrack].wFlags & IN_SYSEX)
                    {
                            // build the MidiEvent
                            lpOutBuf->status = SYSEX;
                            lpOutBuf->data1 = event;
                            lpOutBuf->data2 = 0;
                            lpOutBuf->data3 = 0;

                            // timestamp for sysex data is always zero
                            lpOutBuf->time = 0;

                            // read one of the bytes in block
                            lpSMF->lpTrack[lpSMF->wCurTrack].dwSysexLen--;

                            // found an event
                            return FALSE;
                    }

                    // insert running status
                    lpOutBuf->status = lpSMF->lpTrack[lpSMF->wCurTrack].bStatus;
```

```
                        // else get the number of remaining bytes (after this one)
                        nDataBytes = GetMsgLength(lpOutBuf->status);
                        nDataBytes--;

                        // there is at least one data byte
                        lpOutBuf->data1 = event;
                        lpOutBuf->data2 = (nDataBytes != 0 ? ReadByte(lpSMF) : 0);
                        lpOutBuf->data3 = 0;

                        // found an event
                        return FALSE;
                }
                else
                {
                        // else it must be a status message
                        lpSMF->lpTrack[lpSMF->wCurTrack].bStatus = event;
                        lpOutBuf->status = event;

                        // retrieve any trailing data bytes
                        nDataBytes = GetMsgLength(event);

                        lpOutBuf->data1 = (nDataBytes != 0 ? nDataBytes--, ReadByte(lpSMF) :
0);

                        lpOutBuf->data2 = (nDataBytes != 0 ? ReadByte(lpSMF) : 0);
                        lpOutBuf->data3 = 0;

                        // found an event
                        return FALSE;
                }
        }
    }
}
//-------------------------------------------------------------------------
// ReadNextMeta
//
// This function reads then next specified meta event on the current
// track, pointed to by lpCurTrack.  If found, it returns the length
// of the event and sets *time to the elapsed time since the start of the
// track.  The file is located at the start of the data for the event.
// If not found, it returns -1 and *time is undefined.
//-------------------------------------------------------------------------
DWORD ReadNextMeta(LPSMF lpSMF, LPTRACK lpCurTrack, BYTE MetaEvent, DWORD *time)
{
    BYTE event;       // event byte read from file
    DWORD dwLen;      // length of event data
    UINT nDataBytes;  // count of remaining data bytes

    // initialize the elapsed time
    *time = 0;

    while(TRUE)       // read through file until an event is found
    {
        // read the leading delta time value
        *time += ReadVarLength(lpSMF);

        // read the first event byte
        // process it according to the event type
        //   if it is a status (other than sysex or eox)
        //       skip midi event
        //   if it is a data byte for a midi message
        //       skip midi event - use running status
        //   if it is a 0xFF - it's a meta event
        //       return with file pointer at start of event data
        //       return length of event data
        //   if it is a sysex or eox
        //       skip entire sysex block
        event = ReadByte(lpSMF);

        // is it a meta event?
        if(event == META)
        {
            // read meta event type
            event = ReadByte(lpSMF);

            // length of the meta event
            dwLen = ReadVarLength(lpSMF);

            // is it an end of track?
            if(event == META_EOT)
                return (DWORD)-1;
```

```
                // is it the requested value?
                if(event == MetaEvent)
                    return dwLen;

                // else skip over it and keep looking
                SeekRelative(lpSMF, dwLen);
        }
        else
        // is it a sysex?
        if((event == SYSEX) || (event == EOX))
        {
                // skip over the whole thing
                SeekRelative(lpSMF, ReadVarLength(lpSMF));
        }
        else
        // is it a data byte for a running status message?
        if((event & 0x80) == 0)
        {
                // get the number of remaining bytes (after this one)
                nDataBytes = GetMsgLength(lpCurTrack->bMetaStatus);
                nDataBytes--;

                // read and discard any more data for this event
                if(nDataBytes != 0)
                    ReadByte(lpSMF);
        }
        else
        {
                // else it must be a status message
                lpCurTrack->bMetaStatus = event;

                // get number of remaining bytes (after this one)
                nDataBytes = GetMsgLength(event);

                // read and discard any data bytes for this event
                while(nDataBytes-- != 0)
                    ReadByte(lpSMF);
        }
    }
}

//----------------------------------------------------------------------------
// Standard Midi File Write Functions
//----------------------------------------------------------------------------
//----------------------------------------------------------------------------
// WriteSMF
//
// This function writes a block of events to the previously opened SMF.
// It returns the count of MidiEvents written to the SMF or 0 on error.
//----------------------------------------------------------------------------
PREFIX DWORD WINAPI EXPORT WriteSMF(HSMF hSMF, int wTrack, LPMIDIEVENT
lpMidiEventBuffer, DWORD dwBufferLen)
{
    DWORD dwEventsWritten;      // count of MidiEvents written
    DWORD dwBlockSize;          // size of written block in bytes
    LPSMF lpSMF = (LPSMF)hSMF;

    // was this device opened for write?
    if(lpSMF->mode != 'w')
        return 0;

    // check to see if this is a new track
    isNewTrack(lpSMF, wTrack);

    // convert the Midi events into a smf track data
    dwEventsWritten = 0;
    dwBlockSize = 0;

    while(dwEventsWritten < dwBufferLen)
    {
        dwBlockSize += MidiToSMF(lpSMF, (lpMidiEventBuffer + dwEventsWritten));
        dwEventsWritten++;
    }

    // update the track size count
    lpSMF->dwChunkLen += dwBlockSize;

    return dwEventsWritten;
}
//----------------------------------------------------------------------------
```

```
// WriteMetaEvent
//
// This function writes a Meta Event to the selected track.
//-------------------------------------------------------------------------
PREFIX int WINAPI EXPORT WriteMetaEvent(HSMF hSMF, int wTrack, BYTE MetaEvent,
        LPSTR EventValue, DWORD dwTime)
{
    DWORD dwLen;           // length of event data
    DWORD dwEventLength;   // total length of event
    DWORD dwBytesWritten;
    LPSMF lpSMF = (LPSMF)hSMF;

    // check to see if this is a new track
    isNewTrack(lpSMF, wTrack);

    // write the time stamp
    dwEventLength = WriteVarLength(lpSMF, dwTime);

    // write the meta event tag
    WriteByte(lpSMF, META);

    // write the meta event
    WriteByte(lpSMF, MetaEvent);
    dwEventLength += 2;

    // get the length of the event data
    switch(MetaEvent)
    {
        case META_SEQUENCE_NUMBER:
        case META_KEY_SIG:
            dwLen = META_SEQUENCE_NUMBER_LENGTH;
            break;

        case META_CHAN_PREFIX:
            dwLen = META_CHAN_PREFIX_LENGTH;
            break;

        case META_EOT:
            dwLen = META_EOT_LENGTH;
            break;

        case META_TEMPO:
            dwLen = META_TEMPO_LENGTH;
            break;

        case META_SMPTE_OFFSET:
            dwLen = META_SMPTE_OFFSET_LENGTH;
            break;

        case META_TIME_SIG:
            dwLen = META_TIME_SIG_LENGTH;
            break;

        case META_TEXT:
        case META_COPYRIGHT:
        case META_NAME:
        case META_INST_NAME:
        case META_LYRIC:
        case META_MARKER:
        case META_CUE_POINT:
        case META_SEQ_SPECIFIC:
            dwLen = lstrlen(EventValue);
            break;

        default:
            dwLen = 0;
    }

    // write the length, accounting for meta and event
    // number bytes
    dwEventLength += WriteVarLength(lpSMF, dwLen);
    lpSMF->dwChunkLen += dwEventLength;

    // write the data for the event
    if(dwLen != 0)
    {
        WriteFile(lpSMF->hsmf, EventValue, dwLen, &dwBytesWritten, NULL);
        if(dwBytesWritten != dwLen)
            return -1;
    }

    return 0;
}
```

```
//---------------------------------------------------------------------------
// isNewTrack
//
// This function checks to see if a new track is being requested.
// If so, it closes the last track (if any) and writes the track chunk.
//---------------------------------------------------------------------------
void isNewTrack(LPSMF lpSMF, int wTrack)
{
    DWORD dwCurLoc;              // current file position

    // if this is a new track, close out the old track
    // if this is the first track, just open it
    if(lpSMF->wCurTrack != wTrack)
    {
        if(lpSMF->wCurTrack == -1)
        {
            // save the start of this chunk
            lpSMF->dwChunkStart = CurFilePos(lpSMF);

            // write chunk name and dummy length
            WriteChunkName(lpSMF, "MTrk", CurFilePos(lpSMF), 0);

            // this is the new current track
            lpSMF->wCurTrack = wTrack;
        }
        else
        {
            // this is the new current track.  This must be
            // done here since WriteMetaEvent/isNewTrack
            // is recursive
            lpSMF->wCurTrack = wTrack;

            // write the end of track meta event by
            // recursively calline WriteMetaEvent
            WriteMetaEvent((HSMF)lpSMF, wTrack, META_EOT, NULL, 0);

            // save the current location
            dwCurLoc = CurFilePos(lpSMF);

            // seek to the start of the track chunk and
            // update the chunk with the correct length
            WriteChunkName(lpSMF, "MTrk", lpSMF->dwChunkStart, lpSMF->dwChunkLen);

            // start of new chunk is end of old one
            lpSMF->dwChunkStart = dwCurLoc;

            // seek back to the original location and
            // write chunk name and dummy length for new track
            WriteChunkName(lpSMF, "MTrk", lpSMF->dwChunkStart, 0);

            // make sure that format is correct now that more
            // than one track has been written
            lpSMF->wFormat = 1;
        }

        // reset running status for new track
        lpSMF->bStatus = 0;

        // new chunk length is zero
        lpSMF->dwChunkLen = 0;
        lpSMF->wTracks++;
    }
}

//---------------------------------------------------------------------------
// MidiToSMF
//
// This function reads Midi events from the lpMidiEvent buffer and writes
// running-status-compressed, variable-length-timestamped SMF events to
// the disk file.  If the event is part of a sysex, the data is instead
// written to a buffer.  When the EOX is received, the buffer is written
// to the disk file and the memory is freed.  The buffer will grow in 1K
// increments as needed to hold the entire sysex.  This must be done since
// MidiToSMF does not know the size of the buffer in advance, and the
// length of the sysex must be written to the SMF -- as a variable length
// value -- before the data is written.
// It returns the number of bytes written or buffered.
//---------------------------------------------------------------------------
DWORD MidiToSMF(LPSMF lpSMF, LPMIDIEVENT lpMidiEvent)
{
    UINT nDataBytes;            // number of data bytes for event
```

```
DWORD dwBytesWritten = 0; // number of buffer bytes written
DWORD n = 0;

// if the message is the sysex status byte, write it
if(lpMidiEvent->data1 == SYSEX)
{
    // initialize count of bytes in sysex
    lpSMF->dwSxLen = 0;

    // initialize and allocate a buffer to build the sysex
    // this must be done because we don't know the length
    // of the sysex, and the length must be written first as
    // a variable length value
    lpSMF->dwSxBuffSize = 1024;
    lpSMF->lpSxBuff = (LPSTR)GlobalLock(GlobalAlloc(GHND, lpSMF->dwSxBuffSize));

    // if there is an allocation error, return without writing
    if(lpSMF->lpSxBuff == NULL)
        return 0;

    // convert and write a variable length timestamp
    dwBytesWritten = WriteVarLength(lpSMF, lpMidiEvent->time);

    // write the status
    WriteByte(lpSMF, lpMidiEvent->data1);

    return dwBytesWritten + 1;
}

// if the message is the eox for a sysex, write out the buffer
if(lpMidiEvent->data1 == EOX)
{
    // write the length of the sysex as var length
    // account for the eox that will be written
    dwBytesWritten += WriteVarLength(lpSMF, lpSMF->dwSxLen + 1);

    // write the buffer of data to disk
    WriteFile(lpSMF->hsmf, lpSMF->lpSxBuff, lpSMF->dwSxLen, &n, NULL);

    // write the eox
    WriteByte(lpSMF, EOX);

    // free the sysex buffer
    GlobalFree(lpSMF->lpSxBuff);

    return dwBytesWritten + lpSMF->dwSxLen + 1;
}

// if the message is sysex data, just write the data byte
if((lpMidiEvent->status == SYSEX) && (lpMidiEvent->data1 != SYSEX))
{
    // check to see if the buffer needs to be grown
    if(lpSMF->dwSxLen == lpSMF->dwSxBuffSize)
    {
        // grow it in 1K chunks
        lpSMF->dwSxBuffSize += 1024;
        lpSMF->lpSxBuff = (LPSTR)GlobalReAlloc(lpSMF->lpSxBuff,
                lpSMF->dwSxBuffSize, GMEM_MOVEABLE);
    }

    // write the data
    *(lpSMF->lpSxBuff + lpSMF->dwSxLen) = lpMidiEvent->data1;

    // count the number of bytes in sysex
    lpSMF->dwSxLen++;

    return 1;
}

// else convert and write a variable length timestamp
dwBytesWritten = (DWORD)WriteVarLength(lpSMF, lpMidiEvent->time);

// if it is a tempo change event, write the meta event
if(lpMidiEvent->status == 0)
{
    // write the event
    WriteByte(lpSMF, META);
    WriteByte(lpSMF, META_TEMPO);
    WriteByte(lpSMF, META_TEMPO_LENGTH);
    WriteByte(lpSMF, lpMidiEvent->data1);
    WriteByte(lpSMF, lpMidiEvent->data2);
    WriteByte(lpSMF, lpMidiEvent->data3);

    return dwBytesWritten + 6;
```

```
    }

    // if this status is the same as the last (running) skip over it
    if(lpMidiEvent->status != lpSMF->bStatus)
    {
        WriteByte(lpSMF, lpMidiEvent->status);
        dwBytesWritten++;
        lpSMF->bStatus = lpMidiEvent->status;
    }

    // write the data for the event, if any
    nDataBytes = GetMsgLength(lpMidiEvent->status);
    dwBytesWritten += nDataBytes;

    if(nDataBytes != 0)
    {
        WriteByte(lpSMF, lpMidiEvent->data1);
        nDataBytes--;
    }

    if(nDataBytes != 0)
        WriteByte(lpSMF, lpMidiEvent->data2);

    return dwBytesWritten;
}
//-----------------------------------------------------------------------------
// WriteByte
//
// This function writes the byte val to the SMF disk file.
//-----------------------------------------------------------------------------
void WriteByte(LPSMF lpSMF, BYTE val)
{
    DWORD dwBytesWritten = 0;

    WriteFile(lpSMF->hsmf, &val, 1, &dwBytesWritten, NULL);
}
//-----------------------------------------------------------------------------
// WriteVarLength
//
// This function writes a timestamp to the buffer as a variable length
// value.  It returns the number of bytes written to the buffer and the
// buffer pointing to the next location.
//-----------------------------------------------------------------------------
DWORD WriteVarLength(LPSMF lpSMF, DWORD value)
{
    DWORD nBytesWritten = 0;        // count of bytes written
    DWORD dwBuffer;                 // dword to build var length in

    // write up to four bytes to the buffer, stop when byte == 0
    dwBuffer = value & 0x7F;

    while((value >>= 7) > 0)
    {
        dwBuffer <<= 8;
        dwBuffer |= 0x80;
        dwBuffer += (value & 0x7F);
    }

    // copy the bytes, in reverse order to the destination
    while(TRUE)
    {
        WriteByte(lpSMF, (BYTE)dwBuffer);
        nBytesWritten++;
        if(dwBuffer & 0x80)
            dwBuffer >>= 8;
        else
            break;
    }

    return nBytesWritten;
}
//-----------------------------------------------------------------------------
// WriteReversedData
//
// This function writes the data to the file in reverse byte order.
//-----------------------------------------------------------------------------
void WriteReversedData(LPSMF lpSMF, LPVOID lpData, int wSize)
{
    DWORD dwBytesWritten = 0;
```

```
        while(--wSize != -1)
            WriteFile(lpSMF->hsmf, &((LPBYTE)lpData)[wSize], 1, &dwBytesWritten, NULL);
}
//-----------------------------------------------------------------------
// WriteChunkName
//
// This function writes the name and length of the chunk to the file.
//-----------------------------------------------------------------------
void WriteChunkName(LPSMF lpSMF, LPSTR ChunkName, DWORD offset, DWORD len)
{
    DWORD dwBytesWritten = 0;

    // seek to the desired location in the file
    SeekTo(lpSMF, offset);

    // write the name
    WriteFile(lpSMF->hsmf, ChunkName, lstrlen(ChunkName), &dwBytesWritten, NULL);

    // write the chunk size
    WriteReversedData(lpSMF, &len, sizeof(DWORD));
}
//-----------------------------------------------------------------------
// WriteSMFHeader
//
// This function writes the header for the SMF, based on the information
// in the lpSMF structure.
//-----------------------------------------------------------------------
void WriteSMFHeader(LPSMF lpSMF)
{
    // write the 'MThd' chunk type at the start of the file
    WriteChunkName(lpSMF, "MThd", 0, SMF_HEADER_SIZE);

    // write the data to the chunk
    WriteReversedData(lpSMF, &lpSMF->wFormat, sizeof(WORD));
    WriteReversedData(lpSMF, &lpSMF->wTracks, sizeof(WORD));
    WriteReversedData(lpSMF, &lpSMF->resolution, sizeof(WORD));
}
```

# Thunk Script

```
//
//    Thunk Script for MxMidi16 DLL
//

enablemapdirect3216 = true;

#include "types.def"

//-----------------------------------------------------------------------
// Event structures
//-----------------------------------------------------------------------
typedef struct {
    DWORD   time;
    BYTE status;
    BYTE data1;
    BYTE data2;
    BYTE data3;
} MidiEvent;

typedef MidiEvent *LPMIDIEVENT;
typedef DWORD HMIN;
typedef DWORD HMOUT;
typedef DWORD HSYNC;

//-----------------------------------------------------------------------
// Exported MxMidi DLL entry point function prototypes
//-----------------------------------------------------------------------
WORD GetMaxMidiVersion16(void)
{
}

BOOL GetMidiOutDescription16(WORD wDeviceID, LPSTR lpzDesc)
{
    lpzDesc = inout;
}
```

```
HMOUT OpenMidiOut16(HWND hWnd, WORD wDeviceID, HSYNC hSync, DWORD dwFlags)
{
}

WORD ResetMidiOut16(HMOUT hMidiOut)
{
}

void FlushMidiOut16(HMOUT hMidiOut)
{
}

WORD CloseMidiOut16(HMOUT hMidiOut)
{
}

WORD PutMidiOut16(HMOUT hMidiOut, LPMIDIEVENT lpMidiEvent)
{
}

BOOL GetMidiInDescription16(WORD wDeviceID, LPSTR lpzDesc)
{
    lpzDesc = inout;
}

HMIN OpenMidiIn16(HWND hWnd, WORD wDeviceID, HSYNC hSync, DWORD dwFlags)
{
}

WORD StartMidiIn16(HMIN hMidiIn)
{
}

WORD StopMidiIn16(HMIN hMidiIn)
{
}

WORD CloseMidiIn16(HMIN hMidiIn)
{
}

LPMIDIEVENT GetMidiIn16(HMIN hMidiIn)
{
}

HSYNC OpenSync16(HSYNC hSync, HWND hWnd, UINT mode, UINT timerPeriod)
{
}

WORD CloseSync16(HSYNC hSync)
{
}

void StopSync16(HSYNC hSync)
{
}

void StartSync16(HSYNC hSync)
{
}

void PauseSync16(HSYNC hSync, BOOL reset)
{
}

void ReStartSync16(HSYNC hSync)
{
}

WORD SetTempo16(HSYNC hSync, DWORD uSPerBeat)
{
}

void SetResolution16(HSYNC hSync, UINT resolution)
{
}

DWORD GetTempo16(HSYNC hSync)
{
}

WORD GetResolution16(HSYNC hSync)
{
}
```

# APPENDIX C

# *MaxMidi C++ Classes Source Code*

# CMaxMidiIn

```
//----------------------------------------------------------------------------
//   CMaxMidiIn Class Definition
//
//   (C) Copyright, Paul A. Messick, 1996
//----------------------------------------------------------------------------
class CMaxMidiIn : public CWnd
{
// Class-specific data
protected:
    HMIN      hDevice;          // handle to the MidiIn device
    DWORD     dwFlags;          // current flags for this device
    WORD      wDeviceID;        // device id, in case we need to reopen

    BOOL      fIsOpen;          // true if device is open
    char      Description[MAXPNAMELEN]; // description string
    HWND      hParentWnd;       // parent window handle
#ifdef _SYNC
    CMaxMidiSync* pSync;        // the sync device object
#endif
#ifdef _TRACK
    CMaxMidiTrack* pTrack;      // track object associated with this input (only one)
#endif
    BOOL      fIsStarted;       // true if input started

public:
// Constructors/Destructor
    CMaxMidiIn();               // default constructor
    CMaxMidiIn(HWND hParentWnd, WORD wDeviceID = 0);
    ~CMaxMidiIn();              // destructor

// sync-dependent functions
#ifdef _SYNC
    CMaxMidiIn(HWND hParentWnd, WORD wDeviceID, CMaxMidiSync* pSync = NULL, DWORD
dwFlags = MIDIIN_DEFAULT);
    void Attach(CMaxMidiSync* pSync); // attaches the sync device
    void Detach(CMaxMidiSync* pSync); // detaches the sync device
    CMaxMidiSync* GetSync(void) { return pSync; };
#endif

// track-dependent functions
#ifdef _TRACK
    void Attach(CMaxMidiTrack* pTrack); // attaches the track object
    void Detach(CMaxMidiTrack* pTrack);// detaches the track object
#endif

// Implementation
    WORD GetIDFromName(LPSTR lpszDesc); // find corresponding ID given string name

    BOOL CreateWnd(void);               // creates the hidden window
    void Attach(HWND hParentWnd);       // attaches the parent window

    BOOL IsOpen(void);                  // returns true if device is open
    LPSTR GetDescription(void);         // returns pointer to desc string
    int GetNumDevices(void);            // returns number of input devices available

    BOOL Open(WORD wDeviceID, DWORD dwFlags = MIDIIN_DEFAULT);
    void Close(void);           // close the device without destroying class object

    void Start(void);           // start midi in
    void Stop(void);            // stop midi in
    void Reset(void);           // reset the timestamp to zero, if started
    LPMIDIEVENT Get(void);      // get received event, if any

    virtual BOOL ProcessMidiData(LPMIDIEVENT lpEvent) { return TRUE; };

// Generated message map functions
protected:
    //{{AFX_MSG(CMaxMidiIn)
    afx_msg LPARAM OnMidiData(WPARAM wParam, LPARAM lParam);
    //}}AFX_MSG
    DECLARE_MESSAGE_MAP()
};
```

```
//===========================================================================
//   CMaxMidiIn Class Implementation
//
//   (C) Copyright, Paul A. Messick, 1996
//===========================================================================
#include "stdafx.h"
#include "MaxMidi.h"

BEGIN_MESSAGE_MAP(CMaxMidiIn, CWnd)
    //{{AFX_MSG_MAP(CMaxMidiIn)
    ON_MESSAGE(MIDI_DATA, OnMidiData)
    //}}AFX_MSG_MAP
END_MESSAGE_MAP()

//---------------------------------------------------------------------------
//   CMaxMidiIn Constructors
//---------------------------------------------------------------------------
CMaxMidiIn::CMaxMidiIn()
{
    hDevice = 0;
    fIsOpen = FALSE;
    Description[0] = 0;
    hParentWnd = NULL;

#ifdef _SYNC
    pSync = 0;
#endif
#ifdef _TRACK
    pTrack = 0;
#endif
}

CMaxMidiIn::CMaxMidiIn(HWND hParentWnd, WORD wDeviceID)
{
    hDevice = 0;
    fIsOpen = FALSE;
    Description[0] = 0;
#ifdef _SYNC
    pSync = 0;
#endif
#ifdef _TRACK
    pTrack = 0;
#endif

    Attach(hParentWnd);
    Open(wDeviceID);
}

#ifdef _SYNC
CMaxMidiIn::CMaxMidiIn(HWND hParentWnd, WORD wDeviceID, CMaxMidiSync* pSync, DWORD
dwFlags)
{
#ifdef _TRACK
    pTrack = 0;
#endif

    Attach(hParentWnd);
    Attach(pSync);
    Open(wDeviceID, dwFlags);
}
#endif

BOOL CMaxMidiIn::CreateWnd(void)
{
    RECT r;

    r.left = r.top = r.right = r.bottom = 0;

    return Create(NULL, "CMaxMidiInWnd", WS_CHILD, r, FromHandlePermanent(hParentWnd),
0);
}
//---------------------------------------------------------------------------
//   GetIDFromName
//---------------------------------------------------------------------------
WORD CMaxMidiIn::GetIDFromName(LPSTR lpszDesc)
{
    WORD id;
    char thisDesc[MAXPNAMELEN];
```

```
        WORD MaxDevs = GetNumInDevices();

        for(id = 0; id < MaxDevs; id++)
        {
            GetMidiInDescription(id, thisDesc);
            if(strcmp(thisDesc, lpszDesc) == 0)
                return id;

            id++;
        }

        return ERR_NOMATCH;
}
//-----------------------------------------------------------------------------
//    Attach/Detach
//-----------------------------------------------------------------------------
void CMaxMidiIn::Attach(HWND hParentWnd)
{
    CMaxMidiIn::hParentWnd = hParentWnd;
    CreateWnd();
}

#ifdef _SYNC
void CMaxMidiIn::Attach(CMaxMidiSync* pSync)
{
    CMaxMidiIn::pSync = pSync;
}

void CMaxMidiIn::Detach(CMaxMidiSync* pSync)
{
    // detach this sync device, if it is attached
    if(pSync == CMaxMidiIn::pSync)
        pSync = NULL;

    // close and reopen the device
    if(fIsOpen)
    {
        Close();
        Open(wDeviceID, dwFlags);
    }
}
#endif

#ifdef _TRACK
void CMaxMidiIn::Attach(CMaxMidiTrack* pTrack)
{
    // detach the track if one was already attached
    if(CMaxMidiIn::pTrack != NULL)
        CMaxMidiIn::pTrack->Detach(this);

    // attach the new track
    CMaxMidiIn::pTrack = pTrack;

    // tell the track about this input device
    pTrack->Attach(this);
}

void CMaxMidiIn::Detach(CMaxMidiTrack* pTrack)
{
    // detach this track, if it is attached
    if(pTrack == CMaxMidiIn::pTrack)
        pTrack = NULL;
}
#endif

//-----------------------------------------------------------------------------
//    CMaxMidiIn Destructor
//-----------------------------------------------------------------------------
CMaxMidiIn::~CMaxMidiIn()
{
    Close();
}

//-----------------------------------------------------------------------------
//    Open
//-----------------------------------------------------------------------------
BOOL CMaxMidiIn::Open(WORD wDeviceID, DWORD dwFlags)
{
    HSYNC hSync = 0;

    // get the description of the device
    GetMidiInDescription(wDeviceID, Description);
```

```
#ifdef _SYNC
    // get the sync device handle
    if(CMaxMidiIn::pSync)
        hSync = CMaxMidiIn::pSync->GetHSync();
#endif

    if(!fIsOpen)
    {
        CMaxMidiIn::dwFlags = dwFlags;
        CMaxMidiIn::wDeviceID = wDeviceID;
        hDevice = OpenMidiIn(m_hWnd, wDeviceID, hSync, dwFlags);
    }

    if(hDevice > MXMIDIERR_MAXERR)
        fIsOpen = TRUE;
    else
        hDevice = 0;

    return fIsOpen;
}
//-------------------------------------------------------------------------
//  Close
//-------------------------------------------------------------------------
void CMaxMidiIn::Close(void)
{
    if(fIsOpen)
    {
        Stop();
        CloseMidiIn(hDevice);
    }

    fIsOpen = FALSE;
}
//-------------------------------------------------------------------------
//  Information Functions
//-------------------------------------------------------------------------
BOOL CMaxMidiIn::IsOpen(void)
{
    return fIsOpen;
}

LPSTR CMaxMidiIn::GetDescription(void)
{
    return Description;
}

int CMaxMidiIn::GetNumDevices(void)
{
    return GetNumInDevices();
}
//-------------------------------------------------------------------------
//  Start/Stop
//-------------------------------------------------------------------------
void CMaxMidiIn::Start(void)
{
    if(fIsOpen)
    {
        fIsStarted = TRUE;
        StartMidiIn(hDevice);
    }
}

void CMaxMidiIn::Stop(void)
{
    if(fIsOpen)
    {
        fIsStarted = FALSE;
        StopMidiIn(hDevice);
    }
}

void CMaxMidiIn::Reset(void)
{
    if(fIsOpen && fIsStarted)
    {
        StopMidiIn(hDevice);
        StartMidiIn(hDevice);
    }
```

```
}
//-----------------------------------------------------------------------
//   Get Data
//-----------------------------------------------------------------------
LPMIDIEVENT CMaxMidiIn::Get(void)
{
    return GetMidiIn(hDevice);
}

/////////////////////////////////////////////////////////////////////////
// CMaxMidiIn message handlers
//-----------------------------------------------------------------------
//   OnMimData
//-----------------------------------------------------------------------
LRESULT CMaxMidiIn::OnMidiData(WPARAM wParam, LPARAM lParam)
{
    LPMIDIEVENT lpEvent;

    // send the data to the track object, if attached
    while((lpEvent = Get()) != 0)
    {
        if(ProcessMidiData(lpEvent) == TRUE)
#ifdef _TRACK
            if(pTrack)
                pTrack->Write(lpEvent);
#else
            ;
#endif
    }
    return 0;
}
```

# CMaxMidiOut

```
//-----------------------------------------------------------------------
//   CMaxMidiOut Class Definition
//
//   (C) Copyright, Paul A. Messick, 1996
//-----------------------------------------------------------------------

#ifdef _TRACK
//-----------------------------------------------------------------------
//   TrackMerge structure
//-----------------------------------------------------------------------
typedef struct {
    CMaxMidiTrack*  pTrack;      // track object
    LPMIDIEVENT     pAbsBuf;     // track buffer in absolute time
    DWORD           bufSize;     // number of events in abs buffer
    DWORD           thisEvent;   // index in AbsBuf of next event to read
    DWORD           lastEvent;   // index of last event output from this track
    BOOL            fInSysex;    // true if currently in sysex in this track
} TrackMerge;
#endif

class CMaxMidiOut : public CWnd
{
// Class-specific data
protected:
    HMOUT       hDevice;     // handle to the MidiOut device
    DWORD       dwFlags;     // current flags, in case we reopen
    WORD        wDeviceID;   // device ID of attached device

    BOOL        fIsOpen;     // true if device is open
    char        Description[MAXPNAMELEN]; // description string
    HWND        hParentWnd;  // parent window handle
    DWORD       LastAbs;     // last absolute timestamp used during track merge

#ifdef _SYNC
    CMaxMidiSync* pSync;     // the sync device object
#endif

#ifdef _TRACK
    TrackMerge* pTrackList;  // list of attached track merge structs
```

```
        int         nTracks;        // number of attached tracks
        LPMIDIEVENT lpMerge;         // pointer to the merged output data
        DWORD       numEvents;       // number of events in the merged buffer
        DWORD       outPtr;          // index to retrieve next event from merge buffer
#endif

public:
        CMaxMidiOut();                   // default constructor
        CMaxMidiOut(HWND hParentWnd, WORD wDeviceID = 0);
        ~CMaxMidiOut();                  // destructor

// sync-dependent functions
#ifdef _SYNC
        CMaxMidiOut(HWND hParentWnd, WORD wDeviceID, CMaxMidiSync* pSync = 0, DWORD dwFlags
= MIDIOUT_DEFAULT);
        void Attach(CMaxMidiSync* pSync); // attaches the sync device
        void Detach(CMaxMidiSync* pSync); // detaches the sync device
        CMaxMidiSync* GetSync(void) { return pSync; };
#endif

// track-dependent functions
#ifdef _TRACK
        void Attach(CMaxMidiTrack* pTrack);    // attaches the track object
        BOOL Detach(CMaxMidiTrack* pTrack);    // detaches the track object
        LPMIDIEVENT MergeTracks(void);
        void MergeOut(void);
        void StartOut(void);
#endif

// Implementation
        WORD GetIDFromName(LPSTR lpszDesc); // find corresponding ID given string name

        BOOL CreateWnd(void);            // creates the hidden window
        void Attach(HWND hParentWnd);    // attaches the parent window

        BOOL IsOpen(void);               // returns true if device is open
        LPSTR GetDescription(void);      // returns pointer to desc string
        int GetNumDevices(void);         // returns number of output devices available

        BOOL Open(WORD wDeviceID, DWORD dwFlags = MIDIOUT_DEFAULT);
        void Close(void);                // close the device without destroying class object

        BOOL Put(LPMIDIEVENT lpEvent);   // output an event
        void Reset(void);                // reset the output device
        void Flush(void);                // flush the output queue

        virtual void ProcessOutBufferReady(void) { };

// Generated message map functions
protected:
        //{{AFX_MSG(CMaxMidiOut)
        afx_msg LPARAM OnOutBufferReady(WPARAM wParam, LPARAM lParam);
        //}}AFX_MSG
        DECLARE_MESSAGE_MAP()
};

#define MERGE_BUFFER_SIZE 512 // should be the size of the output device buffer


//=============================================================================
//   CMaxMidiOut Class Implementation
//
//   (C) Copyright, Paul A. Messick, 1996
//=============================================================================
#include "stdafx.h"
#include "MaxMidi.h"

BEGIN_MESSAGE_MAP(CMaxMidiOut, CWnd)
        //{{AFX_MSG_MAP(CMaxMidiOut)
        ON_MESSAGE(OUTBUFFER_READY, OnOutBufferReady)
        //}}AFX_MSG_MAP
END_MESSAGE_MAP()

//-----------------------------------------------------------------------------
//   CMaxMidiOut Constructors
//-----------------------------------------------------------------------------
CMaxMidiOut::CMaxMidiOut()
{
    hDevice = 0;
    fIsOpen = FALSE;
    Description[0] = 0;
    hParentWnd = NULL;
#ifdef _SYNC
```

```
        pSync = NULL;
#endif
#ifdef _TRACK
        pTrackList = NULL;
        nTracks = 0;
        numEvents = 0;
        lpMerge = NULL;
#endif
}

CMaxMidiOut::CMaxMidiOut(HWND hParentWnd, WORD wDeviceID)
{
        hDevice = 0;
        fIsOpen = FALSE;
        Description[0] = 0;
#ifdef _SYNC
        pSync = NULL;
#endif
#ifdef _TRACK
        pTrackList = NULL;
        nTracks = 0;
        numEvents = 0;
        lpMerge = NULL;
#endif

        Attach(hParentWnd);
        Open(wDeviceID);
}

#ifdef _SYNC
CMaxMidiOut::CMaxMidiOut(HWND hParentWnd, WORD wDeviceID, CMaxMidiSync* pSync, DWORD
dwFlags)
{
#ifdef _TRACK
        pTrackList = NULL;
        nTracks = 0;
        numEvents = 0;
        lpMerge = NULL;
#endif
        Attach(hParentWnd);
        Attach(pSync);
        Open(wDeviceID, dwFlags);
}
#endif

BOOL CMaxMidiOut::CreateWnd(void)
{
        RECT r;

        r.left = r.top = r.right = r.bottom = 0;

        return Create(NULL, "CMaxMidiOutWnd", WS_CHILD, r, FromHandlePermanent(hParentWnd),
                      0);
}

void CMaxMidiOut::Attach(HWND hParentWnd)
{
        CMaxMidiOut::hParentWnd = hParentWnd;
        CreateWnd();
}

//-----------------------------------------------------------------------------
//    GetIDFromName
//-----------------------------------------------------------------------------
WORD CMaxMidiOut::GetIDFromName(LPSTR lpszDesc)
{
        WORD id;
        char thisDesc[MAXPNAMELEN];
        WORD MaxDevs = GetNumOutDevices();

        for(id = 0; id < MaxDevs; id++)
        {
            GetMidiOutDescription(id, thisDesc);
            if(strcmp(thisDesc, lpszDesc) == 0)
                return id;

            id++;
        }

        return ERR_NOMATCH;
}
```

```
#ifdef _SYNC
//---------------------------------------------------------------------------
//   Attach/Detach sync
//---------------------------------------------------------------------------
void CMaxMidiOut::Attach(CMaxMidiSync* pSync)
{
    CMaxMidiOut::pSync = pSync;
}

void CMaxMidiOut::Detach(CMaxMidiSync* pSync)
{
    if(pSync == CMaxMidiOut::pSync)
        CMaxMidiOut::pSync = NULL;

    // close and reopen the device
    if(fIsOpen)
    {
        Close();
        Open(wDeviceID, dwFlags);
    }
}
#endif

#ifdef _TRACK
//---------------------------------------------------------------------------
//   Attach/Detach Tracks
//---------------------------------------------------------------------------
void CMaxMidiOut::Attach(CMaxMidiTrack* pTrack)
{
    // expand the track list for one more entry
    nTracks++;
    if(pTrackList)
        // add an entry if list exists
        pTrackList = (TrackMerge*)GlobalReAlloc(pTrackList, nTracks *
                     sizeof(TrackMerge), GPTR | GMEM_MOVEABLE);
    else
        // create the list
        pTrackList = (TrackMerge*)GlobalAlloc(GPTR, sizeof(TrackMerge));

    // append this track to the end of the track list
    pTrackList[nTracks - 1].pTrack = pTrack;
    pTrackList[nTracks - 1].lastEvent = 0;
    pTrackList[nTracks - 1].fInSysex = FALSE;
    pTrackList[nTracks - 1].bufSize = MERGE_BUFFER_SIZE;

    // tell the track about this device
    pTrack->Attach(this);
}

BOOL CMaxMidiOut::Detach(CMaxMidiTrack* pTrack)
{
    int i, j;

    // make sure there is at least one track to delete
    if(nTracks == 0)
        return FALSE;

    // search for the specified track in the track list
    for(i = 0; i < nTracks; i++)
    {
        if(pTrackList[i].pTrack == pTrack)
        {
            // move all of the following tracks down by one entry
            // thus removing the offending track
            nTracks--;
            for(j = i; j < nTracks; j++)
                pTrackList[j] = pTrackList[j + 1];

            // shrink the list
            if(nTracks == 0)
            {
                GlobalFree(pTrackList);
                pTrackList = NULL;
            }
            else
                pTrackList = (TrackMerge*)GlobalReAlloc(pTrackList, nTracks *
                             sizeof(TrackMerge), GPTR | GMEM_MOVEABLE);

            // it's removed!
            return TRUE;
        }
```

```
        }
        // else, this track is not in the list!
        return FALSE;
}
#endif

//-----------------------------------------------------------------------------
//   CMaxMidiOut Destructor
//-----------------------------------------------------------------------------
CMaxMidiOut::~CMaxMidiOut()
{
    Close();

#ifdef _TRACK
    // detach any attached tracks
    for(int i = 0; i < nTracks; i++)
        Detach(pTrackList[i].pTrack);

    // free the merge buffer, if it exists
    if(lpMerge)
        GlobalFree(lpMerge);
#endif
}

//-----------------------------------------------------------------------------
//   Open/Close
//-----------------------------------------------------------------------------
BOOL CMaxMidiOut::Open(WORD wDeviceID, DWORD dwFlags)
{
    HSYNC hSync = 0;

    // get the description of the device
    GetMidiOutDescription(wDeviceID, Description);

#ifdef _SYNC
    // get the sync device handle
    if(pSync)
        hSync = pSync->GetHSync();
#endif

    if(!fIsOpen)
    {
        CMaxMidiOut::dwFlags = dwFlags;
        CMaxMidiOut::wDeviceID = wDeviceID;
        hDevice = OpenMidiOut(m_hWnd, wDeviceID, hSync, dwFlags);
    }

    if(hDevice > MXMIDIERR_MAXERR)
        fIsOpen = TRUE;
    else
        hDevice = 0;

    return fIsOpen;
}

void CMaxMidiOut::Close(void)
{
    if(fIsOpen)
    {
        Reset();
        CloseMidiOut(hDevice);
    }

    fIsOpen = FALSE;
}

//-----------------------------------------------------------------------------
//   Information Functions
//-----------------------------------------------------------------------------
BOOL CMaxMidiOut::IsOpen(void)
{
    return fIsOpen;
}

LPSTR CMaxMidiOut::GetDescription(void)
{
    return Description;
}

int CMaxMidiOut::GetNumDevices(void)
{
    return GetNumOutDevices();
```

```
}
//-------------------------------------------------------------------------------
//   Put
//-------------------------------------------------------------------------------
BOOL CMaxMidiOut::Put(LPMIDIEVENT lpEvent)
{
    if(fIsOpen)
        return (PutMidiOut(hDevice, lpEvent) == 0);

    return TRUE;        // act as though it accepts everything
                        // in case Put is called when not open
}
//-------------------------------------------------------------------------------
//   Reset/Flush
//-------------------------------------------------------------------------------
void CMaxMidiOut::Reset(void)
{
    if(fIsOpen)
        ResetMidiOut(hDevice);
}

void CMaxMidiOut::Flush(void)
{
    if(fIsOpen)
        FlushMidiOut(hDevice);
}

#ifdef _TRACK
//-------------------------------------------------------------------------------
//   Track Merge
//-------------------------------------------------------------------------------
LPMIDIEVENT CMaxMidiOut::MergeTracks(void)
{
    int track;
    DWORD time;
    int minTrack;
    int outEvents;
    BOOL tracksDone = FALSE;
    int i;
    BOOL fAnyInSysex = FALSE;
    int SysexTrack;
    DWORD NewLastAbs;

    // create the merge buffer that will receive the merged events
    if(lpMerge == NULL)
        lpMerge = (LPMIDIEVENT)GlobalAlloc(GPTR, MERGE_BUFFER_SIZE * sizeof(MidiEvent));

    // get a block of events from each of the tracks, in absolute time
    for(track = 0; track < nTracks; track++)
    {
        // always try to read something, even if the buffer was empty last time
        pTrackList[track].bufSize = MERGE_BUFFER_SIZE;
        pTrackList[track].pAbsBuf = pTrackList[track].pTrack->GetAbsBuffer
                            (pTrackList[track].lastEvent, &pTrackList[track].bufSize);

        // initialize the track structs for the search
        pTrackList[track].thisEvent = 0;

        // if this track is currently playing sysex, it blocks all other tracks
        if(pTrackList[track].pAbsBuf && pTrackList[track].fInSysex)
         {
            fAnyInSysex = TRUE;
            SysexTrack = track;
        }
    }
    // search through the tracks, merging events in ascending order, based on
    // abs time, into the merge buffer
    outEvents = 0;

    while(outEvents < MERGE_BUFFER_SIZE && !tracksDone)
    {
        // assume the tracks are empty to start
        tracksDone = TRUE;

        // if one of the tracks is in the middle of a sysex, stick on that track
        if(fAnyInSysex)
        {
            minTrack = SysexTrack;
```

```
                if(pTrackList[minTrack].pAbsBuf != NULL &&
                    pTrackList[minTrack].thisEvent < pTrackList[minTrack].bufSize)
                {
                    time =
                        pTrackList[minTrack].pAbsBuf[pTrackList[minTrack].thisEvent].time;
                    tracksDone = FALSE;
                }
        }
        else
        // get the time of the first event in the first track that has an event
        for(minTrack = 0; minTrack < nTracks; minTrack++)
        {
                if(pTrackList[minTrack].pAbsBuf != NULL &&
                    pTrackList[minTrack].thisEvent < pTrackList[minTrack].bufSize)
                {
                    time =
                        pTrackList[minTrack].pAbsBuf[pTrackList[minTrack].thisEvent].time;
                    tracksDone = FALSE;
                    break;
                }
        }

        if(!tracksDone)
        {
                // start the search from the next track, but
                // if one of the tracks is in the middle of a sysex,
                // remain on that track
                if(!fAnyInSysex)
                    for(track = minTrack + 1; track < nTracks; track++)
                    {
                        // skip tracks that are empty
                        if(pTrackList[track].pAbsBuf != NULL &&
                            pTrackList[track].thisEvent != pTrackList[track].bufSize)
                        {
                            // if the time of the next event in this track is less than
                            // the current time, this is the new event
                            if(pTrackList[track].pAbsBuf[pTrackList[track].thisEvent].time
                                < time)
                            {
                                minTrack = track;
                                time =
                                pTrackList[track].pAbsBuf[pTrackList[track].thisEvent].time;
                            }
                        }
                    }

                // found the next event, copy it over
                lpMerge[outEvents] =
                        pTrackList[minTrack].pAbsBuf[pTrackList[minTrack].thisEvent];
                pTrackList[minTrack].thisEvent++;

                // is this the start or end of a sysex in this track?
                switch(lpMerge[outEvents].data1)
                {
                    case SYSEX:
                        pTrackList[minTrack].fInSysex = TRUE;
                        fAnyInSysex = TRUE;
                        SysexTrack = minTrack;
                        break;

                    case EOX:
                        pTrackList[minTrack].fInSysex = FALSE;
                        fAnyInSysex = FALSE;
                        break;
                }

                outEvents++;
        }
}
// update all of the lastEvent indices and free the abs buffers
for(track = 0; track < nTracks; track++)
{
    pTrackList[track].lastEvent += pTrackList[track].thisEvent;
    if(pTrackList[track].pAbsBuf)
        GlobalFree(pTrackList[track].pAbsBuf);
}
// convert the merge buffer back to delta times
```

```
        if(outEvents)
        {
            NewLastAbs = lpMerge[outEvents - 1].time;

            for(i = outEvents - 1; i >= 1; i--)
            {
                lpMerge[i].time -= lpMerge[i - 1].time;

                // if one of the tracks was playing a large sysex, the timestamp
                // for the next event in the stream might end up with a negative
                // timestamp, since its time would logically be during the sysex.
                // We have to catch up the tracks here... it stinks, I know, but it
                // is the best we can do under the circumstances (sysex, that is).
                if((int)lpMerge[i].time < 0)
                    lpMerge[i].time = 0;
            }

            lpMerge[0].time -= LastAbs;
            LastAbs = NewLastAbs;
        }

        numEvents = outEvents;
        return lpMerge;
}

void CMaxMidiOut::MergeOut(void)
{
    if(nTracks)
    {
        // any events still in merge buffer?
        if(numEvents == outPtr)
        {
            // no, need to merge some more tracks
            // numEvents is set in MergeTracks()
            MergeTracks();
            outPtr = 0;
        }

        // pump out as much data as the MidiOut will accept
        while(outPtr < numEvents && Put(&lpMerge[outPtr]))
        {
            outPtr++;

            // merge more if needed
            if(numEvents == outPtr)
            {
                MergeTracks();
                outPtr = 0;
            }
        }
    }
}

void CMaxMidiOut::StartOut(void)
{
    int track;

    // rewind the tracks and start again
    for(track = 0; track < nTracks; track++)
    {
        pTrackList[track].lastEvent = 0;
        pTrackList[track].fInSysex = FALSE;
        pTrackList[track].bufSize = MERGE_BUFFER_SIZE;
    }

    LastAbs = 0;
    numEvents = outPtr = 0;
    MergeOut();
}
#endif
/////////////////////////////////////////////////////////////////////////////
// CMaxMidiOut message handlers

//-----------------------------------------------------------------------------
//   OnOutBufferReady
//-----------------------------------------------------------------------------
LRESULT CMaxMidiOut::OnOutBufferReady(WPARAM wParam, LPARAM hMidiOut)
{
#ifdef _TRACK
    // output events from any attached tracks
```

```
      MergeOut();
#endif

      ProcessOutBufferReady();
      return 0;
}
```

# CMaxMidiSync

```
//---------------------------------------------------------------------------
//    CMaxMidiSync Class Definition
//
//    (C) Copyright, Paul A. Messick, 1996
//---------------------------------------------------------------------------
class CMaxMidiSync : public CWnd
{
// Class-specific data
protected:
      HSYNC        hDevice;        // handle to the Sync device
      BOOL     fIsOpen;            // true if device is open
      WORD     CurrentMode;        // current sync mode
      WORD     CurrentPeriod;      // current timer period
      HWND     hParentWnd;         // hWnd for sync messages
      BOOL     fRunning;           // true is sync is active

public:
// Constructors/Destructor
      CMaxMidiSync();                      // default constructor
      CMaxMidiSync(HWND hParentWnd);
      CMaxMidiSync(HWND hParentWnd, WORD mode = S_INT, WORD timerPeriod = 10);
      ~CMaxMidiSync();                     // destructor

// Implementation
      BOOL CreateWnd(void);           // creates the hidden window
      void Attach(HWND hParentWnd);   // attaches the parent window

      BOOL IsOpen(void);              // returns true if device is open
      BOOL IsRunning(void) { return fRunning; };
      HSYNC GetHSync(void) { return hDevice; };

      BOOL Open(WORD mode = S_INT, WORD timerPeriod = 10);
      void Close(void);          // close the device without destroying class object

      BOOL Mode(WORD mode);        // set new sync mode
      WORD Mode(void) { return CurrentMode; };
      BOOL Period(WORD period); // set new timer period
      WORD Period(void) { return CurrentPeriod; };

      void Start(void);          // start sync
      void ReStart(void);        // restart sync after pause
      void Stop(void);           // stop sync
      void Pause(BOOL reset = FALSE); // pause sync, send note offs if reset = true

      BOOL Tempo(DWORD tempo);       // set the tempo in uS/beat
      DWORD Tempo(void);             // get the current tempo in uS/beat
      DWORD Convert(double tempo);   // convert bpm to uS/beat
      double Convert(DWORD tempo);   // convert uS/beat to bpm

      WORD Resolution(void);         // get the current resolution in tpb
      void Resolution(WORD res);     // set the current resolution in tpb

      virtual void ProcessMidiBeat(void) { };
      virtual void ProcessSyncDone(void) { };

// Generated message map functions
protected:
      //{{AFX_MSG(CMaxMidiSync)
      afx_msg LPARAM OnMidiBeat(WPARAM wParam, LPARAM lParam);
      afx_msg LPARAM OnSyncDone(WPARAM wParam, LPARAM lParam);
      //}}AFX_MSG
      DECLARE_MESSAGE_MAP()
};
```

```
//================================================================================
//   CMaxMidiSync Class Implementation
//
//   (C) Copyright, Paul A. Messick, 1996
//================================================================================
#include "stdafx.h"
#include "MaxMidi.h"

BEGIN_MESSAGE_MAP(CMaxMidiSync, CWnd)
    //{{AFX_MSG_MAP(CMaxMidiSync)
    ON_MESSAGE(MIDI_BEAT, OnMidiBeat)
    ON_MESSAGE(SYNC_DONE, OnSyncDone)
    //}}AFX_MSG_MAP
END_MESSAGE_MAP()

//--------------------------------------------------------------------------------
//   CMaxMidiSync Constructors
//--------------------------------------------------------------------------------
CMaxMidiSync::CMaxMidiSync()
{
    hDevice = 0;
    fIsOpen = FALSE;
    fRunning = FALSE;
    hParentWnd = NULL;
}

CMaxMidiSync::CMaxMidiSync(HWND hParentWnd)
{
    hDevice = 0;
    fIsOpen = FALSE;
    fRunning = FALSE;
    Attach(hParentWnd);
}

CMaxMidiSync::CMaxMidiSync(HWND hParentWnd, WORD mode, WORD timerPeriod)
{
    fRunning = FALSE;
    Attach(hParentWnd);
    Open(mode, timerPeriod);
}

BOOL CMaxMidiSync::CreateWnd(void)
{
    RECT r;

    r.left = r.top = r.right = r.bottom = 0;

    return Create(NULL, "CMaxMidiSyncWnd", WS_CHILD, r, FromHandlePermanent(hParentWnd),
                  0);
}

void CMaxMidiSync::Attach(HWND hParentWnd)
{
    CMaxMidiSync::hParentWnd = hParentWnd;
    CreateWnd();
}

//--------------------------------------------------------------------------------
//   CMaxMidiSync Destructors
//--------------------------------------------------------------------------------
CMaxMidiSync::~CMaxMidiSync()
{
    Stop();
    Close();
}

//--------------------------------------------------------------------------------
//   Open/Close
//--------------------------------------------------------------------------------
BOOL CMaxMidiSync::Open(WORD mode, WORD timerPeriod)
{
    if(!fIsOpen)
        hDevice = OpenSync(0, m_hWnd, mode, timerPeriod);

    if(hDevice > MXMIDIERR_MAXERR)
    {
        fIsOpen = TRUE;
        CurrentMode = mode;
        CurrentPeriod = timerPeriod;
    }
    else
```

```
        hDevice = 0;
    return fIsOpen;
}
void CMaxMidiSync::Close(void)
{
    if(fIsOpen)
        CloseSync(hDevice);

    fRunning = FALSE;
    fIsOpen = FALSE;
}
//----------------------------------------------------------------------------
//   Mode/Period
//----------------------------------------------------------------------------
BOOL CMaxMidiSync::Mode(WORD mode)
{
    if(fIsOpen)
    {
        hDevice = OpenSync(hDevice, m_hWnd, mode, USE_CURRENT);

        if(hDevice > MXMIDIERR_MAXERR)
        {
            fIsOpen = TRUE;
            CurrentMode = mode;
        }
        else
        {
            hDevice = 0;
            fIsOpen = FALSE;
        }
    }

    return fIsOpen;
}
BOOL CMaxMidiSync::Period(WORD period)
{
    if(fIsOpen)
    {
        hDevice = OpenSync(hDevice, m_hWnd, USE_CURRENT, period);

        if(hDevice > MXMIDIERR_MAXERR)
        {
            fIsOpen = TRUE;
            CurrentPeriod = period;
        }
        else
        {
            hDevice = 0;
            fIsOpen = FALSE;
        }
    }

    return fIsOpen;
}
//----------------------------------------------------------------------------
//   Information Functions
//----------------------------------------------------------------------------
BOOL CMaxMidiSync::IsOpen(void)
{
    return fIsOpen;
}
//----------------------------------------------------------------------------
//   Start/ReStart
//----------------------------------------------------------------------------
void CMaxMidiSync::Start(void)
{
    if(fIsOpen)
    {
        StartSync(hDevice);
        fRunning = TRUE;
    }
}
void CMaxMidiSync::ReStart(void)
{
    if(fIsOpen)
```

```
        {
            ReStartSync(hDevice);
            fRunning = TRUE;
        }
    }

    //------------------------------------------------------------------------
    //   Stop/Pause
    //------------------------------------------------------------------------
    void CMaxMidiSync::Stop(void)
    {
        if(fIsOpen)
        {
            StopSync(hDevice);
            fRunning = FALSE;
        }
    }

    void CMaxMidiSync::Pause(BOOL reset)
    {
        if(fIsOpen)
        {
            PauseSync(hDevice, reset);
            fRunning = FALSE;
        }
    }

    //------------------------------------------------------------------------
    //   Tempo
    //------------------------------------------------------------------------
    DWORD CMaxMidiSync::Tempo(void)
    {
        return GetTempo(hDevice);
    }

    BOOL CMaxMidiSync::Tempo(DWORD tempo)
    {
        return (SetTempo(hDevice, tempo) == 0);
    }

    //------------------------------------------------------------------------
    //   Resolution
    //------------------------------------------------------------------------
    WORD CMaxMidiSync::Resolution(void)
    {
        return GetResolution(hDevice);
    }

    void CMaxMidiSync::Resolution(WORD res)
    {
        SetResolution(hDevice, res);
    }

    //------------------------------------------------------------------------
    //   Convert Tempo
    //------------------------------------------------------------------------
    DWORD CMaxMidiSync::Convert(double tempo)
    {
        // can't allow zero tempo!
        if(tempo == 0.0)
            tempo = 120.0;

        return (DWORD)(60000000.0/tempo);
    }

    double CMaxMidiSync::Convert(DWORD tempo)
    {
        return (60000000.0/(double)tempo);
    }

    ////////////////////////////////////////////////////////////////////////////
    // CMaxMidiSync message handlers

    //------------------------------------------------------------------------
    //   OnMidiBeat
    //------------------------------------------------------------------------
    LRESULT CMaxMidiSync::OnMidiBeat(WPARAM wParam, LPARAM lParam)
    {
        ProcessMidiBeat();
        return 0;
    }
```

```
//--------------------------------------------------------------------------
//  OnSyncDone
//--------------------------------------------------------------------------
LRESULT CMaxMidiSync::OnSyncDone(WPARAM wParam, LPARAM lParam)
{
    ProcessSyncDone();
    return 0;
}
```

# CMaxMidiTrack

```
//--------------------------------------------------------------------------
//  CMaxMidiTrack Class Definition
//
//  (C) Copyright, Paul A. Messick, 1996
//--------------------------------------------------------------------------
#define DEFAULT_BUFFER_SIZE 8192
#define BUFFER_GROW_SIZE DEFAULT_BUFFER_SIZE

class CMaxMidiTrack
{
// Class-specific data
protected:
#ifdef _SMF
    CMaxMidiSMF* pSMF;                      // SMF connected to this track
#endif
#ifdef _MIDIOUT
    CMaxMidiOut* pMidiOut;                  // MidiOut device connected to this track
#endif
#ifdef _MIDIIN
    CMaxMidiIn*  pMidiIn;                   // MidiIn device connected to this track
#endif

    LPMIDIEVENT lpBuffer;                   // buffer for events
    DWORD       dwBufSize;                  // size of buffer, in events
    DWORD       inPtr;                      // buffer write index
    DWORD       outPtr;                     // buffer read index
    BOOL        fRecord;                    // true if recording into this track
    BOOL        fMute;                      // true if playback is muted
    LPSTR       lpName;                     // track name string

public:
// Constructors/Destructor
    CMaxMidiTrack();                        // default constructor
    ~CMaxMidiTrack();                       // destructor

// Implementation
// smf-dependent functions
#ifdef _SMF
    void Attach(CMaxMidiSMF* pSMF);
    void Detach(CMaxMidiSMF* pSMF);
    CMaxMidiSMF* GetSMF(void) { return pSMF; };
#endif

// midi out-dependent functions
#ifdef _MIDIOUT
    void Attach(CMaxMidiOut* pMidiOut);
    void Detach(CMaxMidiOut* pMidiOut);
    CMaxMidiOut* GetMidiOut(void) { return pMidiOut; };
#endif

// midi in-dependent functions
#ifdef _MIDIIN
    void Attach(CMaxMidiIn* pMidiIn);
    void Detach(CMaxMidiIn* pMidiIn);
    CMaxMidiIn* GetMidiIn(void) { return pMidiIn; };
#endif

    void Detach(void);

    BOOL IsEmpty(void) { return (inPtr - outPtr) == 0; };
    BOOL IsRecording(void) { return fRecord; };
    void IsRecording(BOOL record) { fRecord = record; };

    void Mute(BOOL mute) { fMute = mute; };
    BOOL Mute(void) { return fMute; };
```

```
        LPSTR GetName(void);
        void SetName(LPSTR name);

        DWORD GetNumEvents(void) { return (DWORD)(inPtr - outPtr); };
        void SetNumEvents(DWORD nEvents) { Flush(); inPtr = nEvents; };

        BOOL CreateBuffer(DWORD dwBufEvents = DEFAULT_BUFFER_SIZE);
        LPMIDIEVENT GetBuffer(void) { return lpBuffer; };
        void SetBuffer(LPMIDIEVENT lpNewBuf) { lpBuffer = lpNewBuf; };
        DWORD GetBufferSize(void) { return dwBufSize; };
        void SetBufferSize(DWORD dwBufEvents) { dwBufSize = dwBufEvents; };
        void FreeBuffer(void);

        LPMIDIEVENT GetEvent(DWORD eventNum);
        void SetEvent(LPMIDIEVENT lpEvent, DWORD eventNum);
        DWORD GetTime(DWORD eventNum);

        LPMIDIEVENT Read(void);
        void Write(LPMIDIEVENT lpEvent);
        void Flush(void) { inPtr = outPtr = 0; };
        void Rewind(void) { outPtr = 0; };

        BOOL Load(void);
        BOOL Save(void);

        LPMIDIEVENT GetAbsBuffer(DWORD startEvent, DWORD* numEvents);
        DWORD AbsNow(DWORD eventNum);
        void AbsToDelta(LPMIDIEVENT lpBuf, DWORD startEvent, DWORD numEvents);
        void DeltaToAbs(LPMIDIEVENT lpBuf, DWORD startEvent, DWORD numEvents);

        void InsertEvent(LPMIDIEVENT lpEvent, DWORD beforeEvent);
        void DeleteEvent(DWORD eventNum);
        void SlideTrack(DWORD eventNum, int delta);
};


//=============================================================================
//   CMaxMidiTrack Class Implementation
//
//   (C) Copyright, Paul A. Messick, 1996
//=============================================================================
#include "stdafx.h"
#include "MaxMidi.h"
//-----------------------------------------------------------------------------
//   CMaxMidiTrack Constructors
//-----------------------------------------------------------------------------
CMaxMidiTrack::CMaxMidiTrack()
{
    lpBuffer = NULL;
    lpName = NULL;
#ifdef _SMF
    pSMF = NULL;
#endif
#ifdef _MIDIOUT
    pMidiOut = NULL;
#endif
#ifdef _MIDIIN
    pMidiIn = NULL;
#endif
    inPtr = outPtr = 0;
    IsRecording(FALSE);
    Mute(FALSE);

    CreateBuffer();
}

//-----------------------------------------------------------------------------
//   CMaxMidiTrack Destructor
//-----------------------------------------------------------------------------
CMaxMidiTrack::~CMaxMidiTrack()
{
    // detach the track from any smf, input, or output devices
    Detach();
    FreeBuffer();
}

//-----------------------------------------------------------------------------
//   Attach/Detach
//-----------------------------------------------------------------------------
#ifdef _SMF
```

```
void CMaxMidiTrack::Attach(CMaxMidiSMF* pSMF)
{
    CMaxMidiTrack::pSMF = pSMF;
}
void CMaxMidiTrack::Detach(CMaxMidiSMF* pSMF)
{
    if(pSMF == CMaxMidiTrack::pSMF)
        CMaxMidiTrack::pSMF = NULL;
}
#endif

#ifdef _MIDIOUT
void CMaxMidiTrack::Attach(CMaxMidiOut* pMidiOut)
{
    CMaxMidiTrack::pMidiOut = pMidiOut;
}
void CMaxMidiTrack::Detach(CMaxMidiOut* pMidiOut)
{
    if(pMidiOut == CMaxMidiTrack::pMidiOut)
        pMidiOut = NULL;
}
#endif

#ifdef _MIDIIN
void CMaxMidiTrack::Attach(CMaxMidiIn* pMidiIn)
{
    CMaxMidiTrack::pMidiIn = pMidiIn;
}
void CMaxMidiTrack::Detach(CMaxMidiIn* pMidiIn)
{
    if(pMidiIn == CMaxMidiTrack::pMidiIn)
        pMidiIn = NULL;
}
#endif

void CMaxMidiTrack::Detach(void)
{
    // detach from any attached devices
#ifdef _SMF
    if(pSMF)
    {
        pSMF->Detach(this);
        pSMF = NULL;
    }
#endif
#ifdef _MIDIOUT
    if(pMidiOut)
    {
        pMidiOut->Detach(this);
        pMidiOut = NULL;
    }
#endif
#ifdef _MIDIIN
    if(pMidiIn)
    {
        pMidiIn->Detach(this);
        pMidiIn = NULL;
        IsRecording(FALSE);
    }
#endif
}
//------------------------------------------------------------------
//   Track Name
//------------------------------------------------------------------
LPSTR CMaxMidiTrack::GetName(void)
{
    if(lpName)
        return lpName;

#ifdef _SMF
    DWORD cbSize;
    // get the name from the smf, if it exists
    if(pSMF && pSMF->GetMode() == READ)
    {
        pSMF->ReadMeta(this, META_NAME, &lpName, &cbSize);
        return lpName;
```

```
    }
#endif
    // currently no name
    return NULL;
}

void CMaxMidiTrack::SetName(LPSTR name)
{
    // free the old name, if there was one
    if(lpName)
        GlobalFree(lpName);

    // allocate space for the new name
    lpName = (LPSTR)GlobalAlloc(GPTR, strlen(name));
    strcpy(lpName, name);
}
//-----------------------------------------------------------------------------
//   Buffer Functions
//-----------------------------------------------------------------------------
LPMIDIEVENT CMaxMidiTrack::GetEvent(DWORD eventNum)
{
    if(eventNum >= dwBufSize)
        return NULL;

    return &lpBuffer[eventNum];
}

void CMaxMidiTrack::SetEvent(LPMIDIEVENT lpEvent, DWORD eventNum)
{
    if(eventNum >= dwBufSize)
        return;

    lpBuffer[eventNum] = *lpEvent;
}

BOOL CMaxMidiTrack::CreateBuffer(DWORD dwBufEvents)
{
    // this can only be called once per open
    if(lpBuffer)
        return FALSE;

    // create buffers for data from each track
    lpBuffer = (LPMIDIEVENT)GlobalAlloc(GPTR, sizeof(MidiEvent) * dwBufEvents);
    dwBufSize = dwBufEvents;

    return TRUE;
}

void CMaxMidiTrack::FreeBuffer(void)
{
    if(lpBuffer)
        GlobalFree(lpBuffer);

    lpBuffer = NULL;
}
//-----------------------------------------------------------------------------
//   Queued Read/Write
//-----------------------------------------------------------------------------
LPMIDIEVENT CMaxMidiTrack::Read(void)
{
    // don't do anything if at end of buffer, or recording or muted
    if(outPtr == inPtr || fMute || fRecord)
        return NULL;

    return &lpBuffer[outPtr++];
}

void CMaxMidiTrack::Write(LPMIDIEVENT lpEvent)
{
    // don't write into the track if not recording
    if(!fRecord)
        return;

    InsertEvent(lpEvent, (DWORD)-1);
}
//-----------------------------------------------------------------------------
//   Event Editing Functions
//-----------------------------------------------------------------------------
void CMaxMidiTrack::InsertEvent(LPMIDIEVENT lpEvent, DWORD beforeEvent)
{
```

```
        // does the buffer need to grow in order to add this event?
        if(inPtr == dwBufSize)
        {
            dwBufSize += BUFFER_GROW_SIZE;
            lpBuffer = (LPMIDIEVENT)GlobalReAlloc(lpBuffer, dwBufSize * sizeof(MidiEvent),
                                        GPTR | GMEM_MOVEABLE);
        }

        // insert at the end (append) if beforeEvent is -1
        if(beforeEvent == (DWORD)-1)
        {
            // put it in the buffer
            lpBuffer[inPtr] = *lpEvent;
            inPtr++;
            return;
        }

        // else, move all of the events following this new one up by one slot
        memmove(&lpBuffer[beforeEvent + 1], &lpBuffer[beforeEvent], inPtr - beforeEvent);

        // add the event to the track by putting in the specified location
        // without adjusting the timestamp of the following event
        lpBuffer[beforeEvent] = *lpEvent;
        inPtr++;
}
void CMaxMidiTrack::DeleteEvent(DWORD eventNum)
{
        // eventNum == -1 will delete the last event
        inPtr--;
        if(eventNum < inPtr)
        {
            // move all of the events following the specfied event down
            // in the track by one, thus deleteing the event
            memmove(&lpBuffer[eventNum], &lpBuffer[eventNum + 1], inPtr - eventNum);
        }
}

void CMaxMidiTrack::SlideTrack(DWORD eventNum, int delta)
{
        // add the delta time to the specified event
        if(eventNum < inPtr)
        {
            lpBuffer[eventNum].time += delta;
            if((int)lpBuffer[eventNum].time < 0)
                lpBuffer[eventNum].time = 0;
        }
}
//----------------------------------------------------------------------------
//   Save/Load
//----------------------------------------------------------------------------
BOOL CMaxMidiTrack::Load(void)
{
#ifdef _SMF
        // if the SMF object is attached, read data into this track
        if(pSMF)
            return pSMF->Read(this);
#endif

        return FALSE;
}

BOOL CMaxMidiTrack::Save(void)
{
#ifdef _SMF
        // if the SMF object is attached, save this track
        // this assumes that the buffer is properly attached to the smf object
        // NOTE: this should only be done in ascending order of tracks
        // muted tracks are not written
        if(pSMF && !fMute)
        {
            // write the name as the first event in the track, if it exists
            if(lpName)
                pSMF->WriteMeta(this, META_NAME, lpName, 0);

            return pSMF->Write(this);
        }
#endif
        // if not attached, return false
```

```
        return FALSE;
}
//-----------------------------------------------------------------------------
//   Absolute Time/Delta Time Functions
//-----------------------------------------------------------------------------
LPMIDIEVENT CMaxMidiTrack::GetAbsBuffer(DWORD startEvent, DWORD* numEvents)
{
    LPMIDIEVENT lpBuf;

    // sanity check: make sure the requested start event is in the buffer
    // and the track is not muted or recording
    if(startEvent >= inPtr || fMute || fRecord)
    {
        *numEvents = 0;
        return NULL;
    }

    // the buffer size will be either the requested number of events
    // or the number remaining in the track, whichever is lower
    *numEvents = ((inPtr - startEvent) < *numEvents ? (inPtr - startEvent) :
                                                    *numEvents);

    // create the buffer
    lpBuf = (LPMIDIEVENT)GlobalAlloc(GPTR, *numEvents * sizeof(MidiEvent));
    memcpy(lpBuf, &lpBuffer[startEvent], *numEvents * sizeof(MidiEvent));

    // convert it to absolute time
    DeltaToAbs(lpBuf, startEvent, *numEvents);

    return lpBuf;
}

DWORD CMaxMidiTrack::AbsNow(DWORD eventNum)
{
    DWORD time;
    int i;

    // sanity check: make sure the specified event is in the buffer
    // if not, return zero as the time
    if(eventNum >= inPtr)
        return 0;

    // add up the elapsed number of ticks since the beginning
    // of the track till this event
    time = lpBuffer[0].time;
    for(i = 1; i <= (int)eventNum; i++)
        time += lpBuffer[i].time;

    return time;
}

void CMaxMidiTrack::AbsToDelta(LPMIDIEVENT lpBuf, DWORD startEvent, DWORD numEvents)
{
    DWORD now;
    DWORD start;
    int i;

    // get the abs time of the previous event (since we need the delta from it
    // for the time for the first event is this buffer)
    // if this is the first event in the track (i.e. startEvent == 0) then we know
    // the start time is zero
    if(startEvent == 0)
        start = 0;
    else
        start = AbsNow(startEvent - 1);

    // convert each abs time to delta time by subtracting the abs time from
    // the start time of the event prior event
    for(i = 0; i < (int)numEvents; i++)
    {
        // save the abs time of this event
        // it will become the start for the next event
        now = lpBuffer[i].time;
        lpBuffer[i].time -= start;
        start = now;
    }
}

void CMaxMidiTrack::DeltaToAbs(LPMIDIEVENT lpBuf, DWORD startEvent, DWORD numEvents)
{
    DWORD now;
    int i;
```

```
        // get the abs time of the first event in the buffer
        now = AbsNow(startEvent);

        // we know the abs time for the first one -- its the startEvent
        lpBuf[0].time = now;

        // convert each time stamp to abs by setting it to the
        // time since the beginning of the track
        for(i = 1; i < (int)numEvents; i++)
        {
            now += lpBuf[i].time;
            lpBuf[i].time = now;
        }
}

DWORD CMaxMidiTrack::GetTime(DWORD eventNum)
{
        // sanity check: make sure the specified event is in the buffer
        // if not, return zero as the time
        if(eventNum >= inPtr)
            return 0;

        // return the time for the requested event in track
        return lpBuffer[eventNum].time;
}
```

# CMaxMidiSMF

```
//---------------------------------------------------------------------------
//   CMaxMidiSMF Class Definition
//
//   (C) Copyright, Paul A. Messick, 1996
//---------------------------------------------------------------------------
class CMaxMidiSMF
{
// Class-specific data
protected:
    HMIN hSMF;                          // handle to the SMF
    BOOL fIsOpen;                       // true if device is open
    char Mode;                          // 'r' for read, 'w' for write
    int      Format;                    // SMF format type
    int      nTracksInSMF;              // number of tracks in SMF
    int      nTracksAttached;           // number of tracks attached to object
    CMaxMidiTrack** pTrackList;         // array of track object pointers

public:
// Constructors/Destructor
    CMaxMidiSMF();                      // default constructor
    CMaxMidiSMF(LPCTSTR filename, const char Mode);
    CMaxMidiSMF(LPSTR filename, const char Mode);
    ~CMaxMidiSMF();                     // destructor

// Implementation
    void Attach(CMaxMidiTrack* pTrack);
    void Attach(CMaxMidiTrack* pTrack, int position);
    BOOL Detach(CMaxMidiTrack* pTrack);

    BOOL IsOpen(void) { return fIsOpen; }; // returns true if device is open
    int NumTracks(void) { return nTracksInSMF; };
    int GetFormat(void) { return Format; };
    char GetMode(void) { return Mode; };

    BOOL Open(LPCTSTR filename, const char Mode, int Format = 1);
    BOOL Open(LPSTR filename, const char Mode, int Format = 1);
    void Close(void);                   // close the device without destroying class object

    WORD Resolution(void) { return GetSMFResolution(hSMF); };
    WORD Resolution(WORD res) { return SetSMFResolution(hSMF, res); };
    virtual BOOL Read(CMaxMidiTrack* pTrack);
    virtual BOOL Write(CMaxMidiTrack* pTrack);
    DWORD ReadMeta(CMaxMidiTrack* pTrack, BYTE type, LPSTR* Value, DWORD* cbSize);
    BOOL WriteMeta(CMaxMidiTrack* pTrack, BYTE type, LPSTR Value, DWORD time);
    BOOL Rewind(void) { return RewindSMF(hSMF) == 0; };

    BOOL Load(void);
```

```
    BOOL Save(void);
};

#define READ 'r'
#define WRITE 'w'


//=============================================================================
//   CMaxMidiSMF Class Implementation
//
//   (C) Copyright, Paul A. Messick, 1996
//=============================================================================
#include "stdafx.h"
#include "MaxMidi.h"
//-----------------------------------------------------------------------------
//   CMaxMidiSMF Constructors
//-----------------------------------------------------------------------------
CMaxMidiSMF::CMaxMidiSMF()
{
    fIsOpen = FALSE;
    nTracksInSMF = 0;
    nTracksAttached = 0;
    pTrackList = NULL;
}

CMaxMidiSMF::CMaxMidiSMF(LPSTR filename, const char Mode)
{
    fIsOpen = FALSE;
    nTracksInSMF = 0;
    nTracksAttached = 0;
    pTrackList = NULL;

    Open(filename, Mode);
}

CMaxMidiSMF::CMaxMidiSMF(LPCTSTR filename, const char Mode)
{
    CMaxMidiSMF((LPSTR)filename, Mode);
}

//-----------------------------------------------------------------------------
//   Attach/Detach Track
//-----------------------------------------------------------------------------
void CMaxMidiSMF::Attach(CMaxMidiTrack* pTrack)
{
    // attach this track to the end of the list
    Attach(pTrack, -1);
}

void CMaxMidiSMF::Attach(CMaxMidiTrack* pTrack, int position)
{
    int i;

    // adjust the format type if more than one track is attached
    nTracksAttached++;
    if(nTracksAttached > 1)
        Format = 1;

    // expand the track list for one more entry
    if(pTrackList)
        // add an entry if list exists
        pTrackList = (CMaxMidiTrack**)GlobalReAlloc(pTrackList, nTracksAttached *
                                    sizeof(CMaxMidiTrack*), GPTR | GMEM_MOVEABLE);
    else
        // create the list
        pTrackList = (CMaxMidiTrack**)GlobalAlloc(GPTR, sizeof(CMaxMidiTrack*));

    // append this track to the end of the track list if the position is -1
    if(position == -1)
        pTrackList[nTracksAttached - 1] = pTrack;
    else
    // move the other tracks up by one and insert this track at position
    {
        for(i = nTracksAttached - 1; i >= position; i--)
            pTrackList[i + 1] = pTrackList[i];

        pTrackList[position] = pTrack;
    }

    pTrack->Attach(this);
}
```

```
BOOL CMaxMidiSMF::Detach(CMaxMidiTrack* pTrack)
{
    int i, j;

    // make sure there is at least one track to detach
    if(nTracksAttached == 0)
        return FALSE;

    // search for the specified track in the track list
    for(i = 0; i < nTracksAttached; i++)
    {
        if(pTrackList[i] == pTrack)
        {
            // move all of the following tracks down by one entry
            // thus removing the offending track
            nTracksAttached--;
            for(j = i; j < nTracksAttached; j++)
                pTrackList[j] = pTrackList[j + 1];

            // shrink the list
            if(nTracksAttached == 0)
            {
                GlobalFree(pTrackList);
                pTrackList = NULL;
            }
            else
                pTrackList = (CMaxMidiTrack**)GlobalReAlloc(pTrackList, nTracksAttached
                                        * sizeof(CMaxMidiTrack*), GPTR | GMEM_MOVEABLE);

            // it's removed!
            return TRUE;
        }
    }

    // else, this track is not in the list!
    return FALSE;
}
//------------------------------------------------------------------------
//   CMaxMidiSMF Destructor
//------------------------------------------------------------------------
CMaxMidiSMF::~CMaxMidiSMF()
{
    Close();
}
//------------------------------------------------------------------------
//   Open
//------------------------------------------------------------------------
BOOL CMaxMidiSMF::Open(LPCTSTR filename, const char Mode, int Format)
{
    return Open((LPSTR)filename, Mode, Format);
}
BOOL CMaxMidiSMF::Open(LPSTR filename, const char Mode, int Format)
{
    // make sure there are no open files attached to this object
    Close();

    // open the file
    CMaxMidiSMF::Mode = Mode;
    CMaxMidiSMF::Format = Format;
    if((hSMF = OpenSMF(filename, &(CMaxMidiSMF::Format), Mode, &nTracksInSMF)) != 0)
        fIsOpen = TRUE;

    return fIsOpen;
}
//------------------------------------------------------------------------
//   Close
//------------------------------------------------------------------------
void CMaxMidiSMF::Close(void)
{
    if(fIsOpen)
    {
        CloseSMF(hSMF);

        // detach any tracks from this file
        while(nTracksAttached)
        {
            pTrackList[0]->Detach(this);
```

```
            Detach(pTrackList[0]);
        }
        nTracksInSMF = 0;
    }
    fIsOpen = FALSE;
}
//-----------------------------------------------------------------------------
//   SMF Functions
//-----------------------------------------------------------------------------
BOOL CMaxMidiSMF::Read(CMaxMidiTrack* pTrack)
{
    DWORD dwEventsRead = 0;
    DWORD dwRead;
    int Track;
    DWORD dwTrackSize;
    LPMIDIEVENT pBuffer;

    // only valid if opened for read
    if(Mode == READ && pTrackList)
    {
        // find the track number corresponding to this track
        for(Track = 0; Track < nTracksAttached; Track++)
            if(pTrackList[Track] == pTrack)
            {
                dwTrackSize = pTrack->GetBufferSize();
                pBuffer = pTrack->GetBuffer();

                do {
                    // expand the track buffer, if necessary
                    if(dwTrackSize - dwEventsRead < DEFAULT_BUFFER_SIZE)
                    {
                        dwTrackSize += dwEventsRead;
                        pBuffer = (LPMIDIEVENT)GlobalReAlloc(pBuffer, dwTrackSize *
                                    sizeof(MidiEvent), GPTR | GMEM_MOVEABLE);
                    }

                    // read a block of events
                    dwRead = ReadSMF(hSMF, Track, &pBuffer[dwEventsRead],
                                    DEFAULT_BUFFER_SIZE);
                    dwEventsRead += dwRead;

                } while(dwRead);

                pTrack->SetNumEvents(dwEventsRead);
                pTrack->SetBufferSize(dwTrackSize);
                pTrack->SetBuffer(pBuffer);
                pTrack->GetName();
                break;
            }
    }

    return dwEventsRead != 0;
}

BOOL CMaxMidiSMF::Write(CMaxMidiTrack* pTrack)
{
    int Track;
    LPSTR lpName;

    // only valid if opened for write
    if(Mode == WRITE && pTrackList)
    {
        // find the track number corresponding to this track
        for(Track = 0; Track < nTracksAttached; Track++)
            if(pTrackList[Track] == pTrack)
            {
                if(lpName = pTrack->GetName())
                    WriteMeta(pTrack, META_NAME, lpName, 0);

                return (WriteSMF(hSMF, Track, pTrack->GetBuffer(),
                        pTrack->GetNumEvents()) == pTrack->GetNumEvents());
            }
    }

    return FALSE;
}

BOOL CMaxMidiSMF::Save(void)
{
    int i;
```

```
            CMaxMidiIn* pMidiIn;
            CMaxMidiSync* pSync;

        // only valid if opened for write
        if(Mode != WRITE || pTrackList == NULL)
            return FALSE;

        // get the resolution sync device, if attached, and set it in the file
        for(i = 0; i < nTracksAttached; i++)
            if(pMidiIn = pTrackList[i]->GetMidiIn())
                if(pSync = pMidiIn->GetSync())
                {
                    CMaxMidiSMF::Resolution(pSync->Resolution());
                    break;
                }

        // save all of the tracks that are attached
        for(i = 0; i < nTracksAttached; i++)
            Write(pTrackList[i]);

        return TRUE;
}

BOOL CMaxMidiSMF::Load(void)
{
        int i;
        CMaxMidiSync* pSync;
        CMaxMidiOut* pMidiOut;

        // only valid if opened for read
        if(Mode != READ || pTrackList == NULL)
            return FALSE;

        // read all of the tracks that are attached
        RewindSMF(hSMF);
        for(i = 0; i < nTracksAttached; i++)
        {
            pTrackList[i]->Flush();
            Read(pTrackList[i]);
        }

        // get the resolution from the file and set it in the sync device, if attached
        if(pMidiOut = pTrackList[0]->GetMidiOut())
            if(pSync = pMidiOut->GetSync())
                pSync->Resolution(CMaxMidiSMF::Resolution());

        return TRUE;
}
//-------------------------------------------------------------------------------
//   Meta Event Functions
//-------------------------------------------------------------------------------
DWORD CMaxMidiSMF::ReadMeta(CMaxMidiTrack* pTrack, BYTE type, LPSTR* Value, DWORD*
cbSize)
{
        int Track;
        LPSTR valbuf;
        DWORD valbufsize;
        DWORD time = (DWORD)-1;

        // only valid if opened for read
        if(Mode == READ && pTrackList)
        {
            // find the track number corresponding to this track
            for(Track = 0; Track < nTracksAttached; Track++)
                if(pTrackList[Track] == pTrack)
                {
                    // look for the event in the track
                    time = ReadMetaEvent(hSMF, Track, type, &valbuf, &valbufsize);
                    if(time != (DWORD)-1)
                    {
                        // create a buffer for the event value and copy it over
                        *Value = (LPSTR)GlobalAlloc(GPTR, valbufsize);
                        memcpy(*Value, valbuf, valbufsize);
                    }
                }
        }
        return time;
}

BOOL CMaxMidiSMF::WriteMeta(CMaxMidiTrack* pTrack, BYTE type, LPSTR Value, DWORD time)
```

```
{
    int Track;
    UINT rc = 1;

    // only valid if opened for write
    if(Mode == WRITE && pTrackList)
    {
        // find the track number corresponding to this track
        for(Track = 0; Track < nTracksAttached; Track++)
            if(pTrackList[Track] == pTrack)
                rc = WriteMetaEvent(hSMF, Track, type, Value, time);
    }
    return rc == 0;
}
```

# CMidiInDeviceMenu

```
//-------------------------------------------------------------------------------
//   CMidiInDeviceMenu Class Definition
//
//   (C) Copyright, Paul A. Messick, 1996
//-------------------------------------------------------------------------------
class CMidiInDeviceMenu
{
protected:
    HMENU     hPopupMenu;
    int       nMaxDevices;
    UINT idm_base;
    CMaxMidiIn* MidiIn;

public:
    CMidiInDeviceMenu() { nMaxDevices = 0; MidiIn = NULL; };
    CMidiInDeviceMenu(HMENU hMenu, UINT position, LPSTR name, UINT baseMsg);
    ~CMidiInDeviceMenu() { };

    void Create(HMENU hMenu, UINT position, LPSTR name, UINT baseMsg);
    void Attach(CMaxMidiIn* Device) { MidiIn = Device; };

    BOOL GetDeviceName(WORD dwDevice, LPSTR name);
    int GetDeviceCount(void) { return nMaxDevices; };
    HMENU GetMenu(void) { return hPopupMenu; };

    virtual BOOL SelectDevice(UINT id);
};


//===============================================================================
//   CMidiInDeviceMenu Class Implementation
//
//   (C) Copyright, Paul A. Messick, 1996
//===============================================================================
#include "stdafx.h"
#include "MaxMidi.h"
//-------------------------------------------------------------------------------
//   Constructors
//-------------------------------------------------------------------------------
CMidiInDeviceMenu::CMidiInDeviceMenu(HMENU hWndMenu, UINT position, LPSTR mname, UINT
baseMsg)
{
    Create(hWndMenu, position, mname, baseMsg);
}

//-------------------------------------------------------------------------------
//   Create
//-------------------------------------------------------------------------------
void CMidiInDeviceMenu::Create(HMENU hWndMenu, UINT position, LPSTR mname, UINT baseMsg)
{
    char name[MAXPNAMELEN];
    WORD wDevID;

    // create a new popup menu
    hPopupMenu = CreateMenu();
    idm_base = baseMsg;

    // and insert in the existing window menu
```

```
        InsertMenu(hWndMenu, position, MF_BYPOSITION | MF_POPUP | MF_ENABLED,
                (UINT)hPopupMenu, mname);

        // add all of the available input devices to the menu
        nMaxDevices = GetNumInDevices();
        for(wDevID = 0; wDevID < nMaxDevices; wDevID++)
        {
                GetDeviceName(wDevID, name);
                AppendMenu(hPopupMenu, MF_ENABLED | MF_STRING, baseMsg + wDevID, name);
        }
}
//-----------------------------------------------------------------------------
//  GetDeviceName
//-----------------------------------------------------------------------------
BOOL CMidiInDeviceMenu::GetDeviceName(WORD wDeviceID, LPSTR name)
{
        return GetMidiInDescription(wDeviceID, name);
}
//-----------------------------------------------------------------------------
//  SelectDevice
//-----------------------------------------------------------------------------
BOOL CMidiInDeviceMenu::SelectDevice(UINT id)
{
        int i;
        CMenu m;

        // ignore this if no device is attached or if the id is not in range
        if(MidiIn == NULL || ((int)id > nMaxDevices && ((int)id < idm_base) || ((int)id >
                idm_base + nMaxDevices)))
                return FALSE;

        // get a temp CMenu to modify the menu state
        CMenu* Menu = m.FromHandle(hPopupMenu);

        // if the id is between 0 and the number of devices
        // then select the input based on the index, otherwise
        // it is a menu selection
        if((int)id <= nMaxDevices)
                id += idm_base;

        for(i = idm_base; i < (int)(idm_base + nMaxDevices); i++)
                if(i == (int)id)
                {
                        //--------------------------------------------------
                        // close the currently open input device
                        //--------------------------------------------------
                        MidiIn->Stop();
                        MidiIn->Close();

                        //--------------------------------------------------
                        // open midi in for use
                        //--------------------------------------------------
                        MidiIn->Open(id - idm_base);
                        MidiIn->Start();
                        Menu->CheckMenuItem(i, MF_CHECKED);
                }
                else
                        Menu->CheckMenuItem(i, MF_UNCHECKED);

        return TRUE;
}
```

# CMidiOutDeviceMenu

```
//-----------------------------------------------------------------------------
//   CMidiOutDeviceMenu Class Definition
//
//   (C) Copyright, Paul A. Messick, 1996
//-----------------------------------------------------------------------------
class CMidiOutDeviceMenu
{
protected:
        HMENU     hPopupMenu;
```

```
            int     nMaxDevices;
            WORD MapperID;
            UINT idm_base;
            CMaxMidiOut* MidiOut;
public:
            CMidiOutDeviceMenu() { nMaxDevices = 0; MidiOut = NULL; };
            CMidiOutDeviceMenu(HMENU hMenu, UINT position, LPSTR name, UINT baseMsg);
            ~CMidiOutDeviceMenu() { };

            void Create(HMENU hMenu, UINT position, LPSTR name, UINT baseMsg);
            void Attach(CMaxMidiOut* Device) { MidiOut = Device; };

            int GetDeviceCount(void) { return nMaxDevices; };
            HMENU GetMenu(void) { return hPopupMenu; };
            BOOL GetDeviceName(WORD dwDevice, LPSTR name);

            virtual BOOL SelectDevice(UINT id);
};


//=============================================================================
//  CMidiOutDeviceMenu Class Implementation
//
//  (C) Copyright, Paul A. Messick, 1996
//=============================================================================
#include "stdafx.h"
#include "MaxMidi.h"
//-----------------------------------------------------------------------------
//  CMidiOutDeviceMenu Constructor
//-----------------------------------------------------------------------------
CMidiOutDeviceMenu::CMidiOutDeviceMenu(HMENU hWndMenu, UINT position, LPSTR mname, UINT
baseMsg)
{
    Create(hWndMenu, position, mname, baseMsg);
}

//-----------------------------------------------------------------------------
//  Create
//-----------------------------------------------------------------------------
void CMidiOutDeviceMenu::Create(HMENU hWndMenu, UINT position, LPSTR mname, UINT
baseMsg)
{
    char name[MAXPNAMELEN];
    WORD wDevID;

    // create a new popup menu
    hPopupMenu = CreateMenu();
    idm_base = baseMsg;

    // and insert in the existing window menu
    InsertMenu(hWndMenu, position, MF_BYPOSITION | MF_POPUP | MF_ENABLED,
            (UINT)hPopupMenu, mname);

    // add all of the available input devices to the menu
    // nMaxItems will hold the total number of devices found
    nMaxDevices = GetNumOutDevices();
    for(wDevID = 0; wDevID < nMaxDevices; wDevID++)
    {
        GetDeviceName(wDevID, name);
        AppendMenu(hPopupMenu, MF_ENABLED | MF_STRING, baseMsg + wDevID, name);
    }

    // try to add the MIDI Mapper, if present
    MapperID = 0;
    if(GetDeviceName((WORD)MIDI_MAPPER, name) == TRUE)
    {
        AppendMenu(hPopupMenu, MF_ENABLED | MF_STRING, baseMsg + nMaxDevices, name);
        MapperID = baseMsg + nMaxDevices;
        nMaxDevices++;
    }
}

//-----------------------------------------------------------------------------
//  GetDeviceName
//-----------------------------------------------------------------------------
BOOL CMidiOutDeviceMenu::GetDeviceName(WORD wDeviceID, LPSTR name)
{
    return GetMidiOutDescription(wDeviceID, name);
}
```

```
//------------------------------------------------------------------------
//   SelectDevice
//------------------------------------------------------------------------
BOOL CMidiOutDeviceMenu::SelectDevice(UINT id)
{
    int i;
    CMenu m;
    BOOL ItsOpen;

    // ignore this if no device is attached or if the id is not in range
    if(MidiOut == NULL || ((int)id > nMaxDevices && ((int)id < idm_base) || ((int)id >
                 idm_base + nMaxDevices)))
        return FALSE;

    // get a temp CMenu to modify the menu state
    CMenu* Menu = m.FromHandle(hPopupMenu);

    // if the id is between 0 and the number of devices
    // then select the input based on the index, otherwise
    // it is a menu selection
    if((int)id <= nMaxDevices)
        id += idm_base;

    for(i = idm_base; i < (int)(idm_base + nMaxDevices); i++)
        if(i == (int)id)
        {
            //--------------------------------------------------
            // close the currently open output device
            //--------------------------------------------------
            MidiOut->Reset();
            MidiOut->Close();

            //--------------------------------------------------
            // open midi out for use
            //--------------------------------------------------
            if(id == MapperID)
                ItsOpen = MidiOut->Open((WORD)MIDI_MAPPER);
            else
                ItsOpen = MidiOut->Open(id - idm_base);

            Menu->CheckMenuItem(i, (ItsOpen ? MF_CHECKED : MF_UNCHECKED));
        }
        else
            Menu->CheckMenuItem(i, MF_UNCHECKED);

    return TRUE;
}
```

# APPENDIX D

# *MidiSpy, SxLib, and MaxSeq Source Code*

# MidiSpy

## MidiSpy App

```
// MidiSpy.h : main header file for the MIDISPY application

#ifndef __AFXWIN_H__
    #error include 'stdafx.h' before including this file for PCH
#endif

#include "resource.h"          // main symbols

/////////////////////////////////////////////////////////////////////////
// CMidiSpyApp:
// See MidiSpy.cpp for the implementation of this class

class CMidiSpyApp : public CWinApp
{
public:
    WORD MaxMidiVersion;

    CMidiSpyApp();

// Overrides
    // ClassWizard generated virtual function overrides
    //{{AFX_VIRTUAL(CMidiSpyApp)
    public:
    virtual BOOL InitInstance();
    //}}AFX_VIRTUAL

// Implementation

    //{{AFX_MSG(CMidiSpyApp)
    afx_msg void OnAppAbout();
        // NOTE - the ClassWizard will add and remove member functions here.
        //    DO NOT EDIT what you see in these blocks of generated code !
    //}}AFX_MSG
    DECLARE_MESSAGE_MAP()
};


// MidiSpy.cpp : Defines the class behaviors for the application.
#include "stdafx.h"
#include "MidiSpy.h"

#include "MaxMidi.h"

#include "MainFrm.h"
#include "MidiSpyDoc.h"
#include "MidiSpyView.h"

#ifdef _DEBUG
#define new DEBUG_NEW
#undef THIS_FILE
static char THIS_FILE[] = __FILE__;
#endif
/////////////////////////////////////////////////////////////////////////
// CMidiSpyApp

BEGIN_MESSAGE_MAP(CMidiSpyApp, CWinApp)
    //{{AFX_MSG_MAP(CMidiSpyApp)
    ON_COMMAND(ID_APP_ABOUT, OnAppAbout)
        // NOTE - the ClassWizard will add and remove mapping macros here.
        //    DO NOT EDIT what you see in these blocks of generated code!
    //}}AFX_MSG_MAP
    // Standard file based document commands
    ON_COMMAND(ID_FILE_NEW, CWinApp::OnFileNew)
    ON_COMMAND(ID_FILE_OPEN, CWinApp::OnFileOpen)
END_MESSAGE_MAP()
/////////////////////////////////////////////////////////////////////////
// CMidiSpyApp construction

CMidiSpyApp::CMidiSpyApp()
{
}
/////////////////////////////////////////////////////////////////////////
```

```
    // The one and only CMidiSpyApp object

CMidiSpyApp theApp;

/////////////////////////////////////////////////////////////////////////////
// CMidiSpyApp initialization

BOOL CMidiSpyApp::InitInstance()
{
    // get the version before doing anything else, since this
    // resizes the message queue
    MaxMidiVersion = GetMaxMidiVersion();

    // Standard initialization
    // If you are not using these features and wish to reduce the size
    //  of your final executable, you should remove from the following
    //  the specific initialization routines you do not need.

#ifdef _AFXDLL
    Enable3dControls();          // Call this when using MFC in a shared DLL
#else
    Enable3dControlsStatic(); // Call this when linking to MFC statically
#endif

    LoadStdProfileSettings();  // Load standard INI file options (including MRU)

    // Register the application's document templates.  Document templates
    //  serve as the connection between documents, frame windows and views.

    CSingleDocTemplate* pDocTemplate;
    pDocTemplate = new CSingleDocTemplate(
        IDR_MAINFRAME,
        RUNTIME_CLASS(CMidiSpyDoc),
        RUNTIME_CLASS(CMainFrame),       // main SDI frame window
        RUNTIME_CLASS(CMidiSpyView));
    AddDocTemplate(pDocTemplate);

    // Parse command line for standard shell commands, DDE, file open
    CCommandLineInfo cmdInfo;
    ParseCommandLine(cmdInfo);

    // Dispatch commands specified on the command line
    if (!ProcessShellCommand(cmdInfo))
        return FALSE;

    return TRUE;
}

/////////////////////////////////////////////////////////////////////////////
// CAboutDlg dialog used for App About

class CAboutDlg : public CDialog
{
public:
    CAboutDlg();

// Dialog Data
    //{{AFX_DATA(CAboutDlg)
    enum { IDD = IDD_ABOUTBOX };
    CString m_Version;
    //}}AFX_DATA

    // ClassWizard generated virtual function overrides
    //{{AFX_VIRTUAL(CAboutDlg)
    protected:
    virtual void DoDataExchange(CDataExchange* pDX);     // DDX/DDV support
    //}}AFX_VIRTUAL

// Implementation
protected:
    //{{AFX_MSG(CAboutDlg)
        // No message handlers
    //}}AFX_MSG
    DECLARE_MESSAGE_MAP()
};

CAboutDlg::CAboutDlg() : CDialog(CAboutDlg::IDD)
{
    //{{AFX_DATA_INIT(CAboutDlg)
    m_Version = _T("");
    //}}AFX_DATA_INIT
}

void CAboutDlg::DoDataExchange(CDataExchange* pDX)
{
```

```
        CDialog::DoDataExchange(pDX);
        //{{AFX_DATA_MAP(CAboutDlg)
        DDX_Text(pDX, IDC_VERSION, m_Version);
        DDV_MaxChars(pDX, m_Version, 40);
        //}}AFX_DATA_MAP
}
BEGIN_MESSAGE_MAP(CAboutDlg, CDialog)
        //{{AFX_MSG_MAP(CAboutDlg)
            // No message handlers
        //}}AFX_MSG_MAP
END_MESSAGE_MAP()

// App command to run the dialog
void CMidiSpyApp::OnAppAbout()
{
        CAboutDlg aboutDlg;

        // set the version string
        aboutDlg.m_Version.Format("MaxMidi DLL V%d.%02.2d", HIBYTE(MaxMidiVersion),
                                    LOBYTE(MaxMidiVersion));

        aboutDlg.DoModal();
}
```

# MainFrm

```
// MainFrm.h : interface of the CMainFrame class

class CMainFrame : public CFrameWnd
{
protected: // create from serialization only
    CMainFrame();
    DECLARE_DYNCREATE(CMainFrame)

// Attributes
public:

// Operations
public:

// Overrides
    // ClassWizard generated virtual function overrides
    //{{AFX_VIRTUAL(CMainFrame)
    public:
    virtual BOOL PreCreateWindow(CREATESTRUCT& cs);
    //}}AFX_VIRTUAL

// Implementation
public:
    virtual ~CMainFrame();
#ifdef _DEBUG
    virtual void AssertValid() const;
    virtual void Dump(CDumpContext& dc) const;
#endif

protected:  // control bar embedded members
    CStatusBar  m_wndStatusBar;
    CToolBar    m_wndToolBar;

// Generated message map functions
protected:
    //{{AFX_MSG(CMainFrame)
    afx_msg int OnCreate(LPCREATESTRUCT lpCreateStruct);
    //}}AFX_MSG
    DECLARE_MESSAGE_MAP()
};


//MainFrm.cpp : implementation of the CMainFrame class

#include "stdafx.h"
#include "MidiSpy.h"

#include "MaxMidi.h"
#include "MainFrm.h"

#ifdef _DEBUG
#define new DEBUG_NEW
#undef THIS_FILE
static char THIS_FILE[] = __FILE__;
#endif
```

```
////////////////////////////////////////////////////////////////////////
// CMainFrame

IMPLEMENT_DYNCREATE(CMainFrame, CFrameWnd)

BEGIN_MESSAGE_MAP(CMainFrame, CFrameWnd)
    //{{AFX_MSG_MAP(CMainFrame)
    ON_WM_CREATE()
    //}}AFX_MSG_MAP
END_MESSAGE_MAP()
////////////////////////////////////////////////////////////////////////
// CMainFrame construction/destruction

CMainFrame::CMainFrame()
{
}

CMainFrame::~CMainFrame()
{
}

int CMainFrame::OnCreate(LPCREATESTRUCT lpCreateStruct)
{
    if (CFrameWnd::OnCreate(lpCreateStruct) == -1)
        return -1;

    // since we don't have separate ON_UPDATE_COMMAND_UI handlers
    // or ON_COMMAND handlers for the device menu items we must
    // clear this flag so that the Input Device and Output Device
    // menu items are all enabled
    m_bAutoMenuEnable = FALSE;
    return 0;
}

BOOL CMainFrame::PreCreateWindow(CREATESTRUCT& cs)
{
    // TODO: Modify the Window class or styles here by modifying
    //  the CREATESTRUCT cs

    return CFrameWnd::PreCreateWindow(cs);
}
////////////////////////////////////////////////////////////////////////
// CMainFrame diagnostics

#ifdef _DEBUG
void CMainFrame::AssertValid() const
{
    CFrameWnd::AssertValid();
}

void CMainFrame::Dump(CDumpContext& dc) const
{
    CFrameWnd::Dump(dc);
}

#endif //_DEBUG
```

## MidiSpyDoc

```
// MidiSpyDoc.h : interface of the CMidiSpyDoc class

class CMidiSpyDoc : public CDocument
{
protected: // create from serialization only
    CMidiSpyDoc();
    DECLARE_DYNCREATE(CMidiSpyDoc)

// Attributes
public:

// Operations
public:

// Overrides
    // ClassWizard generated virtual function overrides
    //{{AFX_VIRTUAL(CMidiSpyDoc)
    public:
    virtual BOOL OnNewDocument();
    virtual void Serialize(CArchive& ar);
```

```cpp
    //}}AFX_VIRTUAL

// Implementation
public:
    virtual ~CMidiSpyDoc();
#ifdef _DEBUG
    virtual void AssertValid() const;
    virtual void Dump(CDumpContext& dc) const;
#endif

protected:

// Generated message map functions
protected:
    //{{AFX_MSG(CMidiSpyDoc)
        // NOTE - the ClassWizard will add and remove member functions here.
        //      DO NOT EDIT what you see in these blocks of generated code !
    //}}AFX_MSG
    DECLARE_MESSAGE_MAP()
};


// MidiSpyDoc.cpp : implementation of the CMidiSpyDoc class

#include "stdafx.h"
#include "MidiSpy.h"

#include "MidiSpyDoc.h"

#ifdef _DEBUG
#define new DEBUG_NEW
#undef THIS_FILE
static char THIS_FILE[] = __FILE__;
#endif
/////////////////////////////////////////////////////////////////////////////
// CMidiSpyDoc

IMPLEMENT_DYNCREATE(CMidiSpyDoc, CDocument)

BEGIN_MESSAGE_MAP(CMidiSpyDoc, CDocument)
    //{{AFX_MSG_MAP(CMidiSpyDoc)
        // NOTE - the ClassWizard will add and remove mapping macros here.
        //      DO NOT EDIT what you see in these blocks of generated code!
    //}}AFX_MSG_MAP
END_MESSAGE_MAP()
/////////////////////////////////////////////////////////////////////////////
// CMidiSpyDoc construction/destruction

CMidiSpyDoc::CMidiSpyDoc()
{

}

CMidiSpyDoc::~CMidiSpyDoc()
{
}

BOOL CMidiSpyDoc::OnNewDocument()
{
    if (!CDocument::OnNewDocument())
        return FALSE;

    return TRUE;
}
/////////////////////////////////////////////////////////////////////////////
// CMidiSpyDoc serialization

void CMidiSpyDoc::Serialize(CArchive& ar)
{
    if (ar.IsStoring())
    {
    }
    else
    {
    }
}
```

```
///////////////////////////////////////////////////////////////////////////////
// CMidiSpyDoc diagnostics

#ifdef _DEBUG
void CMidiSpyDoc::AssertValid() const
{
    CDocument::AssertValid();
}

void CMidiSpyDoc::Dump(CDumpContext& dc) const
{
    CDocument::Dump(dc);
}
#endif //_DEBUG
```

## MidiSpyView

```
#include "MaxMidi.h"
#include "MyMidiIn.h"

// MidiSpyView.h : interface of the CMidiSpyView class

class CMidiSpyView : public CView
{
protected: // create from serialization only
    CMidiSpyView();
    DECLARE_DYNCREATE(CMidiSpyView)

// Attributes
public:
    CMidiSpyDoc* GetDocument();

    // MaxMidi Input and Output Device Objects
    CMaxMidiOut MidiOut;
    MyMidiIn MidiIn;

    // Input and Output Device Menus
    CMidiInDeviceMenu InMenu;
    CMidiOutDeviceMenu OutMenu;

// Operations
public:

// Overrides
    // ClassWizard generated virtual function overrides
    //{{AFX_VIRTUAL(CMidiSpyView)
    public:
    virtual void OnDraw(CDC* pDC);  // overridden to draw this view
    virtual BOOL PreCreateWindow(CREATESTRUCT& cs);
    virtual BOOL OnCmdMsg(UINT nID, int nCode, void* pExtra, AFX_CMDHANDLERINFO*
pHandlerInfo);
    //}}AFX_VIRTUAL

// Implementation
public:
    virtual ~CMidiSpyView();
#ifdef _DEBUG
    virtual void AssertValid() const;
    virtual void Dump(CDumpContext& dc) const;
#endif

protected:

// Generated message map functions
protected:
    //{{AFX_MSG(CMidiSpyView)
    afx_msg int OnCreate(LPCREATESTRUCT lpCreateStruct);
    afx_msg void OnRaw();
    afx_msg void OnTrace();
    afx_msg void OnThruoff();
    afx_msg void OnThruon();
    afx_msg void OnUpdateThruon(CCmdUI* pCmdUI);
    afx_msg void OnUpdateThruoff(CCmdUI* pCmdUI);
    afx_msg void OnUpdateRaw(CCmdUI* pCmdUI);
    afx_msg void OnUpdateTrace(CCmdUI* pCmdUI);
    //}}AFX_MSG
    DECLARE_MESSAGE_MAP()
};
```

```cpp
#ifndef _DEBUG  // debug version in MidiSpyView.cpp
inline CMidiSpyDoc* CMidiSpyView::GetDocument()
    { return (CMidiSpyDoc*)m_pDocument; }
#endif


// MidiSpyView.cpp : implementation of the CMidiSpyView class

#include "stdafx.h"
#include "MidiSpy.h"

#include "MidiSpyDoc.h"
#include "MidiSpyView.h"

#ifdef _DEBUG
#define new DEBUG_NEW
#undef THIS_FILE
static char THIS_FILE[] = __FILE__;
#endif
/////////////////////////////////////////////////////////////////////////////
// CMidiSpyView

IMPLEMENT_DYNCREATE(CMidiSpyView, CView)

BEGIN_MESSAGE_MAP(CMidiSpyView, CView)
    //{{AFX_MSG_MAP(CMidiSpyView)
    ON_WM_CREATE()
    ON_COMMAND(IDM_RAW, OnRaw)
    ON_COMMAND(IDM_TRACE, OnTrace)
    ON_COMMAND(IDM_THRUOFF, OnThruoff)
    ON_COMMAND(IDM_THRUON, OnThruon)
    ON_UPDATE_COMMAND_UI(IDM_THRUON, OnUpdateThruon)
    ON_UPDATE_COMMAND_UI(IDM_THRUOFF, OnUpdateThruoff)
    ON_UPDATE_COMMAND_UI(IDM_RAW, OnUpdateRaw)
    ON_UPDATE_COMMAND_UI(IDM_TRACE, OnUpdateTrace)
    //}}AFX_MSG_MAP
END_MESSAGE_MAP()
/////////////////////////////////////////////////////////////////////////////
// CMidiSpyView construction/destruction

CMidiSpyView::CMidiSpyView()
{
}

CMidiSpyView::~CMidiSpyView()
{
}

BOOL CMidiSpyView::PreCreateWindow(CREATESTRUCT& cs)
{
    // TODO: Modify the Window class or styles here by modifying
    //  the CREATESTRUCT cs

    return CView::PreCreateWindow(cs);
}
/////////////////////////////////////////////////////////////////////////////
// CMidiSpyView drawing

void CMidiSpyView::OnDraw(CDC* pDC)
{
    CMidiSpyDoc* pDoc = GetDocument();
    ASSERT_VALID(pDoc);

}
/////////////////////////////////////////////////////////////////////////////
// CMidiSpyView diagnostics

#ifdef _DEBUG
void CMidiSpyView::AssertValid() const
{
    CView::AssertValid();
}

void CMidiSpyView::Dump(CDumpContext& dc) const
{
    CView::Dump(dc);
}

CMidiSpyDoc* CMidiSpyView::GetDocument() // non-debug version is inline
{
```

```
        ASSERT(m_pDocument->IsKindOf(RUNTIME_CLASS(CMidiSpyDoc)));
        return (CMidiSpyDoc*)m_pDocument;
}
#endif //_DEBUG

/////////////////////////////////////////////////////////////////////////////
// CMidiSpyView message handlers

int CMidiSpyView::OnCreate(LPCREATESTRUCT lpCreateStruct)
{
        if (CView::OnCreate(lpCreateStruct) == -1)
            return -1;

        // open the first input and output devices
        MidiIn.Attach(GetSafeHwnd());
        MidiOut.Attach(GetSafeHwnd());

        // get the parent menu
        CMenu* ParentMenu = GetParent()->GetMenu();

        // create the device menus and select the first devices
        InMenu.Create(ParentMenu->GetSafeHmenu(), ParentMenu->GetMenuItemCount() - 1,
                    "&Input Device", IDM_INPUT);
        InMenu.Attach(&MidiIn);
        InMenu.SelectDevice(0);

        OutMenu.Create(ParentMenu->GetSafeHmenu(), ParentMenu->GetMenuItemCount() - 1,
                    "&Output Device", IDM_OUTPUT);
        OutMenu.Attach(&MidiOut);
        OutMenu.SelectDevice(0);
        MidiIn.SetEchoOutput(&MidiOut);

        return 0;
}

BOOL CMidiSpyView::OnCmdMsg(UINT nID, int nCode, void* pExtra, AFX_CMDHANDLERINFO*
pHandlerInfo)
{
        // check to see if one of the device menus has been selected
        if(nCode == 0)
        {
            InMenu.SelectDevice(nID);

            // if it's an output device, change the echo device too
            if(OutMenu.SelectDevice(nID))
                MidiIn.SetEchoOutput(&MidiOut);
        }

        return CView::OnCmdMsg(nID, nCode, pExtra, pHandlerInfo);
}

void CMidiSpyView::OnRaw()
{
        MidiIn.SetDisplayMode(RAWMODE);
}

void CMidiSpyView::OnTrace()
{
        MidiIn.SetDisplayMode(TRACEMODE);
}

void CMidiSpyView::OnThruoff()
{
        MidiIn.SetThru(FALSE);
}

void CMidiSpyView::OnThruon()
{
        MidiIn.SetThru(TRUE);
}

void CMidiSpyView::OnUpdateThruon(CCmdUI* pCmdUI)
{
        pCmdUI->SetCheck(MidiIn.GetThru());
}

void CMidiSpyView::OnUpdateThruoff(CCmdUI* pCmdUI)
{
        pCmdUI->SetCheck(!MidiIn.GetThru());
}

void CMidiSpyView::OnUpdateRaw(CCmdUI* pCmdUI)
{
```

```
    pCmdUI->SetCheck(MidiIn.GetDisplayMode() == RAWMODE);
}
void CMidiSpyView::OnUpdateTrace(CCmdUI* pCmdUI)
{
    pCmdUI->SetCheck(MidiIn.GetDisplayMode() == TRACEMODE);
}
```

# MyMidiIn

```
#ifndef __MYMIDIIN__
#define __MYMIDIIN__
//==========================================================================
//   MyMidiIn Class
//==========================================================================
class MyMidiIn : public CMaxMidiIn
{
public:
    int ThisX;
    int ThisY;

    CMaxMidiOut* EchoOut;
    int DisplayMode;
    BOOL ThruEnabled;

public:
    MyMidiIn();
    void DisplayTrace(CWnd* cWnd, LPMIDIEVENT mMsg);
    void DisplayRawMidi(CWnd* cWnd, LPMIDIEVENT mMsg);
    void SetEchoOutput(CMaxMidiOut* moDevice) { EchoOut = moDevice; };
    void SetDisplayMode(int mode) { DisplayMode = mode; };
    void SetThru(BOOL thru) { ThruEnabled = thru; };
    BOOL GetThru(void) { return ThruEnabled; };
    int GetDisplayMode(void) { return DisplayMode; };

// Overrides
    // ClassWizard generated virtual function overrides
    //{{AFX_VIRTUAL(MyMidiIn)
    virtual BOOL ProcessMidiData(LPMIDIEVENT lpEvent);
    //}}AFX_VIRTUAL

protected:
    //{{AFX_MSG(MyMidiIn)
    //}}AFX_MSG
    DECLARE_MESSAGE_MAP()
};

#define RAWMODE   0
#define TRACEMODE 1
#endif //!__MYMIDIIN__

//==========================================================================
//   MyMidiIn Class
//==========================================================================
#include "stdafx.h"
#include "MaxMidi.h"
#include "MyMidiIn.h"

BEGIN_MESSAGE_MAP(MyMidiIn, CMaxMidiIn)
    //{{AFX_MSG_MAP(MyMidiIn)
    //}}AFX_MSG_MAP
END_MESSAGE_MAP()

// text for each status for interpreted trace
char msgtext[][22] = { "Note Off", "Note On", "Poly Key Pressure",
            "Control Change", "Program Change", "Channel Pressure",
            "Pitch Bend", "System Exclusive", "MTC Quarter Frame",
            "Song Position Pointer", "Song Select", "Undefined",
            "Undefined", "Tune Request", "EOX", "Timing Clock",
            "Undefined", "Start", "Continue", "Stop", "Undefined",
            "Active Sensing", "System Reset" };

// text for each data1 byte for interpreted trace
char data1text[][10] = { "Note", "Note", "Note", "Control #", "Program #",
            "Pressure", "LSB", "", "Value", "LSB", "Song #",
            "", "", "", "", "", "", "", "", "", "", "", "" };

// text for each data2 byte for interpreted trace
char data2text[][9] = { "Velocity", "Velocity", "Pressure", "Value", "", "",
            "MSB", "", "", "MSB",
```

```
                  "", "", "", "", "", "", "", "", "", "", "", "", "" };
// number of data bytes for each status.  Sysex 0xF0 shows 3 since it is always in
data1.
static int msglen[24] = { 2, 2, 2, 2, 1, 1, 2, 0, 1, 2, 1, 0, 0, 0, 0, 0, 0, 0, 0, 0, 0,
0, 0, 3 };

//----------------------------------------------------------------------------
//  Constructor
//----------------------------------------------------------------------------
MyMidiIn::MyMidiIn()
{
    EchoOut = NULL;
    DisplayMode = RAWMODE;
    ThruEnabled = FALSE;
    ThisX = ThisY = 0;
}

//----------------------------------------------------------------------------
//  DisplayTrace
//----------------------------------------------------------------------------
void MyMidiIn::DisplayTrace(CWnd* cWnd, LPMIDIEVENT mMsg)
{
    int index;                  // index corresponding to this status. 0=80, 1=90, etc.
    CDC* cDc;
    CSize TextSize;             // text size structure for char string
    char text[80];              // string to display in window
    RECT rect;                  // rectangle corresponding to window dimensions
    RECT cleararea;             // rectangle corresponding to line to be cleared and
overwritten

    // get the device context and current rectangle size
    cDc = cWnd->GetDC();
    cWnd->GetClientRect(&rect);

    // sysex data is represented in the MidiEvent structure as a
    // status byte of 0xF0 with the data1 element set to the
    // particular byte of the sysex.  Other messages are passed
    // in the MidiEvent structure as status, <data1>, <data2>.

    // get index corresponding to the message status
    // index = 0 for 0x80, 1 for 0x90 ... 8 for 0xF0, 9 for 0xF1...22 for 0xFF
    // account for eox in sysex
    if(mMsg->data1 > 0x7f)
        index = mMsg->data1;
    else
        index = mMsg->status;

    if((index & 0xF0) < SYSEX)                          // is it a channel message?
        index = ((index & 0xF0) >> 4) - 8;
    else                                                // or a sysex data?
        if((index == 0xF0) && (mMsg->data1 < 0x80))
            index = 23;
        else                                            // or system message
            index = (index & 0x0F) + 7;
    // build text string, based on index
    switch(msglen[index])
    {
        case 0:                                         // no data bytes
            wsprintf(text, "%s: time = %lu", msgtext[index], mMsg->time);
            break;

        case 1:                                         // one data byte
            wsprintf(text, "%s: %s = %d time = %lu", msgtext[index], data1text[index],
                    mMsg->data1, mMsg->time);
            break;

        case 2:                                         // two data bytes
            wsprintf(text, "%s: %s = %d  %s = %d time = %lu", msgtext[index],
                    data1text[index], mMsg->data1, data2text[index], mMsg->data2,
mMsg->time);
            break;

        case 3:      // sysex data, no timestamp
            wsprintf(text, "Sysex Data = %2.2Xh", mMsg->data1);
            break;
    }
    // clear the current line and write the new text
    TextSize = cDc->GetTextExtent(text, strlen(text));
    cleararea.left = rect.left;
```

```
        cleararea.right = rect.right;
        cleararea.top = ThisY;
        cleararea.bottom = ThisY + TextSize.cy;
        cDc->ExtTextOut(ThisX, ThisY, ETO_OPAQUE, (LPRECT)&cleararea, (LPSTR)text,
                       strlen(text), NULL);

        // find the new x and y
        // always start at left of screen, if at bottom of screen, go to top
        ThisX = 0;
        ThisY += TextSize.cy;
        if(ThisY > rect.bottom)
            ThisY = 0;

        cWnd->ReleaseDC(cDc);
}
//-----------------------------------------------------------------------------
// This function displays the midi data in raw hexadecimal format in
// the application window.
//-----------------------------------------------------------------------------
void MyMidiIn::DisplayRawMidi(CWnd* cWnd, LPMIDIEVENT mMsg)
{
    char text[30];            // string to display in window
    RECT rect;                // rectangle structure
    int index;                // index corresponding to this status. 0=80, 1=90, etc.
    CDC* cDc;
    CSize TextSize;           // text size structure for char string

    // get the device context and current rectangle size
    cDc = cWnd->GetDC();
    cWnd->GetClientRect(&rect);

    // sysex data is represented in the MidiEvent structure as a
    // status byte of 0xF0 with the data1 element set to the particular byte.
    // Other messages are passed in the MidiEvent structure as status, <data1>, <data2>.

    // get index corresponding to the message status
    // index = 0 for 0x80, 1 for 0x90 ... 8 for 0xF0, 9 for 0xF1...22 for 0xFF
    // account for eox in sysex
    if(mMsg->data1 > 0x7f)
        index = mMsg->status = mMsg->data1;
    else
        index = mMsg->status;

    if((index & 0xF0) < SYSEX)                           // is it a channel message?
        index = ((index & 0xF0) >> 4) - 8;
    else                                                 // or a sysex data?
        if((index == SYSEX) && (mMsg->data1 < 0x80))
            index = 23;
        else                                             // or system message
            index = (index & 0x0F) + 7;

    // build text string, based on index
    switch(msglen[index])
    {
        case 0:                                    // no data bytes
            wsprintf(text, "%2.2X ", mMsg->status);
            break;

        case 1:                                    // one data byte
            wsprintf(text, "%2.2X %2.2X ", mMsg->status, mMsg->data1);
            break;

        case 2:                                    // two data bytes
            wsprintf(text, "%2.2X %2.2X %2.2X ", mMsg->status, mMsg->data1,
                    mMsg->data2);
            break;

        case 3:                                // sysex -- status and data in data1
            wsprintf(text, "%2.2X ", mMsg->data1);
            break;
    }
    // print the string
    cDc->TextOut(ThisX, ThisY, text, strlen(text));

    // find the new x and y
    // if at right of screen, go to left; if at bottom, go to top
    TextSize = cDc->GetTextExtent(text, strlen(text));

    ThisX += TextSize.cx;
    if(ThisX > rect.right)
    {
```

```
            ThisX = 0;
            ThisY += TextSize.cy;
            if(ThisY > rect.bottom)
                ThisY = 0;
        }

    cWnd->ReleaseDC(cDc);
}
///////////////////////////////////////////////////////////////////////////
// MyMidiIn virtual functions
//-------------------------------------------------------------------------
//  ProcessMidiData
//-------------------------------------------------------------------------
BOOL MyMidiIn::ProcessMidiData(LPMIDIEVENT lpEvent)
{
    // display the data, either as hex or trace
    if(DisplayMode == RAWMODE)
        DisplayRawMidi(GetOwner(), lpEvent);
    else
        DisplayTrace(GetOwner(), lpEvent);

        if(EchoOut && ThruEnabled)
            EchoOut->Put(lpEvent);

    return TRUE;
}
```

# SxLib

## SxLib App

```
// SxLib.h : main header file for the SXLIB application

#ifndef __AFXWIN_H__
    #error include 'stdafx.h' before including this file for PCH
#endif

#include "resource.h"         // main symbols

///////////////////////////////////////////////////////////////////////////
// CSxLibApp:
// See SxLib.cpp for the implementation of this class
//
class CSxLibApp : public CWinApp
{
public:
    CSxLibApp();
    WORD MaxMidiVersion;

// Overrides
    // ClassWizard generated virtual function overrides
    //{{AFX_VIRTUAL(CSxLibApp)
    public:
    virtual BOOL InitInstance();
    //}}AFX_VIRTUAL

// Implementation

    //{{AFX_MSG(CSxLibApp)
    afx_msg void OnAppAbout();
    //}}AFX_MSG
    DECLARE_MESSAGE_MAP()
};


// SxLib.cpp : Defines the class behaviors for the application.

#include "stdafx.h"
#include "SxLib.h"

#include "MainFrm.h"
#include "SxLibDoc.h"
#include "SxLibView.h"
```

```cpp
#ifdef _DEBUG
#define new DEBUG_NEW
#undef THIS_FILE
static char THIS_FILE[] = __FILE__;
#endif
/////////////////////////////////////////////////////////////////////////
// CSxLibApp

BEGIN_MESSAGE_MAP(CSxLibApp, CWinApp)
    //{{AFX_MSG_MAP(CSxLibApp)
    ON_COMMAND(ID_APP_ABOUT, OnAppAbout)
    //}}AFX_MSG_MAP
    // Standard file based document commands
    ON_COMMAND(ID_FILE_NEW, CWinApp::OnFileNew)
    ON_COMMAND(ID_FILE_OPEN, CWinApp::OnFileOpen)
END_MESSAGE_MAP()
/////////////////////////////////////////////////////////////////////////
// CSxLibApp construction

CSxLibApp::CSxLibApp()
{
}
/////////////////////////////////////////////////////////////////////////
// The one and only CSxLibApp object

CSxLibApp theApp;
/////////////////////////////////////////////////////////////////////////
// CSxLibApp initialization

BOOL CSxLibApp::InitInstance()
{
    // get the version before doing anything else, since this
    // resizes the message queue
    MaxMidiVersion = GetMaxMidiVersion();

    // Standard initialization

#ifdef _AFXDLL
    Enable3dControls();             // Call this when using MFC in a shared DLL
#else
    Enable3dControlsStatic(); // Call this when linking to MFC statically
#endif

    LoadStdProfileSettings();  // Load standard INI file options (including MRU)

    // Register document templates

    CSingleDocTemplate* pDocTemplate;
    pDocTemplate = new CSingleDocTemplate(
        IDR_MAINFRAME,
        RUNTIME_CLASS(CSxLibDoc),
        RUNTIME_CLASS(CMainFrame),          // main SDI frame window
        RUNTIME_CLASS(CSxLibView));
    AddDocTemplate(pDocTemplate);

    // Parse command line for standard shell commands, DDE, file open
    CCommandLineInfo cmdInfo;
    ParseCommandLine(cmdInfo);

    // Dispatch commands specified on the command line
    if (!ProcessShellCommand(cmdInfo))
        return FALSE;

    return TRUE;
}
/////////////////////////////////////////////////////////////////////////
// CAboutDlg dialog used for App About

class CAboutDlg : public CDialog
{
public:
    CAboutDlg();

// Dialog Data
    //{{AFX_DATA(CAboutDlg)
    enum { IDD = IDD_ABOUTBOX };
    CString m_Version;
    //}}AFX_DATA

    // ClassWizard generated virtual function overrides
```

```
    //{{AFX_VIRTUAL(CAboutDlg)
    protected:
    virtual void DoDataExchange(CDataExchange* pDX);      // DDX/DDV support
    //}}AFX_VIRTUAL
// Implementation
protected:
    //{{AFX_MSG(CAboutDlg)
        // No message handlers
    //}}AFX_MSG
    DECLARE_MESSAGE_MAP()
};
CAboutDlg::CAboutDlg() : CDialog(CAboutDlg::IDD)
{
    //{{AFX_DATA_INIT(CAboutDlg)
    m_Version = _T("");
    //}}AFX_DATA_INIT
}

void CAboutDlg::DoDataExchange(CDataExchange* pDX)
{
    CDialog::DoDataExchange(pDX);
    //{{AFX_DATA_MAP(CAboutDlg)
    DDX_Text(pDX, IDC_VERSION, m_Version);
    DDV_MaxChars(pDX, m_Version, 40);
    //}}AFX_DATA_MAP
}

BEGIN_MESSAGE_MAP(CAboutDlg, CDialog)
    //{{AFX_MSG_MAP(CAboutDlg)
        // No message handlers
    //}}AFX_MSG_MAP
END_MESSAGE_MAP()

// App command to run the dialog
void CSxLibApp::OnAppAbout()
{
    CAboutDlg aboutDlg;

    // set the version string
    aboutDlg.m_Version.Format("MaxMidi DLL V%d.%02.2d", HIBYTE(MaxMidiVersion),
                    LOBYTE(MaxMidiVersion));

    aboutDlg.DoModal();
}
```

## MainFrm

```
// MainFrm.h : interface of the CMainFrame class

class CMainFrame : public CFrameWnd
{
protected: // create from serialization only
    CMainFrame();
    DECLARE_DYNCREATE(CMainFrame)

// Attributes
public:

// Operations
public:

// Overrides
    // ClassWizard generated virtual function overrides
    //{{AFX_VIRTUAL(CMainFrame)
    virtual BOOL PreCreateWindow(CREATESTRUCT& cs);
    //}}AFX_VIRTUAL

// Implementation
public:
    virtual ~CMainFrame();
#ifdef _DEBUG
    virtual void AssertValid() const;
    virtual void Dump(CDumpContext& dc) const;
#endif

// Generated message map functions
protected:
    //{{AFX_MSG(CMainFrame)
```

```
    afx_msg int OnCreate(LPCREATESTRUCT lpCreateStruct);
    //}}AFX_MSG
    DECLARE_MESSAGE_MAP()
};


// MainFrm.cpp : implementation of the CMainFrame class

#include "stdafx.h"
#include "SxLib.h"

#include "MainFrm.h"

#ifdef _DEBUG
#define new DEBUG_NEW
#undef THIS_FILE
static char THIS_FILE[] = __FILE__;
#endif
/////////////////////////////////////////////////////////////////////////////
// CMainFrame

IMPLEMENT_DYNCREATE(CMainFrame, CFrameWnd)

BEGIN_MESSAGE_MAP(CMainFrame, CFrameWnd)
    //{{AFX_MSG_MAP(CMainFrame)
    ON_WM_CREATE()
    //}}AFX_MSG_MAP
END_MESSAGE_MAP()
/////////////////////////////////////////////////////////////////////////////
// CMainFrame construction/destruction

CMainFrame::CMainFrame()
{
}

CMainFrame::~CMainFrame()
{
}

BOOL CMainFrame::PreCreateWindow(CREATESTRUCT& cs)
{
    return CFrameWnd::PreCreateWindow(cs);
}
/////////////////////////////////////////////////////////////////////////////
// CMainFrame diagnostics

#ifdef _DEBUG
void CMainFrame::AssertValid() const
{
    CFrameWnd::AssertValid();
}

void CMainFrame::Dump(CDumpContext& dc) const
{
    CFrameWnd::Dump(dc);
}

#endif //_DEBUG
/////////////////////////////////////////////////////////////////////////////
// CMainFrame message handlers

int CMainFrame::OnCreate(LPCREATESTRUCT lpCreateStruct)
{
    if (CFrameWnd::OnCreate(lpCreateStruct) == -1)
        return -1;

    // since we don't have separate ON_UPDATE_COMMAND_UI handlers
    // or ON_COMMAND handlers for the device menu items we must
    // clear this flag so that the Input Device and Output Device
    // menu items are all enabled
    m_bAutoMenuEnable = FALSE;
    return 0;
}
```

# SxLibDoc

```
// SxLibDoc.h : interface of the CSxLibDoc class

class CSxLibDoc : public CDocument
{
protected: // create from serialization only
    CSxLibDoc();
    DECLARE_DYNCREATE(CSxLibDoc)

// Attributes
public:
    LPBYTE pData;
    DWORD cbDataSize;
    DWORD cbNumBytes;

// Operations
public:

// Overrides
    // ClassWizard generated virtual function overrides
    //{{AFX_VIRTUAL(CSxLibDoc)
    public:
    virtual BOOL OnNewDocument();
    virtual void Serialize(CArchive& ar);
    virtual BOOL OnOpenDocument(LPCTSTR lpszPathName);
    virtual BOOL OnSaveDocument(LPCTSTR lpszPathName);
    //}}AFX_VIRTUAL

// Implementation
public:
    virtual ~CSxLibDoc();
#ifdef _DEBUG
    virtual void AssertValid() const;
    virtual void Dump(CDumpContext& dc) const;
#endif

protected:

// Generated message map functions
protected:
    //{{AFX_MSG(CSxLibDoc)
    //}}AFX_MSG
    DECLARE_MESSAGE_MAP()
};


// SxLibDoc.cpp : implementation of the CSxLibDoc class

#include "stdafx.h"
#include "SxLib.h"

#include "SxLibDoc.h"

#ifdef _DEBUG
#define new DEBUG_NEW
#undef THIS_FILE
static char THIS_FILE[] = __FILE__;
#endif
/////////////////////////////////////////////////////////////////////////////
// CSxLibDoc

IMPLEMENT_DYNCREATE(CSxLibDoc, CDocument)

BEGIN_MESSAGE_MAP(CSxLibDoc, CDocument)
    //{{AFX_MSG_MAP(CSxLibDoc)
    //}}AFX_MSG_MAP
END_MESSAGE_MAP()
/////////////////////////////////////////////////////////////////////////////
// CSxLibDoc construction/destruction

CSxLibDoc::CSxLibDoc()
{
    pData = NULL;
    cbDataSize = 0;
    cbNumBytes = 0;
}

CSxLibDoc::~CSxLibDoc()
{
    // free any existing buffer
```

```
        if(pData)
            GlobalFree(GlobalHandle(pData));
}
BOOL CSxLibDoc::OnNewDocument()
{
    if (!CDocument::OnNewDocument())
        return FALSE;

    // free any existing buffer
    if(pData)
        GlobalFree(GlobalHandle(pData));

    // allocate a starting buffer to receive the sysex data
    // this buffer will grow as needed, in 8K chunks
    cbDataSize = 8192;
    cbNumBytes = 0;
    pData = (LPBYTE)GlobalLock(GlobalAlloc(GHND, cbDataSize));

    return TRUE;
}
//////////////////////////////////////////////////////////////////////
// CSxLibDoc serialization

void CSxLibDoc::Serialize(CArchive& ar)
{
    if (ar.IsStoring())
    {
    }
    else
    {
    }
}
//////////////////////////////////////////////////////////////////////
// CSxLibDoc diagnostics

#ifdef _DEBUG
void CSxLibDoc::AssertValid() const
{
    CDocument::AssertValid();
}
void CSxLibDoc::Dump(CDumpContext& dc) const
{
    CDocument::Dump(dc);
}
#endif //_DEBUG
//////////////////////////////////////////////////////////////////////
// CSxLibDoc commands

BOOL CSxLibDoc::OnOpenDocument(LPCTSTR lpszPathName)
{
    HANDLE hFile;
    DWORD numRead;

    // open the specified file
    hFile = CreateFile(lpszPathName, GENERIC_READ, 0, NULL,
                OPEN_EXISTING, FILE_ATTRIBUTE_NORMAL, NULL);

    if(hFile == NULL)
        return FALSE;

    // get the size of the data
    cbNumBytes = cbDataSize = GetFileSize(hFile, NULL);

    // allocate a buffer for the sysex
    pData = (LPBYTE)GlobalLock(GlobalAlloc(GHND, cbDataSize));

    // read the sysex
    if(!ReadFile(hFile, pData, cbDataSize, &numRead, NULL))
    {
        // error reading file -- unwind the memory allocations
        GlobalFree(GlobalHandle(pData));
        pData = NULL;
        CloseHandle(hFile);
        return FALSE;
    }
    // sysex file successfully loaded
    CloseHandle(hFile);
```

```
        return TRUE;
    }

    BOOL CSxLibDoc::OnSaveDocument(LPCTSTR lpszPathName)
    {
        HANDLE hFile;
        DWORD numWritten;

        // create the specified file
        hFile = CreateFile(lpszPathName, GENERIC_WRITE, 0, NULL,
                    CREATE_ALWAYS, FILE_ATTRIBUTE_NORMAL, NULL);

        if(hFile == NULL)
            return FALSE;

        // write the block out
        if(!WriteFile(hFile, pData, cbNumBytes, &numWritten, NULL))
        {
            // error writing file
            CloseHandle(hFile);
            return FALSE;
        }

        // file successfully written
        CloseHandle(hFile);
        return TRUE;
    }
```

# SxLibView

```
#include "MaxMidi.h"
#include "MyMidiIn.h"
#include "MyMidiOut.h"

// SxLibView.h : interface of the CSxLibView class

class CSxLibView : public CView
{
protected: // create from serialization only
    CSxLibView();
    DECLARE_DYNCREATE(CSxLibView)

// Attributes
public:
    CSxLibDoc* GetDocument();

    MyMidiOut    MidiOut;
    MyMidiIn MidiIn;

    // Input and Output Device Menus
    CMidiInDeviceMenu InMenu;
    CMidiOutDeviceMenu OutMenu;

// Operations
public:

// Overrides
    // ClassWizard generated virtual function overrides
    //{{AFX_VIRTUAL(CSxLibView)
    public:
    virtual void OnDraw(CDC* pDC);    // overridden to draw this view
    virtual BOOL PreCreateWindow(CREATESTRUCT& cs);
    protected:
    virtual BOOL OnCmdMsg(UINT nID, int nCode, void* pExtra, AFX_CMDHANDLERINFO*
pHandlerInfo);
    //}}AFX_VIRTUAL

// Implementation
public:
    virtual ~CSxLibView();
#ifdef _DEBUG
    virtual void AssertValid() const;
    virtual void Dump(CDumpContext& dc) const;
#endif

protected:

// Generated message map functions
protected:
    //{{AFX_MSG(CSxLibView)
    afx_msg int OnCreate(LPCREATESTRUCT lpCreateStruct);
```

```
        afx_msg void OnReceive();
        afx_msg void OnUpdateReceive(CCmdUI* pCmdUI);
        afx_msg void OnSend();
        afx_msg void OnUpdateSend(CCmdUI* pCmdUI);
        //}}AFX_MSG
        DECLARE_MESSAGE_MAP()
};
#ifndef _DEBUG  // debug version in SxLibView.cpp
inline CSxLibDoc* CSxLibView::GetDocument()
    { return (CSxLibDoc*)m_pDocument; }
#endif


// SxLibView.cpp : implementation of the CSxLibView class

#include "stdafx.h"
#include "SxLib.h"

#include "SxLibDoc.h"
#include "SxLibView.h"

#ifdef _DEBUG
#define new DEBUG_NEW
#undef THIS_FILE
static char THIS_FILE[] = __FILE__;
#endif
/////////////////////////////////////////////////////////////////////////
// CSxLibView

IMPLEMENT_DYNCREATE(CSxLibView, CView)

BEGIN_MESSAGE_MAP(CSxLibView, CView)
    //{{AFX_MSG_MAP(CSxLibView)
    ON_COMMAND(IDM_RECEIVE, OnReceive)
    ON_UPDATE_COMMAND_UI(IDM_RECEIVE, OnUpdateReceive)
    ON_COMMAND(IDM_SEND, OnSend)
    ON_UPDATE_COMMAND_UI(IDM_SEND, OnUpdateSend)
    ON_WM_CREATE()
    //}}AFX_MSG_MAP
END_MESSAGE_MAP()
/////////////////////////////////////////////////////////////////////////
// CSxLibView construction/destruction

CSxLibView::CSxLibView()
{
}

CSxLibView::~CSxLibView()
{
}

BOOL CSxLibView::PreCreateWindow(CREATESTRUCT& cs)
{
    return CView::PreCreateWindow(cs);
}
/////////////////////////////////////////////////////////////////////////
// CSxLibView drawing

void CSxLibView::OnDraw(CDC* pDC)
{
    CSxLibDoc* pDoc = GetDocument();
    ASSERT_VALID(pDoc);
}
/////////////////////////////////////////////////////////////////////////
// CSxLibView diagnostics

#ifdef _DEBUG
void CSxLibView::AssertValid() const
{
    CView::AssertValid();
}

void CSxLibView::Dump(CDumpContext& dc) const
{
    CView::Dump(dc);
}

CSxLibDoc* CSxLibView::GetDocument() // non-debug version is inline
{
    ASSERT(m_pDocument->IsKindOf(RUNTIME_CLASS(CSxLibDoc)));
```

```
        return (CSxLibDoc*)m_pDocument;
}
#endif //_DEBUG

/////////////////////////////////////////////////////////////////////////////
// CSxLibView message handlers

int CSxLibView::OnCreate(LPCREATESTRUCT lpCreateStruct)
{
    if (CView::OnCreate(lpCreateStruct) == -1)
        return -1;

    // attach the input and output devices to this window
    MidiOut.Attach(GetSafeHwnd());
    MidiIn.Attach(GetSafeHwnd());

    // get the parent menu
    CMenu* ParentMenu = GetParent()->GetMenu();

    // create the device menus and select the first devices
    InMenu.Create(ParentMenu->GetSafeHmenu(), ParentMenu->GetMenuItemCount() - 1,
                "&Input Device", IDM_INPUT);
    InMenu.Attach(&MidiIn);
    InMenu.SelectDevice(0);

    OutMenu.Create(ParentMenu->GetSafeHmenu(), ParentMenu->GetMenuItemCount() - 1,
                "&Output Device", IDM_OUTPUT);
    OutMenu.Attach(&MidiOut);
    OutMenu.SelectDevice(0);

    return 0;
}

BOOL CSxLibView::OnCmdMsg(UINT nID, int nCode, void* pExtra, AFX_CMDHANDLERINFO*
pHandlerInfo)
{
    // check to see if one of the device menus has been selected
    if(nCode == 0)
    {
        InMenu.SelectDevice(nID);
        OutMenu.SelectDevice(nID);
    }

    return CView::OnCmdMsg(nID, nCode, pExtra, pHandlerInfo);
}

void CSxLibView::OnReceive()
{
    CSxLibDoc* pDoc = GetDocument();

    if(MidiIn.IsReceiving())
        MidiIn.StopRx();
    else
        MidiIn.Receive(&pDoc->pData, &pDoc->cbNumBytes, &pDoc->cbDataSize);
}

void CSxLibView::OnUpdateReceive(CCmdUI* pCmdUI)
{
    CSxLibDoc* pDoc = GetDocument();
    pCmdUI->Enable(!MidiOut.IsSending());

    if(MidiIn.IsReceiving())
        pCmdUI->SetText("Stop &Receiving");
    else
        pCmdUI->SetText("&Receive Sysex");
}

void CSxLibView::OnSend()
{
    CSxLibDoc* pDoc = GetDocument();
    MidiOut.Send(pDoc->pData, pDoc->cbNumBytes);
}

void CSxLibView::OnUpdateSend(CCmdUI* pCmdUI)
{
    CSxLibDoc* pDoc = GetDocument();
    pCmdUI->Enable(!MidiIn.IsReceiving() && pDoc->cbNumBytes != 0);

    if(MidiOut.IsSending())
        pCmdUI->SetText("Stop S&ending");
    else
        pCmdUI->SetText("S&end Sysex");
}
```

# MyMidiIn

```
#ifndef __MYMIDIIN__
#define __MYMIDIIN__
//=========================================================================
//   MyMidiIn Class
//=========================================================================
class MyMidiIn : public CMaxMidiIn
{
public:
    MyMidiIn();

public:
    LPBYTE* ppData;
    LPDWORD pNumBytes;
    LPDWORD pDataSize;
    BOOL fReceiving;

    void Receive(LPBYTE* ptr, LPDWORD pRxSize, LPDWORD pBufSize);
    void StopRx(void) { fReceiving = FALSE; };
    void StoreEvent(LPMIDIEVENT lpEvent);
    BOOL IsReceiving(void) { return fReceiving; };

// Overrides
    // ClassWizard generated virtual function overrides
    //{{AFX_VIRTUAL(MyMidiIn)
    virtual BOOL ProcessMidiData(LPMIDIEVENT lpEvent);
    //}}AFX_VIRTUAL

protected:
    //{{AFX_MSG(MyMidiIn)
    //}}AFX_MSG
    DECLARE_MESSAGE_MAP()
};
#endif //!__MYMIDIIN__


//=========================================================================
//   MyMidiIn Class
//=========================================================================
#include "stdafx.h"
#include "MaxMidi.h"
#include "MyMidiIn.h"

BEGIN_MESSAGE_MAP(MyMidiIn, CMaxMidiIn)
    //{{AFX_MSG_MAP(MyMidiIn)
    //}}AFX_MSG_MAP
END_MESSAGE_MAP()

//-------------------------------------------------------------------------
//   Constructor
//-------------------------------------------------------------------------
MyMidiIn::MyMidiIn()
{
    fReceiving = FALSE;
}

/////////////////////////////////////////////////////////////////////////
// MyMidiIn virtual functions

//-------------------------------------------------------------------------
//   ProcessMidiData
//-------------------------------------------------------------------------
BOOL MyMidiIn::ProcessMidiData(LPMIDIEVENT lpEvent)
{
    // store the sysex events in the doc buffer
    if(lpEvent->status == SYSEX)
        StoreEvent(lpEvent);

    return TRUE;
}

//-------------------------------------------------------------------------
//   Receive
//-------------------------------------------------------------------------
void MyMidiIn::Receive(LPBYTE* ptr, LPDWORD pRxSize, LPDWORD pBufSize)
{
    ppData = ptr;
    pNumBytes = pRxSize;
    pDataSize = pBufSize;
```

```
        fReceiving = TRUE;
        *pNumBytes = 0;
}
//-----------------------------------------------------------------------------
//  StoreEvent
//-----------------------------------------------------------------------------
void MyMidiIn::StoreEvent(LPMIDIEVENT lpEvent)
{
        // don't do anything if not receiving
        if(!fReceiving)
            return;

        // need to grow the buffer?
        if(*pNumBytes == *pDataSize)
        {
            // grow the buffer in 8K blocks
            *pDataSize += 8192;
            *ppData = (LPBYTE)GlobalLock(GlobalReAlloc(GlobalHandle(*ppData),
                *pDataSize, GMEM_MOVEABLE));

            // did the realloc succeed?
            if(*ppData == NULL)
            {
                // Very Bad News.  Discard everything!
                *pDataSize = *pNumBytes = 0;
            }
        }

        // store the byte -- which is always in the data1 member of the MidiEvent
        // this will include the leading F0 and trailing F7
        (*ppData)[*pNumBytes] = lpEvent->data1;

        // next position in buffer
        (*pNumBytes)++;

        // stop if received the EOX
        if(lpEvent->data1 == EOX)
            StopRx();
}
```

## MyMidiOut

```
#ifndef __MYMIDIOUT__
#define __MYMIDIOUT__
//=============================================================================
//  MyMidiOut Class
//=============================================================================
class MyMidiOut : public CMaxMidiOut
{
public:
        MyMidiOut();
        void Send(LPBYTE ptr, DWORD size);
        BOOL IsSending(void) { return fSending; };
        DWORD NumSent(void) { return cbNumSent; };

public:
        BOOL fSending;
        DWORD cbNumSent;
        LPBYTE pData;
        DWORD cbDataSize;

// Overrides
        // ClassWizard generated virtual function overrides
        //{{AFX_VIRTUAL(MyMidiOut)
        virtual void ProcessOutBufferReady(void);
        //}}AFX_VIRTUAL

protected:
        //{{AFX_MSG(MyMidiOut)
        //}}AFX_MSG
        DECLARE_MESSAGE_MAP()
};
#endif //!__MYMIDIOUT__


//=============================================================================
//  MyMidiOut Class
//=============================================================================
```

```
#include "stdafx.h"
#include "MaxMidi.h"
#include "MyMidiOut.h"

BEGIN_MESSAGE_MAP(MyMidiOut, CMaxMidiOut)
    //{{AFX_MSG_MAP(MyMidiOut)
    //}}AFX_MSG_MAP
END_MESSAGE_MAP()
//-----------------------------------------------------------------------------
//   Constructor
//-----------------------------------------------------------------------------
MyMidiOut::MyMidiOut()
{
    fSending = FALSE;
    cbNumSent = 0;
}
/////////////////////////////////////////////////////////////////////////////
// MyMidiOut virtual functions
//-----------------------------------------------------------------------------
//   ProcessOutBufferReady
//-----------------------------------------------------------------------------
void MyMidiOut::ProcessOutBufferReady(void)
{
    MidiEvent evt;

    evt.status = SYSEX;

    do {
        evt.data1 = pData[cbNumSent];
    } while(Put(&evt) && cbNumSent++ < cbDataSize);

    fSending = (cbNumSent < cbDataSize);
}
//-----------------------------------------------------------------------------
//   Send
//-----------------------------------------------------------------------------
void MyMidiOut::Send(LPBYTE ptr, DWORD size)
{
    pData = ptr;
    cbDataSize = size;
    cbNumSent = 0;
    fSending = TRUE;

    // kick off the output process off by "faking" an OUTBUFFER_READY
    ProcessOutBufferReady();
}
```

# MaxSeq

## MaxSeq App

```
// MaxSeq.h : main header file for the MAXSEQ application

#ifndef __AFXWIN_H__
    #error include 'stdafx.h' before including this file for PCH
#endif

#include "resource.h"        // main symbols
/////////////////////////////////////////////////////////////////////////////
// CMaxSeqApp:
// See MaxSeq.cpp for the implementation of this class
//
class CMaxSeqApp : public CWinApp
{
public:
    CMaxSeqApp();
    WORD MaxMidiVersion;

// Overrides
```

```
    // ClassWizard generated virtual function overrides
    //{{AFX_VIRTUAL(CMaxSeqApp)
    public:
    virtual BOOL InitInstance();
    //}}AFX_VIRTUAL

// Implementation

    //{{AFX_MSG(CMaxSeqApp)
    afx_msg void OnAppAbout();
    //}}AFX_MSG
    DECLARE_MESSAGE_MAP()
};


// MaxSeq.cpp : Defines the class behaviors for the application.
#include "stdafx.h"
#include "MaxSeq.h"

#include "MainFrm.h"
#include "MaxSeqDoc.h"
#include "MaxSeqView.h"

#ifdef _DEBUG
#define new DEBUG_NEW
#undef THIS_FILE
static char THIS_FILE[] = __FILE__;
#endif
/////////////////////////////////////////////////////////////////////////////
// CMaxSeqApp

BEGIN_MESSAGE_MAP(CMaxSeqApp, CWinApp)
    //{{AFX_MSG_MAP(CMaxSeqApp)
    ON_COMMAND(ID_APP_ABOUT, OnAppAbout)
    //}}AFX_MSG_MAP
    // Standard file based document commands
    ON_COMMAND(ID_FILE_NEW, CWinApp::OnFileNew)
    ON_COMMAND(ID_FILE_OPEN, CWinApp::OnFileOpen)
END_MESSAGE_MAP()
/////////////////////////////////////////////////////////////////////////////
// CMaxSeqApp construction

CMaxSeqApp::CMaxSeqApp()
{
}

/////////////////////////////////////////////////////////////////////////////
// The one and only CMaxSeqApp object

CMaxSeqApp theApp;

/////////////////////////////////////////////////////////////////////////////
// CMaxSeqApp initialization

BOOL CMaxSeqApp::InitInstance()
{
    // get the version before doing anything else, since this
    // resizes the message queue
    MaxMidiVersion = GetMaxMidiVersion();

    // Standard initialization

#ifdef _AFXDLL
    Enable3dControls();            // Call this when using MFC in a shared DLL
#else
    Enable3dControlsStatic(); // Call this when linking to MFC statically
#endif

    LoadStdProfileSettings();  // Load standard INI file options (including MRU)

    // Register document templates

    CSingleDocTemplate* pDocTemplate;
    pDocTemplate = new CSingleDocTemplate(
        IDR_MAINFRAME,
        RUNTIME_CLASS(CMaxSeqDoc),
        RUNTIME_CLASS(CMainFrame),      // main SDI frame window
        RUNTIME_CLASS(CMaxSeqView));
    AddDocTemplate(pDocTemplate);

    // Parse command line for standard shell commands, DDE, file open
    CCommandLineInfo cmdInfo;
```

```
    ParseCommandLine(cmdInfo);

    // Dispatch commands specified on the command line
    if (!ProcessShellCommand(cmdInfo))
        return FALSE;

    return TRUE;
}
/////////////////////////////////////////////////////////////////////////////
// CAboutDlg dialog used for App About

class CAboutDlg : public CDialog
{
public:
    CAboutDlg();

// Dialog Data
    //{{AFX_DATA(CAboutDlg)
    enum { IDD = IDD_ABOUTBOX };
    CString m_Version;
    //}}AFX_DATA

    // ClassWizard generated virtual function overrides
    //{{AFX_VIRTUAL(CAboutDlg)
    protected:
    virtual void DoDataExchange(CDataExchange* pDX);      // DDX/DDV support
    //}}AFX_VIRTUAL

// Implementation
protected:
    //{{AFX_MSG(CAboutDlg)
        // No message handlers
    //}}AFX_MSG
    DECLARE_MESSAGE_MAP()
};

CAboutDlg::CAboutDlg() : CDialog(CAboutDlg::IDD)
{
    //{{AFX_DATA_INIT(CAboutDlg)
    m_Version = _T("");
    //}}AFX_DATA_INIT
}

void CAboutDlg::DoDataExchange(CDataExchange* pDX)
{
    CDialog::DoDataExchange(pDX);
    //{{AFX_DATA_MAP(CAboutDlg)
    DDX_Text(pDX, IDC_VERSION, m_Version);
    DDV_MaxChars(pDX, m_Version, 40);
    //}}AFX_DATA_MAP
}
BEGIN_MESSAGE_MAP(CAboutDlg, CDialog)
    //{{AFX_MSG_MAP(CAboutDlg)
        // No message handlers
    //}}AFX_MSG_MAP
END_MESSAGE_MAP()

// App command to run the dialog
void CMaxSeqApp::OnAppAbout()
{
    CAboutDlg aboutDlg;

    // set the version string
    aboutDlg.m_Version.Format("MaxMidi DLL V%d.%02.2d", HIBYTE(MaxMidiVersion),
                            LOBYTE(MaxMidiVersion));
    aboutDlg.DoModal();
}
```

# MainFrm

```
#include "MySync.h"

// MainFrm.h : interface of the CMainFrame class
//
/////////////////////////////////////////////////////////////////////////////

class CMainFrame : public CFrameWnd
{
protected: // create from serialization only
```

```cpp
        CMainFrame();
        DECLARE_DYNCREATE(CMainFrame)

// Attributes
public:
        MySync SyncDev;

// Operations
public:

// Overrides
        // ClassWizard generated virtual function overrides
        //{{AFX_VIRTUAL(CMainFrame)
        virtual BOOL PreCreateWindow(CREATESTRUCT& cs);
        //}}AFX_VIRTUAL

// Implementation
public:
        virtual ~CMainFrame();
#ifdef _DEBUG
        virtual void AssertValid() const;
        virtual void Dump(CDumpContext& dc) const;
#endif

// Generated message map functions
protected:
        //{{AFX_MSG(CMainFrame)
        afx_msg int OnCreate(LPCREATESTRUCT lpCreateStruct);
        afx_msg void On10ms();
        afx_msg void OnUpdate10ms(CCmdUI* pCmdUI);
        afx_msg void On1ms();
        afx_msg void OnUpdate1ms(CCmdUI* pCmdUI);
        afx_msg void OnInternal();
        afx_msg void OnUpdateInternal(CCmdUI* pCmdUI);
        afx_msg void OnMidiClock();
        afx_msg void OnUpdateMidiClock(CCmdUI* pCmdUI);
        afx_msg void OnSetTempo();
        afx_msg void OnResolution();
        //}}AFX_MSG
        DECLARE_MESSAGE_MAP()
};


// MainFrm.cpp : implementation of the CMainFrame class

#include "stdafx.h"
#include "MaxSeq.h"

#include "MainFrm.h"

#include "TempoDialog.h"
#include "ResolutionDialog.h"

#ifdef _DEBUG
#define new DEBUG_NEW
#undef THIS_FILE
static char THIS_FILE[] = __FILE__;
#endif
/////////////////////////////////////////////////////////////////////////////
// CMainFrame

IMPLEMENT_DYNCREATE(CMainFrame, CFrameWnd)

BEGIN_MESSAGE_MAP(CMainFrame, CFrameWnd)
        //{{AFX_MSG_MAP(CMainFrame)
        ON_WM_CREATE()
        ON_COMMAND(IDM_10MS, On10ms)
        ON_UPDATE_COMMAND_UI(IDM_10MS, OnUpdate10ms)
        ON_COMMAND(IDM_1MS, On1ms)
        ON_UPDATE_COMMAND_UI(IDM_1MS, OnUpdate1ms)
        ON_COMMAND(IDM_INTERNAL, OnInternal)
        ON_UPDATE_COMMAND_UI(IDM_INTERNAL, OnUpdateInternal)
        ON_COMMAND(IDM_MIDICLOCK, OnMidiClock)
        ON_UPDATE_COMMAND_UI(IDM_MIDICLOCK, OnUpdateMidiClock)
        ON_COMMAND(IDM_SETTEMPO, OnSetTempo)
        ON_COMMAND(IDM_RESOLUTION, OnResolution)
        //}}AFX_MSG_MAP
END_MESSAGE_MAP()

/////////////////////////////////////////////////////////////////////////////
// CMainFrame construction/destruction
```

```
CMainFrame::CMainFrame()
{
}

CMainFrame::~CMainFrame()
{
}

BOOL CMainFrame::PreCreateWindow(CREATESTRUCT& cs)
{
    return CFrameWnd::PreCreateWindow(cs);
}
/////////////////////////////////////////////////////////////////////////
// CMainFrame diagnostics

#ifdef _DEBUG
void CMainFrame::AssertValid() const
{
    CFrameWnd::AssertValid();
}

void CMainFrame::Dump(CDumpContext& dc) const
{
    CFrameWnd::Dump(dc);
}

#endif //_DEBUG
/////////////////////////////////////////////////////////////////////////
// CMainFrame message handlers

int CMainFrame::OnCreate(LPCREATESTRUCT lpCreateStruct)
{
    // open the sync device with the default settings
    // open it before calling the base OnCreate, since the sync
    // device must be open before the view object is created.
    SyncDev.Attach(GetSafeHwnd());
    SyncDev.Open(S_INT, DEFAULT_TIMERPERIOD);

    if (CFrameWnd::OnCreate(lpCreateStruct) == -1)
        return -1;

    // since we don't have separate ON_UPDATE_COMMAND_UI handlers
    // or ON_COMMAND handlers for the device menu items we must
    // clear this flag so that the Input Device and Output Device
    // menu items are all enabled
    m_bAutoMenuEnable = FALSE;
    return 0;
}

void CMainFrame::On10ms()
{
    SyncDev.Period(10);
}

void CMainFrame::OnUpdate10ms(CCmdUI* pCmdUI)
{
    pCmdUI->SetCheck(SyncDev.Period() == 10);
}

void CMainFrame::On1ms()
{
    SyncDev.Period(1);
}

void CMainFrame::OnUpdate1ms(CCmdUI* pCmdUI)
{
    pCmdUI->SetCheck(SyncDev.Period() == 1);
}

void CMainFrame::OnInternal()
{
    SyncDev.Mode(S_INT);
}

void CMainFrame::OnUpdateInternal(CCmdUI* pCmdUI)
{
    pCmdUI->SetCheck(SyncDev.Mode() == S_INT);
}

void CMainFrame::OnMidiClock()
{
    SyncDev.Mode(S_MIDI);
```

```
}
void CMainFrame::OnUpdateMidiClock(CCmdUI* pCmdUI)
{
    pCmdUI->SetCheck(SyncDev.Mode() == S_MIDI);
}
void CMainFrame::OnSetTempo()
{
    CTempoDialog TempoDialog;

    // get the current tempo
    double dTempo = SyncDev.Convert(SyncDev.Tempo());

    // convert it to asciiz string
    TempoDialog.m_Tempo.Format("%3.3f", dTempo);

    // display the dialog
    if(TempoDialog.DoModal() == IDOK)
    {
        // get the new value and set the tempo
        dTempo = atof((LPCTSTR)TempoDialog.m_Tempo);
        SyncDev.Tempo(SyncDev.Convert(dTempo));
    }
}
void CMainFrame::OnResolution()
{
    ResolutionDialog ResDialog;

    // get the current resolution
    WORD Res = SyncDev.Resolution();

    // convert it to asciiz string
    ResDialog.m_Resolution.Format("%d", Res);

    // display the dialog
    if(ResDialog.DoModal() == IDOK)
    {
        // get the new value and set the resolution
        Res = atoi((LPCTSTR)ResDialog.m_Resolution);
        SyncDev.Resolution(Res);
    }
}
```

## MaxSeqDoc

```
#include "MaxMidi.h"

// MaxSeqDoc.h : interface of the CMaxSeqDoc class
//
/////////////////////////////////////////////////////////////////////////////

class CMaxSeqDoc : public CDocument
{
protected: // create from serialization only
    CMaxSeqDoc();
    DECLARE_DYNCREATE(CMaxSeqDoc)

// Attributes
public:
    CMaxMidiTrack** pTrackList;
    int nTracks;
    CMaxMidiTrack* pRecTrack;
    CMaxMidiSMF SMF;

// Operations
public:
    void CreateNewTrack(CString name);

// Overrides
    // ClassWizard generated virtual function overrides
    //{{AFX_VIRTUAL(CMaxSeqDoc)
    public:
    virtual BOOL OnNewDocument();
    virtual void Serialize(CArchive& ar);
    virtual BOOL OnSaveDocument(LPCTSTR lpszPathName);
    virtual BOOL OnOpenDocument(LPCTSTR lpszPathName);
    //}}AFX_VIRTUAL

// Implementation
```

```
public:
    virtual ~CMaxSeqDoc();
#ifdef _DEBUG
    virtual void AssertValid() const;
    virtual void Dump(CDumpContext& dc) const;
#endif

protected:

// Generated message map functions
protected:
    //{{AFX_MSG(CMaxSeqDoc)
    afx_msg void OnUpdateFileSave(CCmdUI* pCmdUI);
    afx_msg void OnUpdateFileSaveAs(CCmdUI* pCmdUI);
    afx_msg void OnNewTrack();
    //}}AFX_MSG
    DECLARE_MESSAGE_MAP()
};


// MaxSeqDoc.cpp : implementation of the CMaxSeqDoc class

#include "stdafx.h"
#include "MaxSeq.h"

#include "MaxSeqDoc.h"
#include "MaxSeqView.h"
#include "MainFrm.h"

#include "NewTrackDialog.h"

#ifdef _DEBUG
#define new DEBUG_NEW
#undef THIS_FILE
static char THIS_FILE[] = __FILE__;
#endif
/////////////////////////////////////////////////////////////////////////////
// CMaxSeqDoc

IMPLEMENT_DYNCREATE(CMaxSeqDoc, CDocument)

BEGIN_MESSAGE_MAP(CMaxSeqDoc, CDocument)
    //{{AFX_MSG_MAP(CMaxSeqDoc)
    ON_UPDATE_COMMAND_UI(ID_FILE_SAVE, OnUpdateFileSave)
    ON_UPDATE_COMMAND_UI(ID_FILE_SAVE_AS, OnUpdateFileSaveAs)
    ON_COMMAND(IDM_NEWTRACK, OnNewTrack)
    //}}AFX_MSG_MAP
END_MESSAGE_MAP()
/////////////////////////////////////////////////////////////////////////////
// CMaxSeqDoc construction/destruction

CMaxSeqDoc::CMaxSeqDoc()
{
    pTrackList = NULL;
    nTracks = 0;
    pRecTrack = NULL;
}

CMaxSeqDoc::~CMaxSeqDoc()
{
    int i;

    // free the tracks
    if(pTrackList)
    {
        for(i = 0; i < nTracks; i++)
            delete pTrackList[i];

        GlobalFree(pTrackList);
        pTrackList = NULL;
    }
}

BOOL CMaxSeqDoc::OnNewDocument()
{
    int i;

    if (!CDocument::OnNewDocument())
        return FALSE;

    // close the SMF, if open
    SMF.Close();
```

```
    // close all existing tracks
    if(pTrackList)
    {
        for(i = 0; i < nTracks; i++)
            delete pTrackList[i];

        GlobalFree(pTrackList);
        pTrackList = NULL;
    }

    // open an initial record track
    nTracks = 0;
    CreateNewTrack("New Track");

    // get the pointer to the view (we only have one since this is SDI)
    POSITION pos = GetFirstViewPosition();
    CMaxSeqView* pView = (CMaxSeqView*)GetNextView(pos);

    // get a pointer to the sync device
    CFrameWnd* pMainFrm = pView->GetParentFrame();
    CMaxMidiSync* pSync = &((CMainFrame*)pMainFrm)->SyncDev;

    // reset the default resolution and tempo
    pSync->Resolution(480);
    pSync->Tempo(pSync->Convert(120.0));

    return TRUE;
}
///////////////////////////////////////////////////////////////////////////
// CMaxSeqDoc serialization

void CMaxSeqDoc::Serialize(CArchive& ar)
{
    if (ar.IsStoring())
    {
    }
    else
    {
    }
}
///////////////////////////////////////////////////////////////////////////
// CMaxSeqDoc diagnostics

#ifdef _DEBUG
void CMaxSeqDoc::AssertValid() const
{
    CDocument::AssertValid();
}

void CMaxSeqDoc::Dump(CDumpContext& dc) const
{
    CDocument::Dump(dc);
}
#endif //_DEBUG
///////////////////////////////////////////////////////////////////////////
// CMaxSeqDoc commands

void CMaxSeqDoc::CreateNewTrack(CString name)
{
    // get the pointer to the view (we only have one since this is SDI)
    POSITION pos = GetFirstViewPosition();
    CMaxSeqView* pView = (CMaxSeqView*)GetNextView(pos);

    // create a new track
    nTracks++;
    if(pTrackList)
        pTrackList = (CMaxMidiTrack**)GlobalReAlloc(pTrackList, sizeof(CMaxMidiTrack*) *
                        nTracks, GPTR | GMEM_MOVEABLE);
    else
        pTrackList = (CMaxMidiTrack**)GlobalAlloc(GPTR, sizeof(CMaxMidiTrack*));

    pTrackList[nTracks - 1] = new CMaxMidiTrack;
    pView->MidiOut.Attach(pTrackList[nTracks - 1]);
    pView->MidiIn.Attach(pTrackList[nTracks - 1]);

    // get the new value and set the track name
    pTrackList[nTracks - 1]->SetName((LPSTR)(LPCTSTR)name);

    // the new track is the record track
    pRecTrack = pTrackList[nTracks - 1];
}
```

```
void CMaxSeqDoc::OnNewTrack()
{
    NewTrackDialog NTDialog;

    // display the dialog
    NTDialog.m_Name.Format("New Track");
    if(NTDialog.DoModal() == IDOK)
        CreateNewTrack(NTDialog.m_Name);
}

BOOL CMaxSeqDoc::OnSaveDocument(LPCTSTR lpszPathName)
{
    CMaxMidiSMF wSMF;
    int i;
    // open an smf for writing and output the recorded track
    if(pTrackList)
    {
        SMF.Close();
        wSMF.Open(lpszPathName, WRITE);

        for(i = 0; i < nTracks; i++)
            wSMF.Attach(pTrackList[i]);

        wSMF.Save();
        wSMF.Close();
    }

    return TRUE;
}

void CMaxSeqDoc::OnUpdateFileSave(CCmdUI* pCmdUI)
{
    BOOL saveable = FALSE;
    int i;

    for(i = 0; i < nTracks; i++)
        saveable |= !pTrackList[i]->IsEmpty();

    pCmdUI->Enable(saveable);
}

void CMaxSeqDoc::OnUpdateFileSaveAs(CCmdUI* pCmdUI)
{
    OnUpdateFileSave(pCmdUI);
}

BOOL CMaxSeqDoc::OnOpenDocument(LPCTSTR lpszPathName)
{
    int i;

    // get the pointer to the view (we only have one since this is SDI)
    POSITION pos = GetFirstViewPosition();
    CMaxSeqView* pView = (CMaxSeqView*)GetNextView(pos);

    // get a pointer to the sync device
    CFrameWnd* pMainFrm = pView->GetParentFrame();
    CMaxMidiSync* pSync = &((CMainFrame*)pMainFrm)->SyncDev;

    // close any open tracks
    if(pTrackList)
    {
        for(i = 0; i < nTracks; i++)
            if(pTrackList[i])
                delete pTrackList[i];

        GlobalFree(pTrackList);
        pTrackList = NULL;
    }

    // open the new SMF
    SMF.Open(lpszPathName, READ);

    nTracks = SMF.NumTracks();
    pTrackList = (CMaxMidiTrack**)GlobalAlloc(GPTR, sizeof(CMaxMidiTrack*) * nTracks);

    for(i = 0; i < nTracks; i++)
    {
        pTrackList[i] = new CMaxMidiTrack;
        SMF.Attach(pTrackList[i]);
        pView->MidiOut.Attach(pTrackList[i]);
        pView->MidiIn.Attach(pTrackList[i]);
    }
```

```
    // load 'em up
    SMF.Load();

    // set the default tempo
    pSync->Tempo(pSync->Convert(120.0));

    // create a new track to record into, if desired
    CreateNewTrack("New Track");

    return TRUE;
}
```

## MaxSeqView

```cpp
#include "MaxMidi.h"
#include "MySync.h"
#include "MyMidiIn.h"

// MaxSeqView.h : interface of the CMaxSeqView class
//
/////////////////////////////////////////////////////////////////////////////

class CMaxSeqView : public CView
{
protected: // create from serialization only
    CMaxSeqView();
    DECLARE_DYNCREATE(CMaxSeqView)

// Attributes
public:
    CMaxSeqDoc* GetDocument();

    // MaxMidi Sync Device
    MySync* Sync;

    // MaxMidi Input and Output Device Objects
    MyMidiIn MidiIn;
    CMaxMidiOut MidiOut;

    // Input and Output Device Menus
    CMidiInDeviceMenu InMenu;
    CMidiOutDeviceMenu OutMenu;

// Operations
public:

// Overrides
    // ClassWizard generated virtual function overrides
    //{{AFX_VIRTUAL(CMaxSeqView)
    public:
    virtual void OnDraw(CDC* pDC);  // overridden to draw this view
    virtual BOOL PreCreateWindow(CREATESTRUCT& cs);
    virtual BOOL OnCmdMsg(UINT nID, int nCode, void* pExtra, AFX_CMDHANDLERINFO*
pHandlerInfo);
    //}}AFX_VIRTUAL

// Implementation
public:
    virtual ~CMaxSeqView();
#ifdef _DEBUG
    virtual void AssertValid() const;
    virtual void Dump(CDumpContext& dc) const;
#endif

protected:

// Generated message map functions
protected:
    //{{AFX_MSG(CMaxSeqView)
    afx_msg int OnCreate(LPCREATESTRUCT lpCreateStruct);
    afx_msg void OnRecordStart();
    afx_msg void OnUpdateRecordStart(CCmdUI* pCmdUI);
    afx_msg void OnRecordStop();
    afx_msg void OnUpdateRecordStop(CCmdUI* pCmdUI);
    afx_msg void OnPlayStart();
    afx_msg void OnUpdatePlayStart(CCmdUI* pCmdUI);
    afx_msg void OnThruOn();
    afx_msg void OnUpdateThruOn(CCmdUI* pCmdUI);
    afx_msg void OnThruOff();
    afx_msg void OnUpdateThruOff(CCmdUI* pCmdUI);
    afx_msg void OnPlayStop();
```

```
        afx_msg void OnUpdatePlayStop(CCmdUI* pCmdUI);
    //}}AFX_MSG
    DECLARE_MESSAGE_MAP()
};
#ifndef _DEBUG  // debug version in MaxSeqView.cpp
inline CMaxSeqDoc* CMaxSeqView::GetDocument()
    { return (CMaxSeqDoc*)m_pDocument; }
#endif


// MaxSeqView.cpp : implementation of the CMaxSeqView class

#include "stdafx.h"
#include "MaxSeq.h"

#include "MaxSeqDoc.h"
#include "MaxSeqView.h"
#include "MainFrm.h"

#ifdef _DEBUG
#define new DEBUG_NEW
#undef THIS_FILE
static char THIS_FILE[] = __FILE__;
#endif
/////////////////////////////////////////////////////////////////////////////
// CMaxSeqView

IMPLEMENT_DYNCREATE(CMaxSeqView, CView)

BEGIN_MESSAGE_MAP(CMaxSeqView, CView)
    //{{AFX_MSG_MAP(CMaxSeqView)
    ON_WM_CREATE()
    ON_COMMAND(IDM_RSTART, OnRecordStart)
    ON_UPDATE_COMMAND_UI(IDM_RSTART, OnUpdateRecordStart)
    ON_COMMAND(IDM_RSTOP, OnRecordStop)
    ON_UPDATE_COMMAND_UI(IDM_RSTOP, OnUpdateRecordStop)
    ON_COMMAND(IDM_PSTART, OnPlayStart)
    ON_UPDATE_COMMAND_UI(IDM_PSTART, OnUpdatePlayStart)
    ON_COMMAND(IDM_THRUON, OnThruOn)
    ON_UPDATE_COMMAND_UI(IDM_THRUON, OnUpdateThruOn)
    ON_COMMAND(IDM_THRUOFF, OnThruOff)
    ON_UPDATE_COMMAND_UI(IDM_THRUOFF, OnUpdateThruOff)
    ON_COMMAND(IDM_PSTOP, OnPlayStop)
    ON_UPDATE_COMMAND_UI(IDM_PSTOP, OnUpdatePlayStop)
    //}}AFX_MSG_MAP
END_MESSAGE_MAP()
/////////////////////////////////////////////////////////////////////////////
// CMaxSeqView construction/destruction

CMaxSeqView::CMaxSeqView()
{
}

CMaxSeqView::~CMaxSeqView()
{
}

BOOL CMaxSeqView::PreCreateWindow(CREATESTRUCT& cs)
{
    return CView::PreCreateWindow(cs);
}
/////////////////////////////////////////////////////////////////////////////
// CMaxSeqView drawing

void CMaxSeqView::OnDraw(CDC* pDC)
{
    char text[30];
    CMaxSeqDoc* pDoc = GetDocument();
    ASSERT_VALID(pDoc);

    // display the beat count
    wsprintf(text, "Beats = %d      ", Sync->beats);
    pDC->TextOut(10, 10, text, strlen(text));
}
/////////////////////////////////////////////////////////////////////////////
// CMaxSeqView diagnostics

#ifdef _DEBUG
void CMaxSeqView::AssertValid() const
```

```
{
    CView::AssertValid();
}

void CMaxSeqView::Dump(CDumpContext& dc) const
{
    CView::Dump(dc);
}

CMaxSeqDoc* CMaxSeqView::GetDocument() // non-debug version is inline
{
    ASSERT(m_pDocument->IsKindOf(RUNTIME_CLASS(CMaxSeqDoc)));
    return (CMaxSeqDoc*)m_pDocument;
}
#endif //_DEBUG
///////////////////////////////////////////////////////////////////////////
// CMaxSeqView message handlers

int CMaxSeqView::OnCreate(LPCREATESTRUCT lpCreateStruct)
{
    if (CView::OnCreate(lpCreateStruct) == -1)
        return -1;

    CMaxSeqDoc* pDoc = GetDocument();

    // get a pointer to the sync device
    CFrameWnd* pMainFrm = GetParentFrame();
    Sync = &((CMainFrame*)pMainFrm)->SyncDev;

    // open the first input and output devices
    MidiIn.Attach(GetSafeHwnd());
    MidiOut.Attach(GetSafeHwnd());

    // attach the sync device to the input and output devices
    MidiIn.Attach(Sync);
    MidiOut.Attach(Sync);

    // get the parent menu
    CMenu* ParentMenu = GetParent()->GetMenu();

    // create the device menus and select the first devices
    InMenu.Create(ParentMenu->GetSafeHmenu(), ParentMenu->GetMenuItemCount() - 1,
                "&Input Device", IDM_INPUT);
    InMenu.Attach(&MidiIn);
    InMenu.SelectDevice(0);

    OutMenu.Create(ParentMenu->GetSafeHmenu(), ParentMenu->GetMenuItemCount() - 1,
                "&Output Device", IDM_OUTPUT);
    OutMenu.Attach(&MidiOut);
    OutMenu.SelectDevice(0);
    MidiIn.SetEchoOutput(&MidiOut);
    return 0;
}

BOOL CMaxSeqView::OnCmdMsg(UINT nID, int nCode, void* pExtra, AFX_CMDHANDLERINFO*
pHandlerInfo)
{
    // check to see if one of the device menus has been selected
    if(nCode == 0)
    {
        InMenu.SelectDevice(nID);

        // if it's an output device, change the echo device too
        if(OutMenu.SelectDevice(nID))
            MidiIn.SetEchoOutput(&MidiOut);
    }

    return CView::OnCmdMsg(nID, nCode, pExtra, pHandlerInfo);
}

void CMaxSeqView::OnRecordStart()
{
    CMaxSeqDoc* pDoc = GetDocument();

    // initialize the beat counter
    Sync->beats = 0;

    // reset the timestamp for the input device since
    // input is always active (for echo while idle)
    MidiIn.Reset();

    // enable record for the selected track
    pDoc->pRecTrack->Flush();
```

```
        pDoc->pRecTrack->IsRecording(TRUE);

        // start input
        Sync->IsRecording(TRUE);
        Sync->Start();

        // start merging (non-record) tracks into the output device
        MidiOut.StartOut();
}
void CMaxSeqView::OnUpdateRecordStart(CCmdUI* pCmdUI)
{
        CMaxSeqDoc* pDoc = GetDocument();
        BOOL rec = TRUE;

        // don't allow recording if record track does not exist
        if(pDoc->pRecTrack)
            rec = pDoc->pRecTrack->IsRecording();

        pCmdUI->Enable(!rec && !Sync->IsRunning());
}
void CMaxSeqView::OnRecordStop()
{
        CMaxSeqDoc* pDoc = GetDocument();

        // stop recording
        pDoc->pRecTrack->IsRecording(FALSE);

        // stop input
        Sync->IsRecording(FALSE);
        Sync->Stop();
}
void CMaxSeqView::OnUpdateRecordStop(CCmdUI* pCmdUI)
{
        CMaxSeqDoc* pDoc = GetDocument();

        pCmdUI->Enable(pDoc->pRecTrack->IsRecording());
}
void CMaxSeqView::OnPlayStart()
{
        // start playback
        Sync->beats = 0;

        // sync must be started before any data is sent
        // to midi out so that data is sent with proper timing.
        Sync->Start();

        // start merging tracks into the output device
        MidiOut.StartOut();
}
void CMaxSeqView::OnUpdatePlayStart(CCmdUI* pCmdUI)
{
        CMaxSeqDoc* pDoc = GetDocument();
        BOOL playable = FALSE;
        int i;

        for(i = 0; i < pDoc->nTracks; i++)
            playable |= !pDoc->pTrackList[i]->IsEmpty();

        pCmdUI->Enable(playable && !Sync->IsRunning());
}
void CMaxSeqView::OnPlayStop()
{
        // stop playback
        Sync->Stop();
}
void CMaxSeqView::OnUpdatePlayStop(CCmdUI* pCmdUI)
{
        CMaxSeqDoc* pDoc = GetDocument();

        pCmdUI->Enable(Sync->IsRunning() && !pDoc->pRecTrack->IsRecording());
}
void CMaxSeqView::OnThruOn()
{
        MidiIn.SetThru(TRUE);
}
void CMaxSeqView::OnUpdateThruOn(CCmdUI* pCmdUI)
{
```

```
        pCmdUI->SetCheck(MidiIn.GetThru());
}
void CMaxSeqView::OnThruOff()
{
        MidiIn.SetThru(FALSE);
}
void CMaxSeqView::OnUpdateThruOff(CCmdUI* pCmdUI)
{
        pCmdUI->SetCheck(!MidiIn.GetThru());
}
```

# MyMidiIn

```
//============================================================================
//   MyMidiIn Class
//============================================================================
#ifndef __MYMIDIIN__
#define __MYMIDIIN__
class MyMidiIn : public CMaxMidiIn
{
public:
        CMaxMidiOut* EchoOut;
        BOOL ThruEnabled;

public:
        MyMidiIn();
        void SetEchoOutput(CMaxMidiOut* moDevice) { EchoOut = moDevice; };
        void SetThru(BOOL thru) { ThruEnabled = thru; };
        BOOL GetThru(void) { return ThruEnabled; };

// Overrides
        // ClassWizard generated virtual function overrides
        //{{AFX_VIRTUAL(MyMidiIn)
        virtual BOOL ProcessMidiData(LPMIDIEVENT lpEvent);
        //}}AFX_VIRTUAL

protected:
        //{{AFX_MSG(MyMidiIn)
        //}}AFX_MSG
        DECLARE_MESSAGE_MAP()
};

#endif //!__MYMIDIIN__


//============================================================================
//   MyMidiIn Class
//============================================================================
#include "stdafx.h"
#include "MaxMidi.h"
#include "MyMidiIn.h"

BEGIN_MESSAGE_MAP(MyMidiIn, CMaxMidiIn)
        //{{AFX_MSG_MAP(MyMidiIn)
        //}}AFX_MSG_MAP
END_MESSAGE_MAP()

//----------------------------------------------------------------------------
//   Constructor
//----------------------------------------------------------------------------
MyMidiIn::MyMidiIn()
{
        EchoOut = NULL;
        ThruEnabled = FALSE;
}

////////////////////////////////////////////////////////////////////////////
// MyMidiIn virtual functions

//----------------------------------------------------------------------------
//   ProcessMimData
//----------------------------------------------------------------------------
BOOL MyMidiIn::ProcessMidiData(LPMIDIEVENT lpEvent)
{
        MidiEvent EchoEvent;

        // echo the event, if enabled
        if(EchoOut && ThruEnabled)
```

```
    {
        // echo it now by setting time to -1
        EchoEvent = *lpEvent;
        EchoEvent.time = (DWORD)-1;
        EchoOut->Put(&EchoEvent);
    }
    // return TRUE to append this event to any attached tracks
    return TRUE;
}
```

# MySync

```
#include "MaxMidi.h"
//===========================================================================
//  MySync Class
//===========================================================================
#ifndef __MYSYNC__
#define __MYSYNC__
class MySync : public CMaxMidiSync
{
public:
    int        beats;              // beat count since start

protected:
    BOOL fRecord;       // true if recording

public:
    MySync();

    void IsRecording(BOOL record) { fRecord = record; };
    BOOL IsRecording(void) { return fRecord; };

// Overrides
    // ClassWizard generated virtual function overrides
    //{{AFX_VIRTUAL(MySync)
    virtual void ProcessSyncDone(void);
    virtual void ProcessMidiBeat(void);
    //}}AFX_VIRTUAL

protected:
    //{{AFX_MSG(MySync)
    //}}AFX_MSG
    DECLARE_MESSAGE_MAP()
};

#endif //!__MYSYNC__


//===========================================================================
//  MySync Class
//===========================================================================
#include "stdafx.h"
#include "MaxSeqDoc.h"
#include "MaxSeqView.h"
BEGIN_MESSAGE_MAP(MySync, CMaxMidiSync)
    //{{AFX_MSG_MAP(MySync)
    //}}AFX_MSG_MAP
END_MESSAGE_MAP()
//---------------------------------------------------------------------------
//  Constructor
//---------------------------------------------------------------------------
MySync::MySync()
{
    beats = 0;
    IsRecording(FALSE);
}
/////////////////////////////////////////////////////////////////////////////
// MySync virtual functions

//---------------------------------------------------------------------------
//  ProcessSyncDone
//---------------------------------------------------------------------------
void MySync::ProcessSyncDone(void)
{
    // stop playback, but only if not recording
    if(!IsRecording())
```

```
        Stop();
}
//-----------------------------------------------------------------------
//    ProcessMidiBeat
//-----------------------------------------------------------------------
void MySync::ProcessMidiBeat(void)
{
    beats++;

    // force any and all views to update the beats display
    CFrameWnd* pMainFrm = GetParentFrame();
    CDocument* pDoc = pMainFrm->GetActiveDocument();
    pDoc->UpdateAllViews(NULL);
}
```

# NewTrackDialog

```
// NewTrackDialog.h : header file
/////////////////////////////////////////////////////////////////////////////
// NewTrackDialog dialog

class NewTrackDialog : public CDialog
{
// Construction
public:
    NewTrackDialog(CWnd* pParent = NULL);   // standard constructor

// Dialog Data
    //{{AFX_DATA(NewTrackDialog)
    enum { IDD = IDD_NEWTRACK };
    CString  m_Name;
    //}}AFX_DATA


// Overrides
    // ClassWizard generated virtual function overrides
    //{{AFX_VIRTUAL(NewTrackDialog)
    protected:
    virtual void DoDataExchange(CDataExchange* pDX);   // DDX/DDV support
    //}}AFX_VIRTUAL

// Implementation
protected:

    // Generated message map functions
    //{{AFX_MSG(NewTrackDialog)
        // NOTE: the ClassWizard will add member functions here
    //}}AFX_MSG
    DECLARE_MESSAGE_MAP()
};


// NewTrackDialog.cpp : implementation file

#include "stdafx.h"
#include "MaxSeq.h"
#include "NewTrackDialog.h"

#ifdef _DEBUG
#define new DEBUG_NEW
#undef THIS_FILE
static char THIS_FILE[] = __FILE__;
#endif

/////////////////////////////////////////////////////////////////////////////
// NewTrackDialog dialog

NewTrackDialog::NewTrackDialog(CWnd* pParent /*=NULL*/)
    : CDialog(NewTrackDialog::IDD, pParent)
{
    //{{AFX_DATA_INIT(NewTrackDialog)
    m_Name = _T("");
    //}}AFX_DATA_INIT
}

void NewTrackDialog::DoDataExchange(CDataExchange* pDX)
{
    CDialog::DoDataExchange(pDX);
    //{{AFX_DATA_MAP(NewTrackDialog)
```

```
        DDX_Text(pDX, IDC_TRACKNAME, m_Name);
        //}}AFX_DATA_MAP
}
BEGIN_MESSAGE_MAP(NewTrackDialog, CDialog)
    //{{AFX_MSG_MAP(NewTrackDialog)
        // NOTE: the ClassWizard will add message map macros here
    //}}AFX_MSG_MAP
END_MESSAGE_MAP()
```

# ResolutionDialog

```
// ResolutionDialog.h : header file
/////////////////////////////////////////////////////////////////////////////
// ResolutionDialog dialog

class ResolutionDialog : public CDialog
{
// Construction
public:
    ResolutionDialog(CWnd* pParent = NULL);    // standard constructor

// Dialog Data
    //{{AFX_DATA(ResolutionDialog)
    enum { IDD = IDD_RESOLUTION };
    CString m_Resolution;
    //}}AFX_DATA


// Overrides
    // ClassWizard generated virtual function overrides
    //{{AFX_VIRTUAL(ResolutionDialog)
    protected:
    virtual void DoDataExchange(CDataExchange* pDX);    // DDX/DDV support
    //}}AFX_VIRTUAL

// Implementation
protected:

    // Generated message map functions
    //{{AFX_MSG(ResolutionDialog)
        // NOTE: the ClassWizard will add member functions here
    //}}AFX_MSG
    DECLARE_MESSAGE_MAP()
};


// ResolutionDialog.cpp : implementation file

#include "stdafx.h"
#include "MaxSeq.h"
#include "ResolutionDialog.h"

#ifdef _DEBUG
#define new DEBUG_NEW
#undef THIS_FILE
static char THIS_FILE[] = __FILE__;
#endif
/////////////////////////////////////////////////////////////////////////////
// ResolutionDialog dialog

ResolutionDialog::ResolutionDialog(CWnd* pParent /*=NULL*/)
    : CDialog(ResolutionDialog::IDD, pParent)
{
    //{{AFX_DATA_INIT(ResolutionDialog)
    m_Resolution = _T("");
    //}}AFX_DATA_INIT
}
void ResolutionDialog::DoDataExchange(CDataExchange* pDX)
{
    CDialog::DoDataExchange(pDX);
    //{{AFX_DATA_MAP(ResolutionDialog)
    DDX_Text(pDX, IDC_RESOLUTION, m_Resolution);
    DDV_MaxChars(pDX, m_Resolution, 4);
    //}}AFX_DATA_MAP
}
BEGIN_MESSAGE_MAP(ResolutionDialog, CDialog)
    //{{AFX_MSG_MAP(ResolutionDialog)
```

```
        // NOTE: the ClassWizard will add message map macros here
    //}}AFX_MSG_MAP
END_MESSAGE_MAP()
```

# TempoDialog

```
// TempoDialog.h : header file
//////////////////////////////////////////////////////////////////////////////
// CTempoDialog dialog

class CTempoDialog : public CDialog
{
// Construction
public:
    CTempoDialog(CWnd* pParent = NULL);    // standard constructor

// Dialog Data
    //{{AFX_DATA(CTempoDialog)
    enum { IDD = IDD_TEMPO };
    CString  m_Tempo;
    //}}AFX_DATA


// Overrides
    // ClassWizard generated virtual function overrides
    //{{AFX_VIRTUAL(CTempoDialog)
    protected:
    virtual void DoDataExchange(CDataExchange* pDX);    // DDX/DDV support
    //}}AFX_VIRTUAL

// Implementation
protected:

    // Generated message map functions
    //{{AFX_MSG(CTempoDialog)
        // NOTE: the ClassWizard will add member functions here
    //}}AFX_MSG
    DECLARE_MESSAGE_MAP()
};


// TempoDialog.cpp : implementation file

#include "stdafx.h"
#include "MaxSeq.h"
#include "TempoDialog.h"

#ifdef _DEBUG
#define new DEBUG_NEW
#undef THIS_FILE
static char THIS_FILE[] = __FILE__;
#endif

//////////////////////////////////////////////////////////////////////////////
// CTempoDialog dialog

CTempoDialog::CTempoDialog(CWnd* pParent /*=NULL*/)
    : CDialog(CTempoDialog::IDD, pParent)
{
    //{{AFX_DATA_INIT(CTempoDialog)
    m_Tempo = _T("");
    //}}AFX_DATA_INIT
}

void CTempoDialog::DoDataExchange(CDataExchange* pDX)
{
    CDialog::DoDataExchange(pDX);
    //{{AFX_DATA_MAP(CTempoDialog)
    DDX_Text(pDX, IDC_TEMPO, m_Tempo);
    DDV_MaxChars(pDX, m_Tempo, 8);
    //}}AFX_DATA_MAP
}

BEGIN_MESSAGE_MAP(CTempoDialog, CDialog)
    //{{AFX_MSG_MAP(CTempoDialog)
        // NOTE: the ClassWizard will add message map macros here
    //}}AFX_MSG_MAP
END_MESSAGE_MAP()
```

# MaxMidi ToolKit License Agreement

You may use the Maximum MIDI ToolKit in the development of any software, whether for personal use, public domain consumption, or commercial use. However, you may not use the ToolKit, in part or in whole, to develop or publish another toolkit or other software that substantially duplicates the functionality of the Maximum MIDI ToolKit.

If you use any part of the ToolKit or any modified part of the ToolKit, all that is required is that you recognize my copyright. You must do this by including the statement "Maximum MIDI Programmer's ToolKit Copyright © 1993-1997 by Paul Messick" in a manner visible to the user of your software, and by including the same statement along with your copyright notice if you provide one.

# GLOSSARY

*Abstract base class*   A C++ class that contains one or more pure virtual functions. An abstract class can only serve as a base of another class.

*Accuracy*   See **timing accuracy**.

*API*   An acronym for *Application Programming Interface*. An API specifies the function names, functionality, and parameters for a set of functions that can be called by applications.

*Asynchronous*   Not coincident in time. For example, an asynchronous function returns control to the caller before the function's operation is complete. The function's processing continues independently from the calling client. See **synchronous**.

*Basic channel*   The particular channel on which an instrument will respond to Channel messages, if it is set to Omni Off mode. Also known as the *Global Channel*.

*Baud*   Symbols per second. This is not the same as bits per second, although the term is often misused in this way. For example, a high-speed modem might transfer data at 28,800 bits per second. The audio signal sent through the telephone line by the modem sends data at 2,400 *baud*; each symbol is made up of 12 bits, to achieve a 28,800 bits-per-second data rate.

*Big-Endian*   A byte-ordering method where the most significant bits of a multibyte value comes first in memory. Motorola 68K and PPC CPUs are Big-Endian processors. See **Little-Endian**.

*Boilerplate*   Source code that does not change from version to version.

*Callback function*   A function that is called at interrupt time by a timer or device driver.

*Channel*   A number that specifies to which instrument or section of an instrument a given Channel message is directed. MIDI channels are analogous to channels on a television; if a television is tuned to channel 4, it will only receive information directed at channel 4. There are 16 possible MIDI channels.

*Channel message*   A classification of a MIDI message that is directed at a particular channel of a receiving device. The channel number is encoded in four bits of a status byte where 0000 binary (0 decimal) corresponds to channel 1, and 1111 binary (15 decimal) corresponds to channel 16. Channel messages are further subdivided into Channel Voice messages and Channel Mode messages.

*Channel Mode message*   A Channel message that configures a receiving device. Four different modes are possible: Omni On/Poly, Omni On/Mono, Omni Off/Poly, and Omni Off/Mono.

*Channel Voice message*   A Channel message that specifies or modifies a note. Examples include Note Off, Note On, Aftertouch, and Pitch Bend.

*Chase*   To calculate and locate a new position in a sequence, during synchronization, given a SMPTE frame or Song Position Pointer. Chasing is usually done while starting to play or record while synchronizing to tape at a location other than the beginning of a sequence.

*Chunk*   A data structure used in Standard MIDI Files. A chunk is made up of a four-character type, a 32-bit byte count, and data. See **track chunk** and **header chunk**.

*Circular queue*   A queue whose input and output pointers wrap around. Such queues are needed when handling streaming data, such as MIDI events, since the length of the queued data—over time—may exceed the size of the queue. See **linear queue**.

*Data byte*   An 8-bit byte in a MIDI message that specifies a data value for a corresponding status byte. The upper bit of a data byte is always zero, leaving seven bits to hold the data. See **status byte**.

*Data flow diagram*   A flowchart-like diagram that illustrates the logical flow of data through an algorithm or program.

*Delta ticks*   The difference in time, measured in units of ticks, between one event and the next.

*Derived class*   A class that includes one or more other classes as base classes. A derived class has access to all of the public and protected class members of its base classes.

*Device driver*   A system-level program, usually in the form of a DLL, that presents a known programming interface to a client (such as MMSYSTEM) and provides access to a hardware peripheral. The device driver hides the particulars of a hardware device from the calling client. Therefore, all instances of a given kind of device look identical to the client, even though the hardware controlled by a driver may be radically different from device to device.

*Device ID*   A number, ranging from 0 up to one less than the number of MIDI devices available on a system, that identifies a particular device.

*DLL*   Windows-*ese* for *dynamic link library*. A DLL is a module containing functions that applications can call without knowing the functions' addresses. A DLL may not even load until an application calls one of its functions.

*Drift*   Long-term timing error. Synchronization can drift from the proper timing due to mathematical and algorithmic errors.

*Drop frame*   A counting scheme used to force frame addresses to match elapsed time for frame rates that are not integer divisible. To make 29.97 fps timecode frame numbers match the actual elapsed time over a long period, the first two frame numbers of each minute are skipped, except during minutes 0, 10, 20, 30, 40, and 50.

*Drum machine*   A MIDI instrument that contains a sound module having a wide variety of percussion sounds and a simple sequencer that is optimized for playing looped patterns.

*Fixed memory*   A block of memory whose physical address will not change and that will not be paged out to disk. Memory that will be accessed at interrupt time must be fixed, since moveable memory may be paged out to disk by Windows' virtual memory manager. Access to paged-out memory at interrupt time causes Windows to attempt to read the block from disk. But since the system cannot properly access the disk during an interrupt, the memory cannot be reloaded, with catastrophic consequences.

*Flat thunk*   See **thunk**.

*Frame*   A logical division of time, corresponding to the duration of a single frame of video or film.

*Frame address*   A serial number, specified as hours, minutes, seconds, and frames, given to a frame to uniquely identify it.

*Frame rate*   The number of frames that occur in one second. Common frame rates are 30 frames per second (fps), 29.97 fps, 25 fps, and 24 fps.

*Granularity*   See **resolution.**

*Greyhound*   A breed of dog, related to the whippet, that is known to chase rabbits and other small furry creatures, often to the accompaniment of cheering crowds and tax-deductible-to-the-extent-of-winnings wagers.

*Header chunk*   A Standard MIDI File chunk (MThd) that defines the file type (format), number of tracks, and timing resolution.

*Import file*   A file that defines the public functions provided by a DLL. An import file is normally included in a program's project to tell the linker how to resolve function calls to the DLL. Alternatively, suitable entries in the program's .def file can resolve the function names. The import file needed to access the MaxMidi DLLs is named MxMidi32.lib.

*Internal sync*   Synchronization based on the internal timer of the computer.

*Irrational number*   The author's checkbook balance at the end of the month. Mathematically, a number that cannot be represented as a quotient of two integers. $\pi$ and $\sqrt{2}$ are examples of irrational numbers.

*Jitter*   Random or ordered inaccuracy without drift, or short-term timing inaccuracy. Events will tend to vary in time from when they should occur, falling on either side of the ideal time. Better accuracy results in events falling closer to the proper time, and thus, less jitter.

*Linear queue*   A queue whose input and output pointers advance until the end of data or the end of the queue is reached, without wrapping around. Linear queues are useful when assembling packets of data whose size is guaranteed to never exceed the queue size. Data is written to the queue, and after the data is read out, the input and output pointers are reset to the beginning of the queue. See **circular queue.**

*Little-Endian*   A byte ordering method where the least significant byte of a multibyte number appears first. The Intel 80x86 CPUs are Little-Endian processors. See **Big-Endian.**

*Magic cookie*   A unique number that provides access to a resource without revealing any information about that resource. The handles used by the MaxMidi ToolKit (HMIN, HMOUT, HSYNC) are all magic cookies.

*Manufacturer ID*　A 1- or 3-byte identifier of a particular instrument manufacturer. The manufacturer of any device that sends or receives sysex messages must have a unique ID. These IDs are assigned by the MIDI Manufacturer's Association. If the first byte following the 0xF0 status byte in a sysex message is nonzero, then that byte is the single-byte ID. Three-byte IDs all begin with a 0 byte, followed by a two-byte (14-bit) value.

*MaxMidi DLLs*　Two dynamic link libraries, MxMidi16 and MxMidi32, which contain all of the low-level MIDI input, output, and synchronization functions needed by a MIDI application.

*Message map*　A jump table, implemented using macros, that MFC-based programs use to connect window messages to message handling functions. A message map replaces the long `switch` statements normally used by Windows programs for message handling.

*Meta event*　A timestamped, non-MIDI event that appears in a Standard MIDI File. Examples include: Set Tempo, Lyric, End of Track, etc.

*MIDI*　Musical Instrument Digital Interface. A specification for connecting musical instruments together to transfer data. Most modern electronic instruments are equipped with MIDI hardware. PCs require a MIDI interface, similar to a serial port, to be able to access external keyboards and sound modules. Most sound cards provide a simple MIDI interface—requiring a special cable to connect to the real world—as well as an on-board synthesizer that is MIDI compatible.

*MIDI File*　See **Standard MIDI File**.

*Midi Mapper*　A system-level program in Windows that routes MIDI events to different output devices based on the channel of the messages. In Windows 95, the Midi Mapper is configured by adding instrument definitions in the MIDI tab of the Multimedia Control Panel applet.

*MIDI sync*　Beat-based synchronization whose tempo is determined by the rate at which MIDI Timing Clock messages are received.

*MIDI Timing Clock*　Often referred to as a MIDI Clock. A System Real-Time message (0xF8) that occurs at a rate of 24 clocks per beat at the current tempo. MIDI Clock messages can be used to synchronize two or more devices, such as a sequencer and a drum machine.

*MIDI Time Code (MTC)*　Frame-based synchronization that is the MIDI representation of SMPTE time code. MTC messages indicate frames and fractions of frames. See **SMPTE**.

*MidiEvent*   An 8-byte structure that holds either a single MIDI event or a single byte of a System Exclusive message.

*MMSYSTEM*   A 16-bit Windows system DLL that provides the basic functionality for multimedia audio, MIDI, and timing.

*Mono*   Short for *monophonic*. A monophonic instrument can only play a single note at a time. If one note is sounding and another note is played, the new note will either cause the other note to stop, or the new note will be ignored, depending on the instrument.

*Multimedia Extensions*   Microsoft's original name for the multimedia API and device-driver architecture, first seen as an add-on for Windows 3.0. These extensions were later added to Windows 3.1 as an integral part of the system.

*Mutex*   A contraction of *mutually exclusive*. A special flag that can only be claimed by a single process at a time. Any subsequent process that tries to claim the mutex will be blocked until it is released by the current holder, thus restricting access to the resource protected by the mutex.

*Omni*   A receiving mode. If On, the receiver will respond to Channel messages sent on any channel. If Off, the receiver will only respond to messages sent on the basic channel.

*Opaque handle*   See **magic cookie**.

*Origin*   See **start frame**.

*Poly*   Short for *polyphonic*. A polyphonic instrument is capable of sounding more than one note at a time. If the number of notes requested exceeds the instrument's polyphony, either one or more already sounding notes will be silenced and reassigned to the new notes, or the new notes will be ignored, depending on the instrument.

*Polyphony*   The number of simultaneous notes that a sound device can play, allocated across all of the channels on which the device is able to respond. Typical polyphonic instruments can play 16 or more notes at once.

*Port*   An independent MIDI input or output. A particular MIDI interface can have one or more input and/or output ports. Each of the ports of a multiport MIDI interface is accessed as a separate device and will have a unique device ID.

*Posted message*   A Windows message that is placed in the application message queue. Posted messages are retrieved when the `GetMessage()` function is called in the application's message loop. See **sent message**.

*Ppqn*   Pulses per quarter note or ticks per beat. Another term for **resolution**.

*Protocol*   An accepted procedure for performing an action.

*Pseudo code*   An alternative to flowcharts as a method for outlining the operation of an algorithm or program. Instead of boxes interconnected by lines and arrows, pseudo code shows the steps needed to implement an algorithm using program-like instructions. The author's pseudo code looks suspiciously like C, since his brain's boot ROM is written using that language.

*Quantize*   To correct the timing of a performance by forcing events to occur only on fixed boundaries.

*Quarter Frame message*   Often referred to as a *MIDI Time Code message*. A two-byte System Common message that occurs at four times the frame rate. Each Quarter Frame message specifies a nibble of a frame address; eight Quarter Frame messages are needed to fully specify a frame address.

*Queue*   A memory block, along with an input and output pointer, that stores data for later retrieval. Data is written at the input pointer location and read from the output pointer location. See **circular queue** and **linear queue**.

*Resolution*   The number of divisions into which a quarter note is divided. The duration of a single tick is that fraction of a quarter note.

*Running status*   A method of improving the throughput of a MIDI stream by omitting redundant status bytes. When using running status, status bytes can be omitted whenever the status stays the same for a string of MIDI events.

*Semitone*   The smallest pitch step in the Western 12-tone musical scale: a half step. The twelve notes of a chromatic scale are each semitones. MIDI notes are specified in units of semitones.

*Sent message*   A Windows message that is directly delivered to the appropriate window procedure without passing through the message queue. See **posted message**.

*SMPTE*   The acronym for *Society of Motion Picture and Television Engineers*. SMPTE is an industry group that generates standards for the audio, broadcast, and film industries. Their best-known specification, "Time and Control Code," outlines the method used to record frame-based timecode onto audio and video tape. So-called SMPTE Time Code is often used to synchronize MIDI sequencers to audio and video programs. See **MIDI Time Code**.

*Sound module*   The sound-generating portion of a MIDI instrument. A sound module can either be an independent unit or part of a keyboard instrument.

*Standard MIDI File (SMF)*   A platform- and program-independent file format, as defined in the MIDI specification, that is used to store and transfer timestamped MIDI data and other non-MIDI events. SMFs can be stored on disk or transferred via MIDI. This format is most commonly used as a common bridge for data between programs and operating systems, but it can also be used as a native format for sequencers and other MIDI applications.

*Start frame*   The SMPTE frame that corresponds to the first beat of a sequence.

*StarWord*   A DOS-based word processor, once popular thoughout the galaxy, now fallen into disfavor due to the spread of the WormHoles operating system and its native word processor, Muck.

*Status byte*   An 8-bit byte that specifies the type of MIDI event being transferred. The upper bit of a status byte is always a 1, making all status bytes greater than 128 in value. See **data byte**.

*Stopwatch time*   Elapsed time, as would be measured using a stopwatch or wall clock.

*Streaming data*   Data that is transmitted as a stream of bytes whose duration is arbitrary.

*Stripe*   To record timecode onto an audio or video tape. This timecode will be later read and used to synchronize other devices to the striped tape.

*Sync*   See **synchronization**.

*Sync engine*   The algorithms or the software that embodies those algorithms that provide synchronization for MIDI programs.

*Synchronization*   The process or mechanism for interlocking two processes in time so that they run at the same rate.

*Synchronous*   Occurring at the same time or within the same period. For example, a synchronous function does not return control to the caller until the function's operation is complete. See **asynchronous**.

*Synthesizer*   A hardware device, available as part of a keyboard, as a standalone unit, or as a plug-in computer card, that makes sound in response to keys being pressed on its keyboard or to data received via MIDI or directly from a computer.

*Sysex*   See **System Exclusive message**.

*Sysex librarian*   Not associated with the private peccadilloes of the bookish. Instead, a program used to receive, store, and send System Exclusive messages between a computer and a MIDI device.

*System Common message*   A MIDI message that is of interest to all devices connected to the system (e.g., Song Position Pointer).

*System Exclusive message*   A multi-byte, free-form message that allows any data to be sent. It starts with a 0xF0 status byte, followed by a 1- or 3-byte Manufacturer ID, and any number of data bytes. The message is terminated by an 0xF7 End Of Exclusive (EOX) status byte, except that System Real-Time messages can occur during a System Exclusive message. All of the bytes between the 0xF0 and 0xF7 status bytes must be values between 0 and 127, inclusive.

*System message*   A classification of a MIDI message that is intended for all devices connected to a MIDI network. There are three kinds of System messages: System Common, System Real-Time, and System Exclusive.

*System Real-Time message*   A single-byte MIDI message that specifies timing information (e.g., Timing Clock). Real-Time messages can occur anywhere in the MIDI stream, even in the middle of other multibyte messages or during a System Exclusive message.

*Tempo*   The rate at which music is played. Tempo is often measured in beats per minute. The MaxMidi ToolKit specifies tempo as microseconds per beat, where a beat is a quarter note, to support fractional tempos as integer values.

*Thread*   In a preemptively multitasking operating system, a portion of an application or process that runs independently from and simultaneously with other applications and processes. In Windows 95, each running application has at least one thread.

*Thunk*   A small piece of code that allows 32-bit code to call 16-bit code and vice versa. There are three kinds of thunks used in Windows: flat thunks work in Windows 95 only and allow calls to occur in either direction; generic thunks allow 16-bit code to call 32-bit code in Windows NT; and universal thunks exist only in Win32s. The MaxMidi DLLs make extensive use of flat thunks.

*Tick*   The smallest division of a beat (or quarter note when using the MaxMidi) at a given resolution.

*Tick generator*   An algorithm that periodically calculates the number of ticks that have elapsed at a given tempo and resolution.

*Timeslice*   The portion of time during which a thread executes. A thread stops executing (and another one takes its place) when either its timeslice expires or the thread relinquishes the remaining time of the timeslice.

*Timestamp*   A number, applied to a MIDI event, that indicates the time when the event occurred or is to be played. Timestamps used by the MaxMidi DLLs are measured in units of delta ticks.

*Timing accuracy*   A measure of the time at which an event occurs relative to when it should have occurred. Factors affecting accuracy are the timer period, interrupt latency, and algorithmic errors.

*Track chunk*   A Standard MIDI File chunk (MTrk) that contains timestamped MIDI and Meta events.

*Variable-length value*   A 28-bit number, encoded into one to four bytes, that compresses the value by eliminating leading 0s. Seven bits are stored in each byte, and the eighth bit, if set, indicates that one or more bytes follow.

*Virtual Device Driver*   A 32-bit program, usually with a file extension of .386 or .vxd, that runs at the highest execution privilege level available on the Intel CPU. *VxDs*, as they are called, are used in Windows 3.x and Windows 95, and do not work at all in Windows NT. A VxD can access any memory or hardware available in the PC, but cannot be easily called from applications.

*Virtual function*   A member function of a class that can be redefined in a **derived class**.

*VxD*   See **Virtual Device Driver**.

*Wall-clock time*   See **stopwatch time**.

*Win16Mutex*   A **mutex** that serializes access to non-reentrant 16-bit code in Windows.

*WINMM*   A 32-bit Windows system DLL that provides Win32 access to the 16-bit functions in MMSYSTEM.

# INDEX

## F

FIXED 54, 68
FlushMidiOut() 52, 57, 232, 340
FlushMidiOut16() 321
Format 0 file 189, 295
Format 1 file 189, 295
Format 2 file 189
frame 23–24, 438
   drop 24, 438
   origin 98, 441
   start 98, 443
frame address 438
frame rate 439
Full 24, 25

## G

General MIDI 26–30
GetIDFromName 369
GetIDFromName() 47, 63
GetMaxMidiVersion() 48, 141, 172,
   249, 339
GetMaxMidiVersion16() 310
GetMidiIn() 64, 70, 78, 83, 233,
   234, 236, 341
GetMidiIn16() 313
GetMidiInDescription() 63, 232, 340
GetMidiInDescription16() 310
GetMidiOutDescription() 47, 228, 340
GetMidiOutDescription16() 319
GetNumInDevices() 232, 339
GetNumOutDevices() 228, 339
GetResolution() 108, 110, 114, 241, 342
GetResolution16() 334
GetSMFResolution() 200, 243, 245, 346
GetTempo() 108, 110, 114, 240, 342
GetTempo16() 334
global channel 19, 436
GM. *See* MIDI: General
GM Sound Set 26, 28
granularity. *See* resolution
greyhound 65, 439

## H

HMIDIIN 39, 80
HMIDIOUT 39, 80
HMIN 64, 68
HMOUT 50, 55

## I

IDM_INPUT 148
IDM_OUTPUT 148
Import file 439
Internal mode 237
internal sync 439
interrupts 54, 86, 94, 107
irrational number 439

## J

jitter 93, 439

## L

Little-Endian 189, 439
Local Control 20

## M

m_bAutoMenuEnable 148, 279, 283
magic cookie 50, 439
manufacturer ID 22, 76, 440
master 100
MaxMidi.h 302
MAXPNAMELEN 228, 233
MaxSeq 11, 219, 225, 417
MC_HOLD 102
MCI. *See* Media Control Interface
MCI Sequencer 6
Media Control Interface 6
_MENUS 276, 280
memory
   fixed 438
message
   All Notes Off 19

System Reset (0xFF) 22

# T

tempo 21, 89, 90–91, 108, 237, 271, 444
  changing 106
tempo change event 108, 133
thread 444
thunk 9, 34–38, 444
  flat 438
  script 360
tick 89, 90–91, 93–97, 444
  absolute 210
  delta 89, 437
  generator 93–97, 115, 118, 444
ticks per beat (tpb) 91
timebase 89
timeslice 37, 444
timestamp 89, 94, 210, 445
timing accuracy 92, 237, 273, 445
timing resolution 237, 243, 273
track 168–70, 187
  playing back 178–85
  recording 171–78
_TRACK 123
TrackMidiOut() 56, 57, 322
Tune Request 20
TurnNotesOff() 322

# U

UPDATE_COMMAND_UI 156
USE_CURRENT 107, 238

# V

variable-length value 188–89, 445
velocity 15–16, 45
Virtual Device Driver 445
virtual function 261, 268, 445
VxD. *See* Virtual Device Driver

# W

wall-clock time 445
waveform audio 2, 73
wavetable synthesis 4
Win16Mutex 35–36, 54, 445
WINMM 9, 36, 445
WRITE 295, 296
WriteByte() 206, 361
WriteMetaEvent() 199, 242, 247, 359
WriteSMF() 198, 244, 248, 355

The CDROM included with this book contains all of the ToolKit files along with a Windows 95 setup program that installs the files in their proper places. The files are also supplied in an uncompressed form for easy access on PC operating systems other than Windows 95.

## *Installing the ToolKit Files*

Installing the ToolKit is simple. Click on the Start button and select Run... . Type in the following path, replacing D: with the drive name for your CDROM drive:

```
D:\ToolKit\Setup
```

Click on OK to launch the installer and display the welcome screen. Click Next to move to the next step. This page shows the destination where the installer will copy the ToolKit files. If desired, click on the Browse button and choose a new destination drive or folder.

Click Next to move to the Setup Type screen, where you can choose which ToolKit files you wish to be installed.

Most users should accept the default Typical setup. This setup type installs all of the ToolKit files, including the C++ classes, source code for the MaxMidi DLLs, the example program

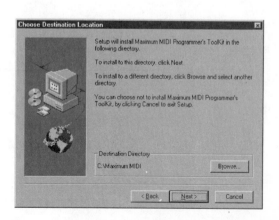

**Choose destination**

source code, executable versions of MidiSpy, SxLib, and MaxSeq, and the system files that are needed to run these examples.

Choosing the Compact setup option will install the C++ classes and the system files, but eliminate the ToolKit source code and example programs. These files can still be accessed directly from the CDROM. By choosing the Custom setup option, particular categories of ToolKit files can be selected for installation. This option provides maximum control for advanced users.

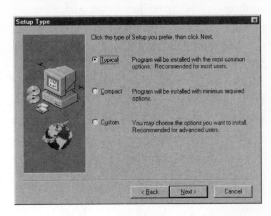

Click the Next button to reach the Select Program Folder page. Specify the folder name where the ToolKit icons will be installed in the Start button. Several icons provide access to the on-line help files, a ReadMe file that contains any last

**Setup Screen**

minute ToolKit changes, a copy of the software license, and the ready-to-run example programs. Most users should accept the default folder name. Click Next to complete the ToolKit installation.

# File Organization

The ToolKit files are organized in a group of folders in the *Maximum MIDI* folder (as installed using the default path suggested by the installer program), or in the uncompressed *Source Files* folder on the CDROM.

The MaxMidi ToolKit includes two help files that document the C-language API and the C++ classes. These help files appear in the *Help* folder. The Win95 installer provides shortcuts to these help files (in the *Maximum MIDI* menu located in the *Start* button).

The ToolKit header files are located in the *Include* folder, while the MxMidi32.lib import library file is in the *Lib* folder. The ToolKit MFC C++ class implementation files are found in the *MFC Classes* folder.

All of the example programs discussed in the book are included in the *Example Apps* folder. The *Book Examples* folder contains the intermediate example programs, while the three main example apps appear in the *MidiSpy*, *SxLib*, and *MaxSeq* folders.

Ready-to-run versions of the MaxMidi DLLs are found in the *Redist* folder. These files are also copied by the installation program to the *Windows/System* folder so that the example programs will execute properly. ToolKit-based applications should be distributed with these two files (or your own modified versions), which must be copied to the *Windows/System* folder in order to work properly.

The source code for these two MaxMidi DLLs is located in the *DLL Source* folder. The 16-bit DLL source code is located in the *MxMidi16* folder, while the 32-bit DLL source is in the *MxMidi32* folder. The thunking source files (explained in Chapter 3) are in the *Thunk* folder.

In addition to the 32-bit MaxMidi ToolKit, an unsupported 16-bit version, *PTKLite*, is included in the *Unsupported* folder. PTKLite comes with all of its DLL source code and several example programs. It can be used to write Windows 3.1 MIDI applications. PTKLite is similar to the MaxMidi ToolKit, but it lacks several

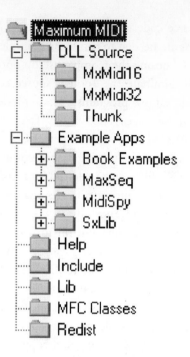

**MaxMidi file organization**

features, most notably the C++ classes and the features that they provide. PTKLite is an expanded version of the freeware ToolKit that was originally distributed on the Internet. As the folder name implies, this ToolKit is unsupported and is included for users who need to support Windows 3.1.